Morning finds me sitting sleepless, scratching my head and at a loss for ideas. My mind races, my thoughts twist back on themselves, my eyes are hollow and sunken, my face is drawn in a scowl and my back is bent like an old crone's.

"Yeaaargh! I'm finished!" I open the door, and there's my cat. And what a cat! With trembling hands, I close the blinds.

This episode I humbly entitle, "I Like My Kitty." In my next life, I want to come back as a cat.

– Yoshiyuki Nishi

Yoshiyuki Nishi was born in Tokyo. Two of his favorite manga series are *Dragon Ball* and the robot-cat comedy *Doraemon*. His latest series, *Muhyo & Roji's Bureau of Supernatural Investigation*, debuted in Japan's *Akamaru Jump* magazine in 2004 and went on to be serialized in *Weekly Shonen Jump*.

MUHYO & ROJI'S
BUREAU OF SUPERNATURAL INVESTIGATION

VOL. 16
SHONEN JUMP Manga Edition

STORY AND ART BY
YOSHIYUKI NISHI

Translation & Adaptation/Alexander O. Smith
Touch-up Art & Lettering/Susan Daigle-Leach and Brian Bilter
Design/Yukiko Whitley
Editor/Amy Yu

VP, Production/Alvin Lu
VP, Sales & Product Marketing/Gonzalo Ferreyra
VP, Creative/Linda Espinosa
Publisher/Hyoe Narita

MUHYO TO ROZY NO MAHORITSU SODAN JIMUSHO © 2004
by Yoshiyuki Nishi. All rights reserved. First published in Japan
in 2004 by SHUEISHA Inc., Tokyo. English translation rights
arranged by SHUEISHA Inc.

Printed in the U.S.A.

Published by VIZ Media, LLC
P.O. Box 77010
San Francisco, CA 94107

10 9 8 7 6 5 4 3 2 1
First printing, April 2010

THE WORLD'S
MOST POPULAR MANGA

SHONEN JUMP

www.viz.com

www.shonenjump.com

SHONEN JUMP MANGA EDITION

Muhyo & Roji's

Bureau of Supernatural Investigation

BSI

Vol. 16   The Stray Spirit

Story & Art by Yoshiyuki Nishi

Dramatis Personae

Toru Muhyo (Muhyo)

Young, genius magic law practitioner with the highest rank of "Executor." Always calm and collected (though sometimes considered cold), Muhyo possesses a strong sense of justice and even has a kind side. Sleeps a lot to recover from the exhaustion caused by his practice. Likes: *Jabin* (a manga). Dislikes: Anything that interrupts his naps.

Jiro Kusano (Roji)

Assistant at Muhyo's office, recently promoted from the lowest rank of "Second Clerk" to that of (provisional) "First Clerk." Roji has a gentle heart and has been known to freak out in the presence of spirits. Lately, he has been devoting himself to the study of magic law so that he can pull his own weight someday. Likes: Tea and cakes. Dislikes: Scary ghosts and scary Muhyo.

Nana Takenouchi (Nana)

High school student, spirit medium and amateur photographer. Working as an assistant photographic investigator.

Seven-Faced Dog

An envoy with the ability to change shape. Specialist at uncovering spectral crimes.

The Story

Magic law is a newly established practice for judging and punishing the increasing crimes committed by spirits; those who use it are called "practitioners."

Muhyo and gang successfully defeat Teeki (forbidden magic law practitioner and the root of much evil), thereby saving their friend Enchu who had fallen into darkness and had become a traitor.

After being released from his forbidden magic law contract, Enchu is given a "lenient" sentence by the Magic Law Association—eternal imprisonment. After saying their farewells to Enchu at the Arcanum prison entrance, Muhyo and Roji return to their office at last, only to find a pesky surprise waiting for them...

Kenji Sato (Kenji)

Muhyo and Roji saved this troublemaker from a ghost, earning his grudging respect.

Ginji Sugakiya (Ginji)

Upperclassman at M.L.S. Boasts the rank of Assistant Judge even though he is still enrolled in school.

Q-la

An envoy who drives a demon carriage. Bound to Ginji through a blood contract.

Muhyo & Roji's

Bureau of Supernatural Investigation

BSI

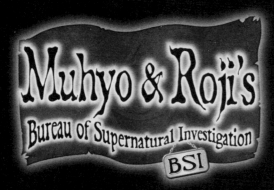

CONTENTS

16

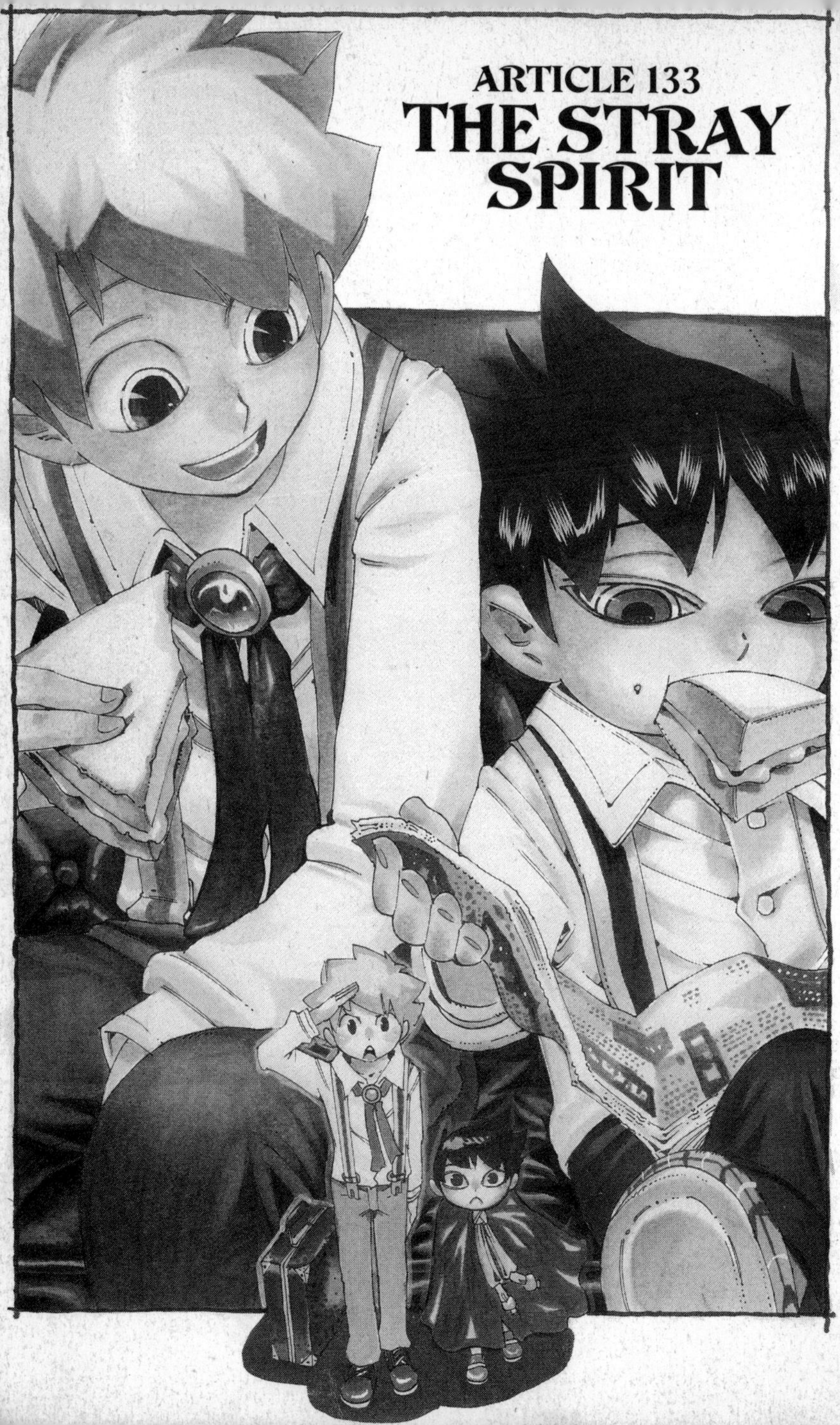
ARTICLE 133
THE STRAY SPIRIT

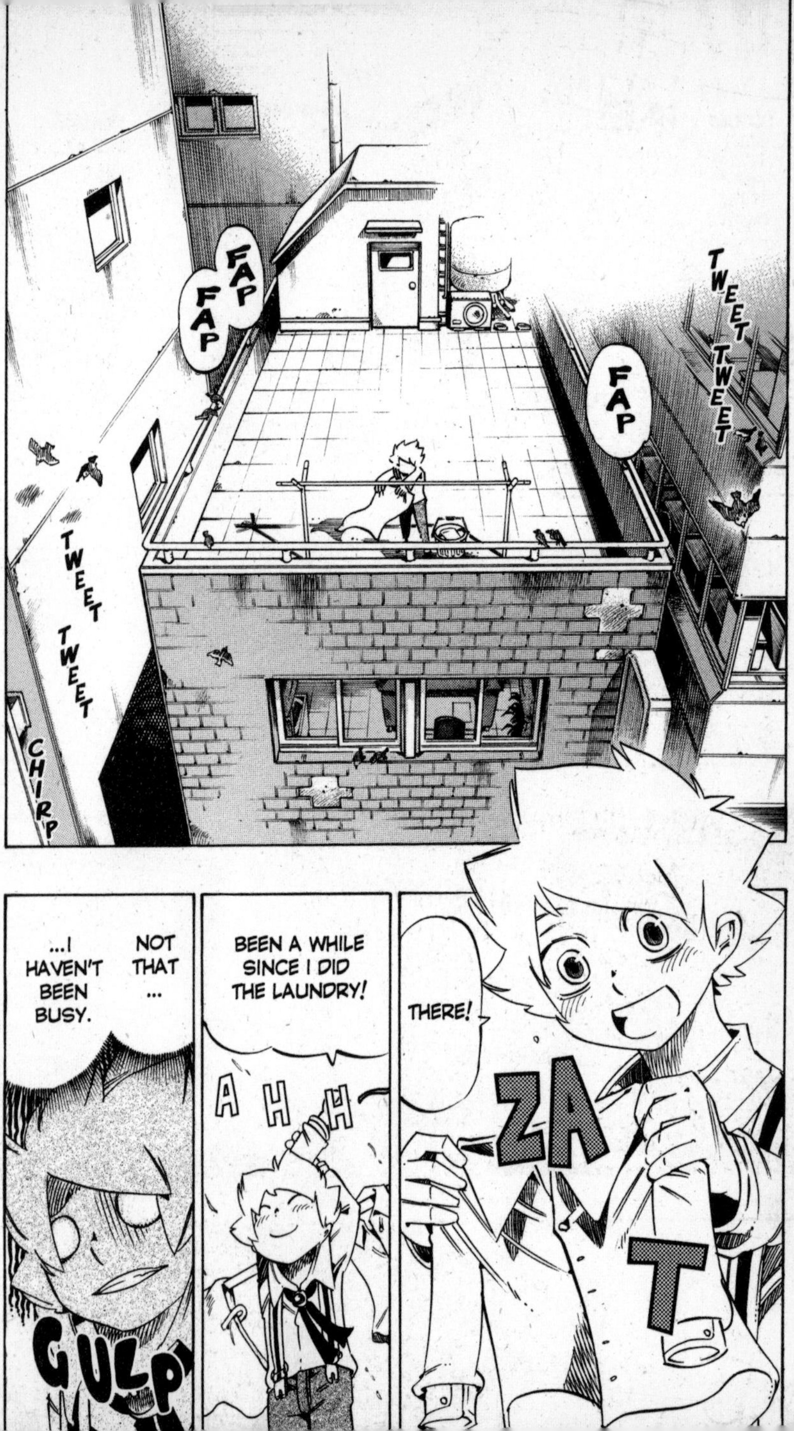
TWEET TWEET
FAP
FAP FAP
TWEET TWEET
CHIRP
THERE!
ZAT
BEEN A WHILE SINCE I DID THE LAUNDRY!
AHH
NOT THAT ...
...I HAVEN'T BEEN BUSY.
GULP

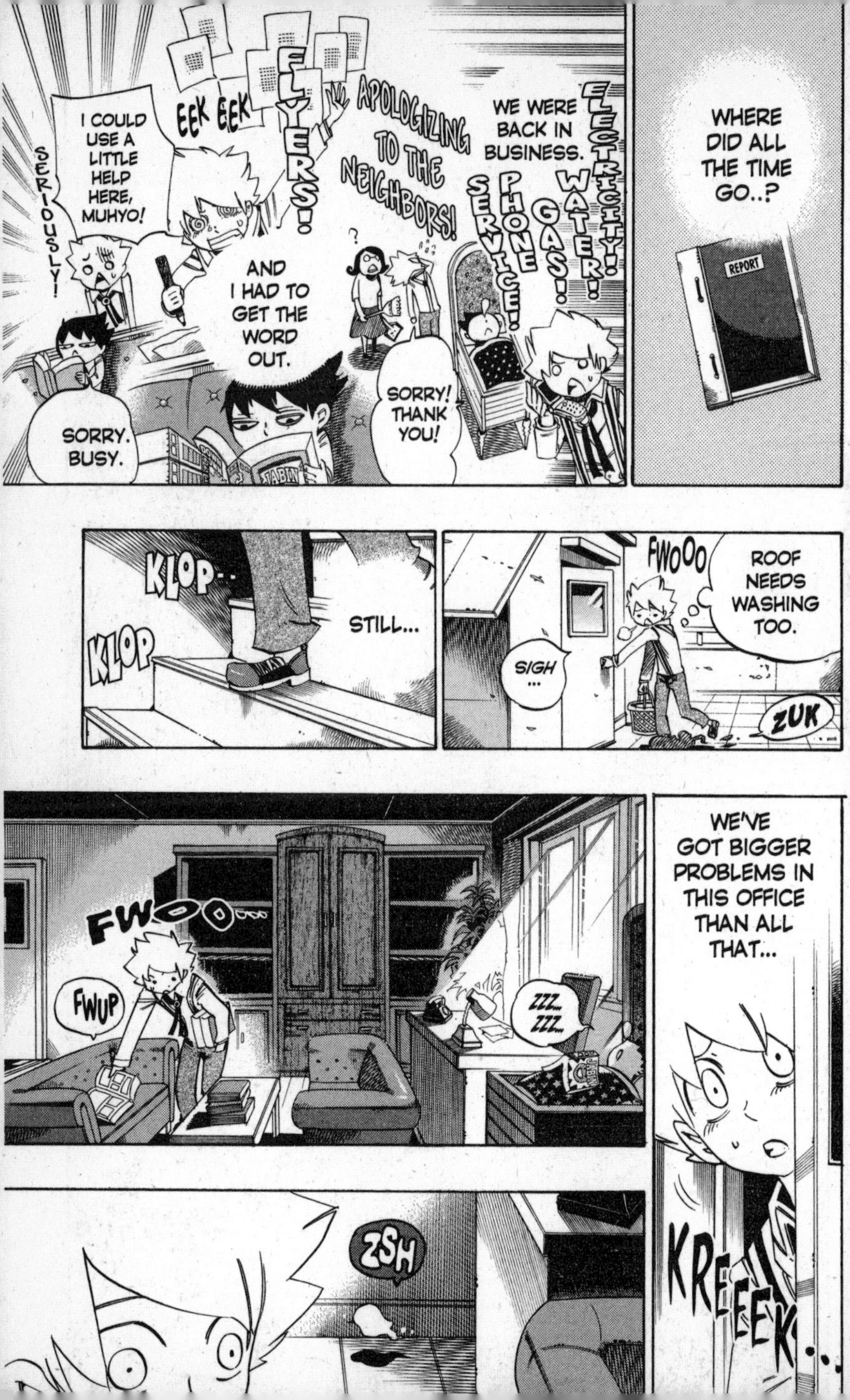

WHERE DID ALL THE TIME GO..?
REPORT
ELECTRICITY!
WATER!
GAS!
PHONE SERVICE!
WE WERE BACK IN BUSINESS.
APOLOGIZING TO THE NEIGHBORS!
FLYERS!
EEK EEK
I COULD USE A LITTLE HELP HERE, MUHYO!
SERIOUSLY!
AND I HAD TO GET THE WORD OUT.
SORRY! THANK YOU!
SORRY. BUSY.
JABIN
FWOOO
ROOF NEEDS WASHING TOO.
SIGH...
ZUK
STILL...
KLOP..
KLOP
WE'VE GOT BIGGER PROBLEMS IN THIS OFFICE THAN ALL THAT...
KREEEK...
ZZZ... ZZZ...
FWOOO
FWUP
ZSH

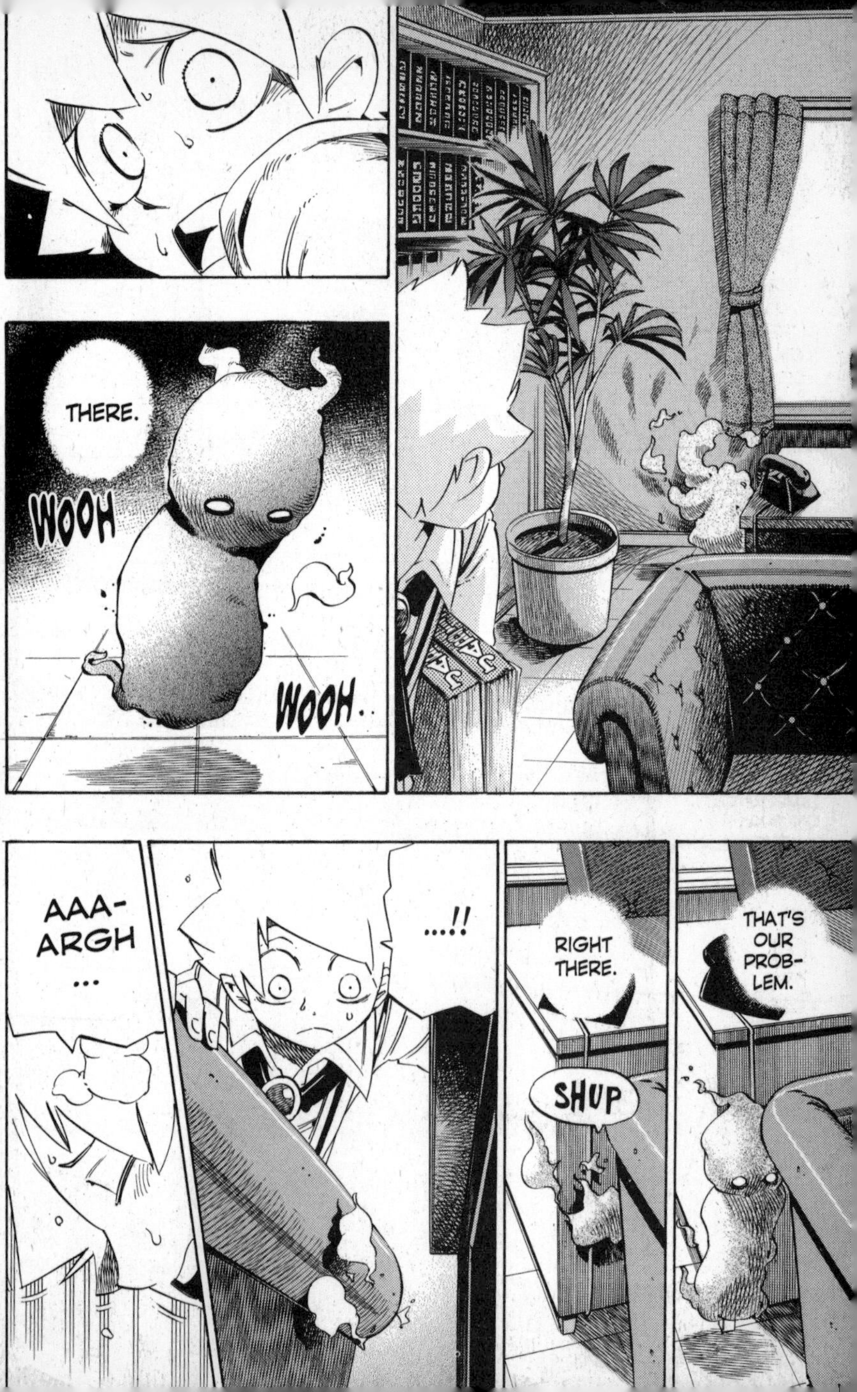
THERE.
WOOH
WOOH..
THAT'S OUR PROB-LEM.
RIGHT THERE.
SHUP
...!!
AAA-ARGH ...

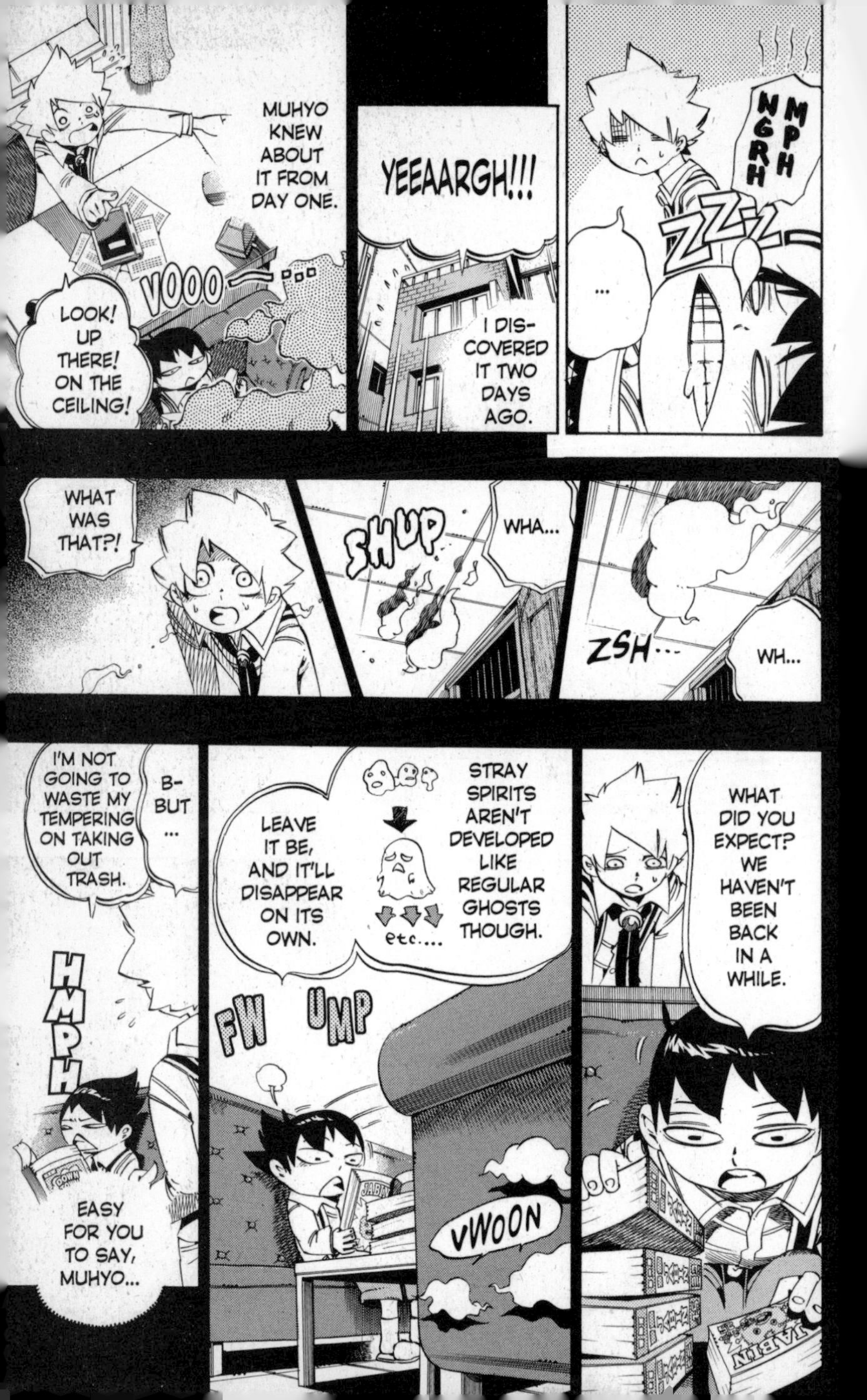
MPH
NGRH
ZZZ
...
YEEAARGH!!!
I DIS-COVERED IT TWO DAYS AGO.
MUHYO KNEW ABOUT IT FROM DAY ONE.
VOOO—
LOOK! UP THERE! ON THE CEILING!
WH...
ZSH...
WHA...
SHUP
WHAT WAS THAT?!
WHAT DID YOU EXPECT? WE HAVEN'T BEEN BACK IN A WHILE.
STRAY SPIRITS AREN'T DEVELOPED LIKE REGULAR GHOSTS THOUGH.
etc....
LEAVE IT BE, AND IT'LL DISAPPEAR ON ITS OWN.
FWUMP
VWOON
B-BUT...
I'M NOT GOING TO WASTE MY TEMPERING ON TAKING OUT TRASH.
HMPH
EASY FOR YOU TO SAY, MUHYO...

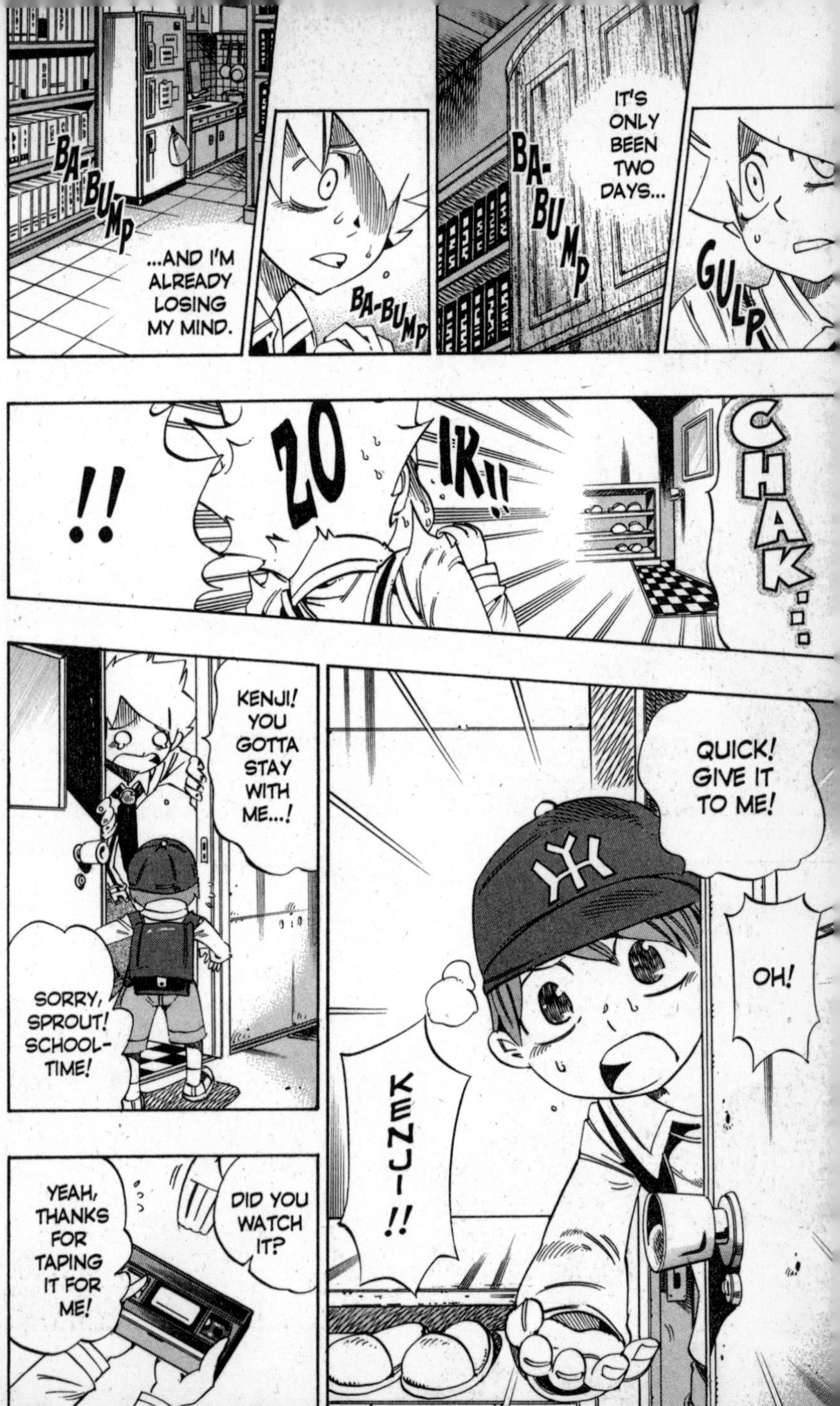
GULP
IT'S ONLY BEEN TWO DAYS...
BA-BUMP
BA-BUMP
BA-BUMP
...AND I'M ALREADY LOSING MY MIND.
CHAK...
ZOIK!!
!!
QUICK! GIVE IT TO ME!
OH!
KENJI!!
KENJI! YOU GOTTA STAY WITH ME...!
SORRY, SPROUT! SCHOOL-TIME!
DID YOU WATCH IT?
YEAH, THANKS FOR TAPING IT FOR ME!

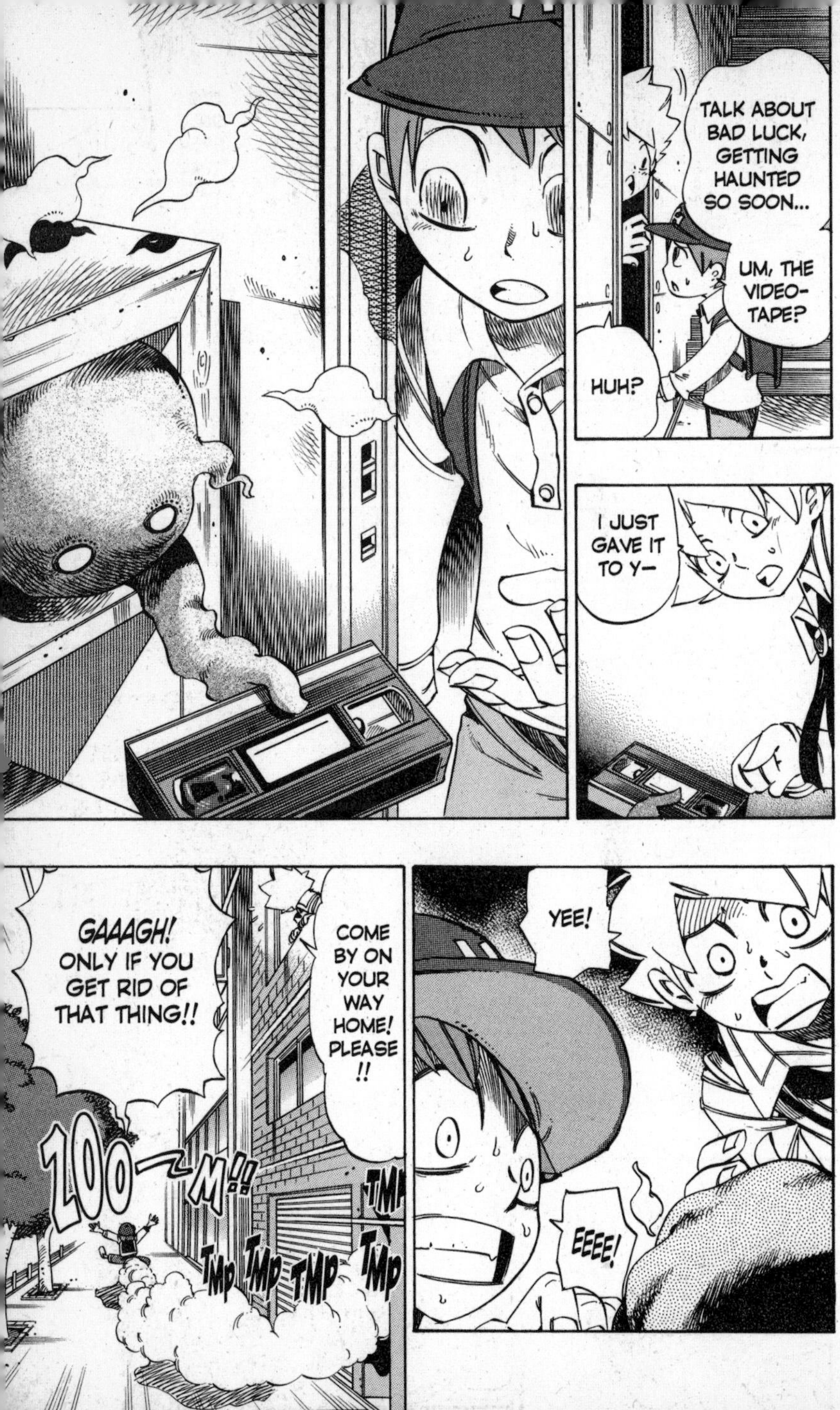

TALK ABOUT BAD LUCK, GETTING HAUNTED SO SOON...
UM, THE VIDEO-TAPE?
HUH?
I JUST GAVE IT TO Y—
YEE!
EEEE!
COME BY ON YOUR WAY HOME! PLEASE!!
GAAAGH! ONLY IF YOU GET RID OF THAT THING!!
ZOO~M!!
TMP TMP TMP TMP TMP

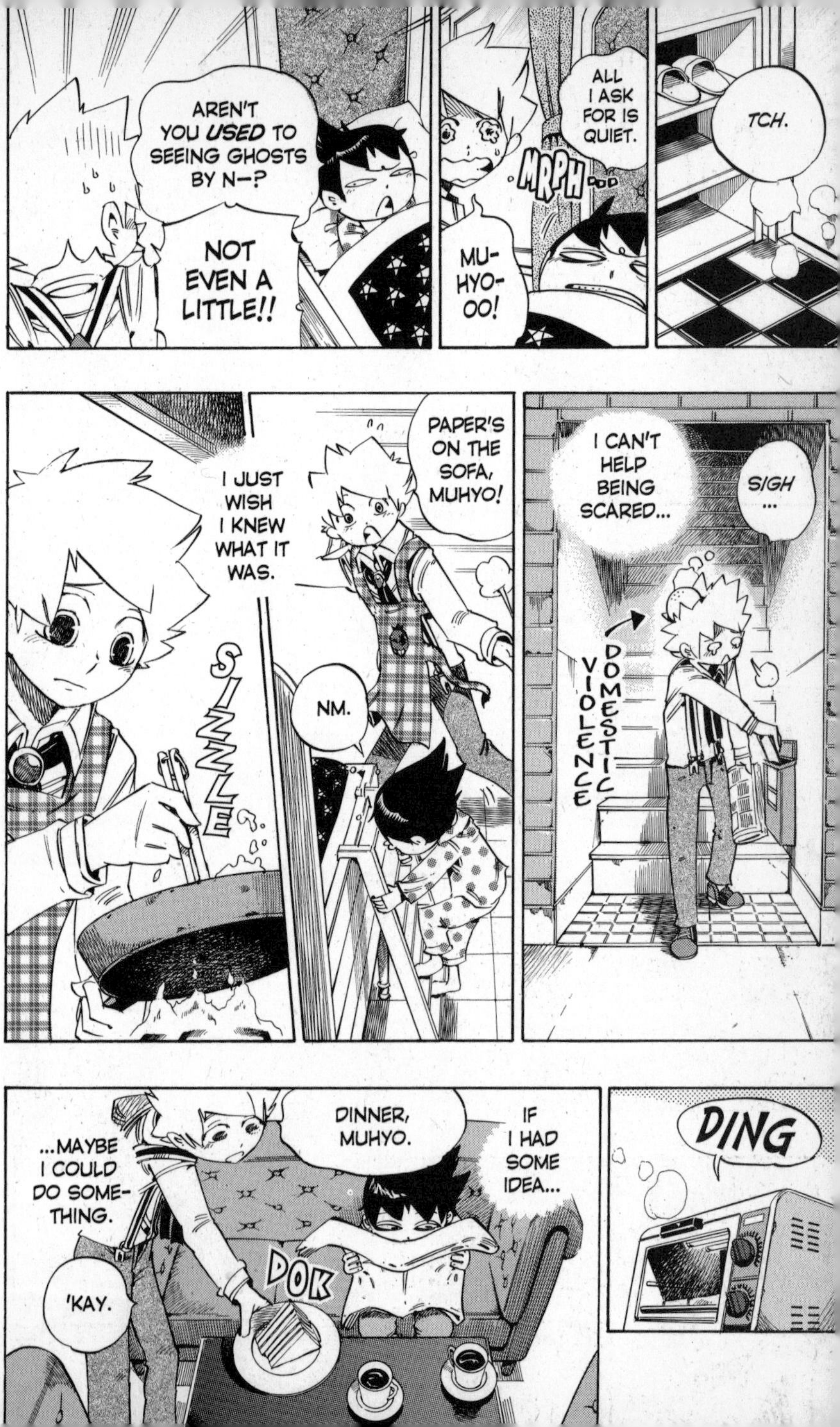
TCH.
ALL I ASK FOR IS QUIET.
MRPH...
MU-HYO-OO!
AREN'T YOU *USED* TO SEEING GHOSTS BY N—?
NOT EVEN A LITTLE!!
SIGH...
I CAN'T HELP BEING SCARED...
DOMESTIC VIOLENCE
PAPER'S ON THE SOFA, MUHYO!
NM.
I JUST WISH I KNEW WHAT IT WAS.
SIZZLE
DING
IF I HAD SOME IDEA...
DINNER, MUHYO.
...MAYBE I COULD DO SOME-THING.
DOK
'KAY.

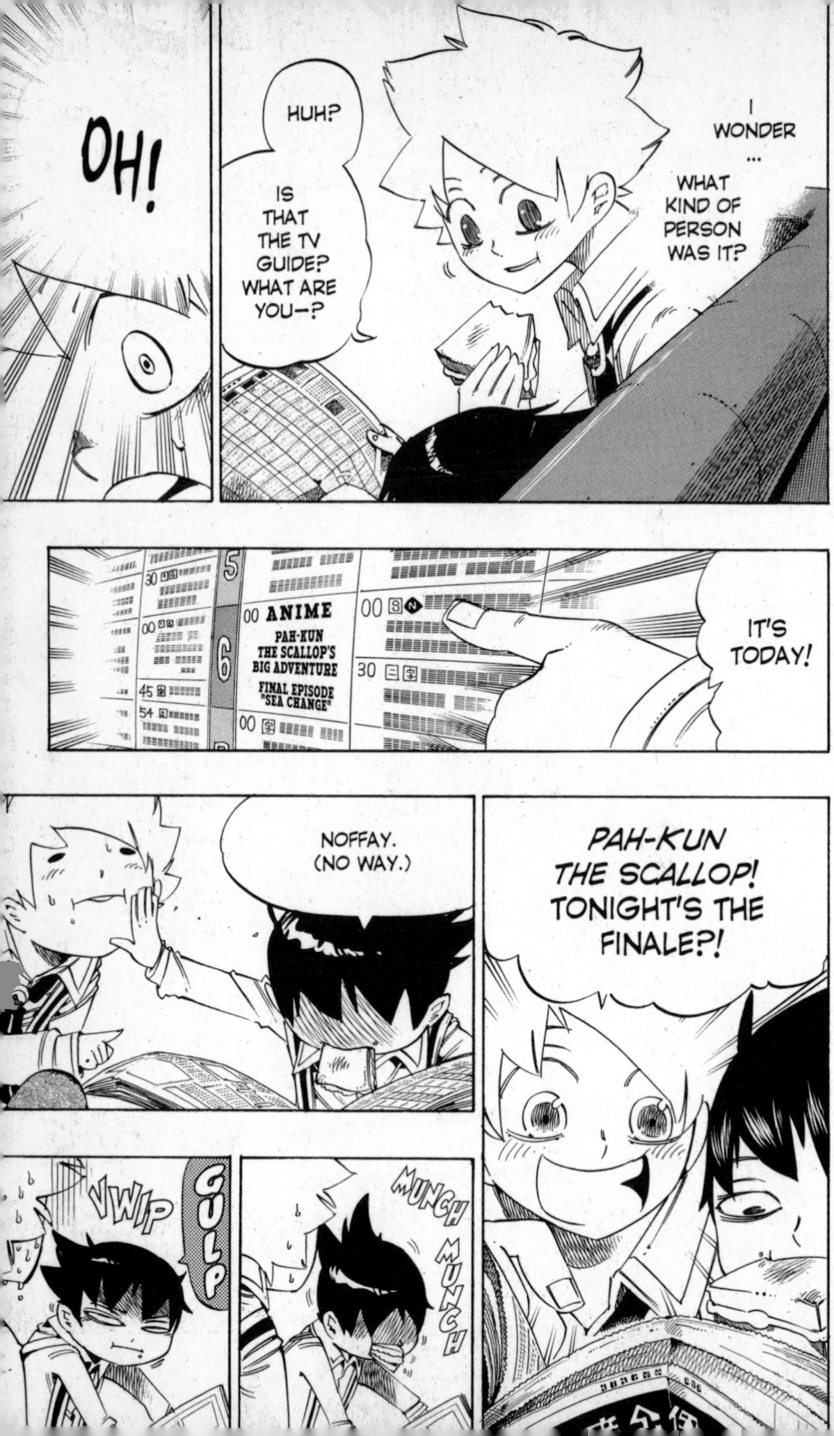
I WONDER ... WHAT KIND OF PERSON WAS IT?
HUH?
IS THAT THE TV GUIDE? WHAT ARE YOU—?
OH!
IT'S TODAY!
00 ANIME
PAH-KUN THE SCALLOP'S BIG ADVENTURE
FINAL EPISODE "SEA CHANGE"
PAH-KUN THE SCALLOP! TONIGHT'S THE FINALE?!
...
NOFFAY. (NO WAY.)
MUNCH
MUNCH
MUNCH
GULP
VWIP

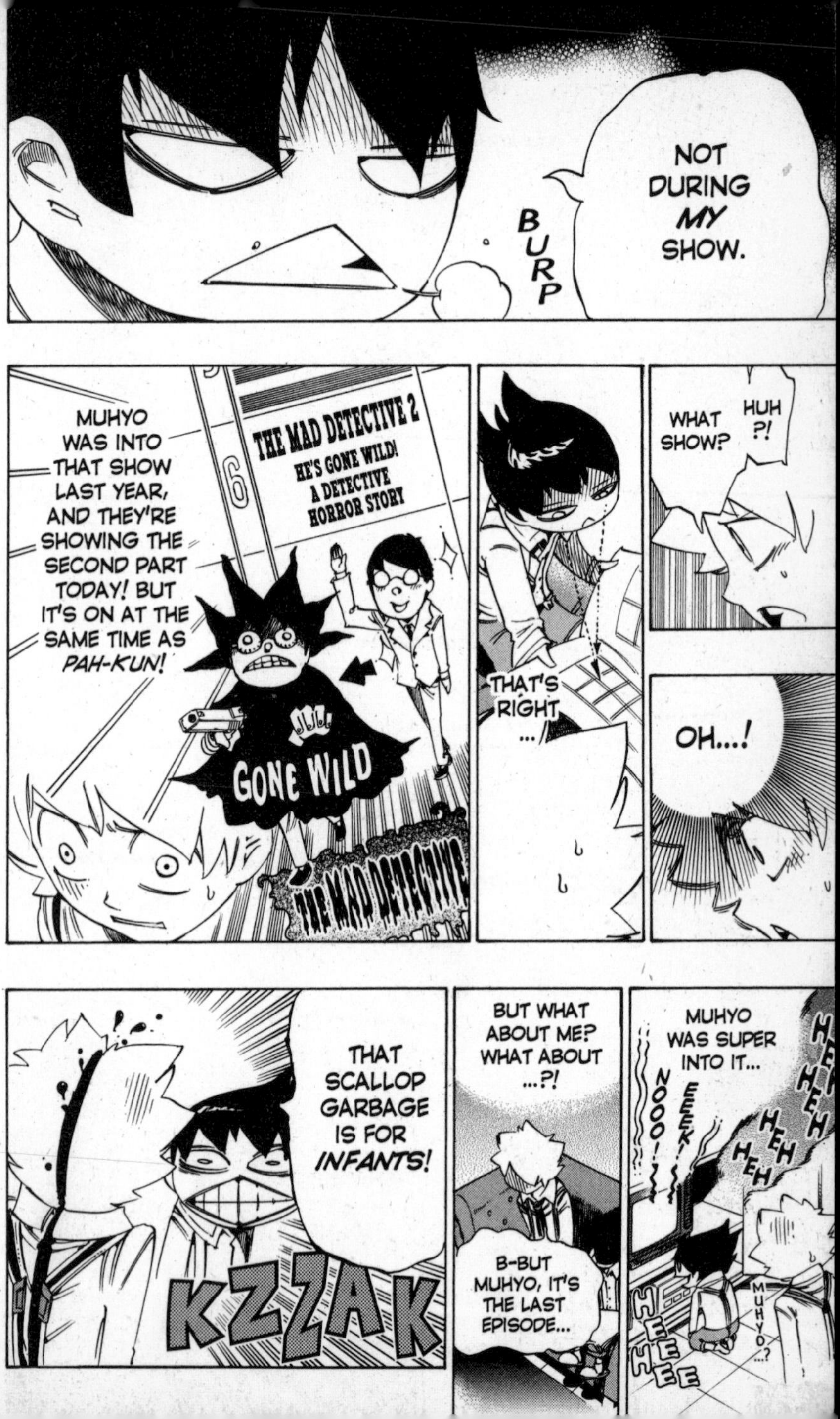
NOT DURING *MY* SHOW.
BURP
HUH ?!
WHAT SHOW?
OH...!
THAT'S RIGHT ...
MUHYO WAS INTO THAT SHOW LAST YEAR, AND THEY'RE SHOWING THE SECOND PART TODAY! BUT IT'S ON AT THE SAME TIME AS *PAH-KUN*!
THE MAD DETECTIVE 2
HE'S GONE WILD! A DETECTIVE HORROR STORY
6
GONE WILD
THE MAD DETECTIVE
MUHYO WAS SUPER INTO IT...
HEH HEH HEH HEH HEH
EEEK!
NOOO!
MUHYO ...?
HEE HEE HEE
BUT WHAT ABOUT ME? WHAT ABOUT ...?!
B-BUT MUHYO, IT'S THE LAST EPISODE...
THAT SCALLOP GARBAGE IS FOR *INFANTS*!
KZZAK

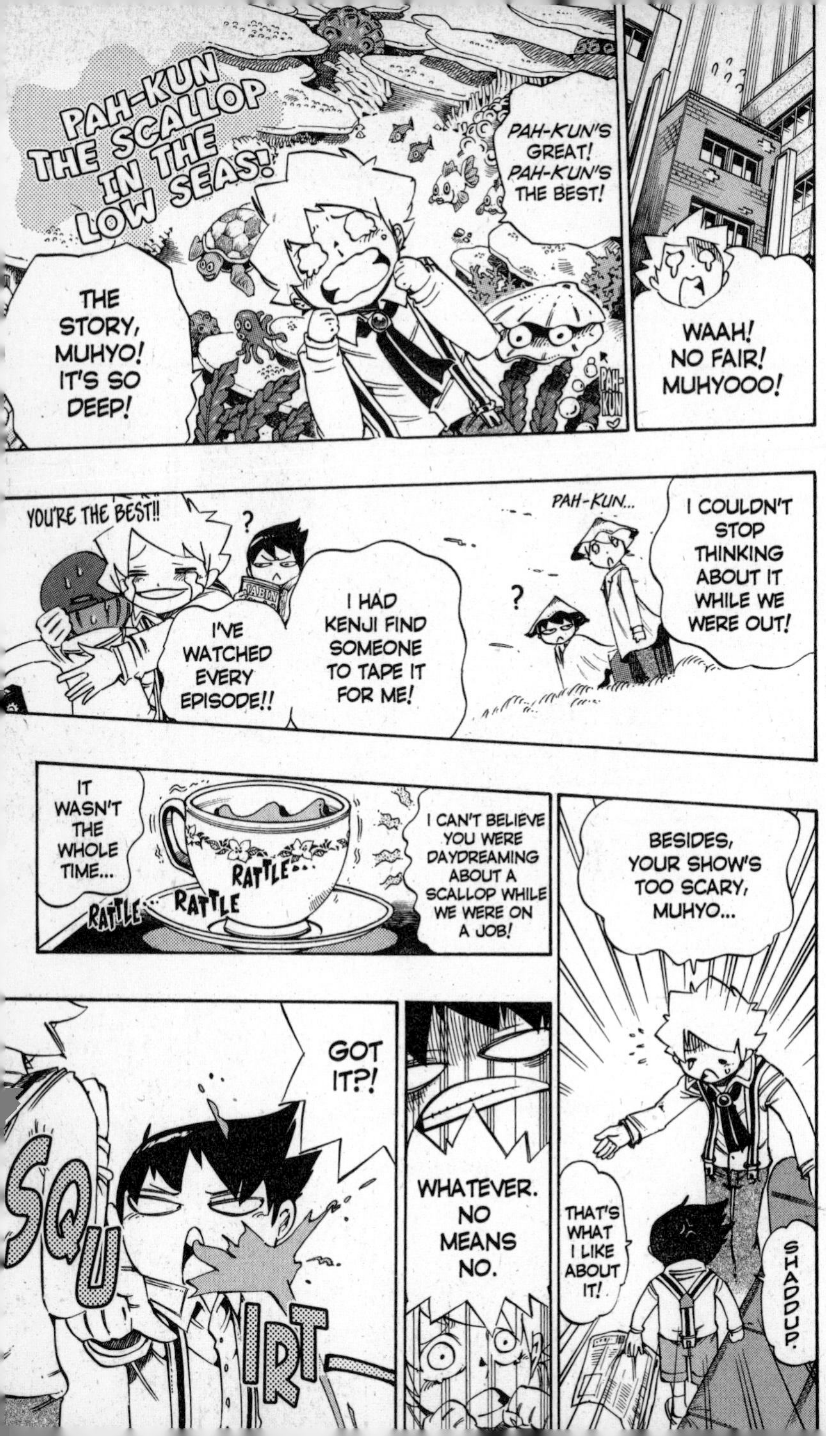
WAAH! NO FAIR! MUHYOOO!
PAH-KUN'S GREAT! PAH-KUN'S THE BEST!
PAH-KUN THE SCALLOP IN THE LOW SEAS!
PAH-KUN
THE STORY, MUHYO! IT'S SO DEEP!
I COULDN'T STOP THINKING ABOUT IT WHILE WE WERE OUT!
PAH-KUN...
I HAD KENJI FIND SOMEONE TO TAPE IT FOR ME!
I'VE WATCHED EVERY EPISODE!!
YOU'RE THE BEST!!
BESIDES, YOUR SHOW'S TOO SCARY, MUHYO...
SHADDUP.
THAT'S WHAT I LIKE ABOUT IT!
I CAN'T BELIEVE YOU WERE DAYDREAMING ABOUT A SCALLOP WHILE WE WERE ON A JOB!
RATTLE...
RATTLE
RATTLE...
IT WASN'T THE WHOLE TIME...
WHATEVER. NO MEANS NO.
GOT IT?!
SQUIRT

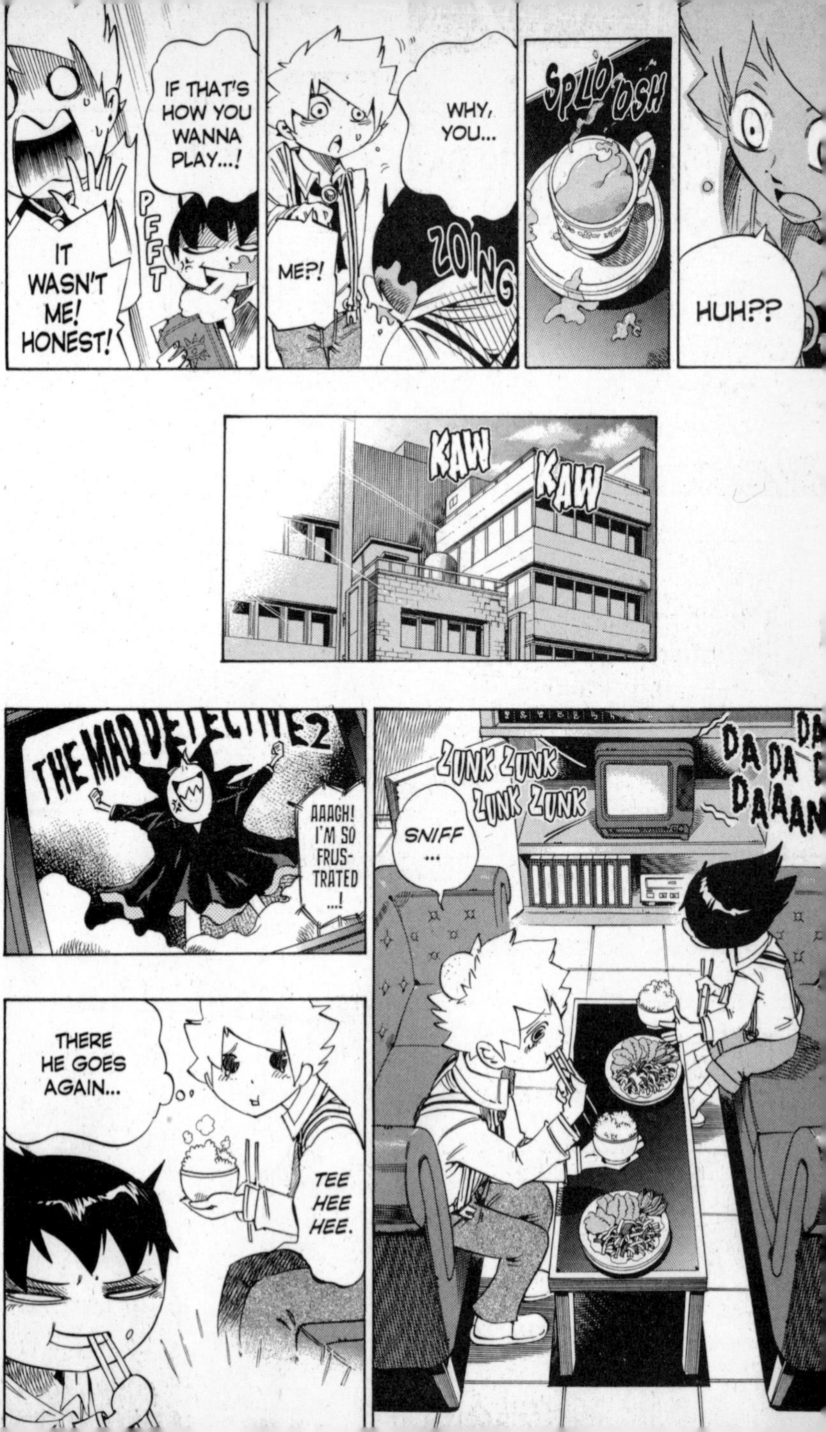
HUH??
SPLOOSH
WHY, YOU...
ME?!
ZOING
IF THAT'S HOW YOU WANNA PLAY...!
PFFT
IT WASN'T ME! HONEST!
KAW
KAW
DA DA DA DAAAN
ZUNK ZUNK
ZUNK ZUNK
SNIFF...
THE MAD DETECTIVE 2
AAAGH! I'M SO FRUS-TRATED...!
THERE HE GOES AGAIN...
TEE HEE HEE.

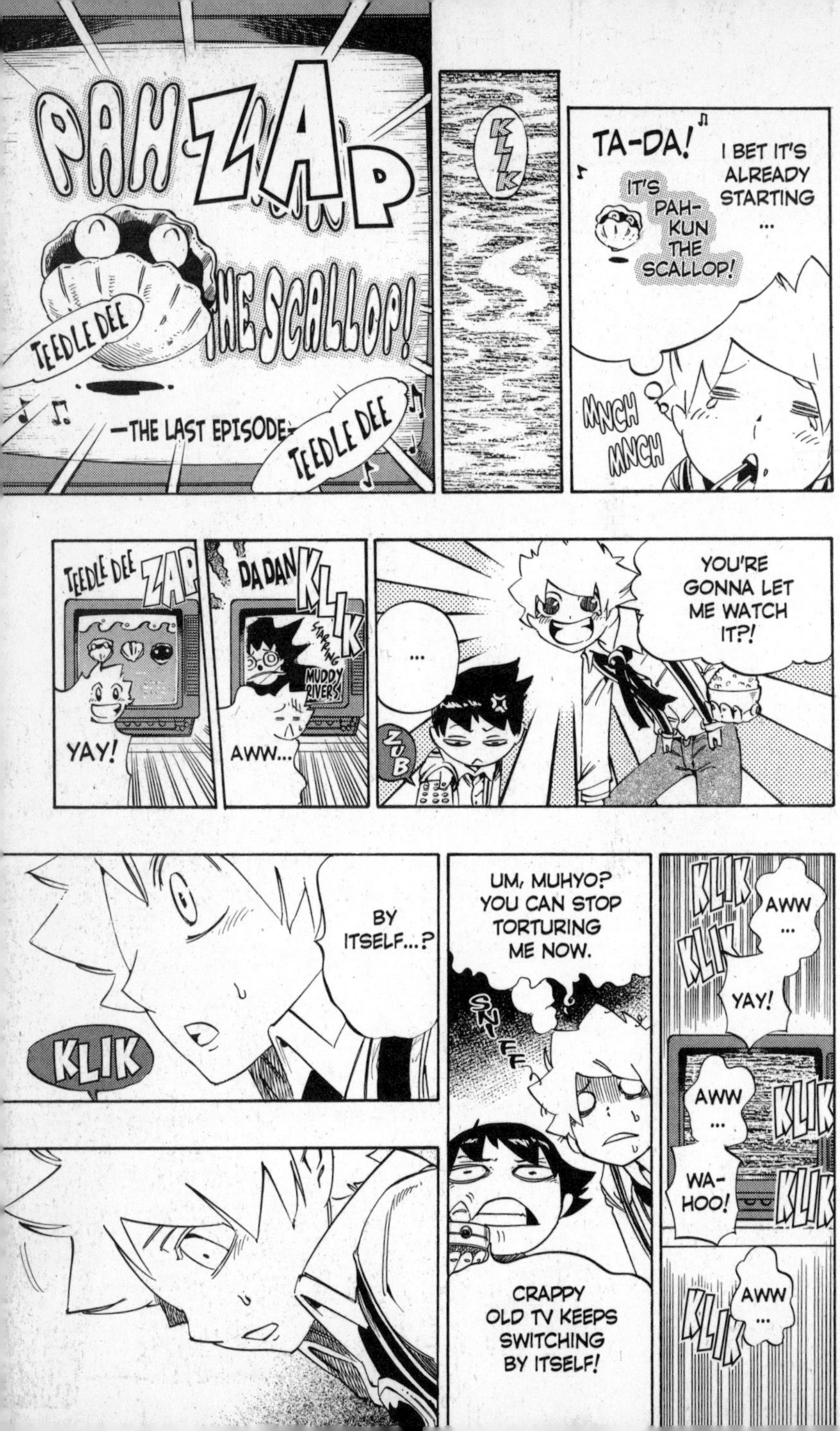
I BET IT'S ALREADY STARTING ...
TA-DA!
IT'S PAH-KUN THE SCALLOP!
MNCH MNCH
KLIK
PAH ZAP
THE SCALLOP!
TEEDLE DEE
—THE LAST EPISODE—
TEEDLE DEE
YOU'RE GONNA LET ME WATCH IT?!
...
ZUB
DA DAN KLIK
STARRING MUDDY RIVERS
AWW...
TEEDLE DEE ZAP
YAY!
KLIK
AWW ...
KLIK
YAY!
AWW ...
KLIK
WA-HOO!
KLIK
KLIK
AWW ...
UM, MUHYO? YOU CAN STOP TORTURING ME NOW.
SNIFF
CRAPPY OLD TV KEEPS SWITCHING BY ITSELF!
BY ITSELF...?
KLIK

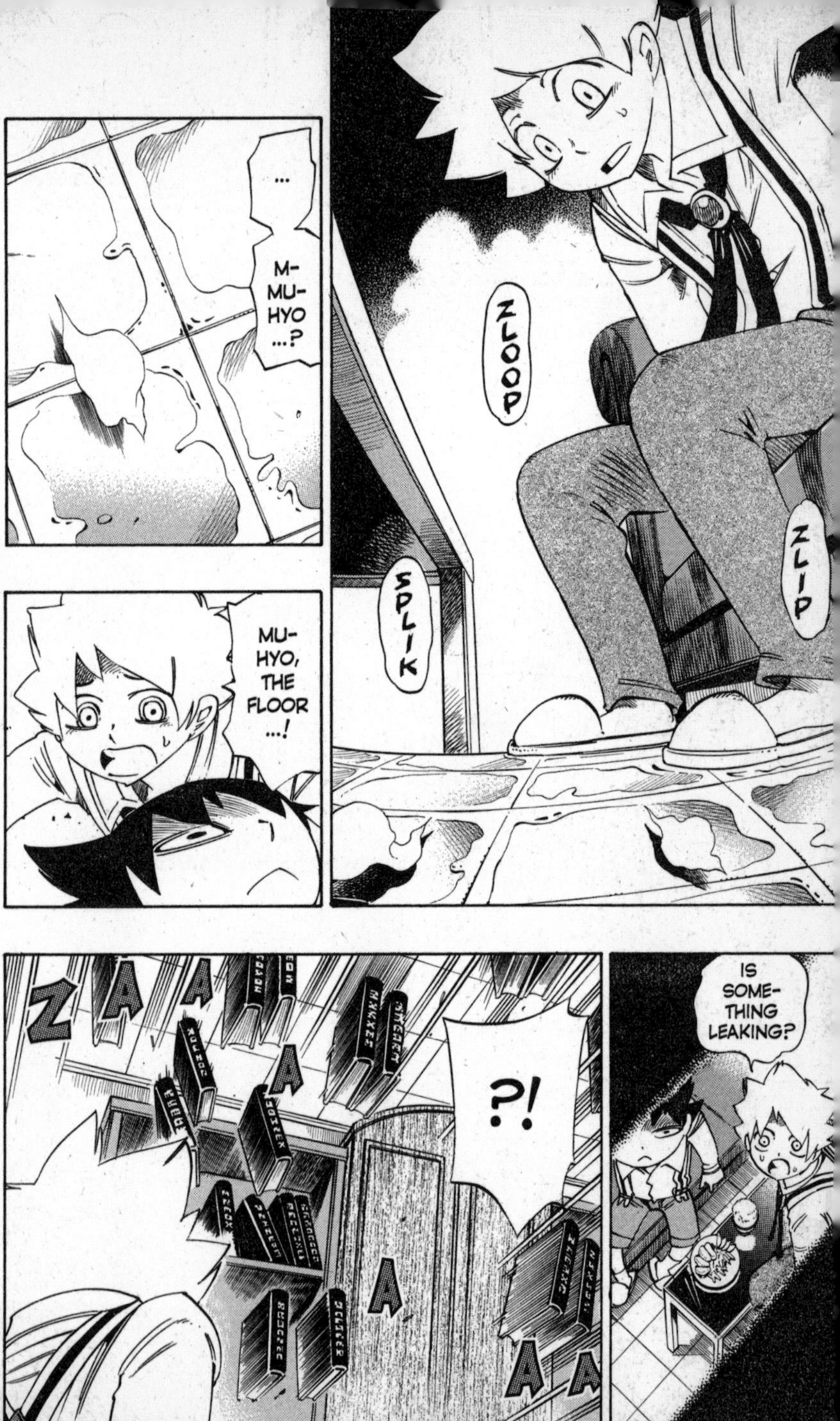
ZLOOP
ZLIP
SPLIK
...
M-MU-HYO ...?
MU-HYO, THE FLOOR ...!
IS SOMETHING LEAKING?
?!
ZAAAAAA

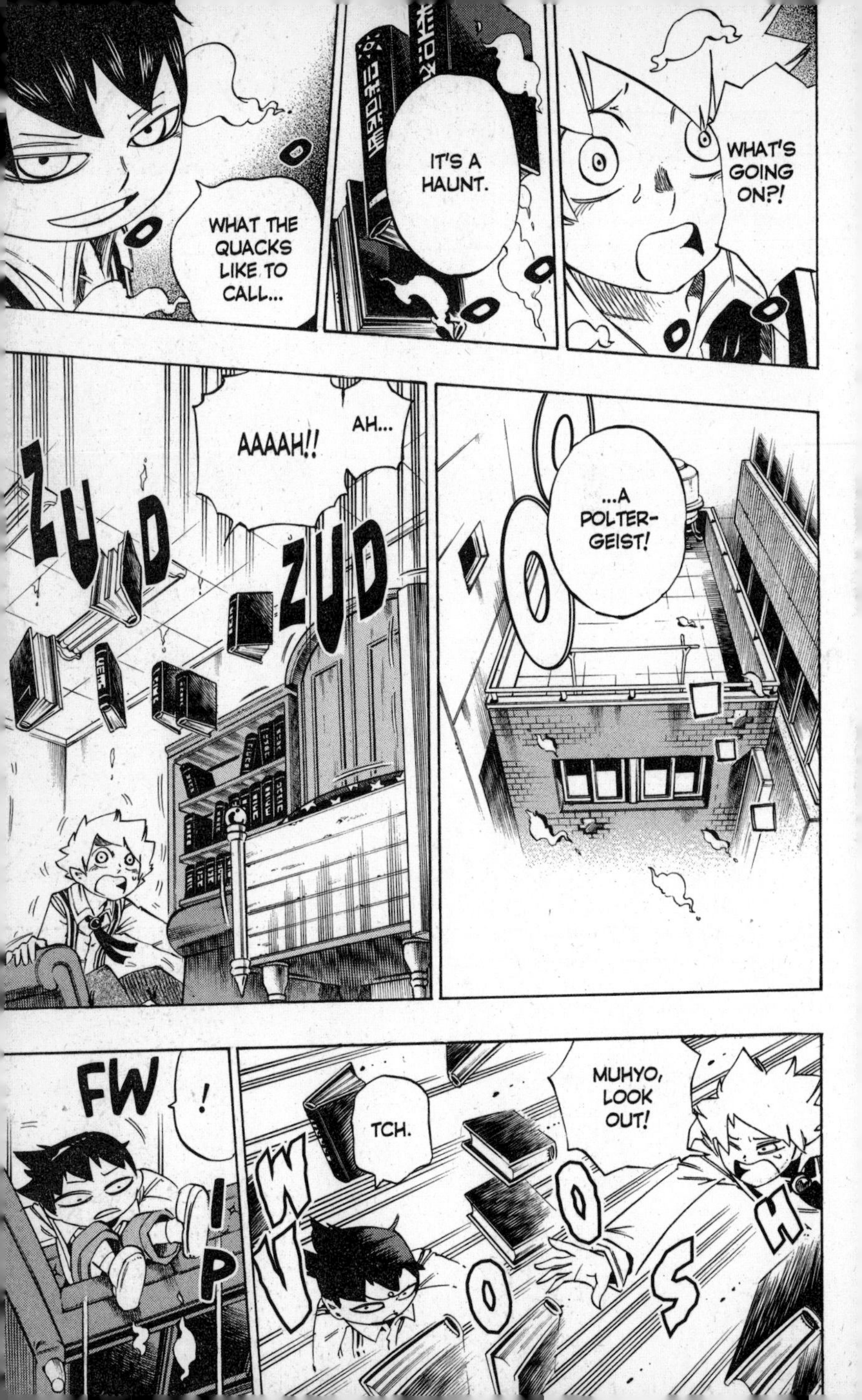
WHAT'S GOING ON?!
IT'S A HAUNT.
WHAT THE QUACKS LIKE TO CALL...
...A POLTER-GEIST!
AH...
AAAAH!!
ZUD
ZUD
MUHYO, LOOK OUT!
WHOOOSH
TCH.
!
FWIP

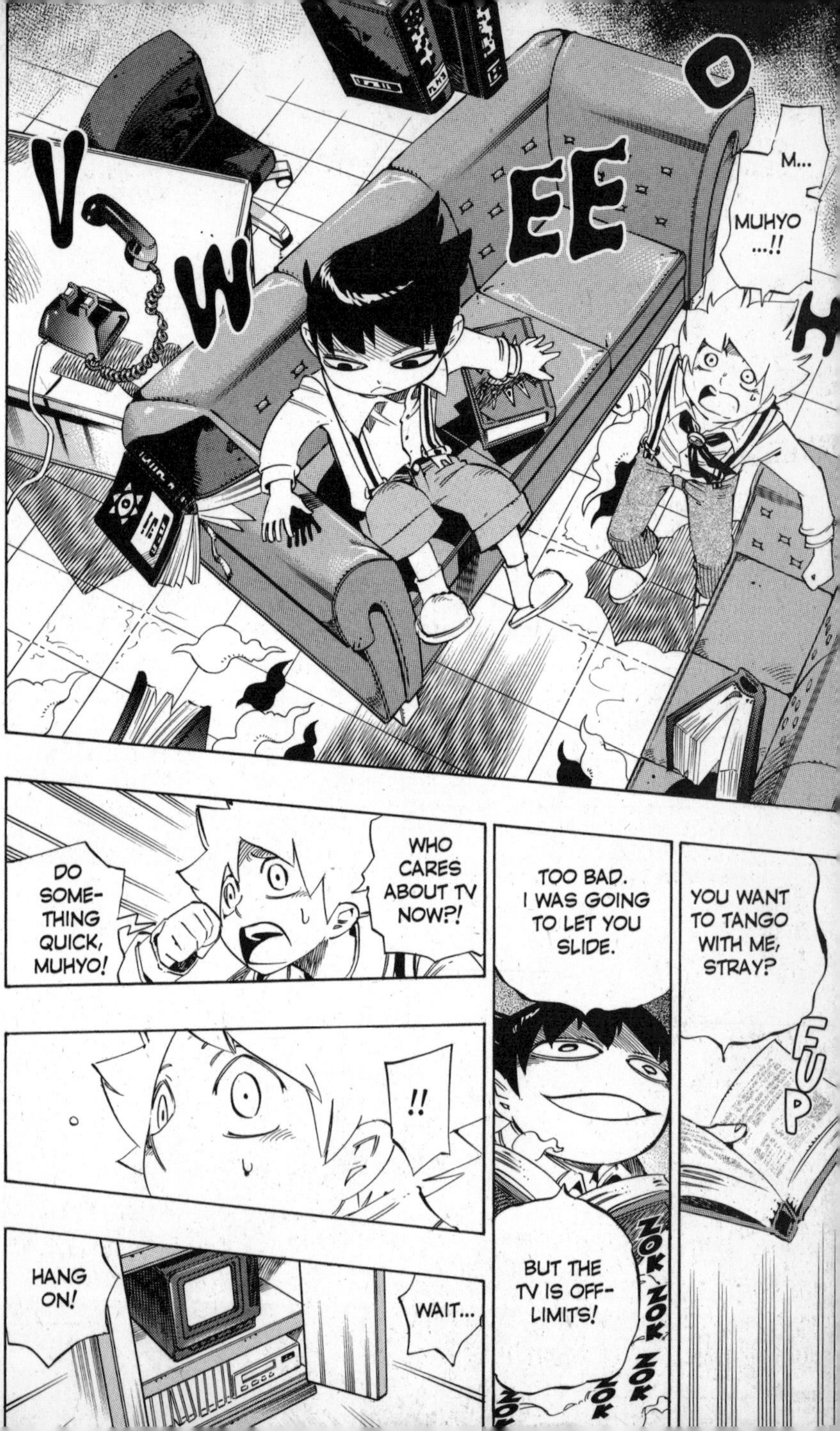
VWEEOH
M...
MUHYO ...!!
YOU WANT TO TANGO WITH ME, STRAY?
FUP
TOO BAD. I WAS GOING TO LET YOU SLIDE.
BUT THE TV IS OFF-LIMITS!
ZOK ZOK ZOK ZOK ZOK
WHO CARES ABOUT TV NOW?!
DO SOMETHING QUICK, MUHYO!
!!
WAIT...
HANG ON!

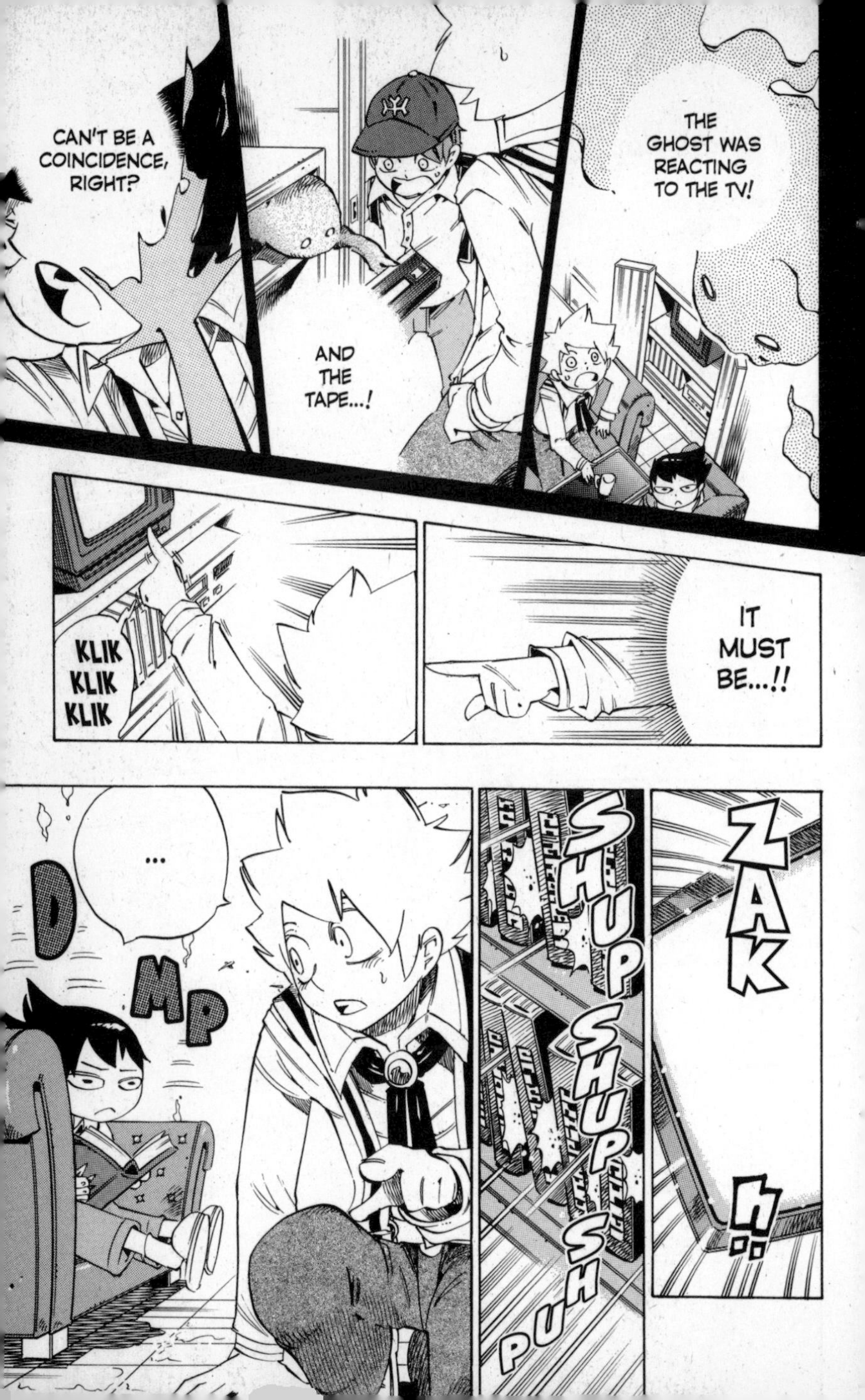

THE GHOST WAS REACTING TO THE TV!
AND THE TAPE...!
CAN'T BE A COINCIDENCE, RIGHT?
IT MUST BE...!!
KLIK KLIK KLIK
ZAK
SHUP SHUP SHUP SH
PUH
...
DMP

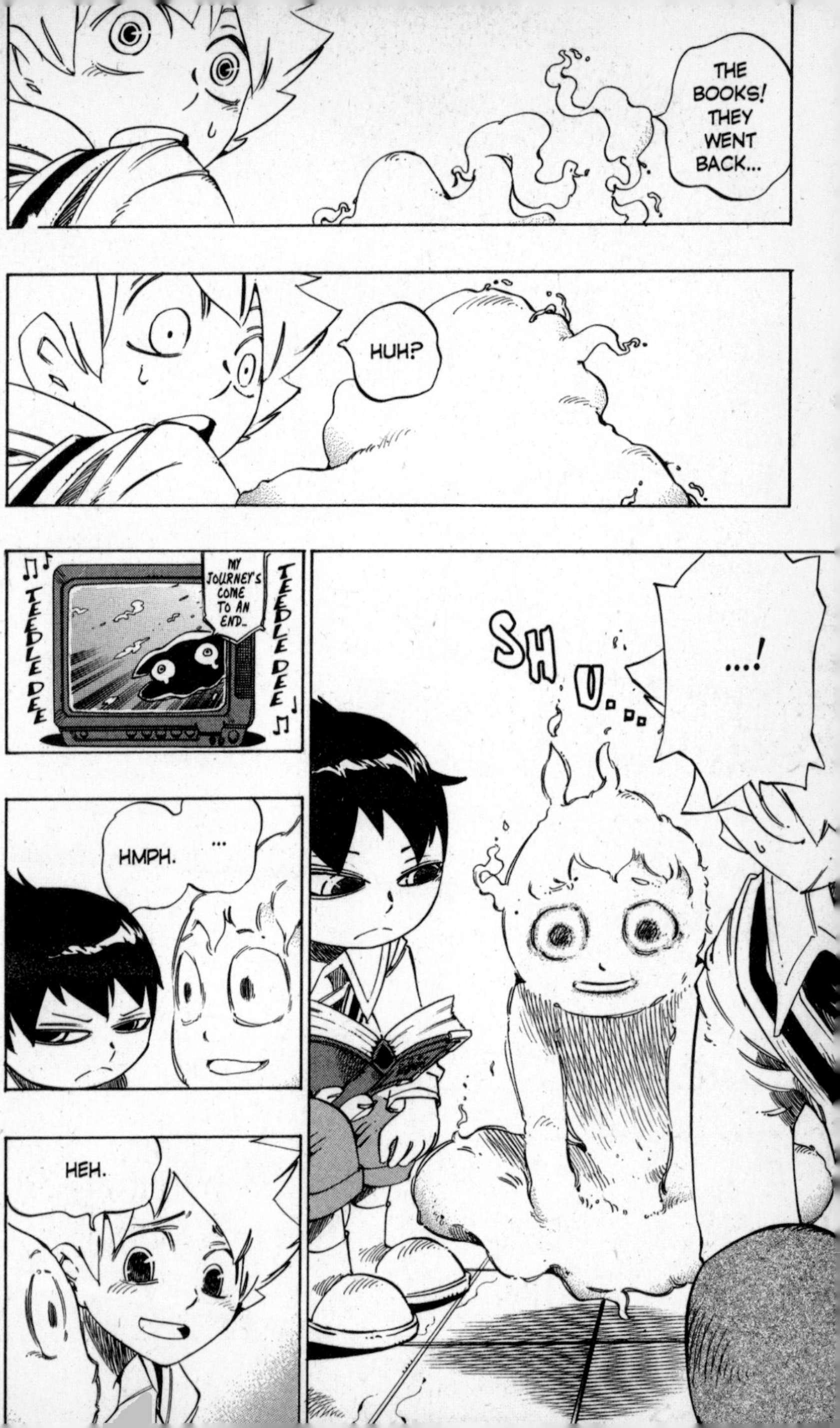
THE BOOKS! THEY WENT BACK...
HUH?
...!
SHU...
TEEDLE DEE
MY JOURNEY'S COME TO AN END...
TEEDLE DEE
...
HMPH.
HEH.

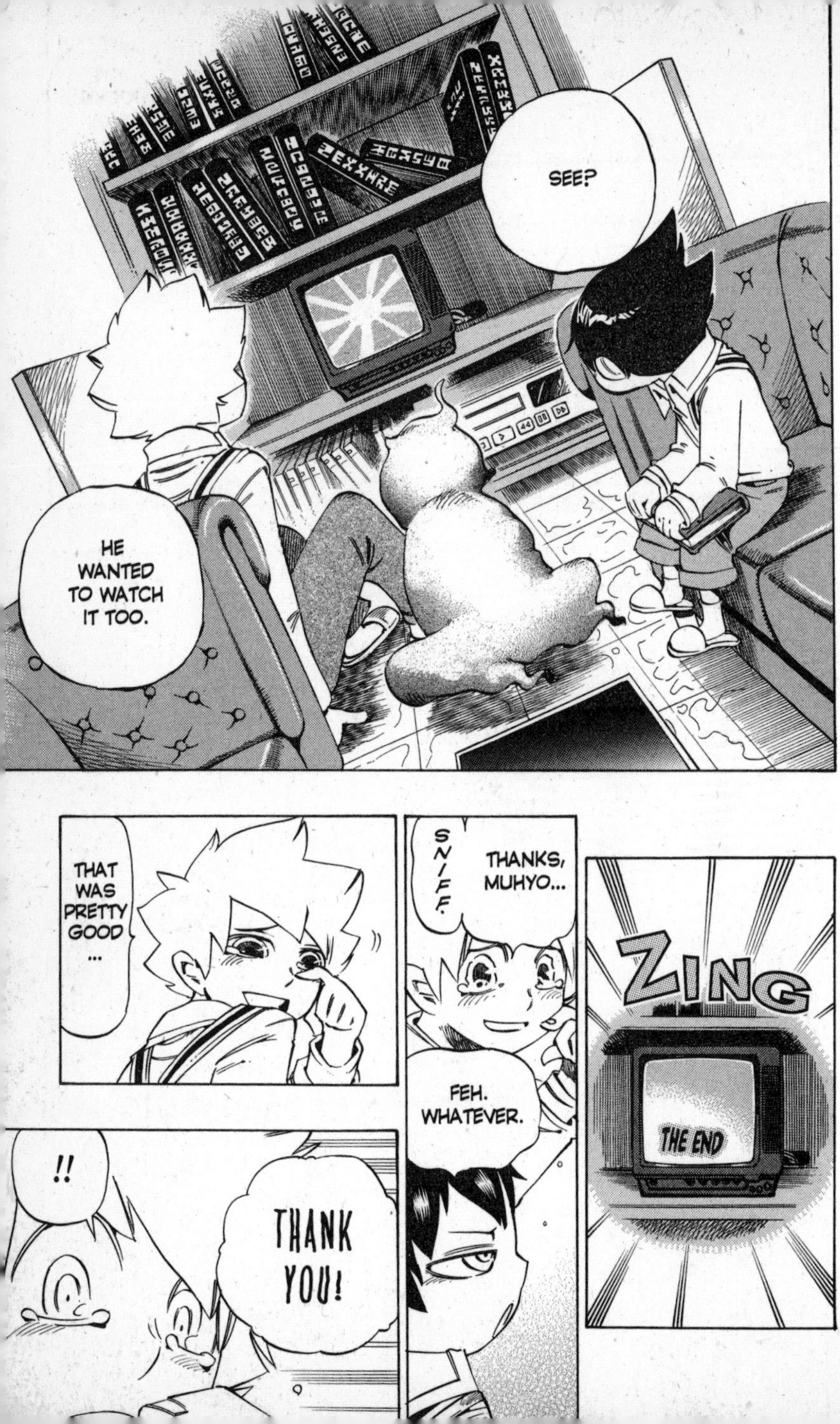
SEE?
HE WANTED TO WATCH IT TOO.
ZING
THE END
SNIFF.
THANKS, MUHYO...
FEH. WHATEVER.
THAT WAS PRETTY GOOD ...
!!
THANK YOU!

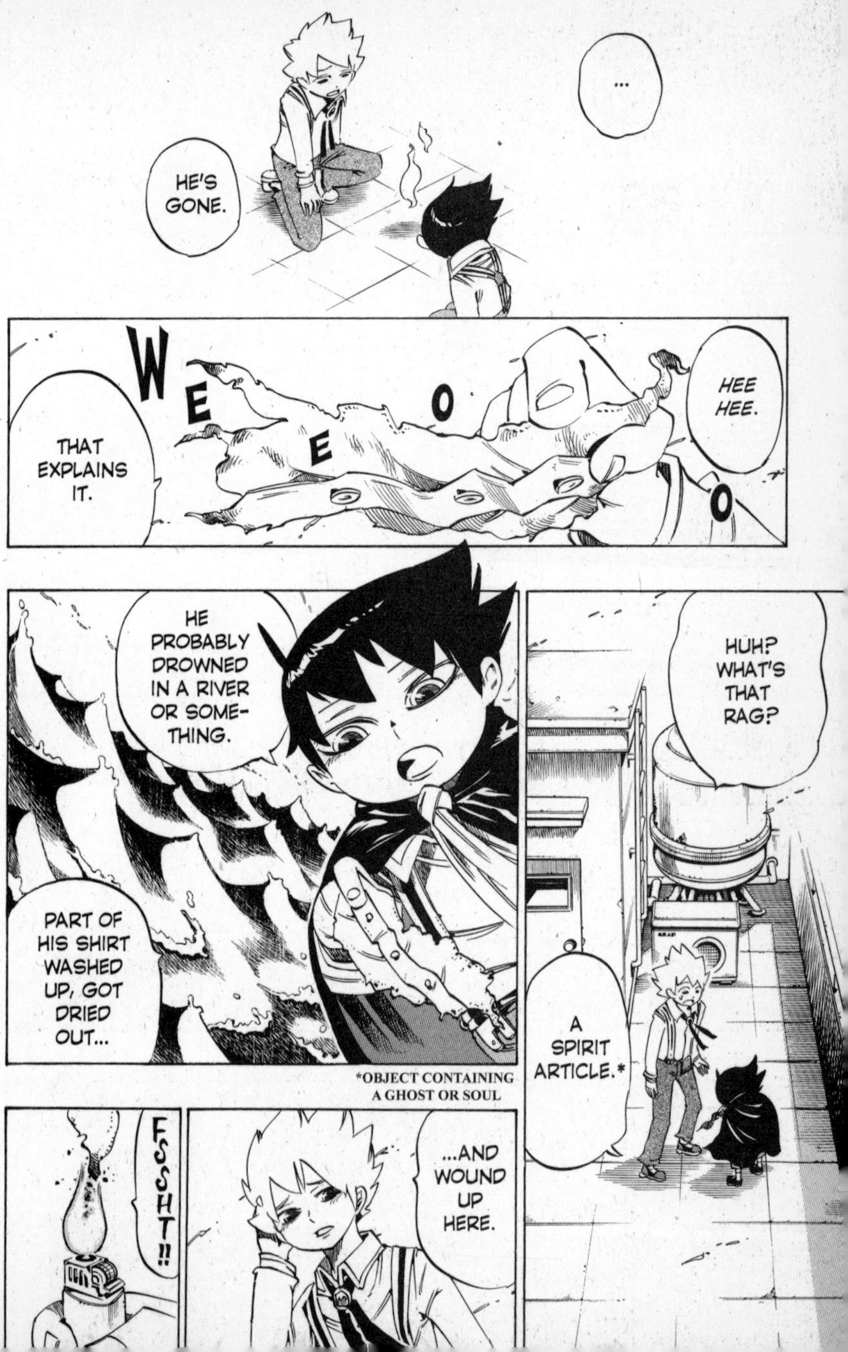
...
HE'S GONE.
HEE HEE.
WEEEOO
THAT EXPLAINS IT.
HUH? WHAT'S THAT RAG?
A SPIRIT ARTICLE.*
HE PROBABLY DROWNED IN A RIVER OR SOME-THING.
PART OF HIS SHIRT WASHED UP, GOT DRIED OUT...
*OBJECT CONTAINING A GHOST OR SOUL
...AND WOUND UP HERE.
FSSHT!!

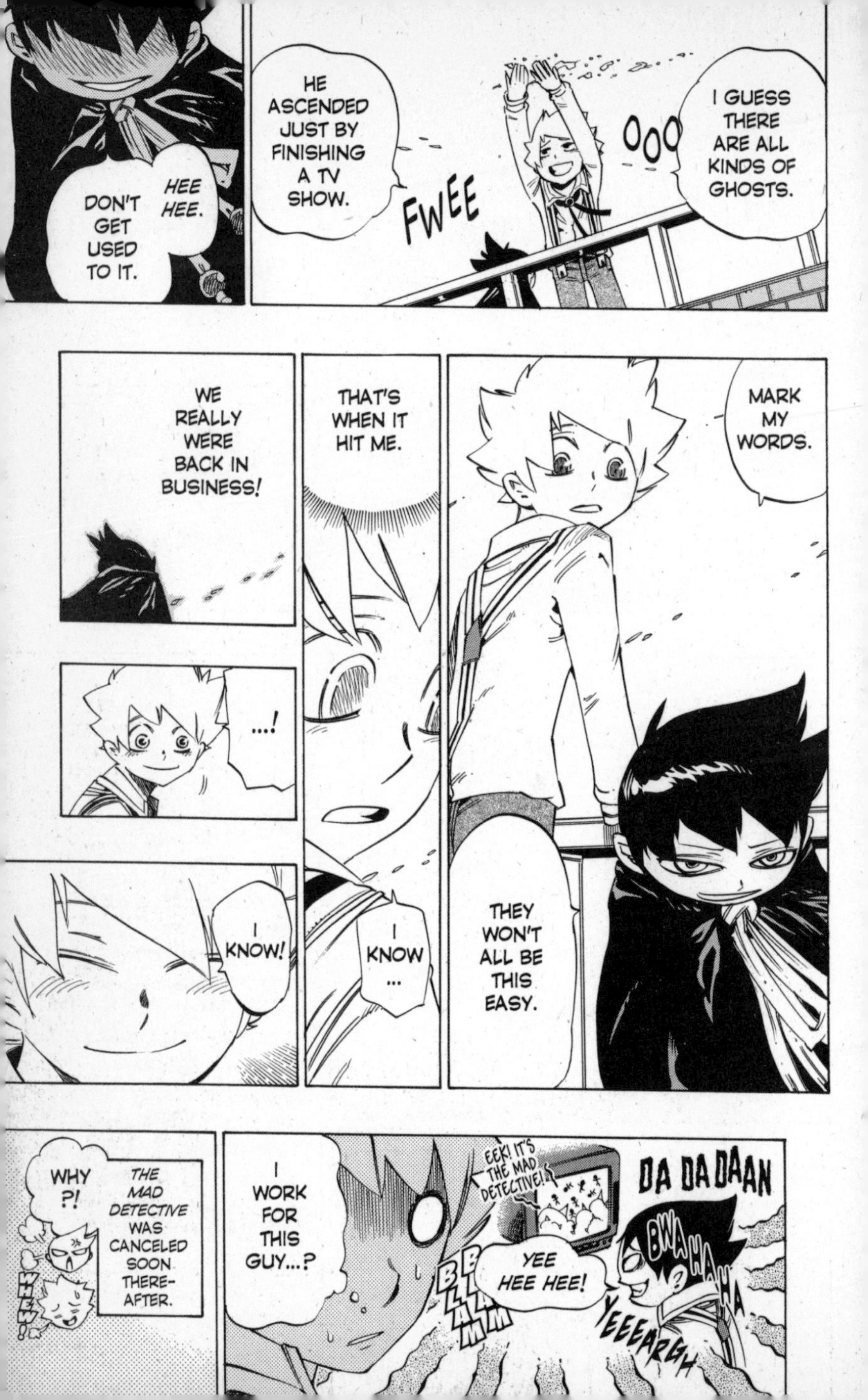
I GUESS THERE ARE ALL KINDS OF GHOSTS.
OOO
HE ASCENDED JUST BY FINISHING A TV SHOW.
FWEE
HEE HEE.
DON'T GET USED TO IT.
MARK MY WORDS.
THEY WON'T ALL BE THIS EASY.
THAT'S WHEN IT HIT ME.
I KNOW...
WE REALLY WERE BACK IN BUSINESS!
...!
I KNOW!
DA DA DAAN
EEK! IT'S THE MAD DETECTIVE!!
BWAHAHAHA
YEE HEE HEE!
YEEEARGH
BBLAAMM
I WORK FOR THIS GUY...?
WHY?!
THE MAD DETECTIVE WAS CANCELED SOON THERE-AFTER.
WHEW!

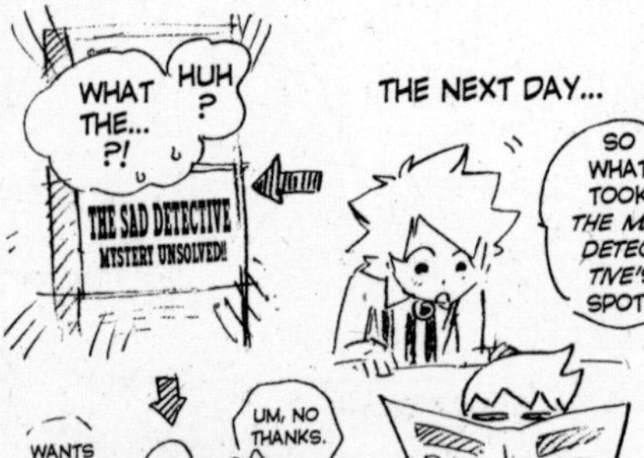
THE NEXT DAY...
SO WHAT TOOK THE MAD DETECTIVE'S SPOT?
...
HUH?
WHAT THE...?!
THE SAD DETECTIVE
MYSTERY UNSOLVED!
UM, NO THANKS.
HEE HEE.
WANTS TO WATCH
I'M SO TIRED.
WHAT A PAIN.

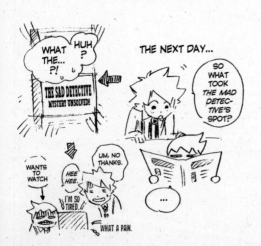

A WORD FROM THE AUTHOR

I'D BEEN DOING SERIOUS STORIES FOR SO LONG... "THE STRAY SPIRIT" WAS MY BREATHER FROM ALL THAT. IT'S FUN TO DO SOMETHING SHORT AND EPISODIC ONCE IN A WHILE! FOR SOME REASON, I'VE BEEN GETTING LOTS OF COMMENTS ABOUT *THE MAD DETECTIVE*. SOME PEOPLE EVEN WANT ME TO DO A MANGA ON HIM... HE'S QUITE A CHARACTER, EH?

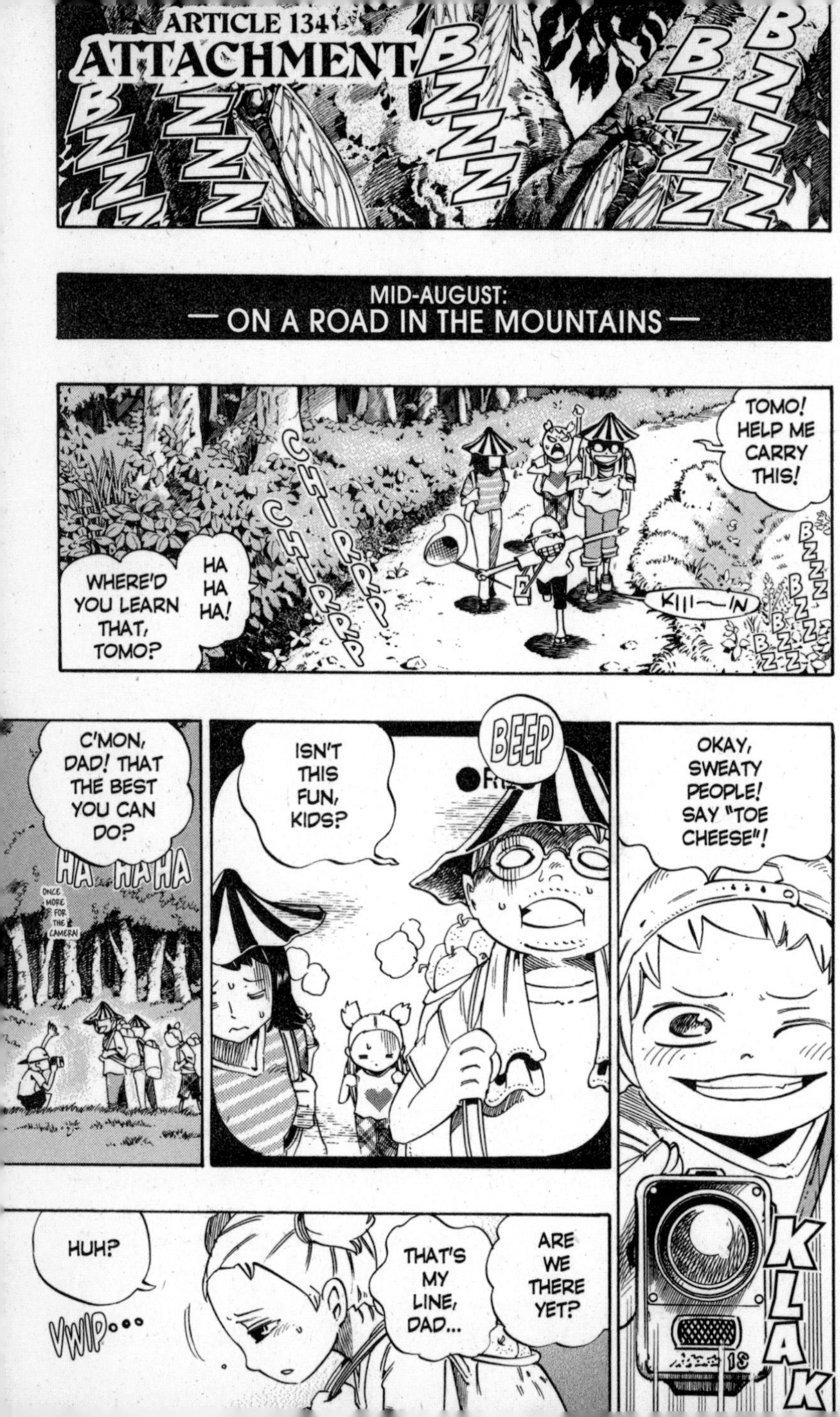
ARTICLE 134
ATTACHMENT
BZZZ
BZZZ
BZZZ
BZZZ
BZZZ
MID-AUGUST:
— ON A ROAD IN THE MOUNTAINS —
TOMO! HELP ME CARRY THIS!
BZZZ
KIII—IN
CHIRRRP
CHIRRRP
HA HA HA!
WHERE'D YOU LEARN THAT, TOMO?
OKAY, SWEATY PEOPLE! SAY "TOE CHEESE"!
KLAK
BEEP
ISN'T THIS FUN, KIDS?
C'MON, DAD! THAT THE BEST YOU CAN DO?
HA HAHA
ONCE MORE FOR THE CAMERA
ARE WE THERE YET?
THAT'S MY LINE, DAD...
HUH?
VWIP...

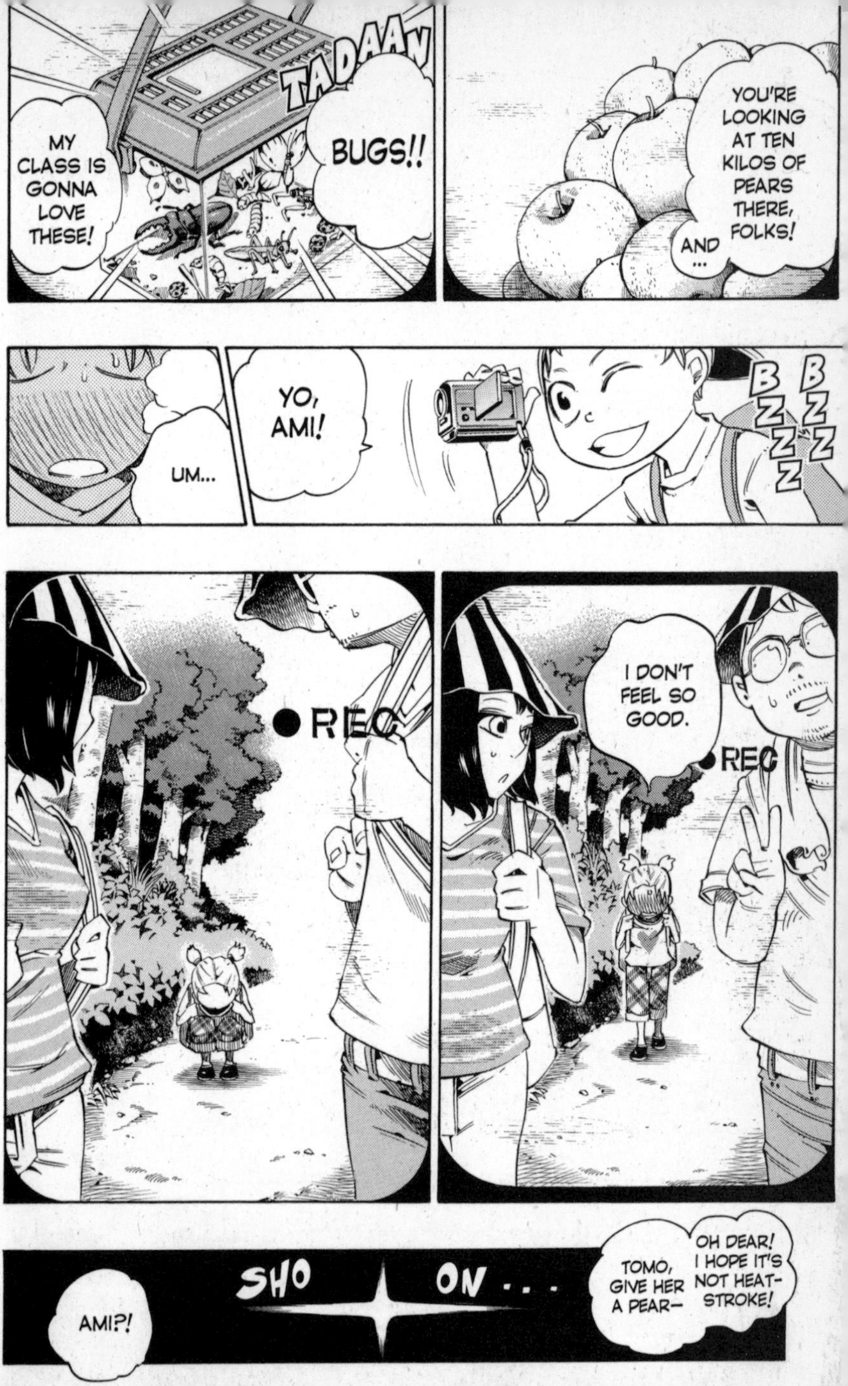
YOU'RE LOOKING AT TEN KILOS OF PEARS THERE, FOLKS!
AND ...
TADAAN
BUGS!!
MY CLASS IS GONNA LOVE THESE!
BZZZ
BZZZZ
YO, AMI!
UM...
I DON'T FEEL SO GOOD.
●REC
●REC
OH DEAR! I HOPE IT'S NOT HEAT-STROKE!
TOMO, GIVE HER A PEAR—
SHO ON . . .
AMI?!

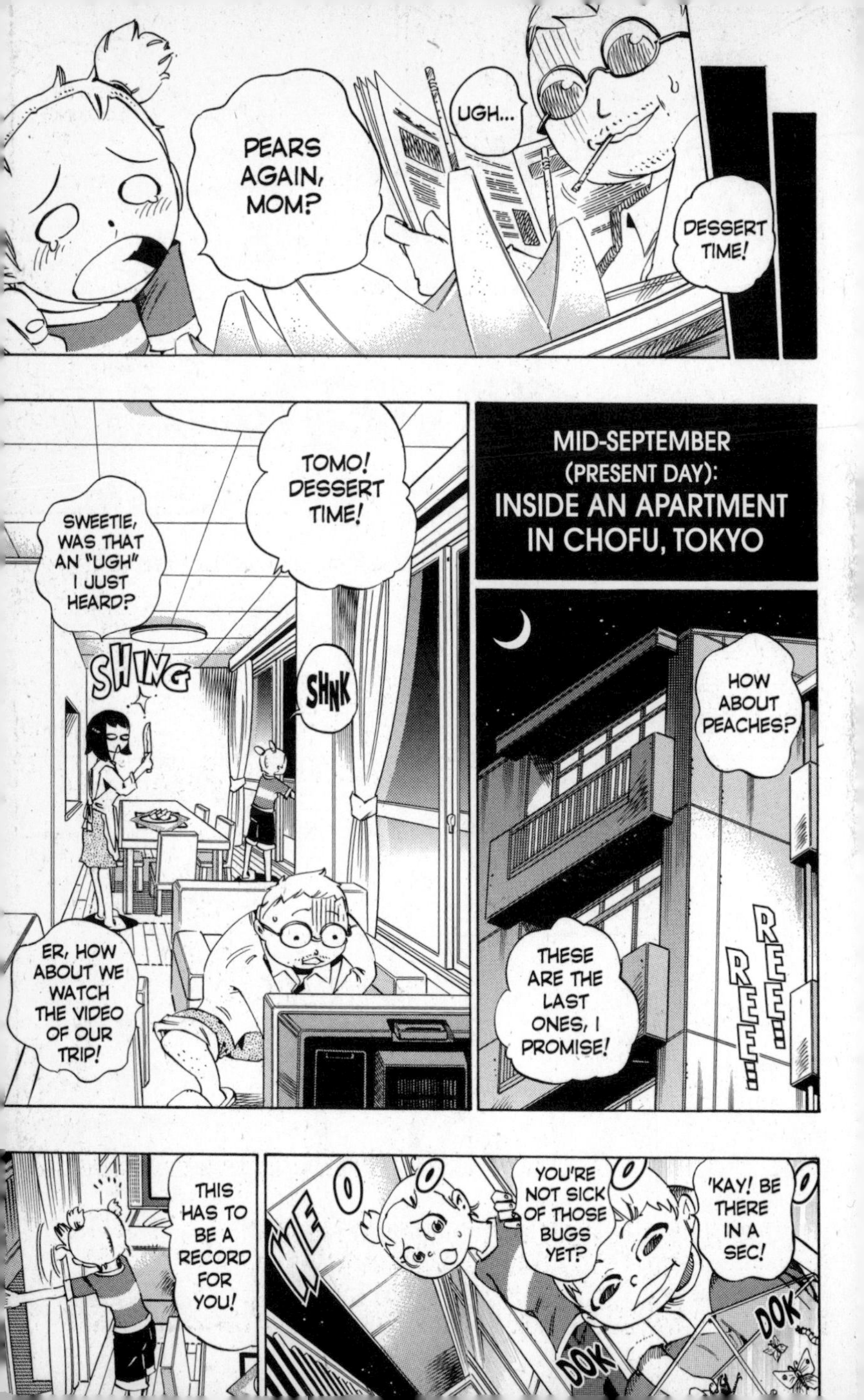
DESSERT TIME!
UGH...
PEARS AGAIN, MOM?
MID-SEPTEMBER (PRESENT DAY): INSIDE AN APARTMENT IN CHOFU, TOKYO
HOW ABOUT PEACHES?
REE REE...
REE...
THESE ARE THE LAST ONES, I PROMISE!
TOMO! DESSERT TIME!
SWEETIE, WAS THAT AN "UGH" I JUST HEARD?
SHNK
SHING
ER, HOW ABOUT WE WATCH THE VIDEO OF OUR TRIP!
'KAY! BE THERE IN A SEC!
YOU'RE NOT SICK OF THOSE BUGS YET?
DOK
DOK
THIS HAS TO BE A RECORD FOR YOU!

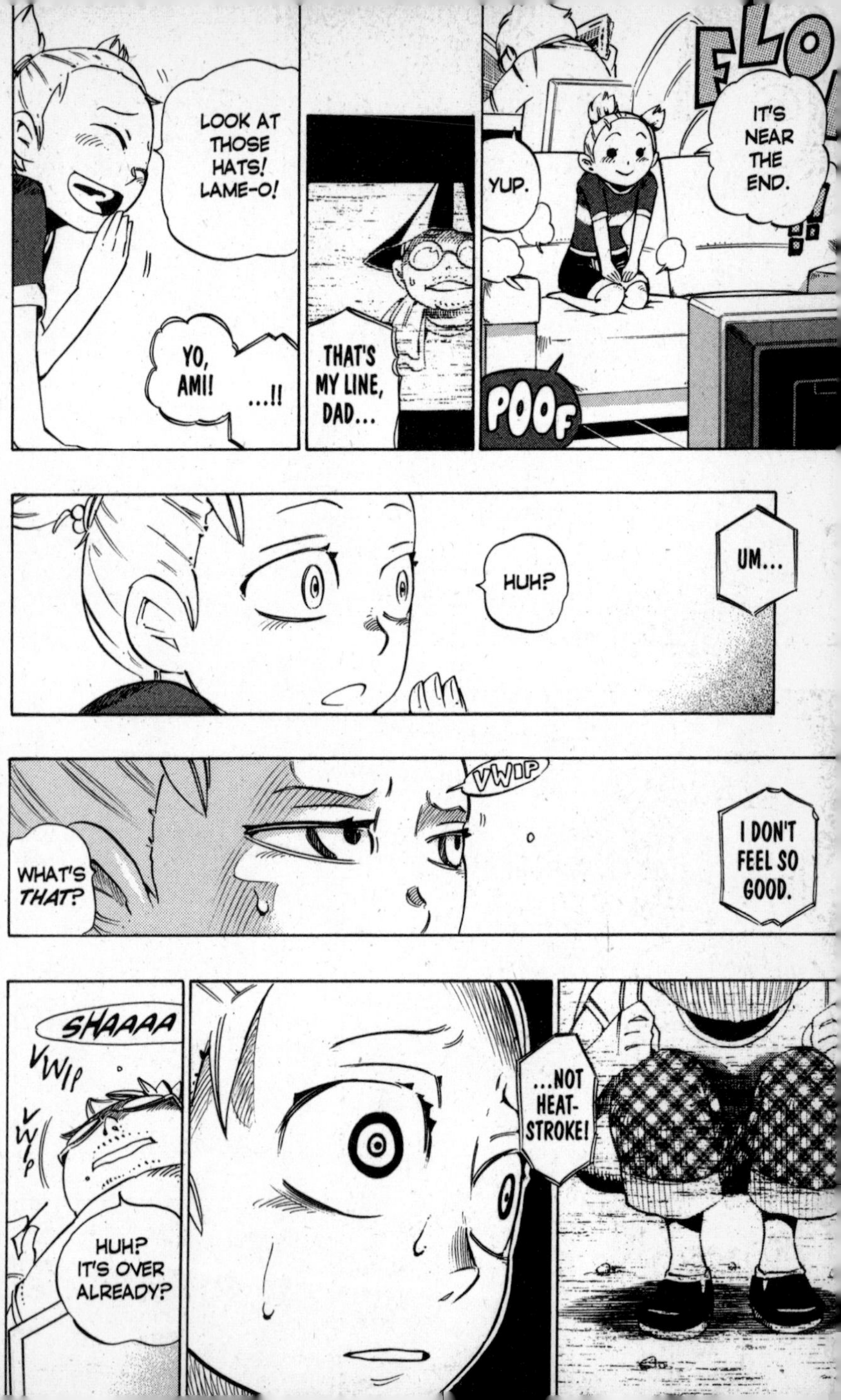
FLO
IT'S NEAR THE END.
YUP.
POOF
THAT'S MY LINE, DAD...
LOOK AT THOSE HATS! LAME-O!
YO, AMI!
...!!
UM...
HUH?
I DON'T FEEL SO GOOD.
VWIP
WHAT'S *THAT?*
...NOT HEAT-STROKE!
SHAAAA
VWIP
VWIP
HUH? IT'S OVER ALREADY?

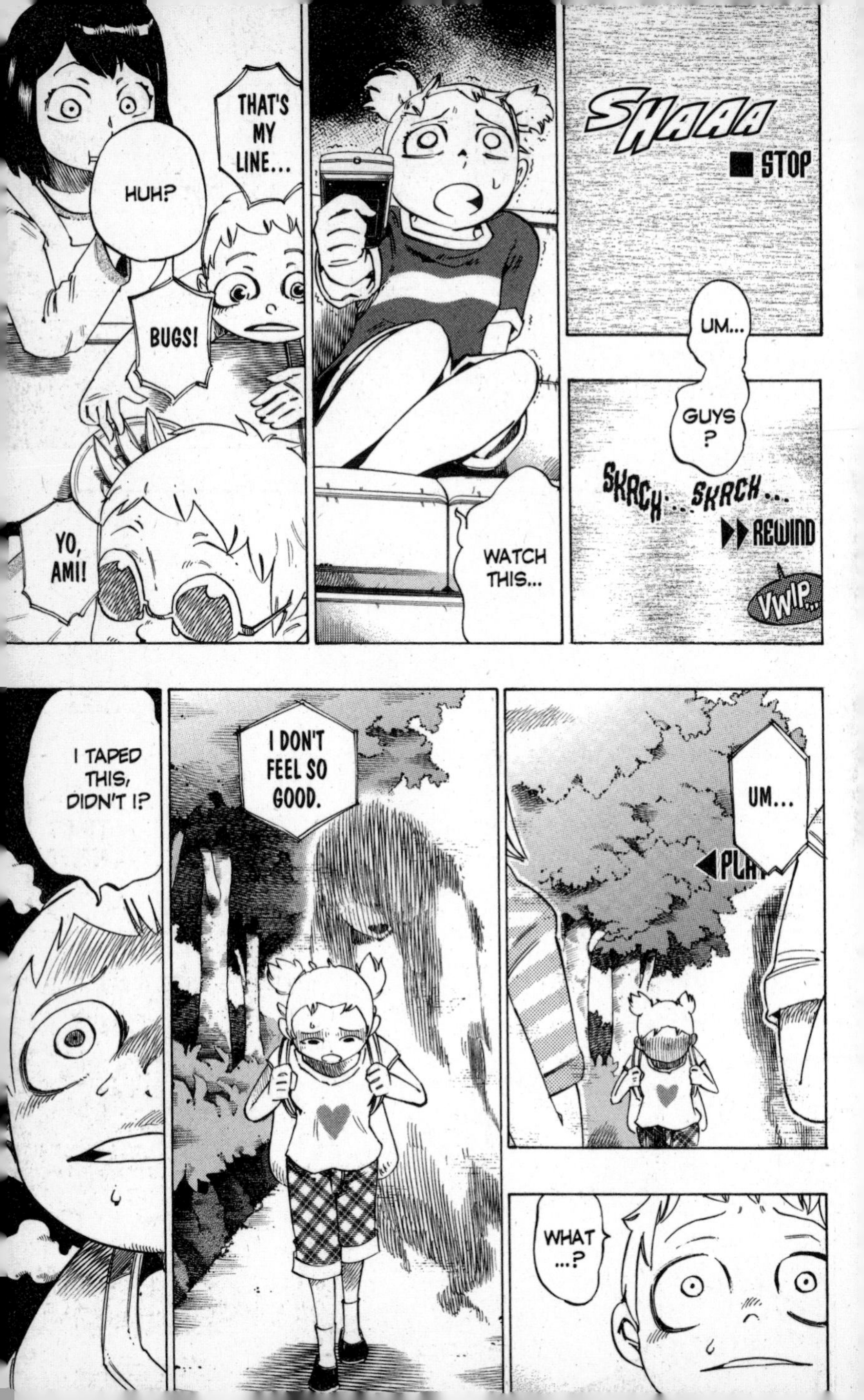
SHAAA
■ STOP
UM... GUYS?
SKRCH... SKRCH...
▶▶ REWIND
VWIP...
WATCH THIS...
THAT'S MY LINE...
HUH?
BUGS!
YO, AMI!
UM...
◀ PLA
WHAT ...?
I DON'T FEEL SO GOOD.
I TAPED THIS, DIDN'T I?

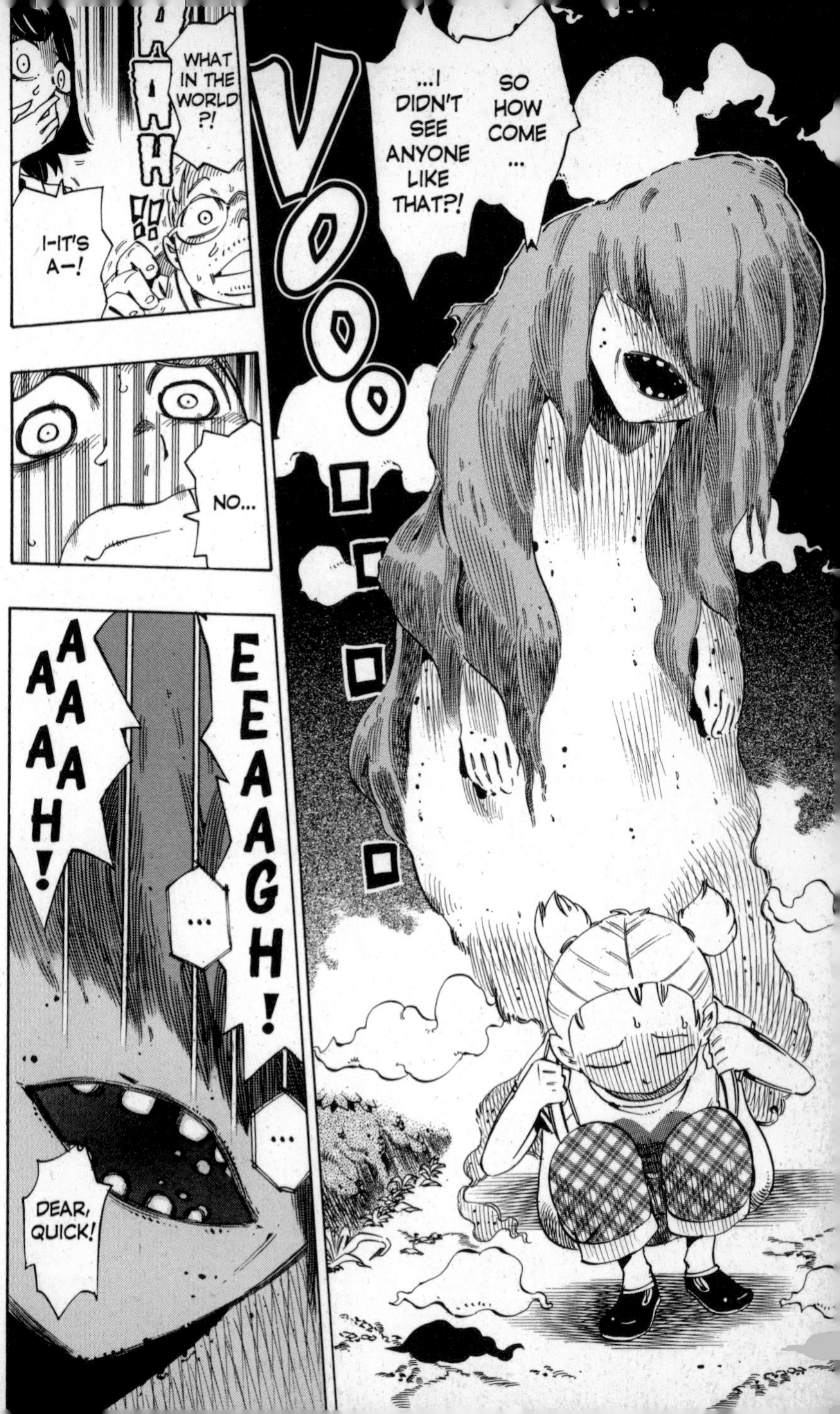
SO HOW COME ...
...I DIDN'T SEE ANYONE LIKE THAT?!
VOOOO
WHAT IN THE WORLD ?!
AAH!!
I-IT'S A—!
NO...
EEAAAGH!
AAAAAH!
...
...
DEAR, QUICK!

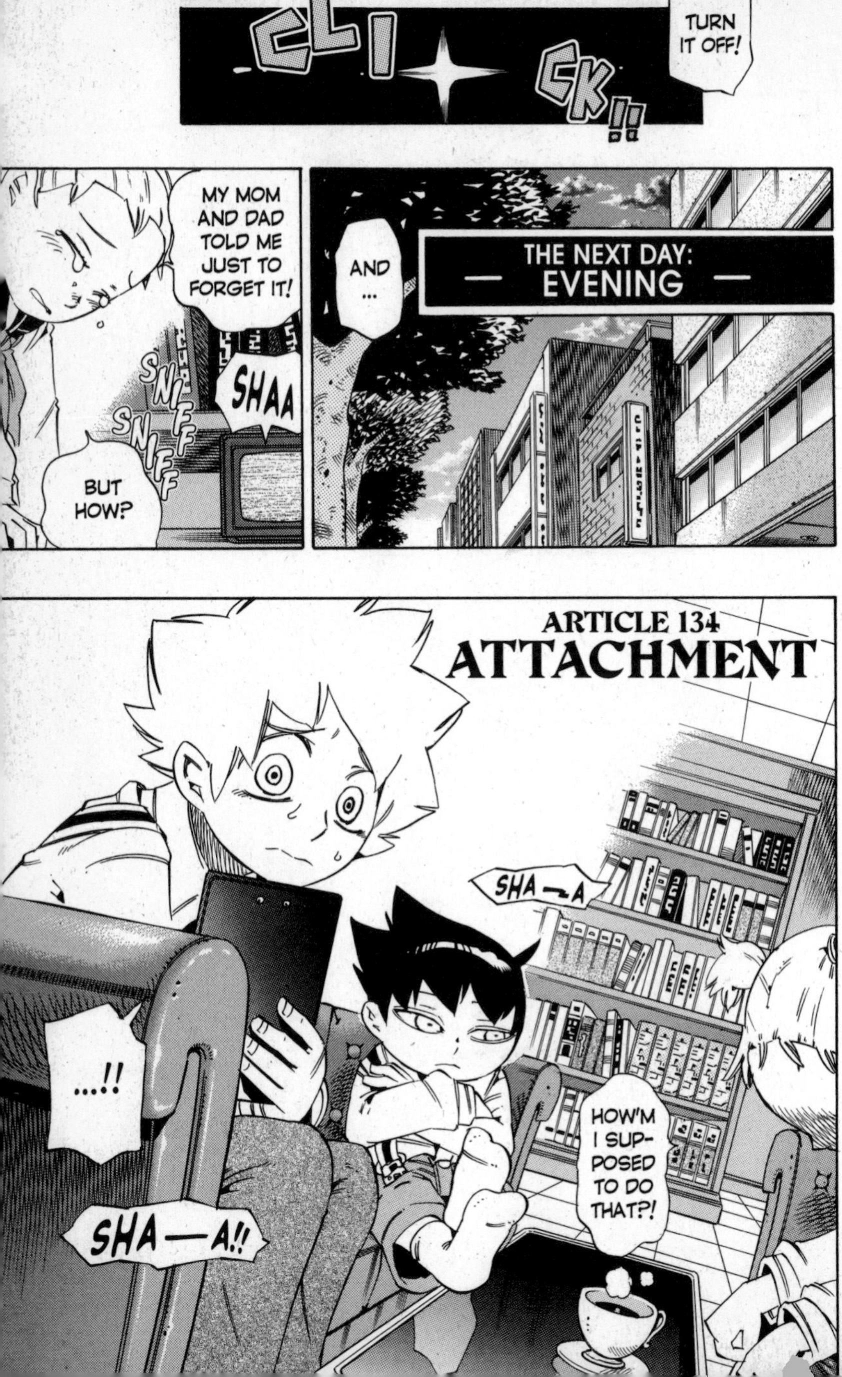
TURN IT OFF!
CLI—CK!!
THE NEXT DAY: — EVENING —
AND ...
MY MOM AND DAD TOLD ME JUST TO FORGET IT!
SHAA
SNIFF SNIFF
BUT HOW?
ARTICLE 134
ATTACHMENT
SHA—A
HOW'M I SUP-POSED TO DO THAT?!
...!!
SHA—A!!

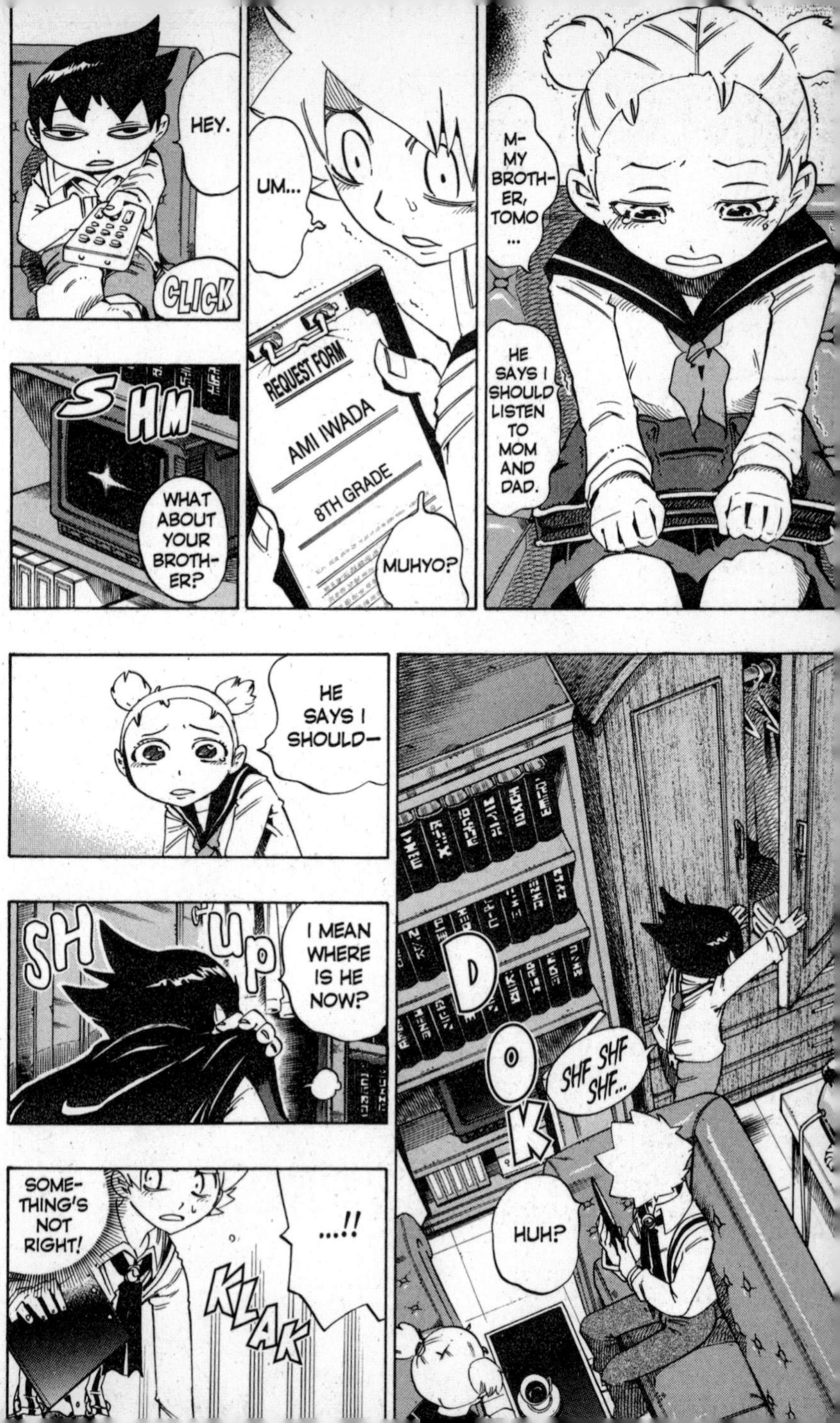
M- MY BROTHER, TOMO ...
HE SAYS I SHOULD LISTEN TO MOM AND DAD.
UM...
REQUEST FORM
AMI IWADA
8TH GRADE
MUHYO?
HEY.
CLICK
SHM
WHAT ABOUT YOUR BROTHER?
DOK
SHF SHF SHF...
HUH?
HE SAYS I SHOULD—
SHUP
I MEAN WHERE IS HE NOW?
...!!
SOME-THING'S NOT RIGHT!
KLAK

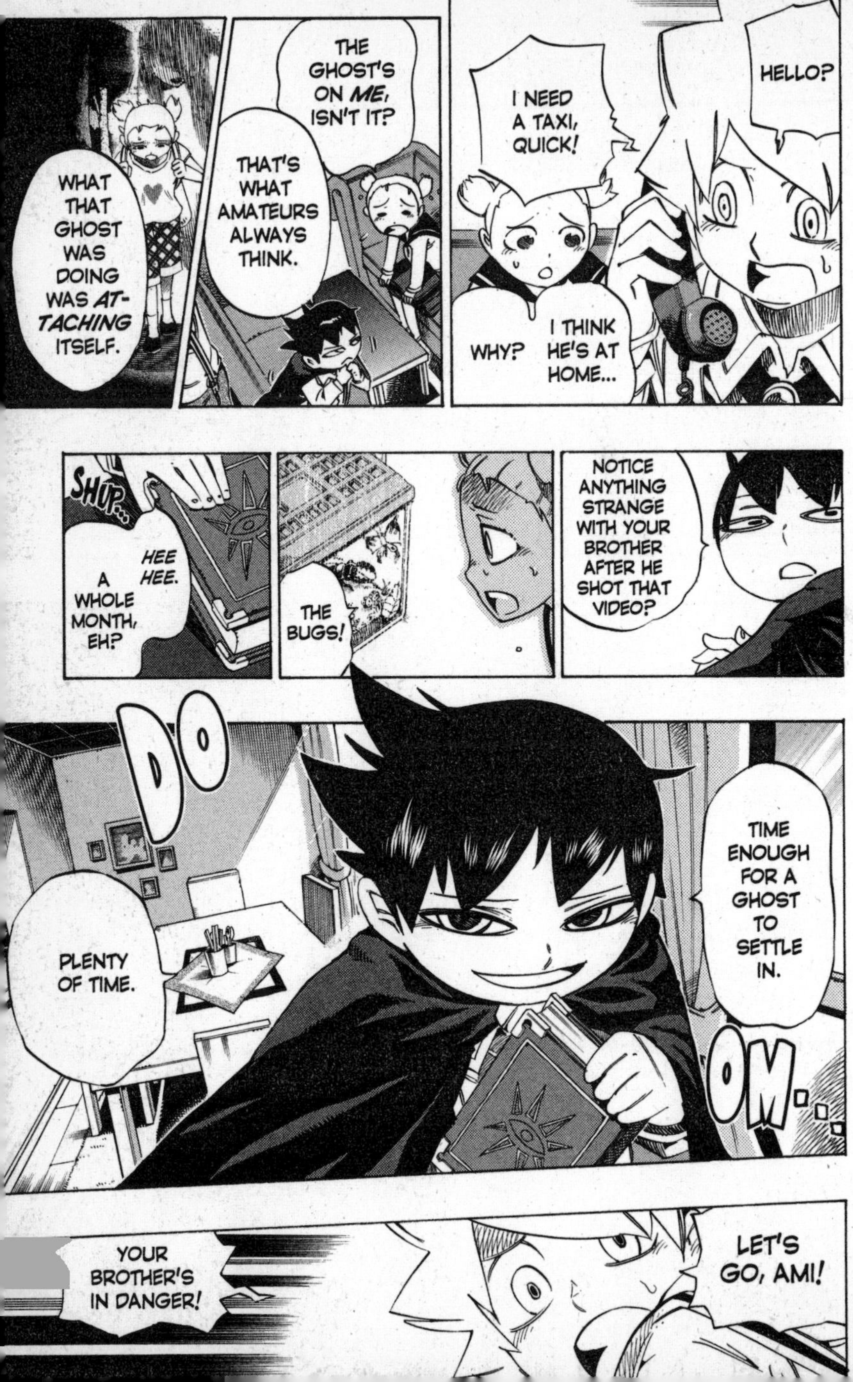
HELLO?
I NEED A TAXI, QUICK!
I THINK HE'S AT HOME...
WHY?
THE GHOST'S ON *ME*, ISN'T IT?
THAT'S WHAT AMATEURS ALWAYS THINK.
WHAT THAT GHOST WAS DOING WAS *ATTACHING* ITSELF.
NOTICE ANYTHING STRANGE WITH YOUR BROTHER AFTER HE SHOT THAT VIDEO?
THE BUGS!
SHUP...
HEE HEE.
A WHOLE MONTH, EH?
DO
TIME ENOUGH FOR A GHOST TO SETTLE IN.
PLENTY OF TIME.
OM...
LET'S GO, AMI!
YOUR BROTHER'S IN DANGER!

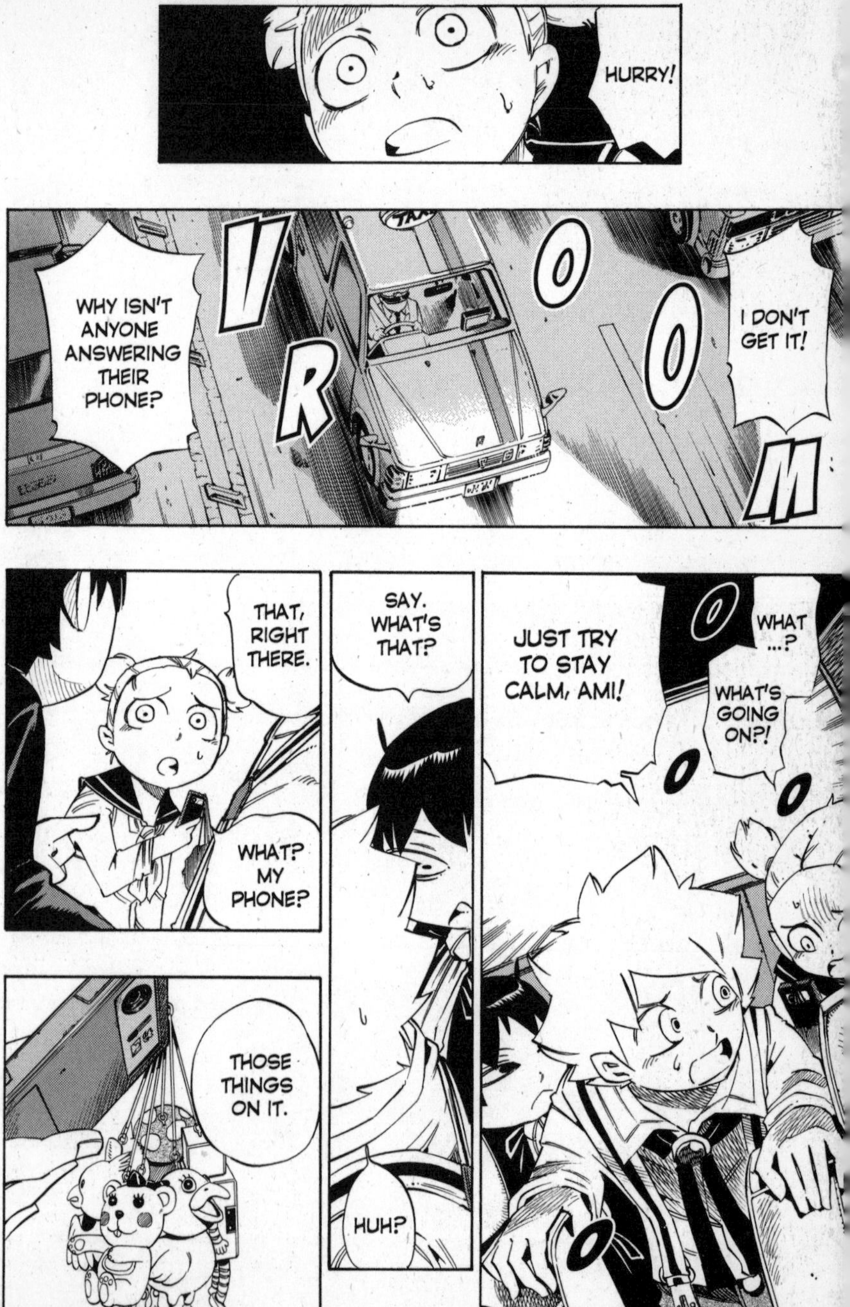
HURRY!
I DON'T GET IT!
VROOOM
WHY ISN'T ANYONE ANSWERING THEIR PHONE?
WHAT ...?
WHAT'S GOING ON?!
JUST TRY TO STAY CALM, AMI!
SAY. WHAT'S THAT?
HUH?
THAT, RIGHT THERE.
WHAT? MY PHONE?
THOSE THINGS ON IT.

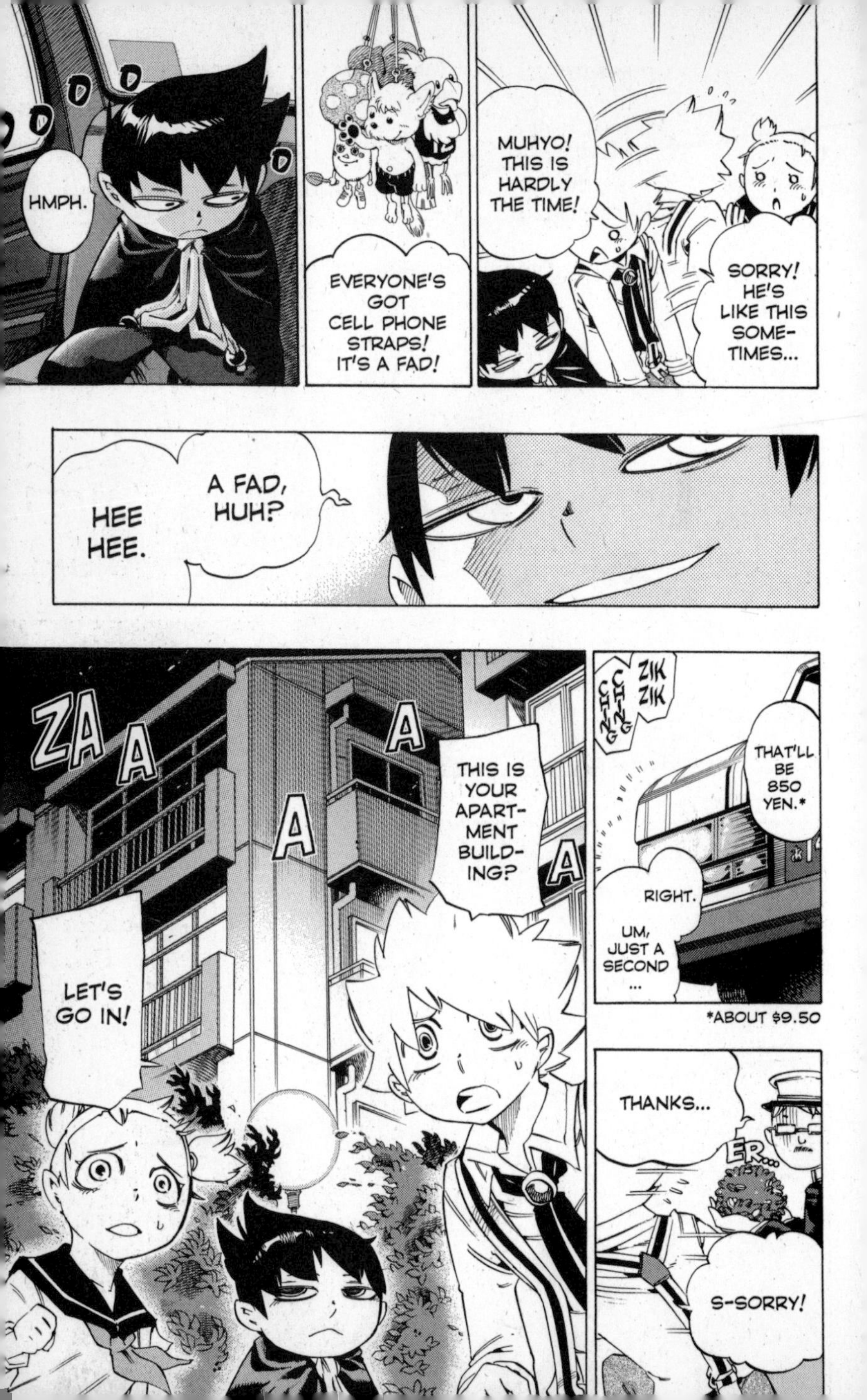
MUHYO! THIS IS HARDLY THE TIME!
SORRY! HE'S LIKE THIS SOME-TIMES...
EVERYONE'S GOT CELL PHONE STRAPS! IT'S A FAD!
HMPH.
A FAD, HUH?
HEE HEE.
ZIK ZIK
CHING CHING
THAT'LL BE 850 YEN.*
RIGHT.
UM, JUST A SECOND ...
*ABOUT $9.50
THANKS...
ER...
S-SORRY!
ZAAAAA
THIS IS YOUR APART-MENT BUILD-ING?
LET'S GO IN!

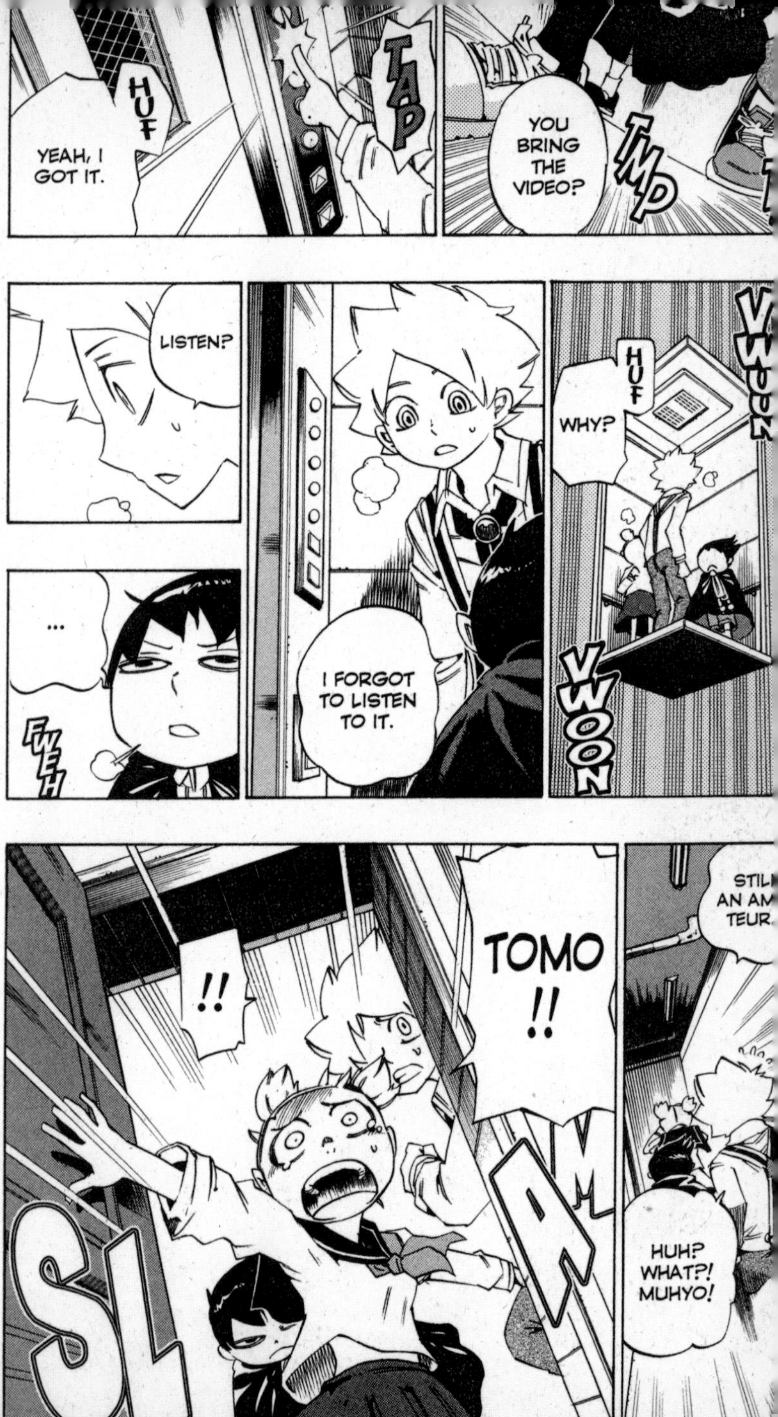
YOU BRING THE VIDEO?
TMP
TAP
HUF
YEAH, I GOT IT.
VWOON
HUF
WHY?
VWOON
I FORGOT TO LISTEN TO IT.
LISTEN?
...
FWEH
STIL AN AM TEUR.
HUH? WHAT?! MUHYO!
TOMO !!
!!
SL
AM

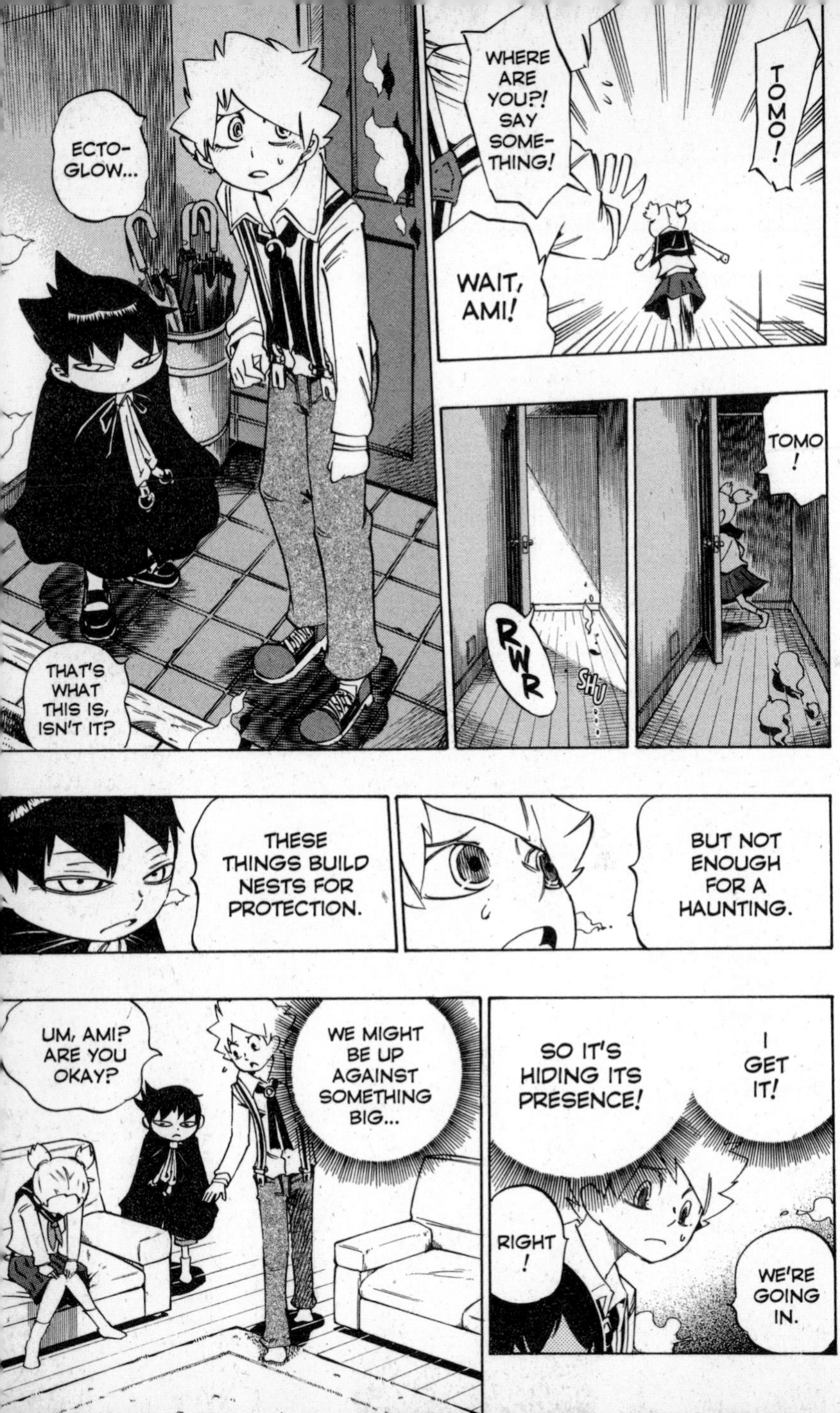
TOMO!
WHERE ARE YOU?! SAY SOMETHING!
WAIT, AMI!
TOMO!
RWR
SHU...
ECTO-GLOW...
THAT'S WHAT THIS IS, ISN'T IT?
BUT NOT ENOUGH FOR A HAUNTING.
THESE THINGS BUILD NESTS FOR PROTECTION.
I GET IT!
SO IT'S HIDING ITS PRESENCE!
WE'RE GOING IN.
RIGHT!
WE MIGHT BE UP AGAINST SOMETHING BIG...
UM, AMI? ARE YOU OKAY?

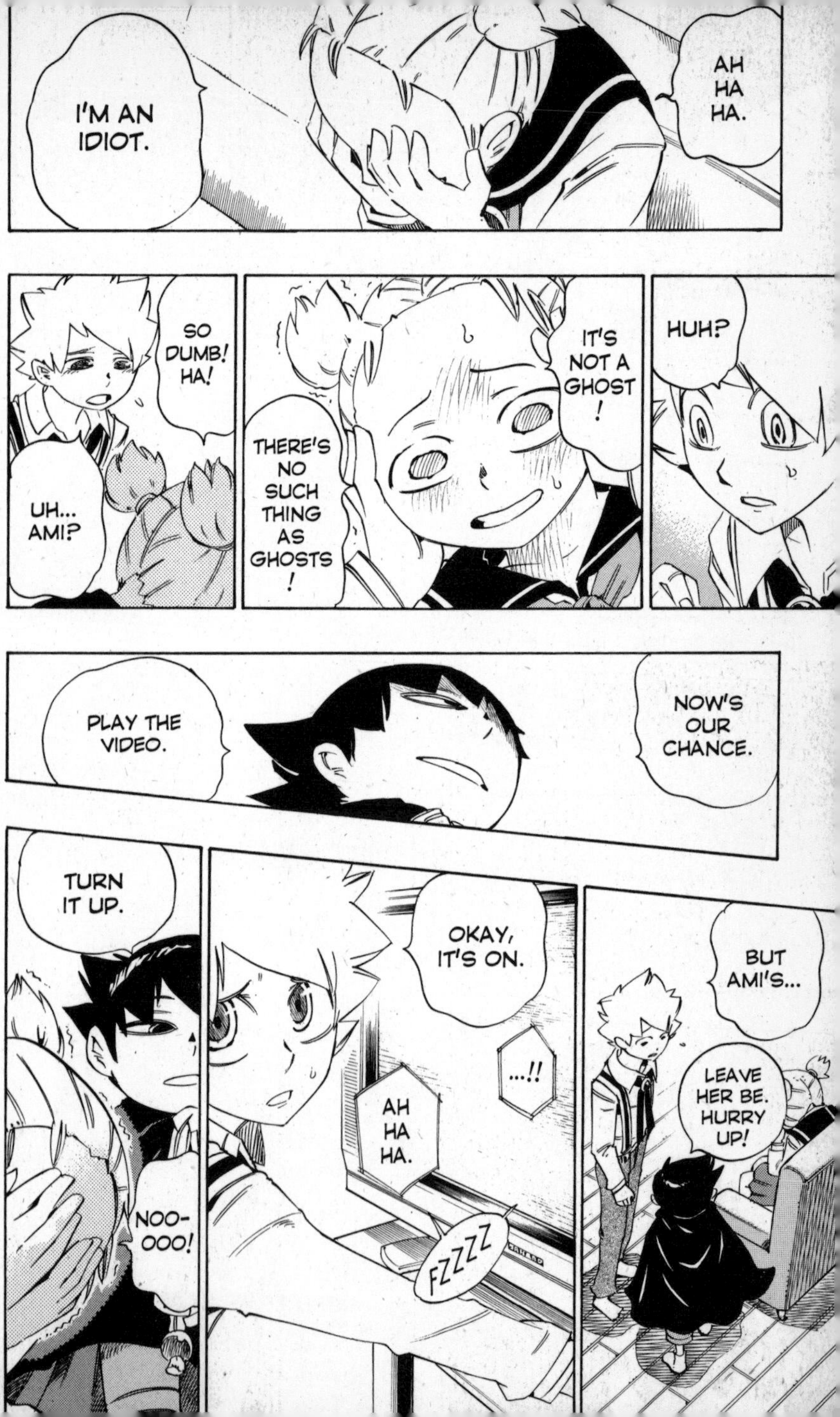
AH HA HA.
I'M AN IDIOT.
HUH?
IT'S NOT A GHOST!
THERE'S NO SUCH THING AS GHOSTS!
SO DUMB! HA!
UH... AMI?
NOW'S OUR CHANCE.
PLAY THE VIDEO.
BUT AMI'S...
LEAVE HER BE. HURRY UP!
OKAY, IT'S ON.
...!!
AH HA HA.
FZZZZ
TURN IT UP.
NOO-OOO!

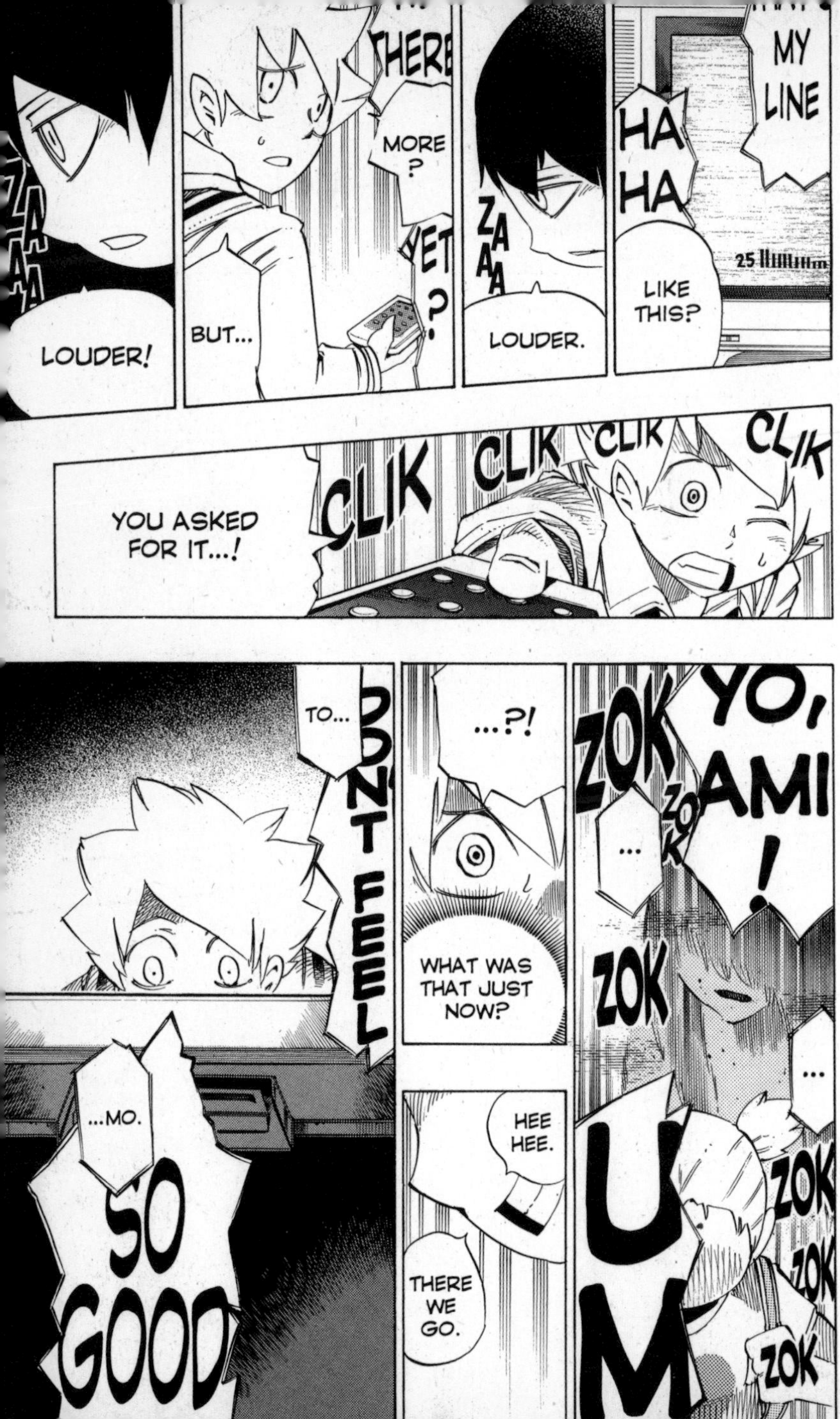
MY LINE
HA HA
LIKE THIS?
ZAAA
LOUDER.
THERE
MORE?
YET?
BUT...
ZAAAA
LOUDER!
CLIK CLIK CLIK CLIK
YOU ASKED FOR IT...!
YO, AMI!
ZOK ZOK
...
ZOK
...
UM
ZOK ZOK ZOK
...?!
WHAT WAS THAT JUST NOW?
HEE HEE.
THERE WE GO.
TO...
DON'T FEEL
...MO.
SO GOOD

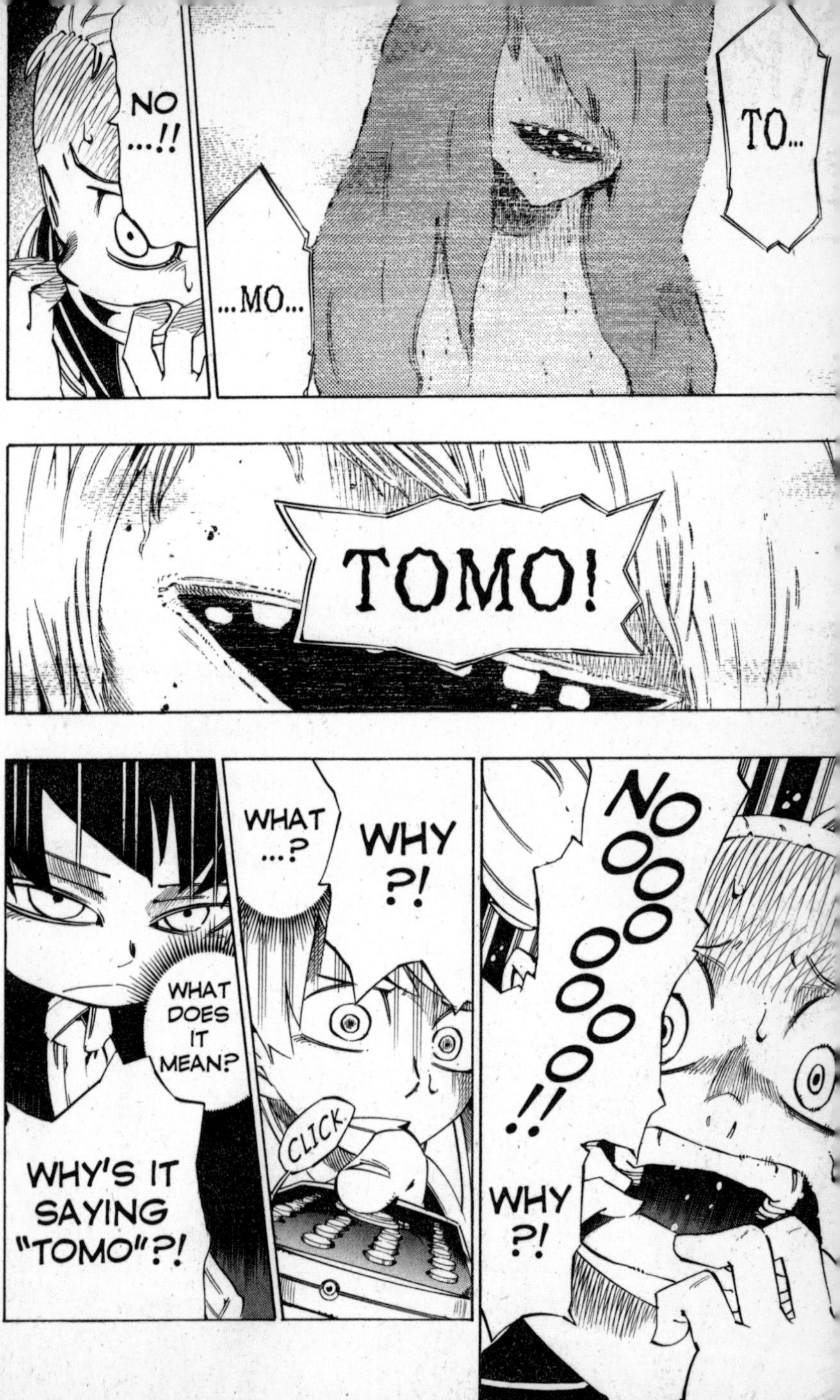
TO...
...MO...
NO ...!!
TOMO!
NOOOOOOOOO!!
WHY ?!
WHY ?!
WHAT ...?
CLICK
WHAT DOES IT MEAN?
WHY'S IT SAYING "TOMO"?!

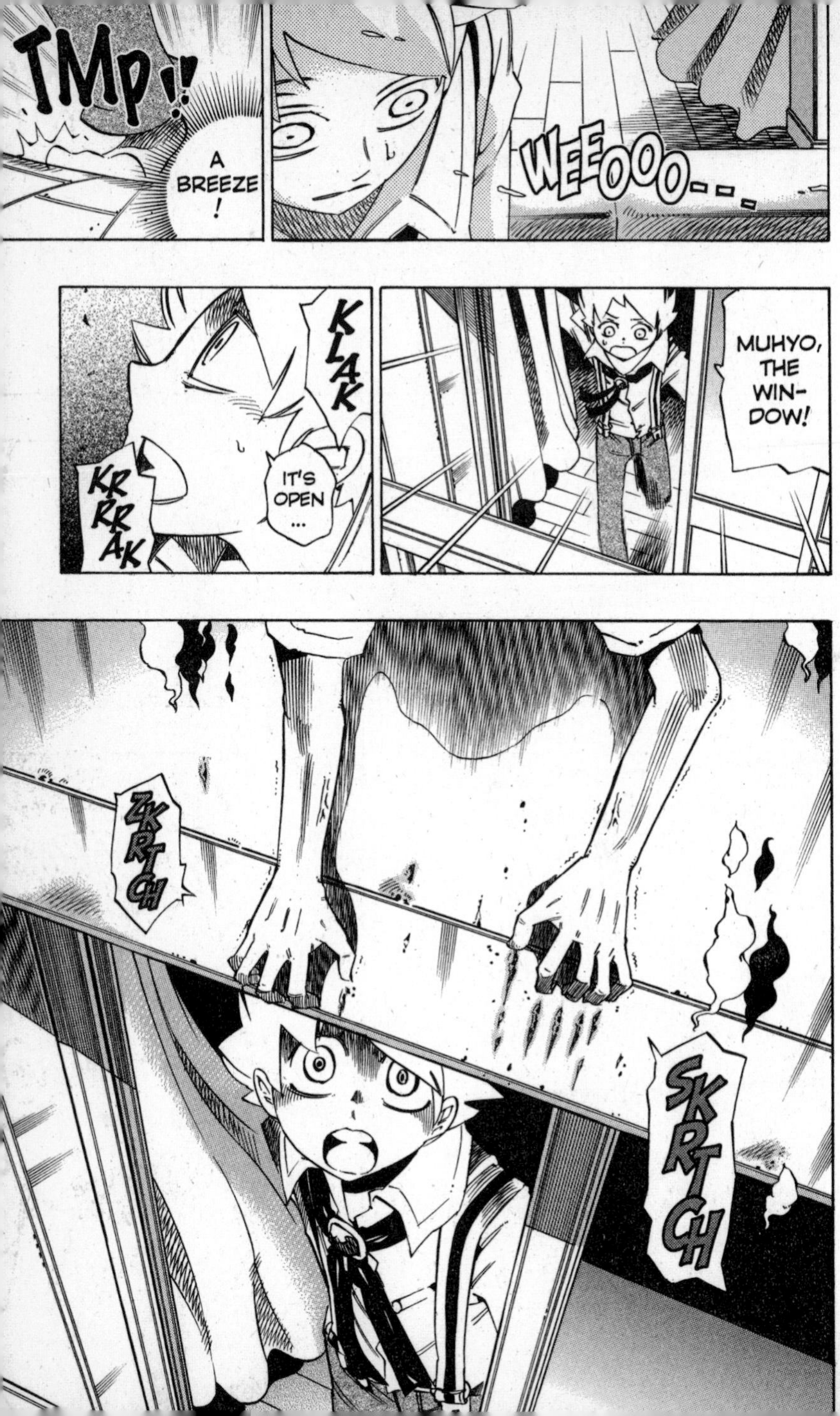
WEEOOO...
TMP!!
A BREEZE!
MUHYO, THE WIN-DOW!
KLAK
IT'S OPEN...
KRRRAK
ZKRTCH
SKRTCH

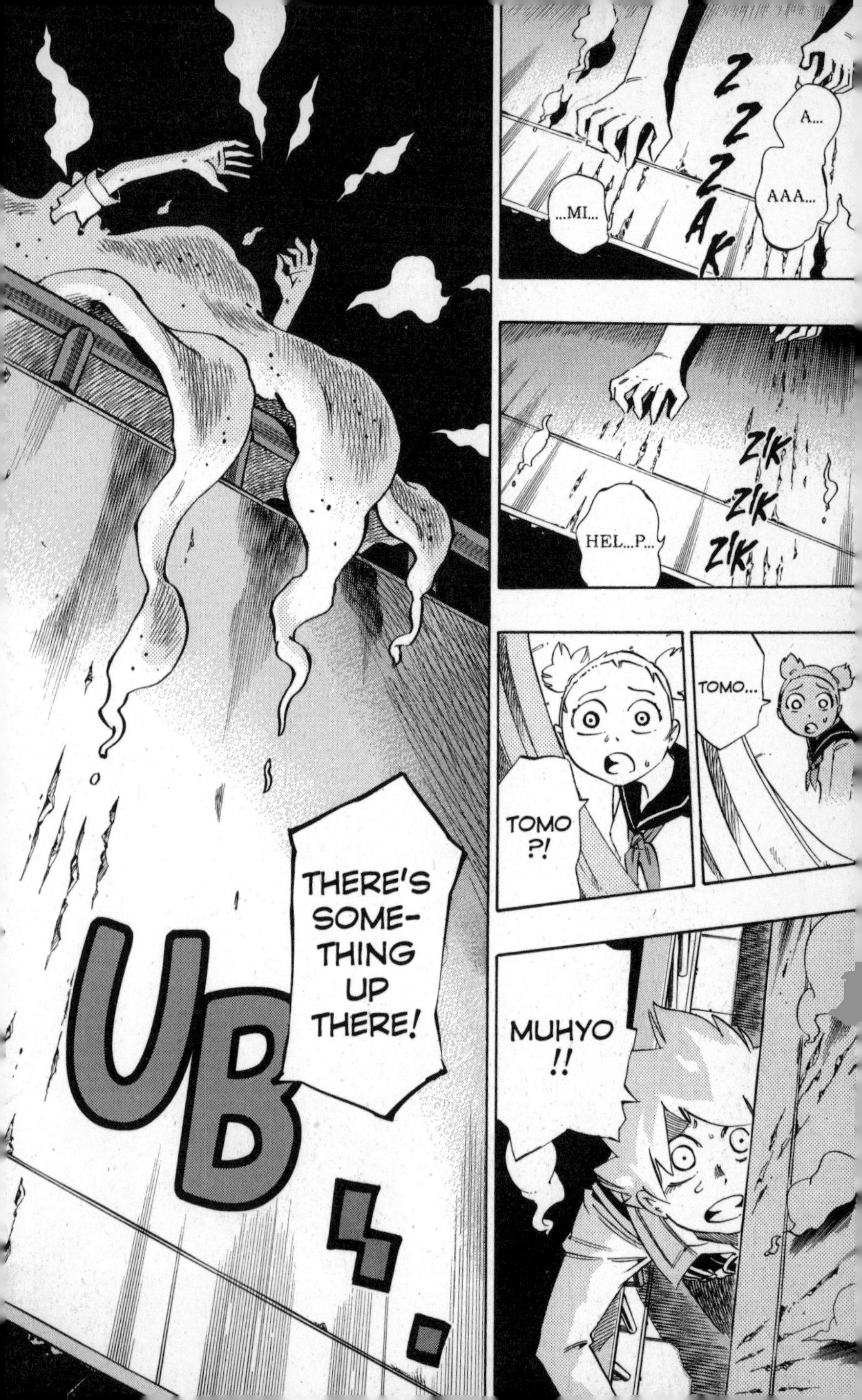

ZZZAAK
A...
AAA...
...MI...
ZIK ZIK ZIK
HEL...P...
TOMO...
TOMO ?!
MUHYO !!
THERE'S SOME-THING UP THERE!
UB

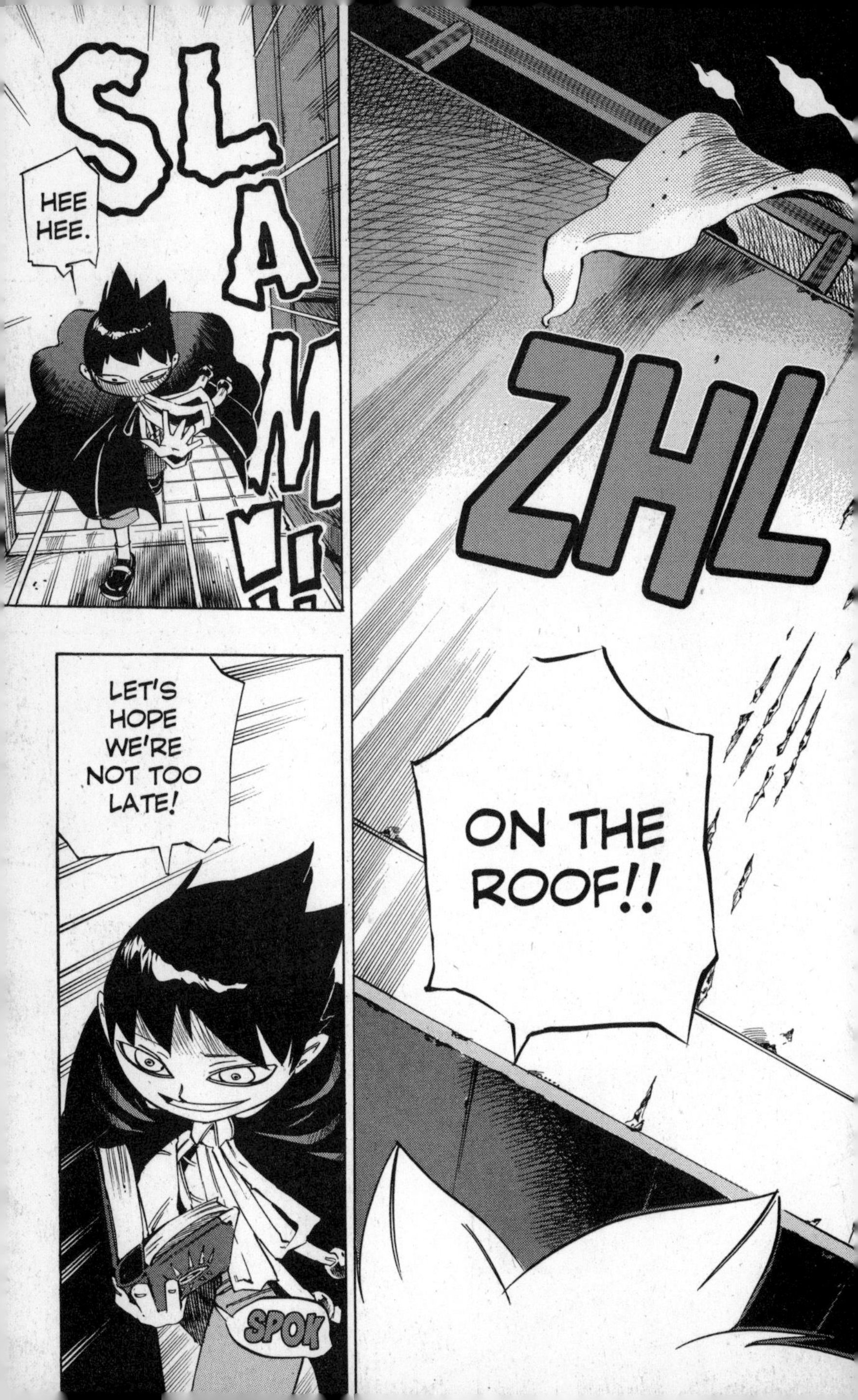
ZHL
ON THE ROOF!!
SLAM!!
HEE HEE.
LET'S HOPE WE'RE NOT TOO LATE!
SPOK

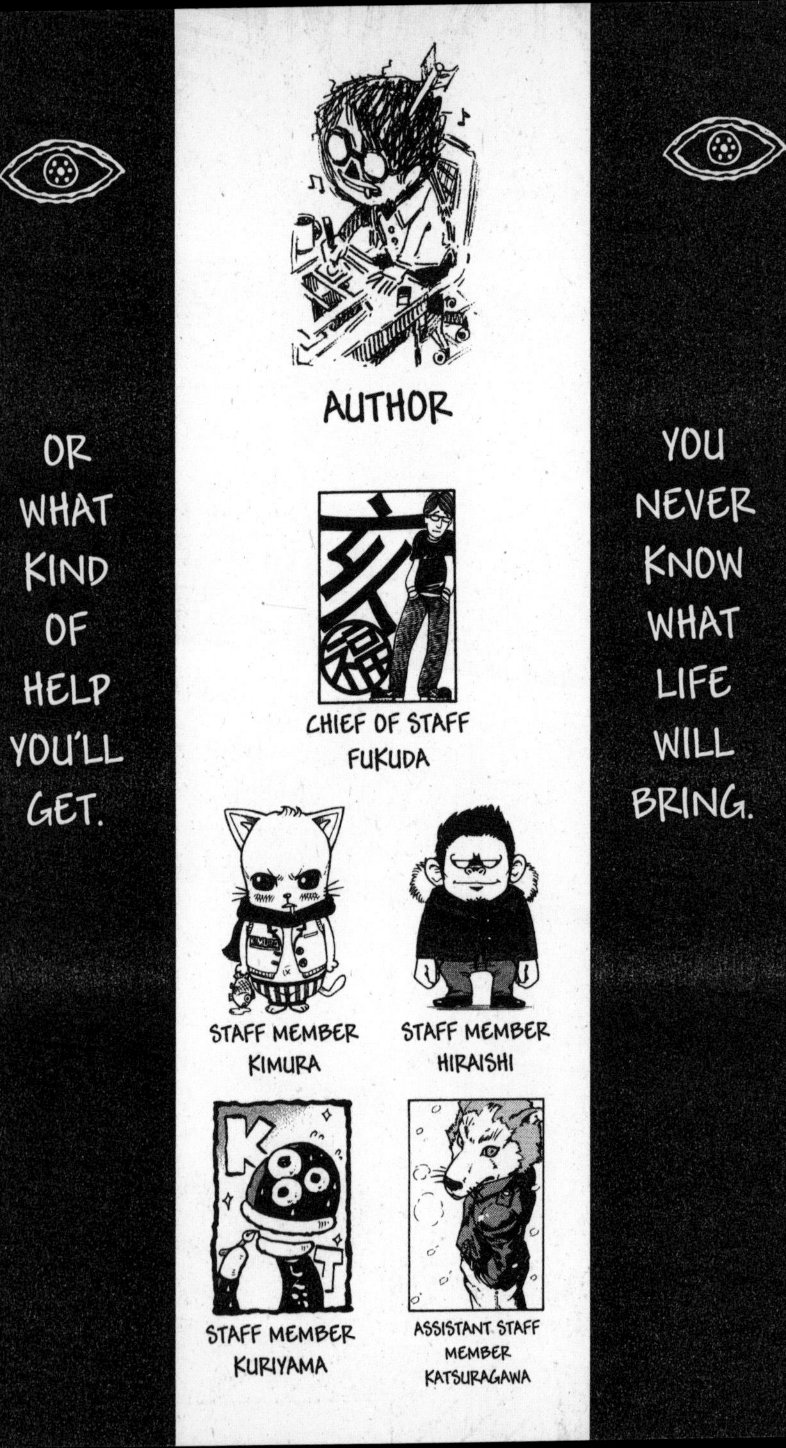
YOU NEVER KNOW WHAT LIFE WILL BRING.
AUTHOR
CHIEF OF STAFF FUKUDA
STAFF MEMBER HIRAISHI
STAFF MEMBER KIMURA
ASSISTANT STAFF MEMBER KATSURAGAWA
STAFF MEMBER KURIYAMA
OR WHAT KIND OF HELP YOU'LL GET.

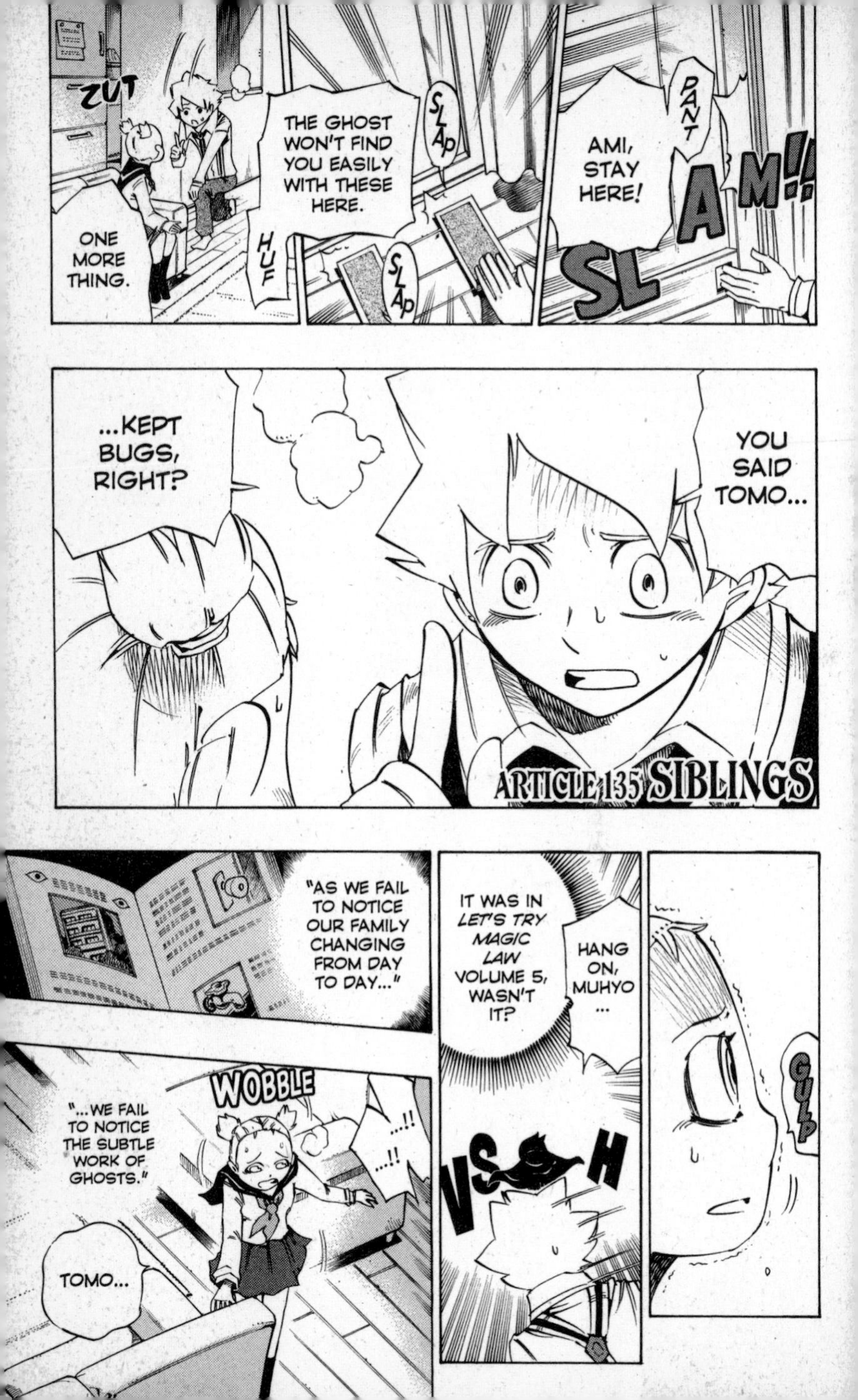
PANT
AMI, STAY HERE!
SLAM!!
SLAP
THE GHOST WON'T FIND YOU EASILY WITH THESE HERE.
HUF
SLAP
ZUT
ONE MORE THING.
YOU SAID TOMO...
...KEPT BUGS, RIGHT?
ARTICLE 135 SIBLINGS
...
GULP
HANG ON, MUHYO...
IT WAS IN *LET'S TRY MAGIC LAW* VOLUME 5, WASN'T IT?
VSSH
"AS WE FAIL TO NOTICE OUR FAMILY CHANGING FROM DAY TO DAY..."
...!!
...!!
WOBBLE
"...WE FAIL TO NOTICE THE SUBTLE WORK OF GHOSTS."
TOMO...

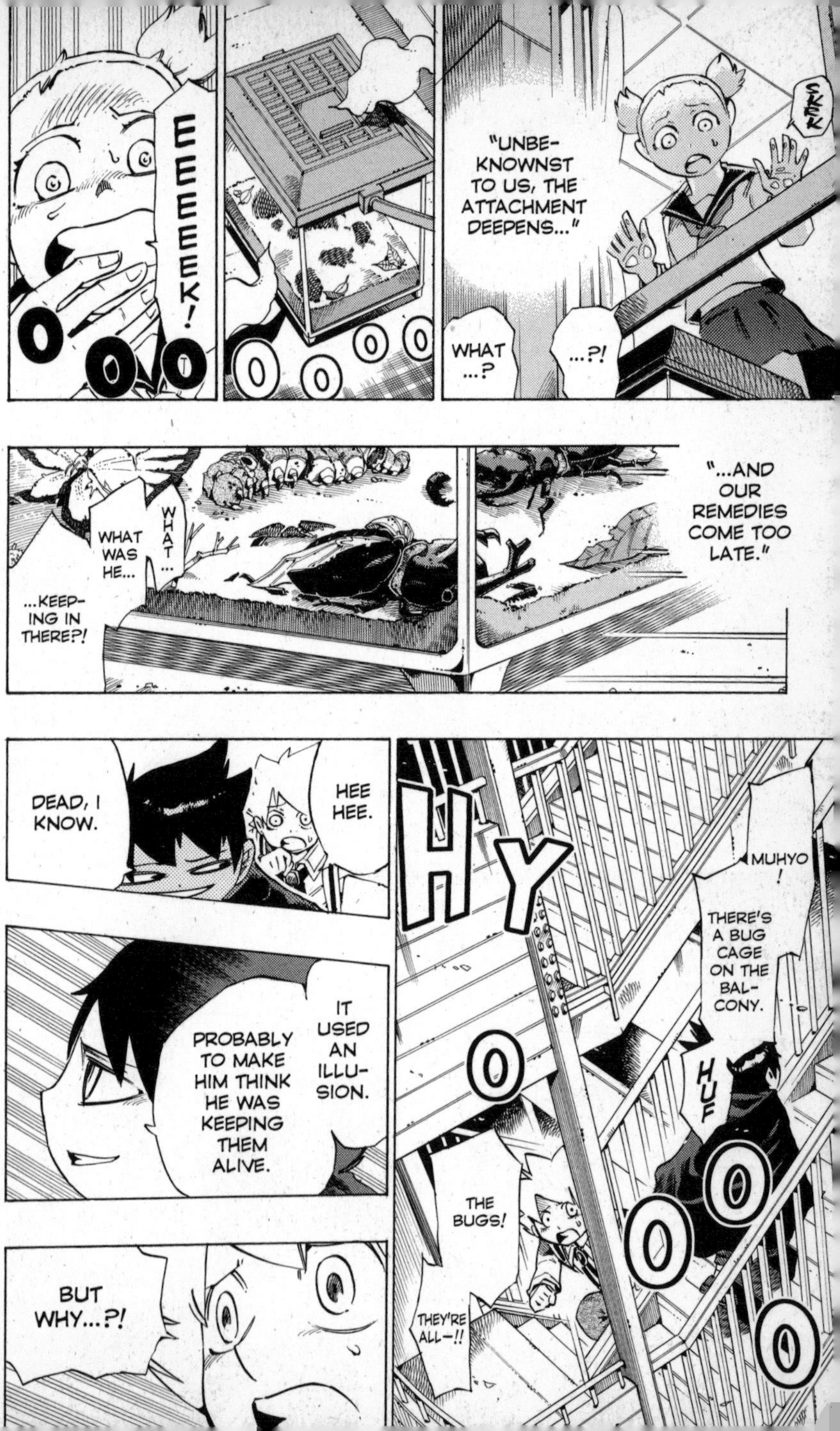

SKEK
"UNBE-KNOWNST TO US, THE ATTACHMENT DEEPENS..."
...?!
WHAT ...?
OOOOO
EEEEEEK!
OOO
"...AND OUR REMEDIES COME TOO LATE."
WHAT...
WHAT WAS HE...
...KEEPING IN THERE?!
HY
MUHYO!
THERE'S A BUG CAGE ON THE BALCONY.
HUF
OOOOO
THE BUGS!
THEY'RE ALL—!!
HEE HEE.
DEAD, I KNOW.
IT USED AN ILLUSION.
PROBABLY TO MAKE HIM THINK HE WAS KEEPING THEM ALIVE.
BUT WHY...?!

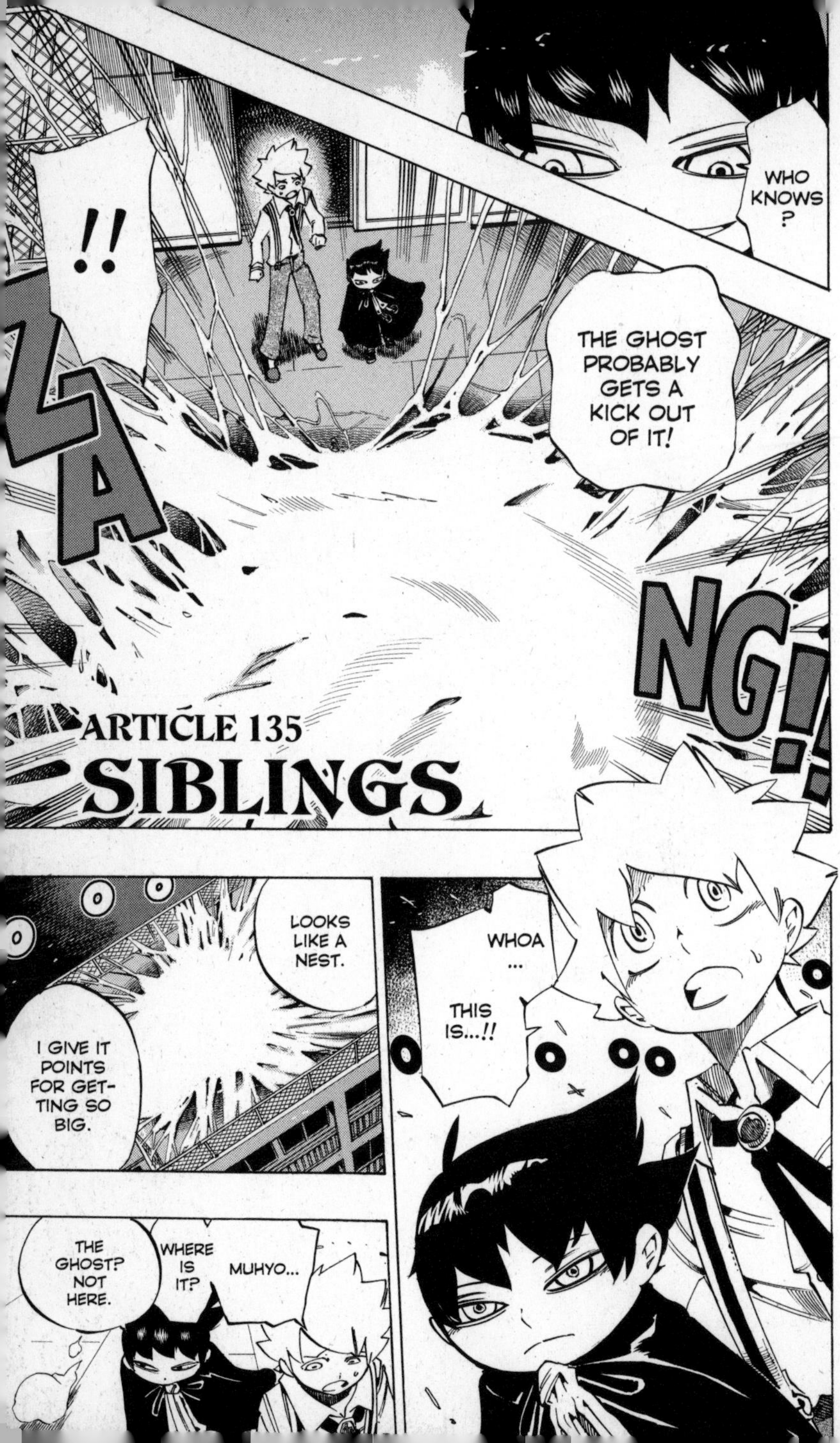
WHO KNOWS?
THE GHOST PROBABLY GETS A KICK OUT OF IT!
!!
ZA
NG!!
ARTICLE 135
SIBLINGS
WHOA ...
THIS IS...!!
LOOKS LIKE A NEST.
I GIVE IT POINTS FOR GET-TING SO BIG.
MUHYO...
WHERE IS IT?
THE GHOST? NOT HERE.

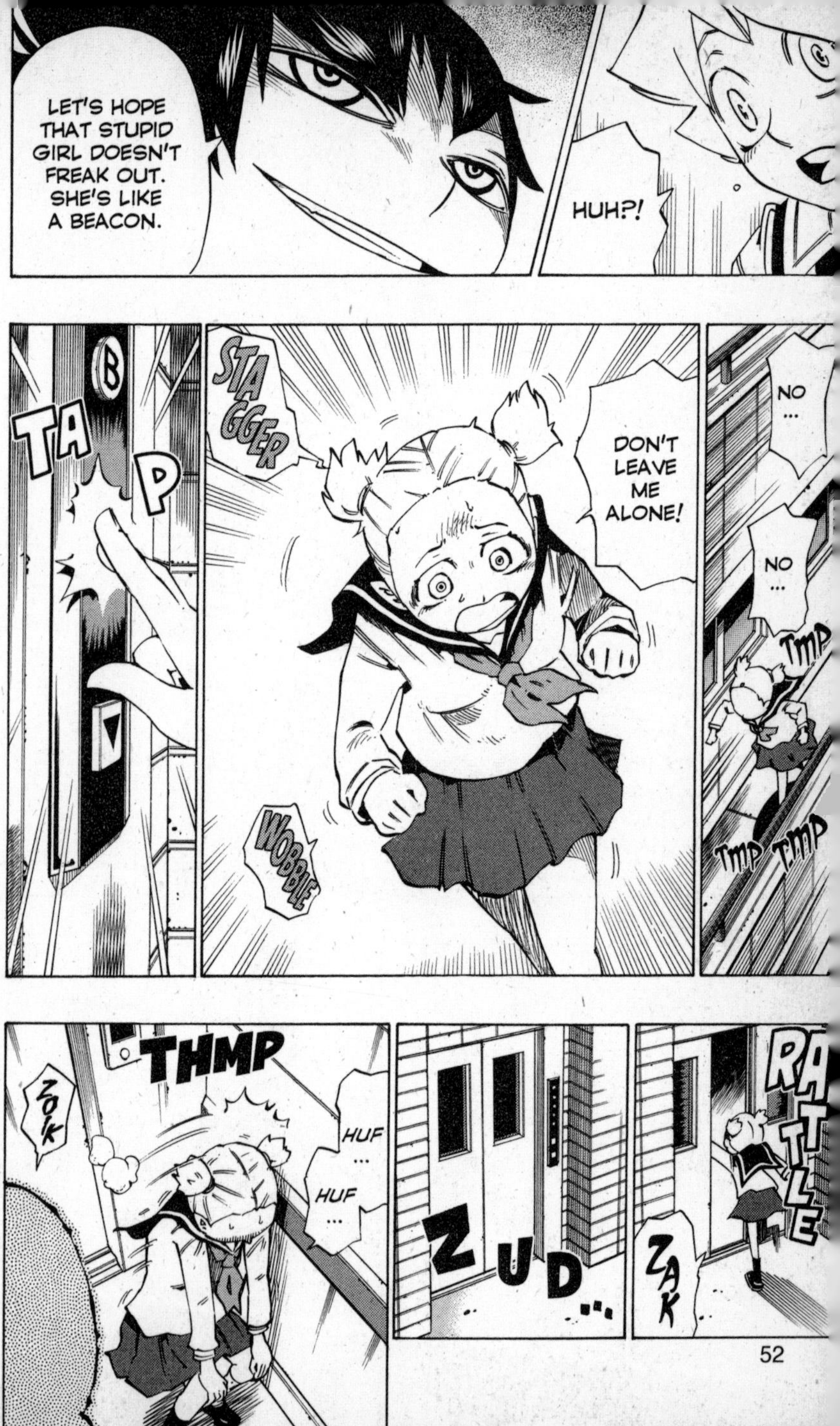
HUH?!
LET'S HOPE THAT STUPID GIRL DOESN'T FREAK OUT. SHE'S LIKE A BEACON.
NO ...
NO ...
TMP
TMP TMP
DON'T LEAVE ME ALONE!
STAGGER
WOBBLE
TAP
RATTLE
ZAK
ZUD...
THMP
ZOIK
HUF ...
HUF ...

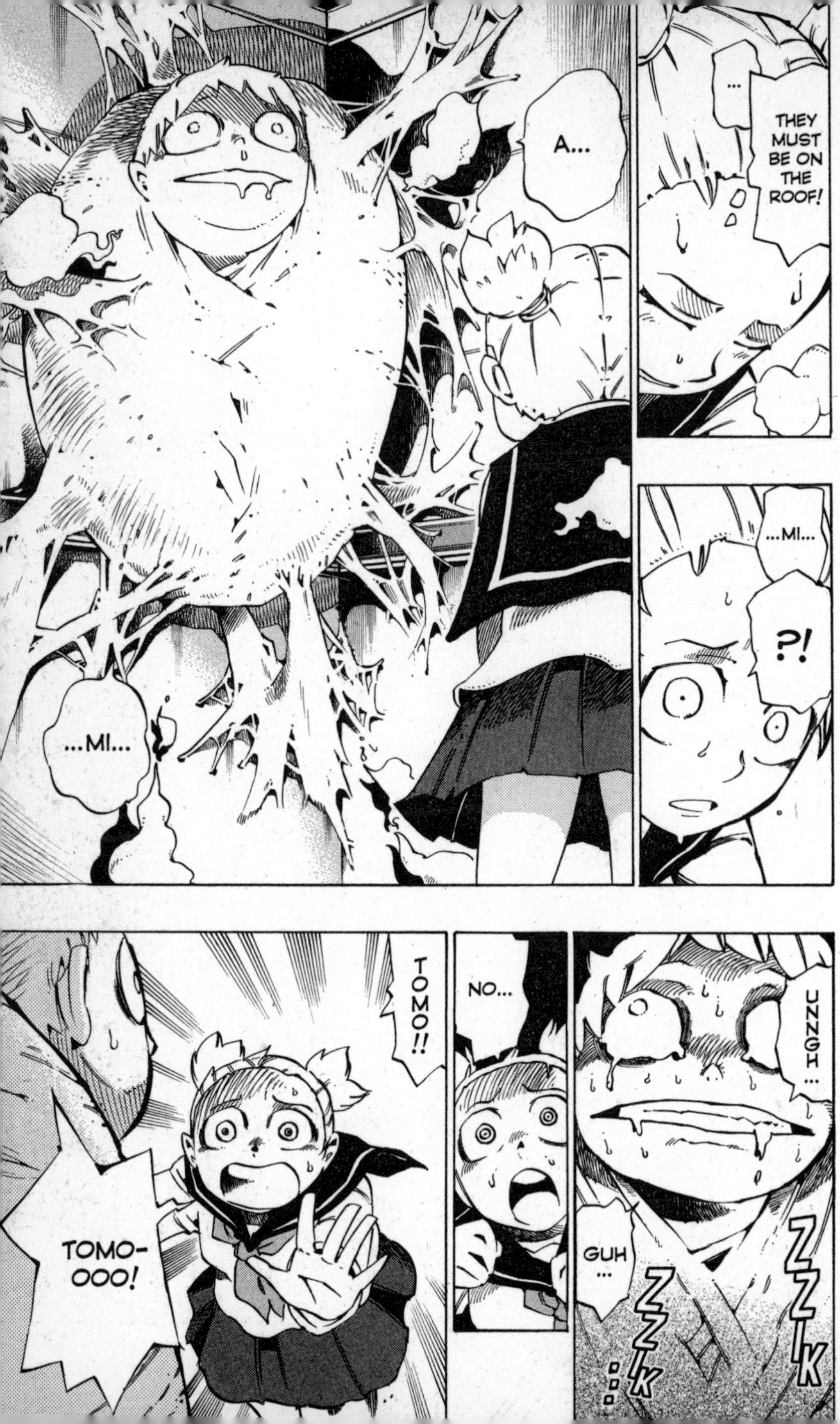
...
THEY MUST BE ON THE ROOF!
...MI...
?!
A...
...MI...
UNNGH...
GUH...
ZZIK
ZZIK...
NO...
TOMO!!
TOMO-OOO!

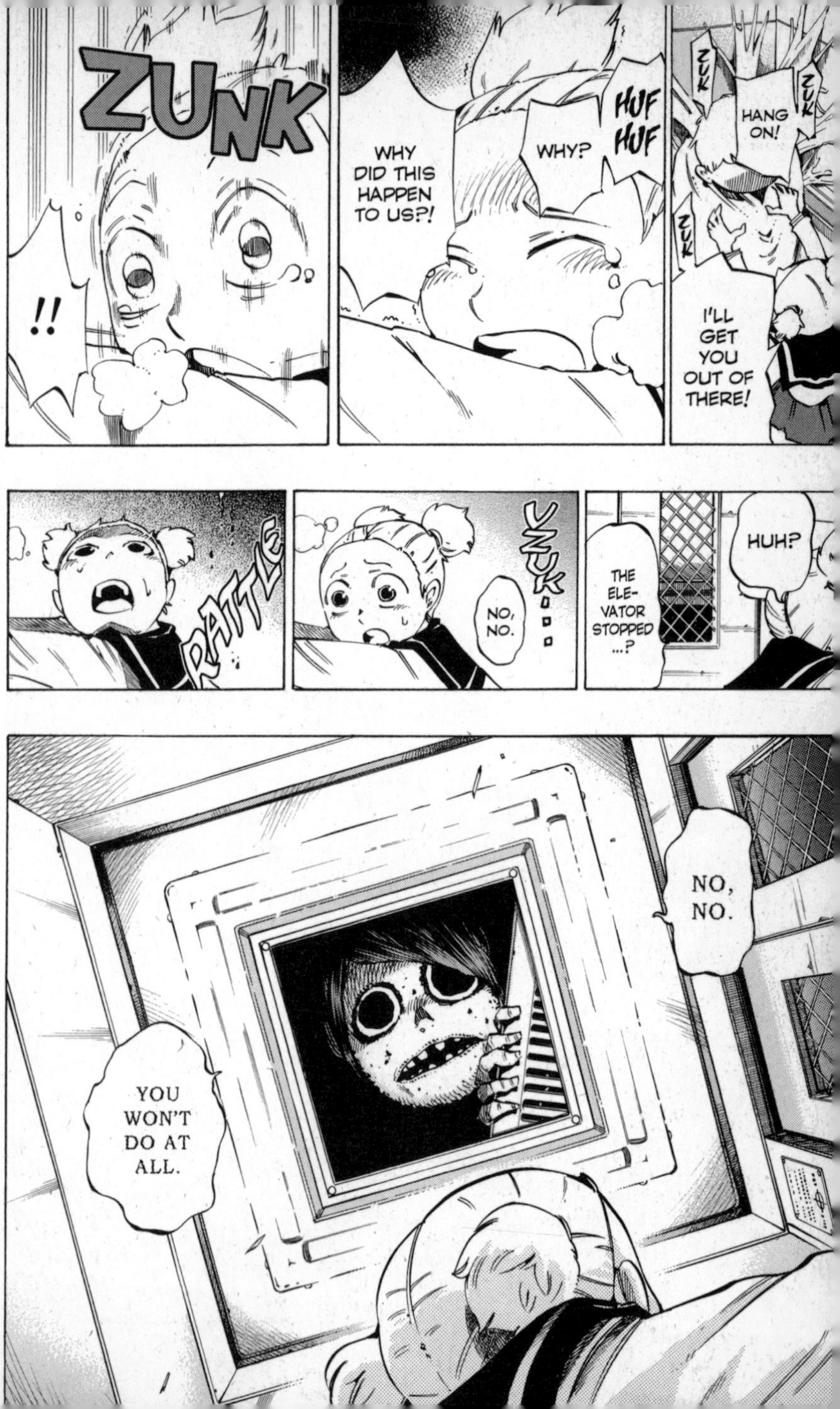
ZUK
ZUK
HANG ON!
ZUK
I'LL GET YOU OUT OF THERE!
HUF HUF
WHY?
WHY DID THIS HAPPEN TO US?!
ZUNK
!!
HUH?
THE ELE-VATOR STOPPED ...?
VZUK...
NO, NO.
RATTLE
NO, NO.
YOU WON'T DO AT ALL.

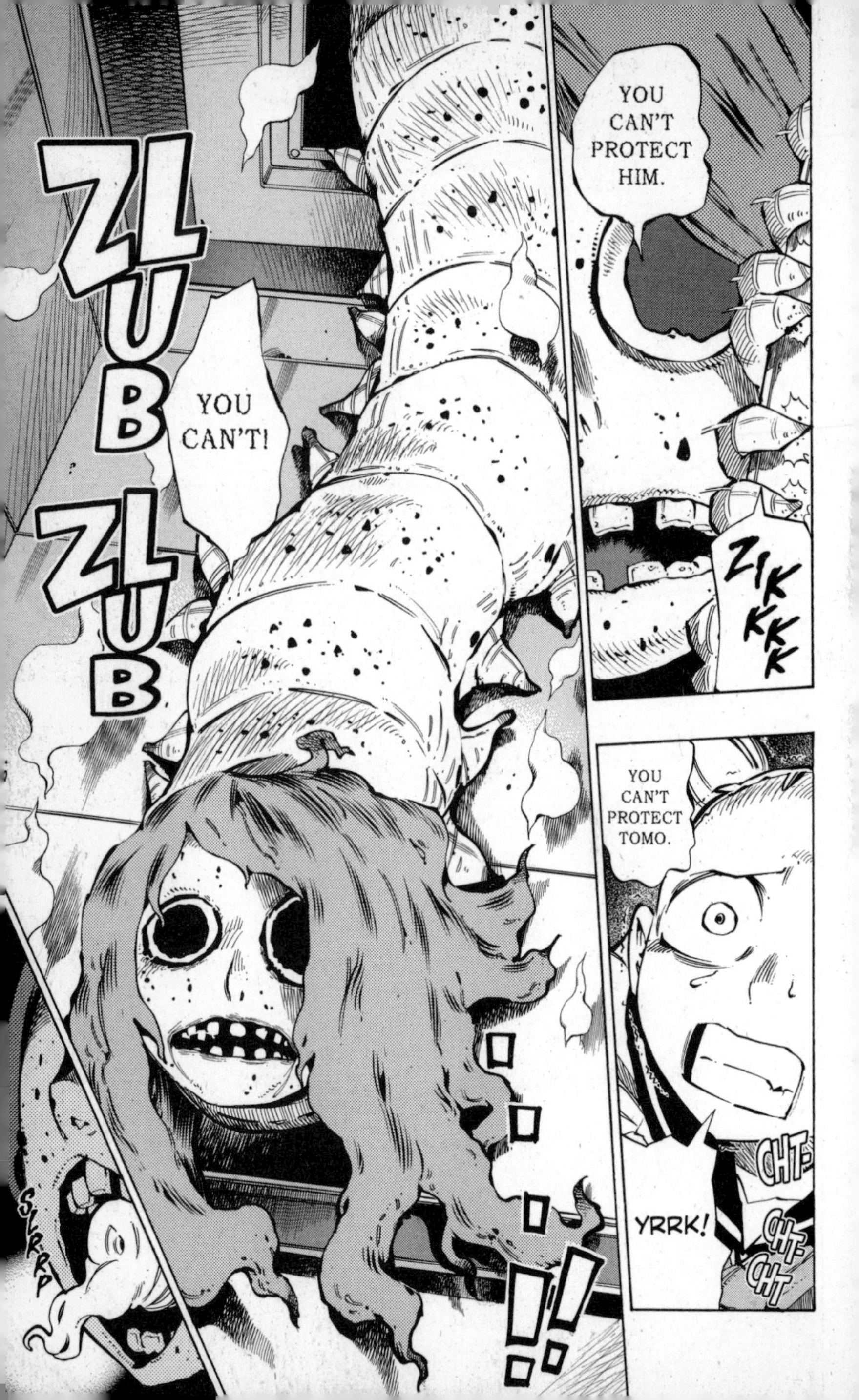
YOU CAN'T PROTECT HIM.
ZIKKKK
YOU CAN'T PROTECT TOMO.
YRRK!
CHT-CHT-CHT
ZLUB ZLUB
YOU CAN'T!
!!
SLRRP

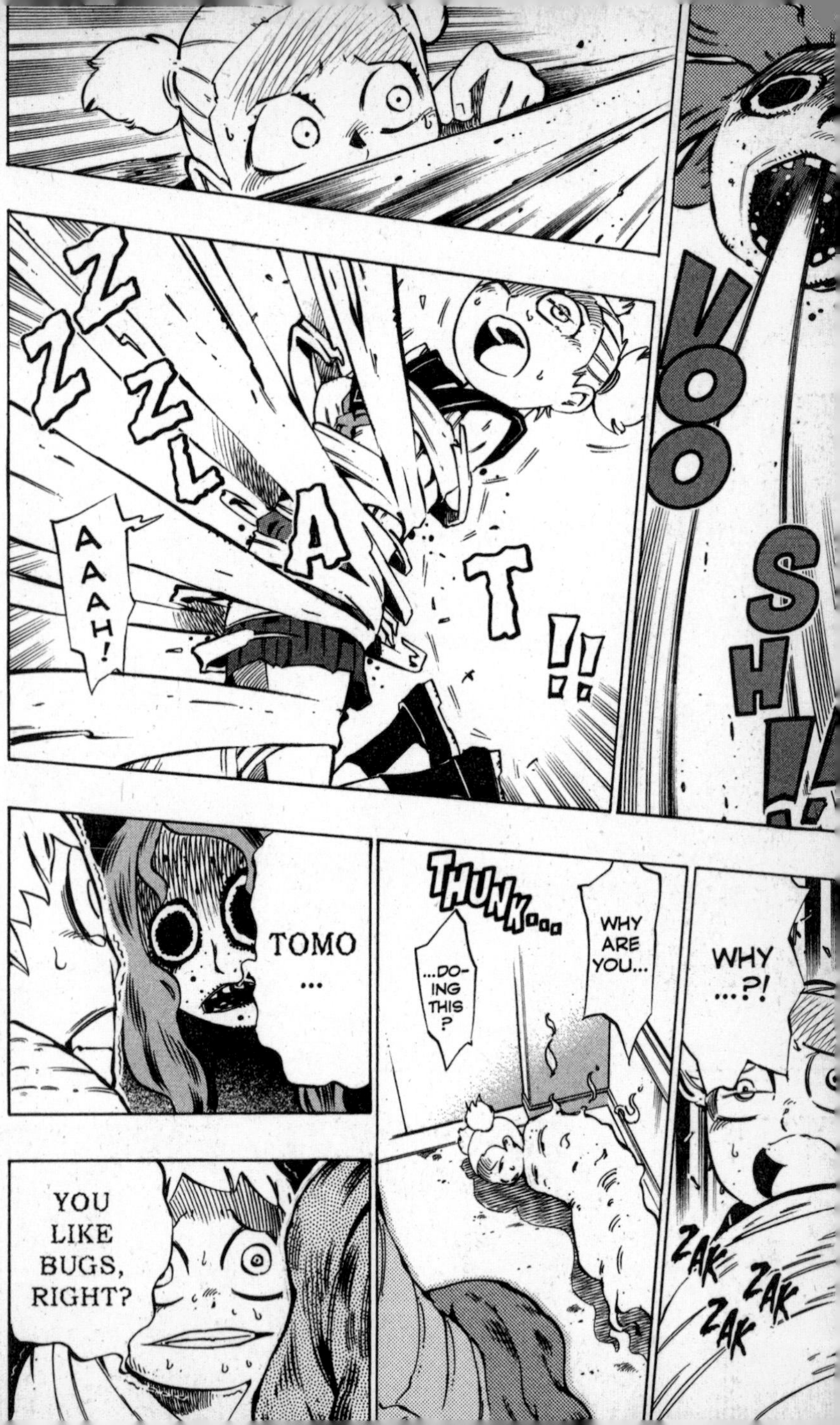
VOOSH!!
ZZZLAT!!
AAAH!
WHY ...?!
ZAK ZAK ZAK
THUNK...
WHY ARE YOU...
...DOING THIS?
TOMO ...
YOU LIKE BUGS, RIGHT?

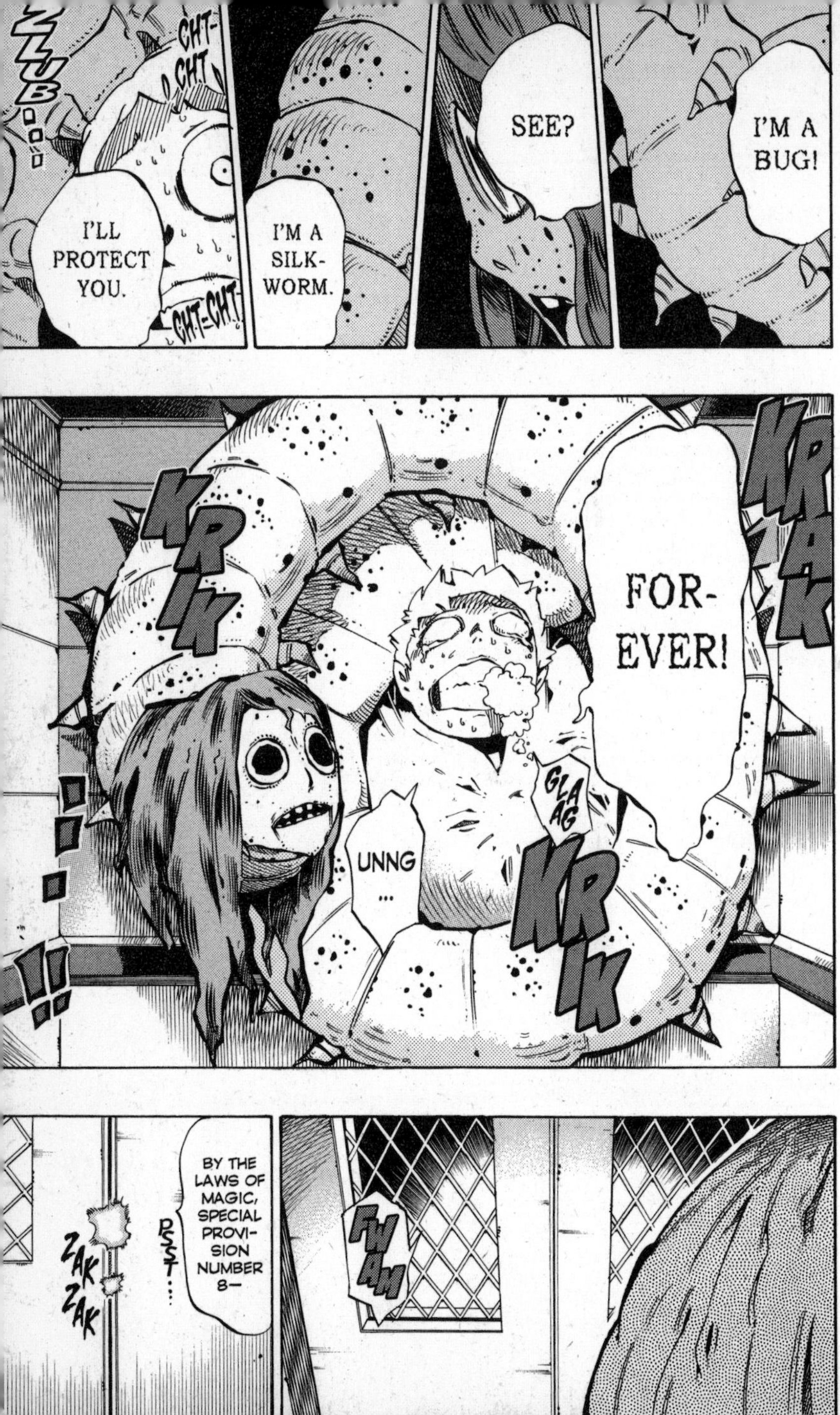
I'M A BUG!
SEE?
I'M A SILKWORM.
CHT-CHT
ZLUB...
I'LL PROTECT YOU.
CHT-CHT
KRAK
FOR-EVER!
KRIK
GLAAG
KRIK
UNNG...
...!!
FWAM
BY THE LAWS OF MAGIC, SPECIAL PROVISION NUMBER 8—
PSST...
ZAK ZAK

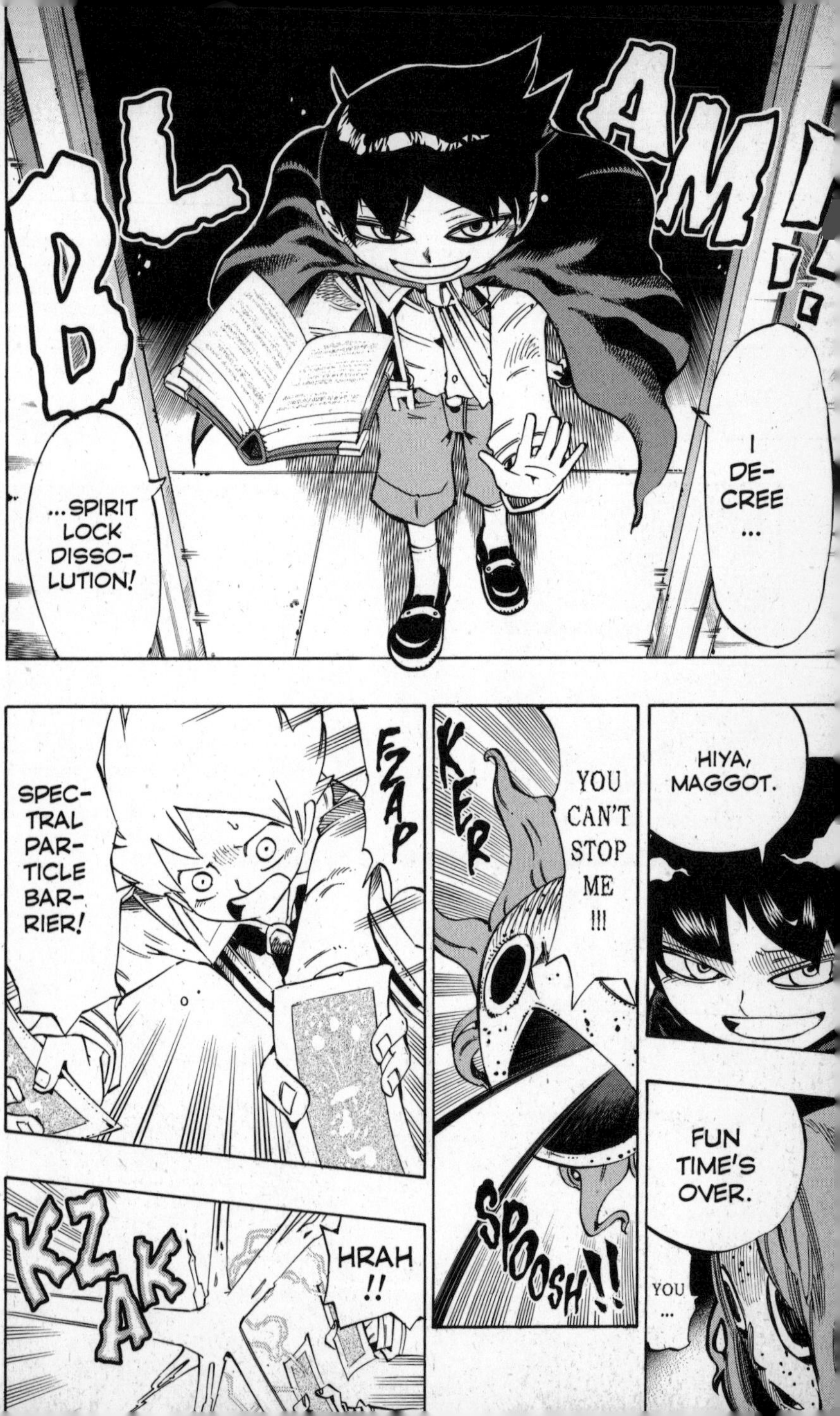
BLAM!!
I DE-CREE...
...SPIRIT LOCK DISSO-LUTION!
HIYA, MAGGOT.
FUN TIME'S OVER.
YOU...
KER
YOU CAN'T STOP ME !!!
SPOOSH!!
FZAP
SPEC-TRAL PAR-TICLE BAR-RIER!
HRAH !!
KZAK

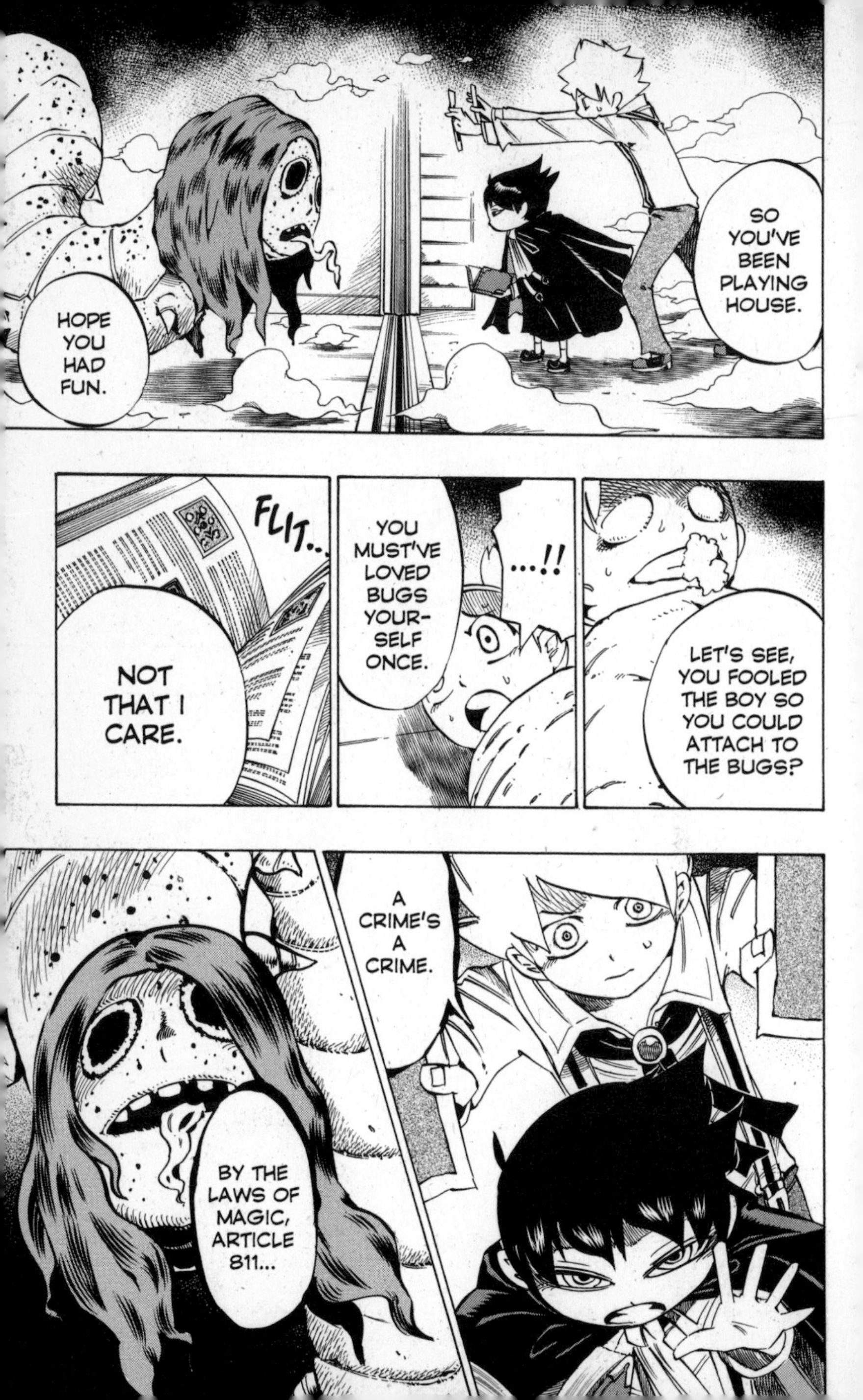
SO YOU'VE BEEN PLAYING HOUSE.
HOPE YOU HAD FUN.
LET'S SEE, YOU FOOLED THE BOY SO YOU COULD ATTACH TO THE BUGS?
YOU MUST'VE LOVED BUGS YOUR-SELF ONCE.
...!!
FLIT...
NOT THAT I CARE.
A CRIME'S A CRIME.
BY THE LAWS OF MAGIC, ARTICLE 811...

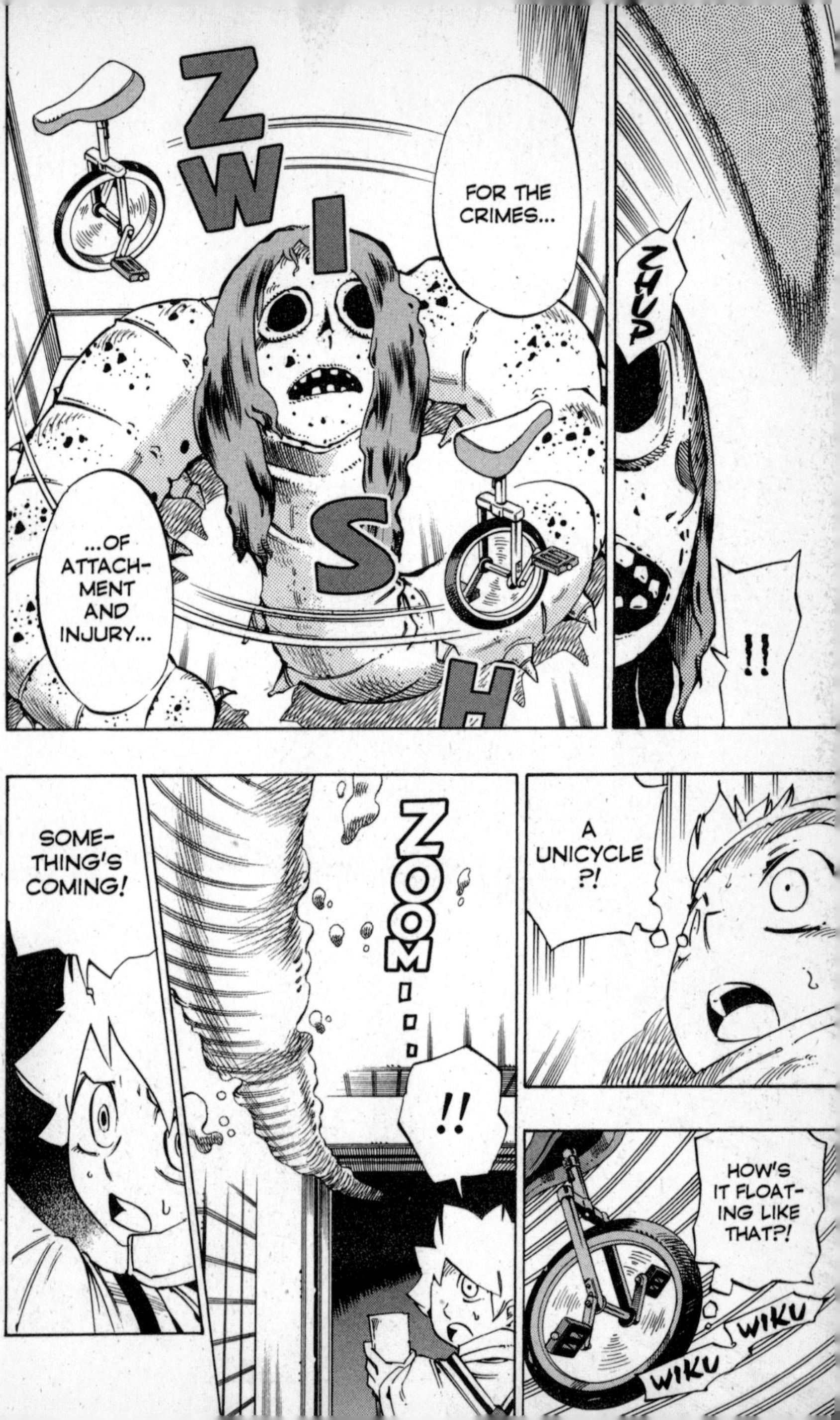
ZHUP
!!
FOR THE CRIMES...
...OF ATTACHMENT AND INJURY...
ZWISH
A UNICYCLE ?!
HOW'S IT FLOATING LIKE THAT?!
WIKU
WIKU
ZOOM...
!!
SOMETHING'S COMING!

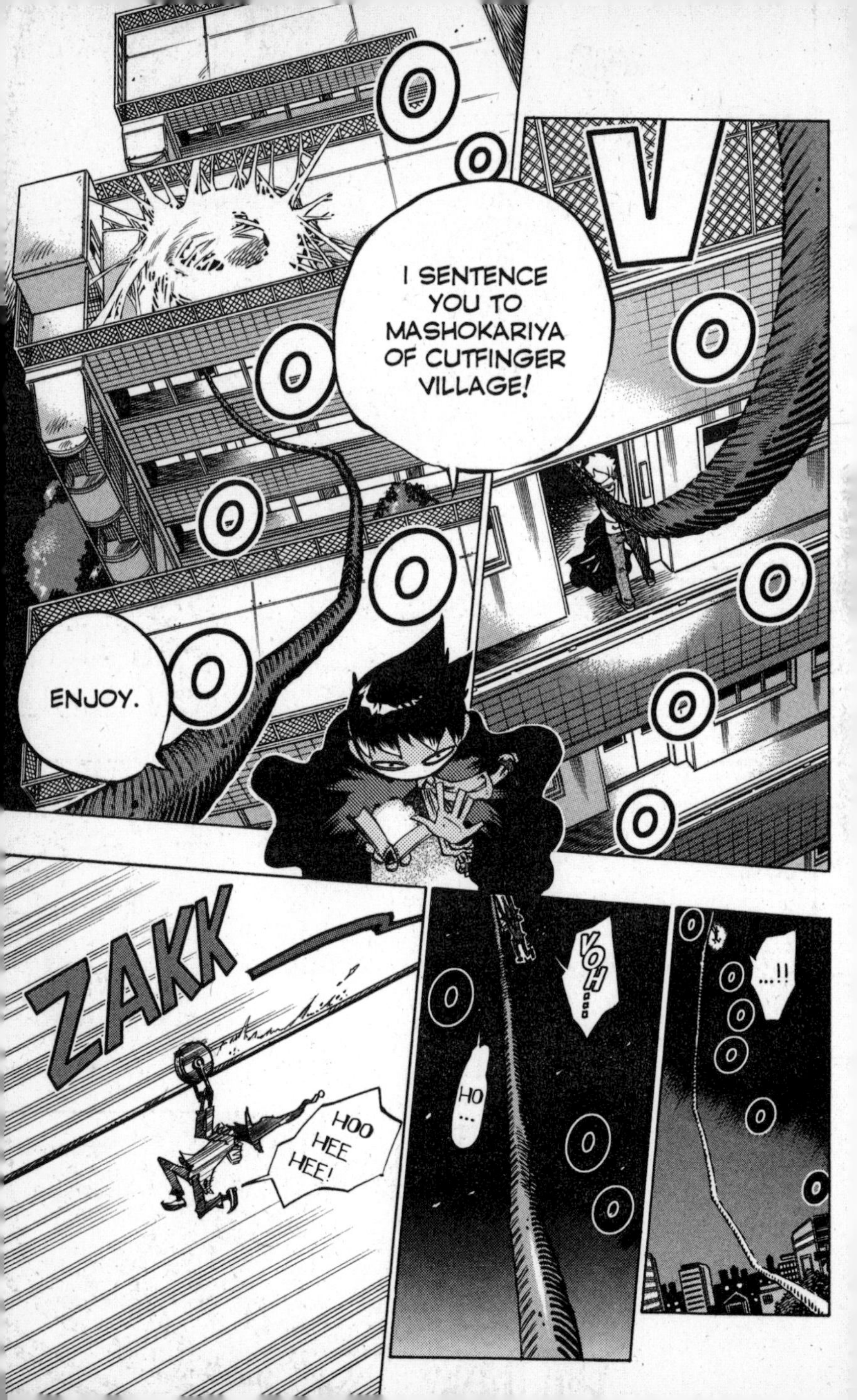
I SENTENCE YOU TO MASHOKARIYA OF CUTFINGER VILLAGE!
ENJOY.
...!!
VOH...
HO...
ZAKK
HOO HEE HEE!

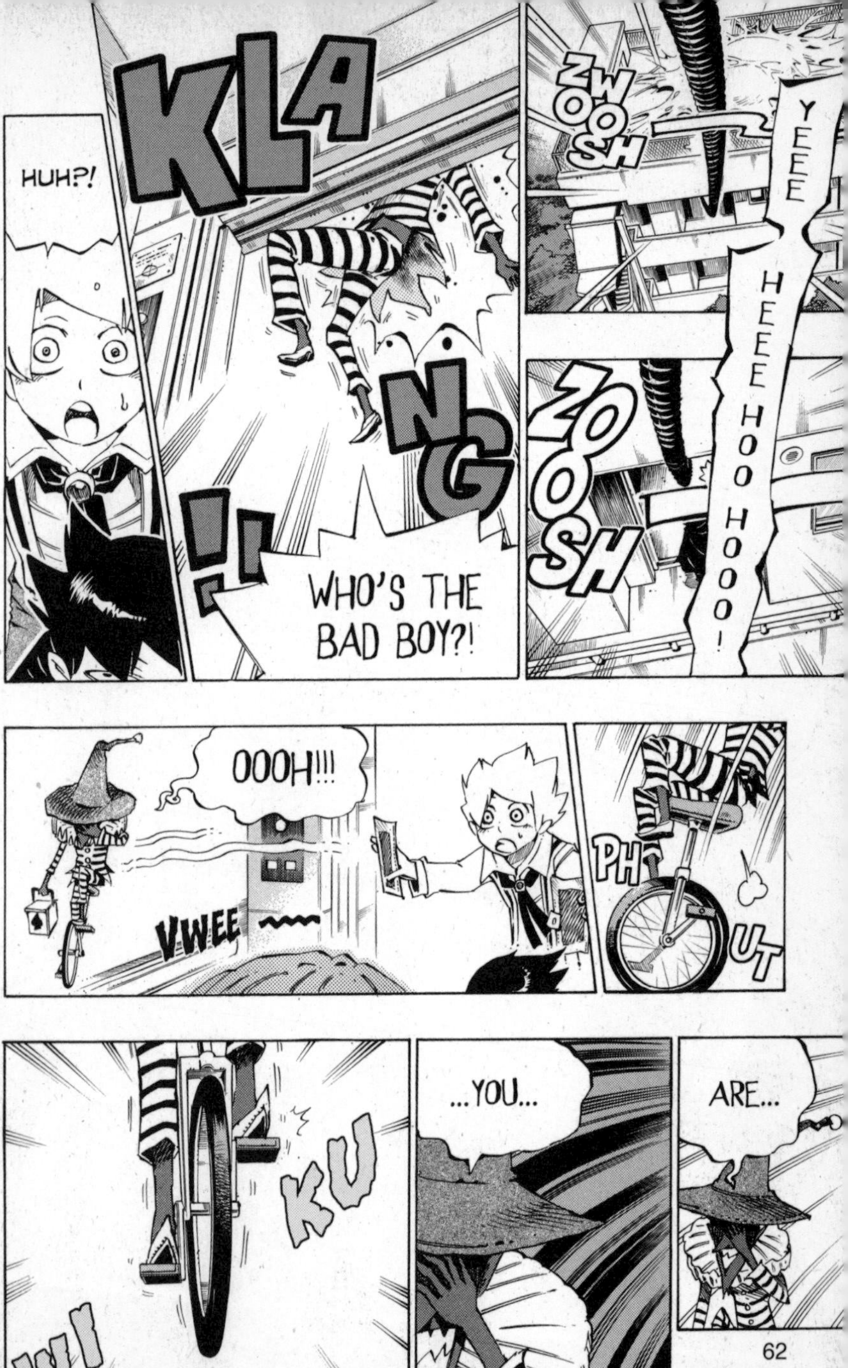
ZWOOSH
YEEE HEEE HOO HOOOO!
ZOOSH
KLANG
!!
WHO'S THE BAD BOY?!
HUH?!
PHUT
OOOH!!!
VWEE ~~
ARE...
...YOU...
KU
WI

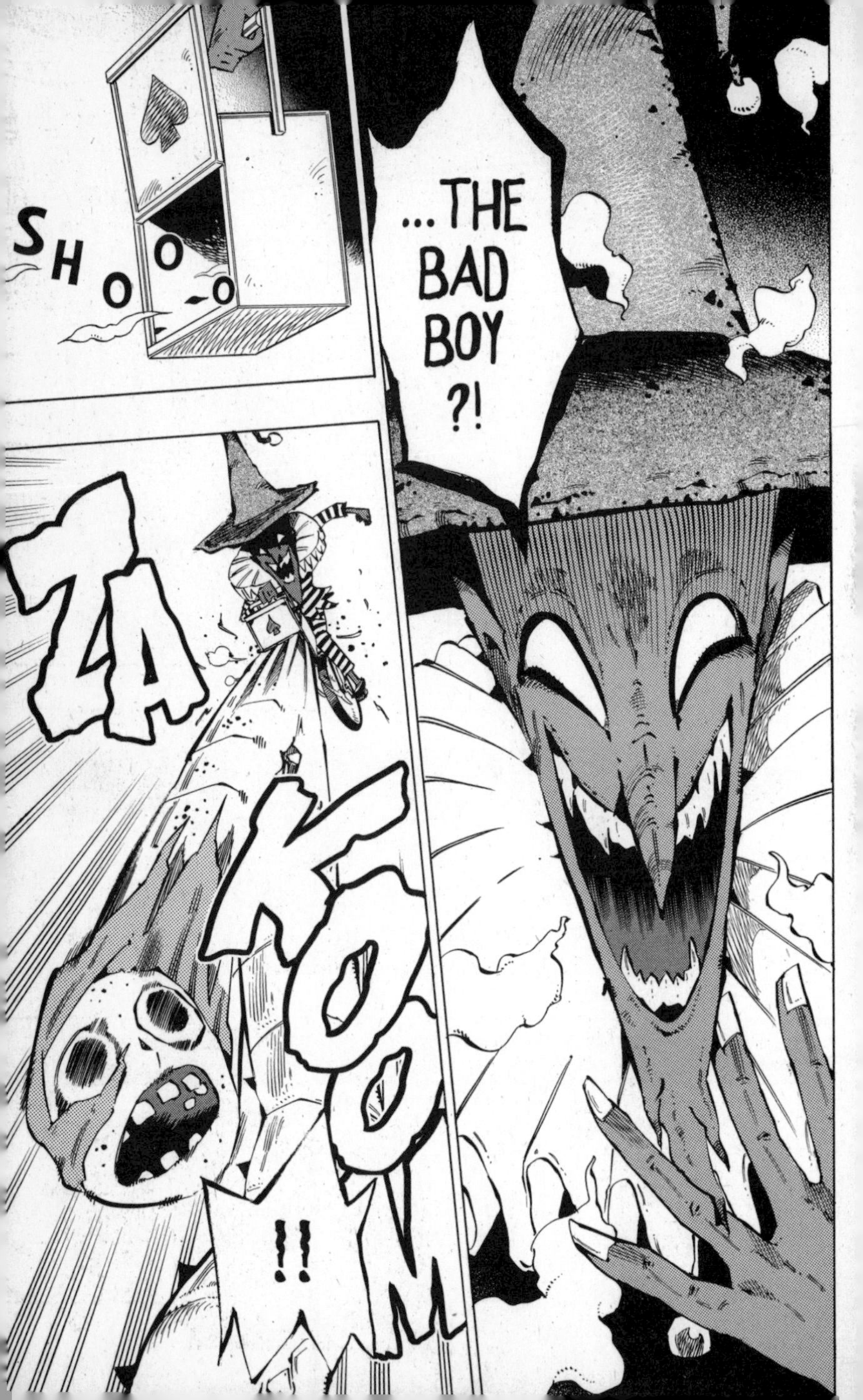
...THE BAD BOY ?!
SHOO-O
ZAKOOM
!!

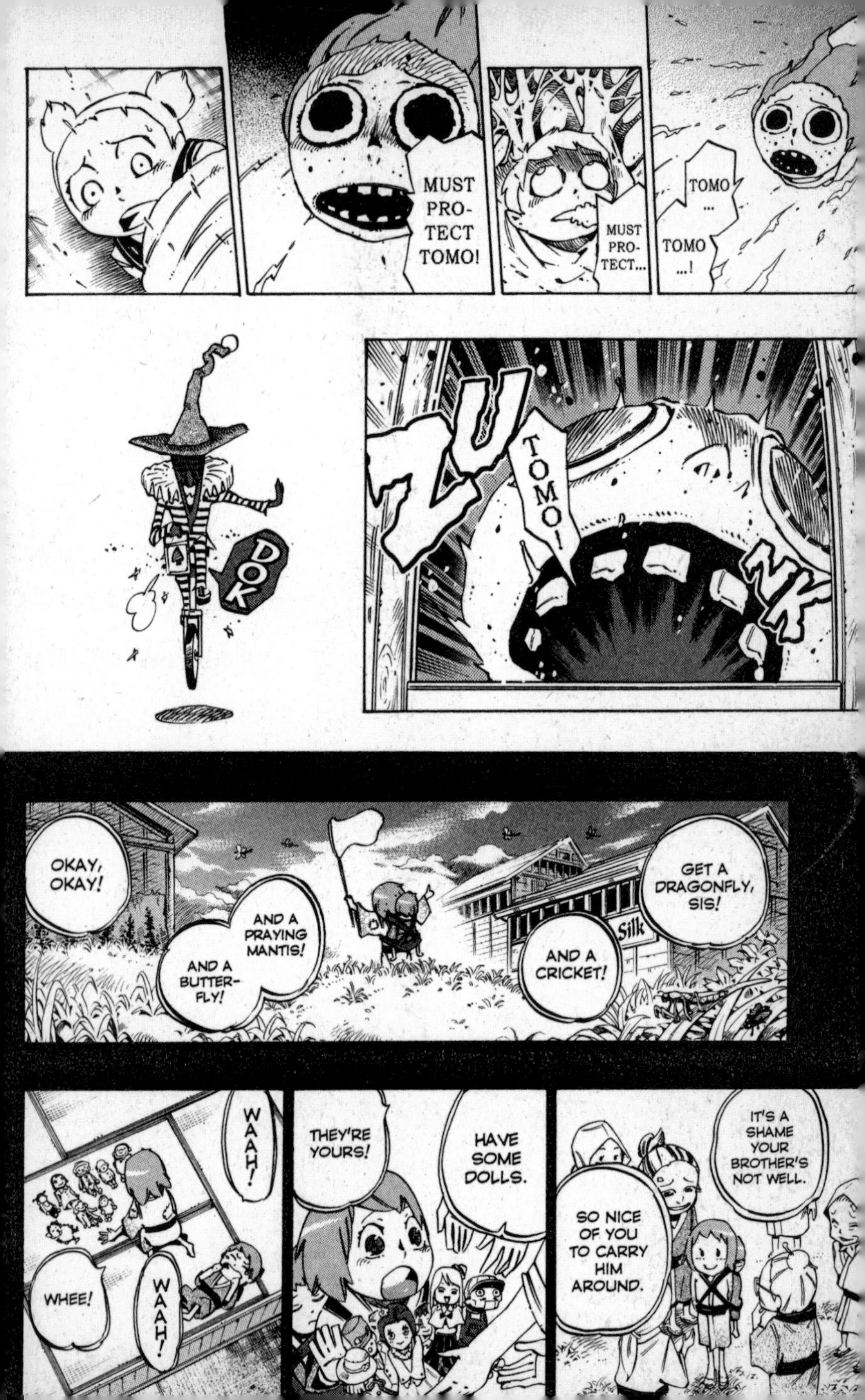

TOMO ... TOMO ...!
MUST PRO-TECT...
MUST PRO-TECT TOMO!
ZUNK
TOMO!
DOK
GET A DRAGONFLY, SIS!
AND A CRICKET!
AND A PRAYING MANTIS!
AND A BUTTER-FLY!
OKAY, OKAY!
IT'S A SHAME YOUR BROTHER'S NOT WELL.
SO NICE OF YOU TO CARRY HIM AROUND.
HAVE SOME DOLLS.
THEY'RE YOURS!
WAAH!
WAAH!
WHEE!

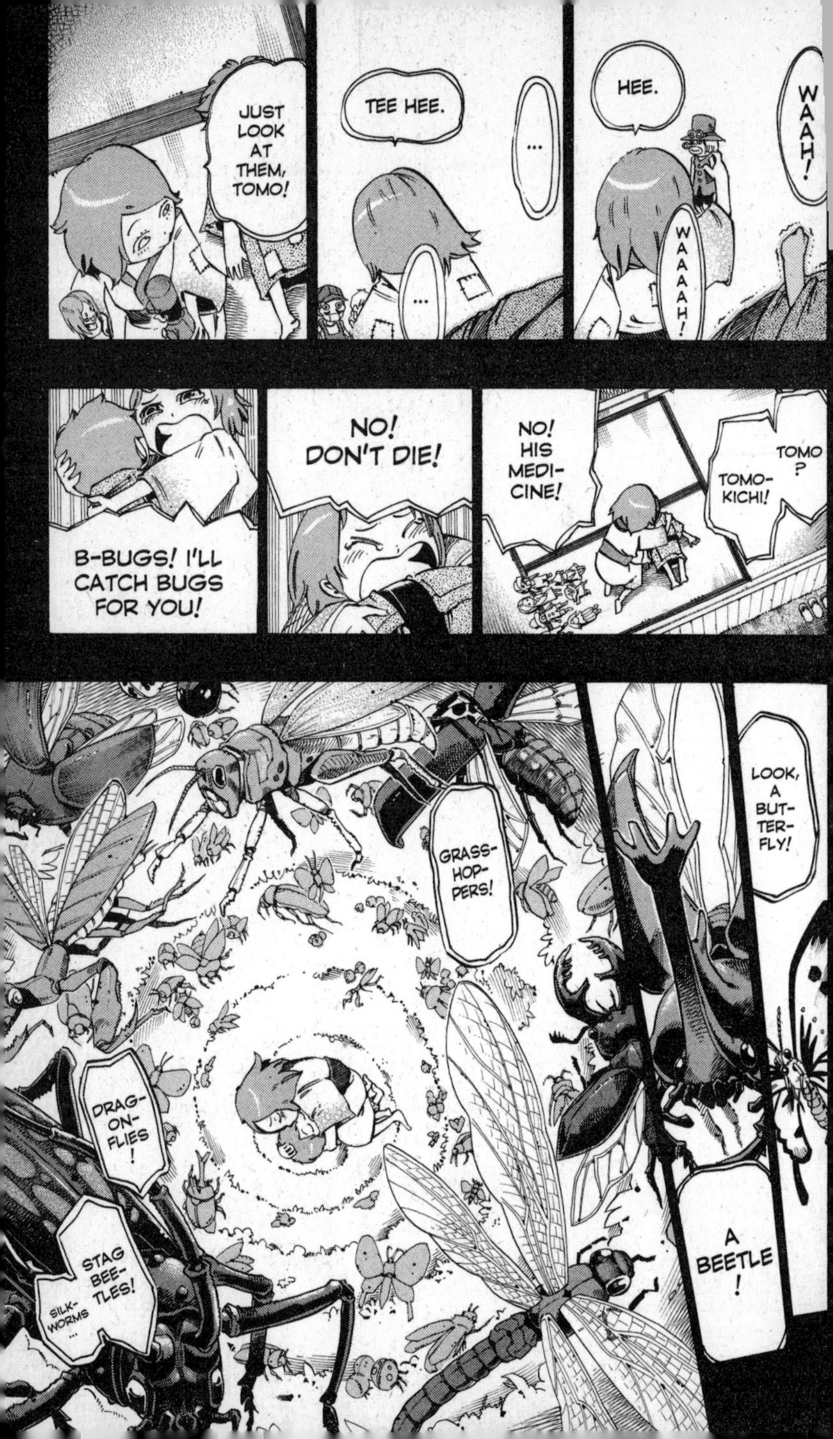

HEE.
WAAH!
WAAAAH!
TEE HEE.
...
...
JUST LOOK AT THEM, TOMO!
TOMO?
TOMOKICHI!
NO! HIS MEDICINE!
NO! DON'T DIE!
B-BUGS! I'LL CATCH BUGS FOR YOU!
LOOK, A BUTTERFLY!
A BEETLE!
GRASSHOPPERS!
DRAGONFLIES!
STAG BEETLES!
SILKWORMS...

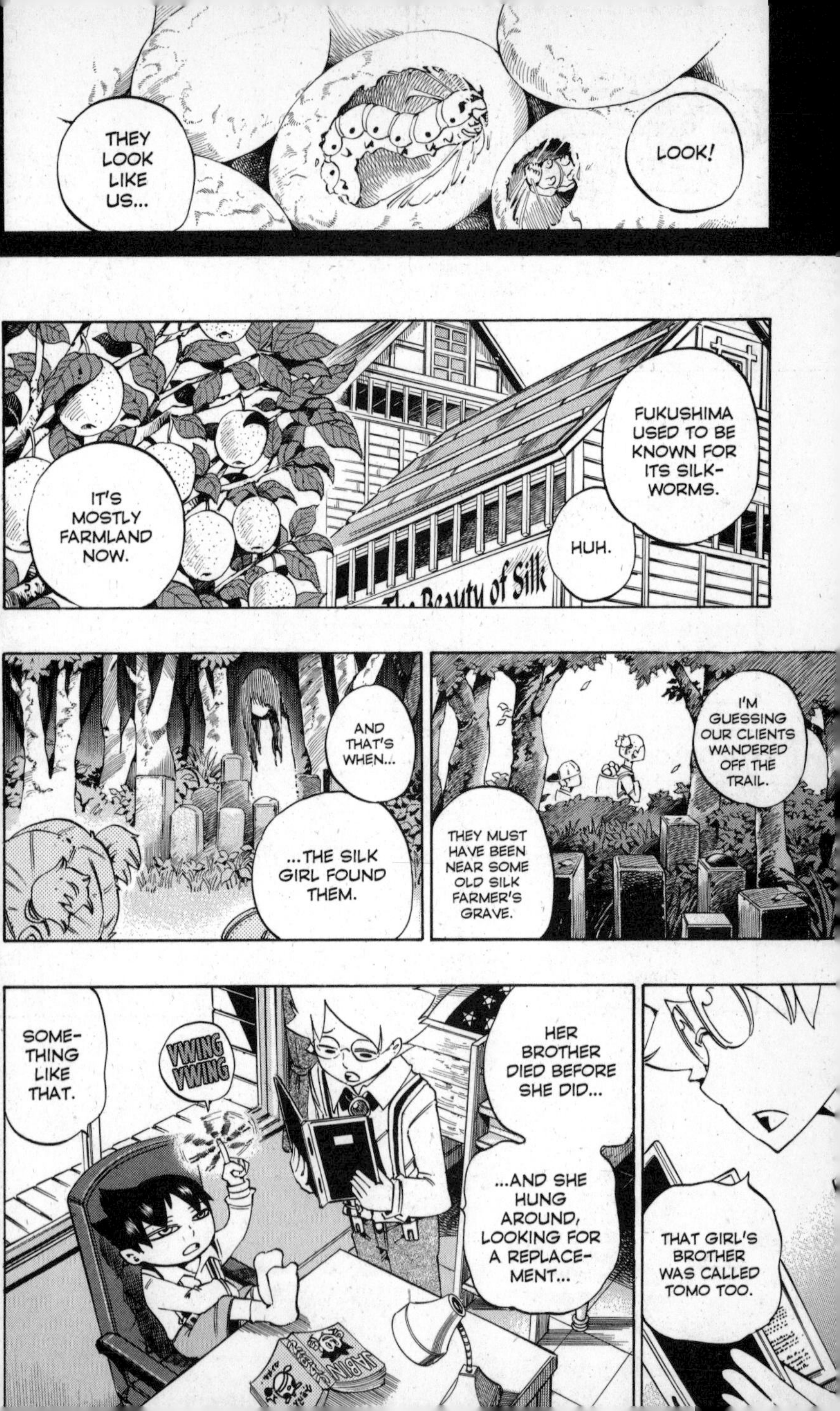
LOOK!
THEY LOOK LIKE US...
FUKUSHIMA USED TO BE KNOWN FOR ITS SILK-WORMS.
HUH.
The Beauty of Silk
IT'S MOSTLY FARMLAND NOW.
I'M GUESSING OUR CLIENTS WANDERED OFF THE TRAIL.
THEY MUST HAVE BEEN NEAR SOME OLD SILK FARMER'S GRAVE.
AND THAT'S WHEN...
...THE SILK GIRL FOUND THEM.
THAT GIRL'S BROTHER WAS CALLED TOMO TOO.
HER BROTHER DIED BEFORE SHE DID...
...AND SHE HUNG AROUND, LOOKING FOR A REPLACE-MENT...
VWING VWING
SOME-THING LIKE THAT.

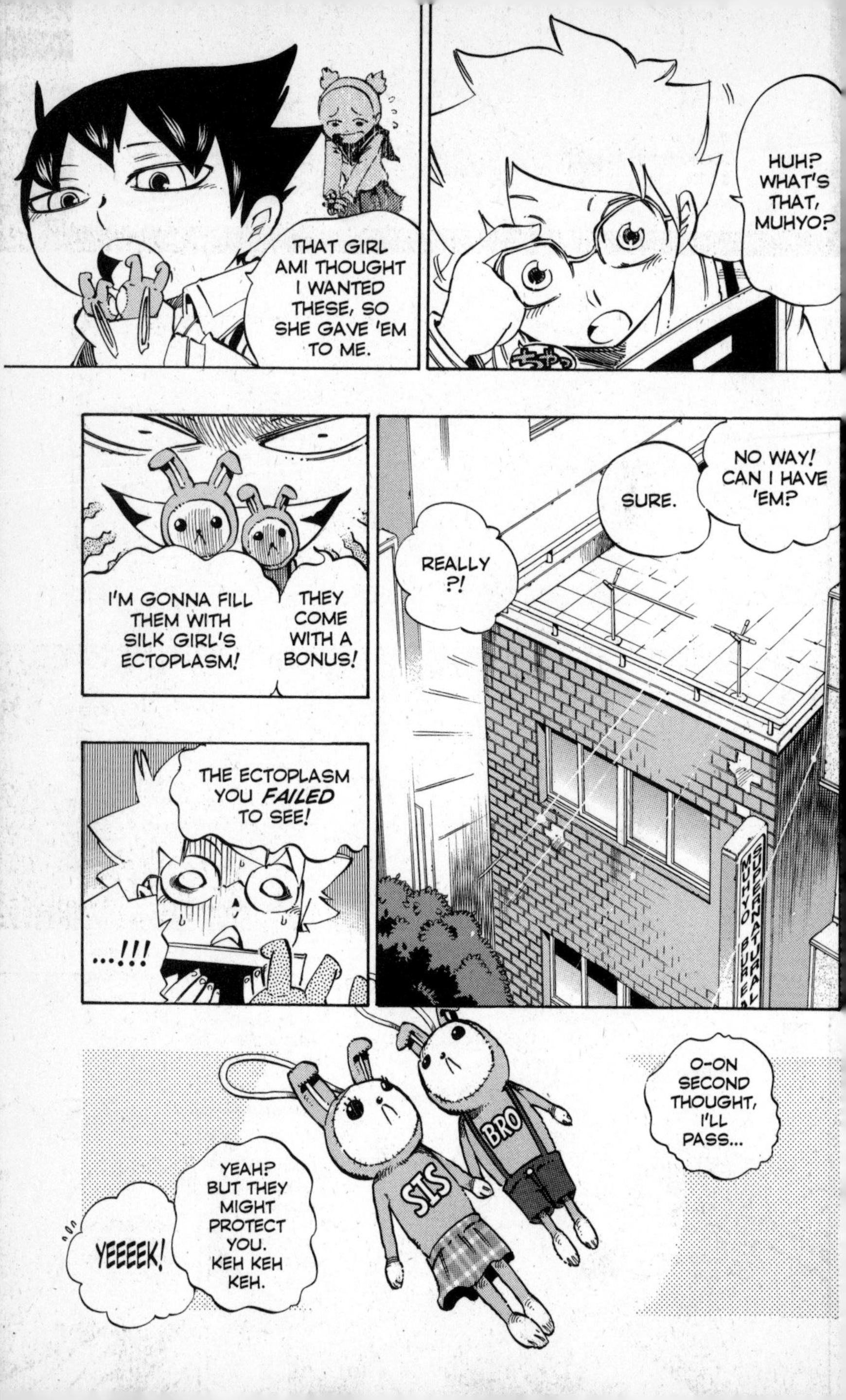
HUH? WHAT'S THAT, MUHYO?
THAT GIRL AMI THOUGHT I WANTED THESE, SO SHE GAVE 'EM TO ME.
NO WAY! CAN I HAVE 'EM?
SURE.
REALLY?!
SUPERNATURAL
THEY COME WITH A BONUS!
I'M GONNA FILL THEM WITH SILK GIRL'S ECTOPLASM!
THE ECTOPLASM YOU *FAILED* TO SEE!
...!!!
O-ON SECOND THOUGHT, I'LL PASS...
BRO
SIS
YEAH? BUT THEY MIGHT PROTECT YOU. KEH KEH KEH.
YEEEEK!

POST-SENTENCING:
DOWN BELOW

QUIVER

OWW ...
I REALLY
HIT MY
HEAD!!

P

___ BY WAY OF ___
EXPLANATION

SO I REALLY WANTED TO
DO SOMETHING WITH A
VIDEOTAPE IN IT. I GOT SO
INVOLVED THAT I TOTALLY
FORGOT HOW FREAKED OUT
I WAS WHEN I SAW THE RING
AND ITS SEQUEL (UNTIL I WAS
WORKING ON THIS STORY LATE
AT NIGHT)! EEE, SCARY!
BY THE WAY, THE ENVOY IN
THIS CHAPTER WAS THE IDEA
OF MR. A.H. FROM AKITA.
THANKS! — ♪

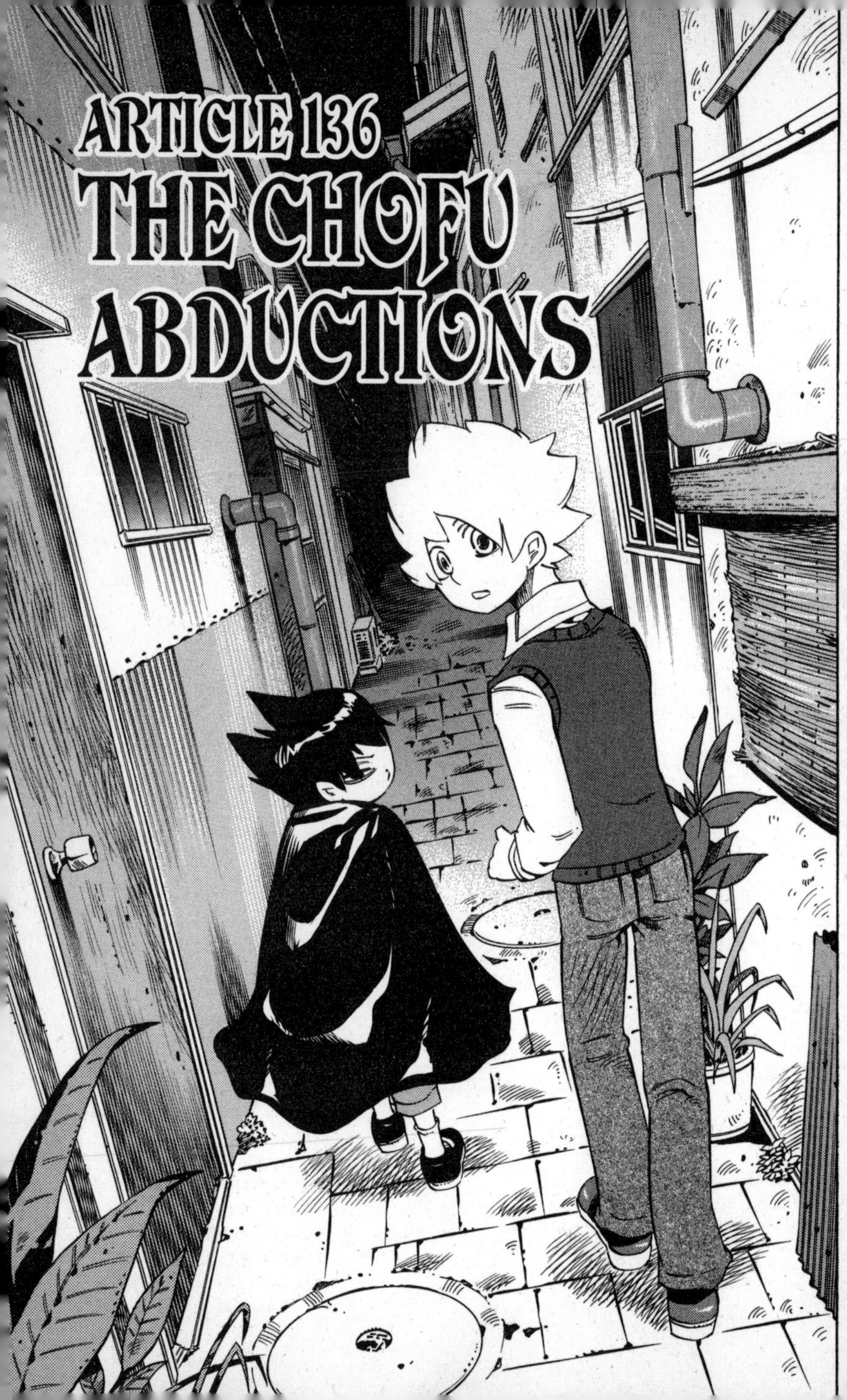
ARTICLE 136
THE CHOFU ABDUCTIONS

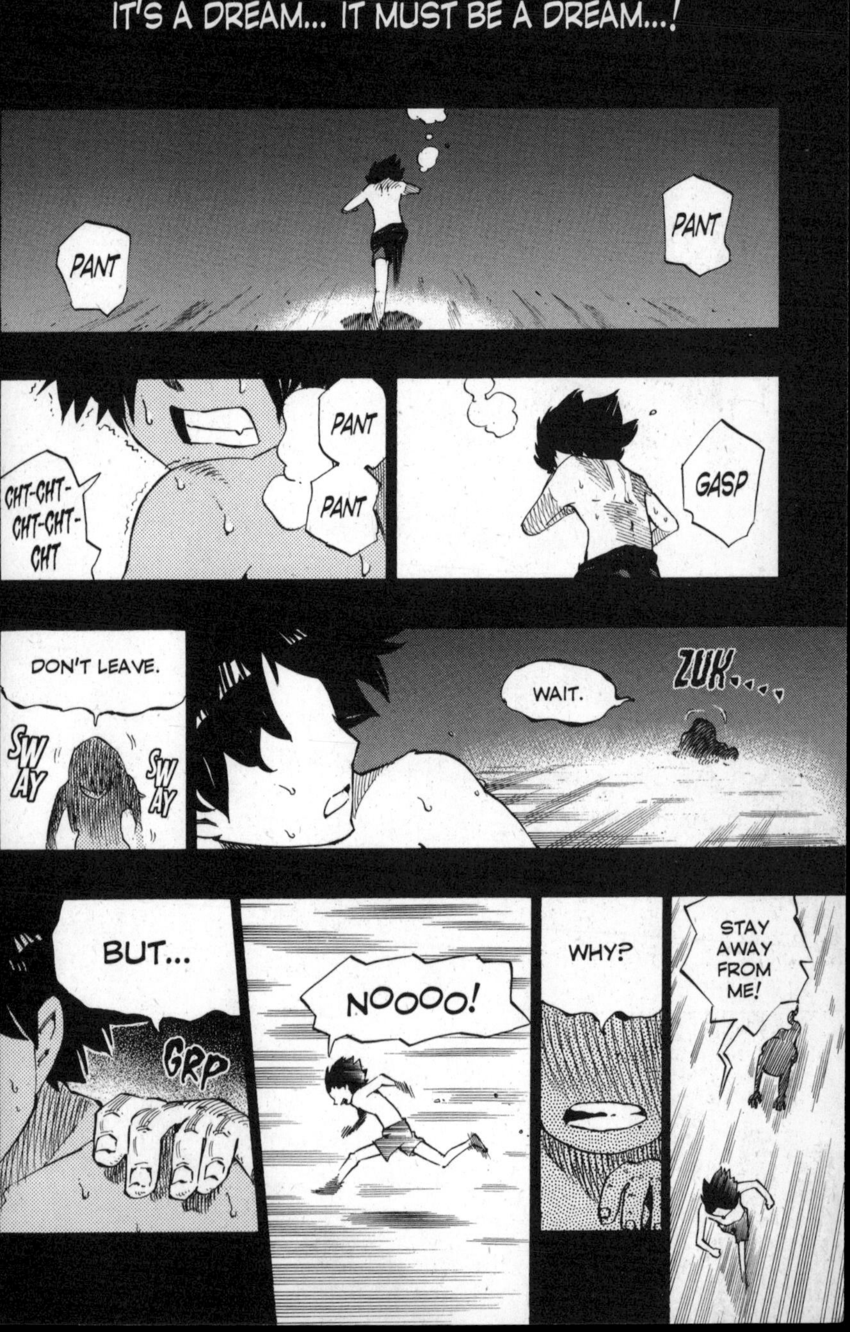
IT'S A DREAM... IT MUST BE A DREAM...!
PANT
PANT
GASP
PANT
PANT
CHT-CHT-CHT-CHT-CHT
ZUK
WAIT.
DON'T LEAVE.
SWAY
SWAY
STAY AWAY FROM ME!
WHY?
NOOOO!
BUT...
GRP

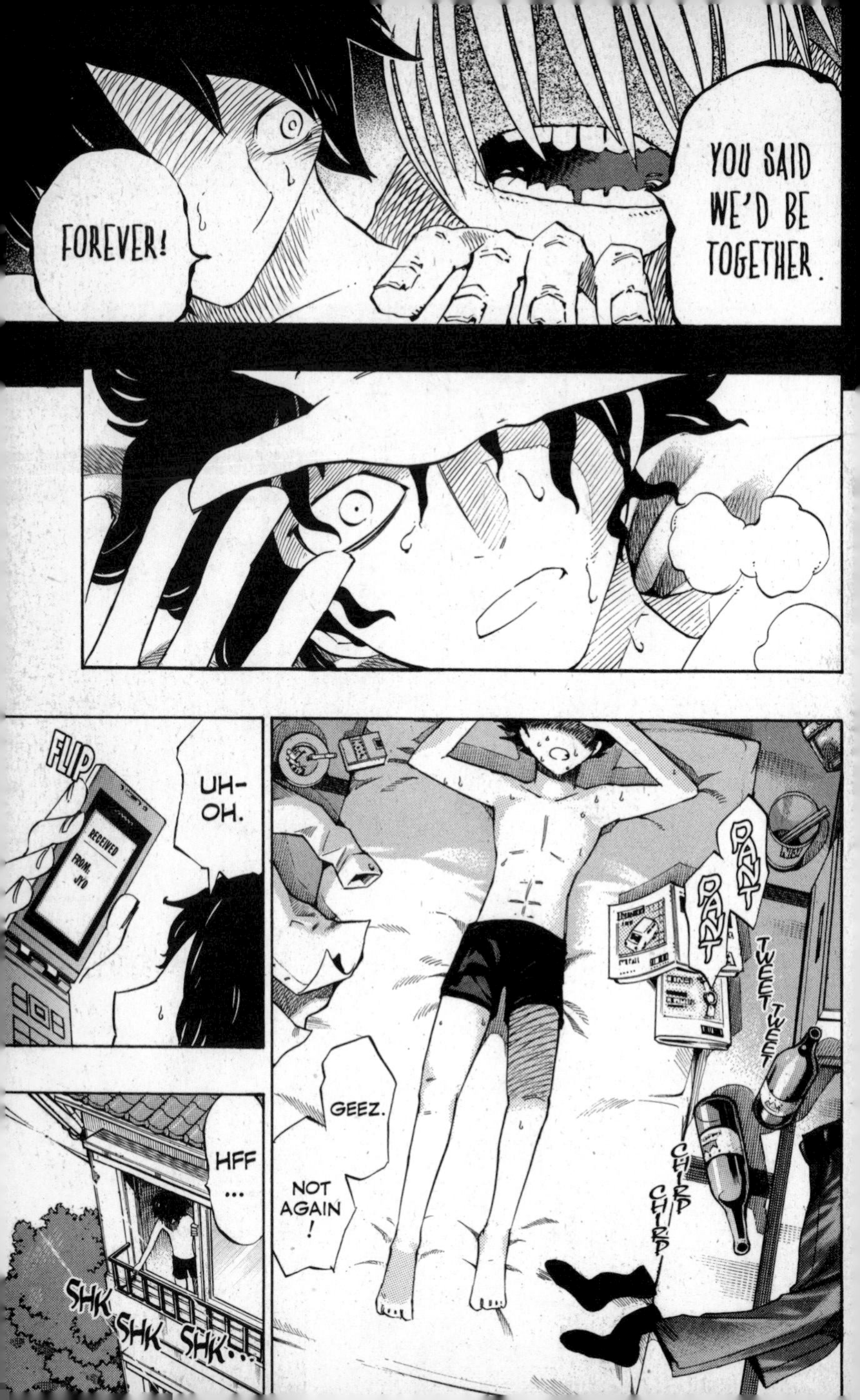
YOU SAID WE'D BE TOGETHER.
FOREVER!
PANT PANT
TWEET TWEET
CHIRP CHIRP
GEEZ.
NOT AGAIN!
FLIP
RECEIVED
FROM: JYO
UH-OH.
HFF...
SHK SHK SHK...

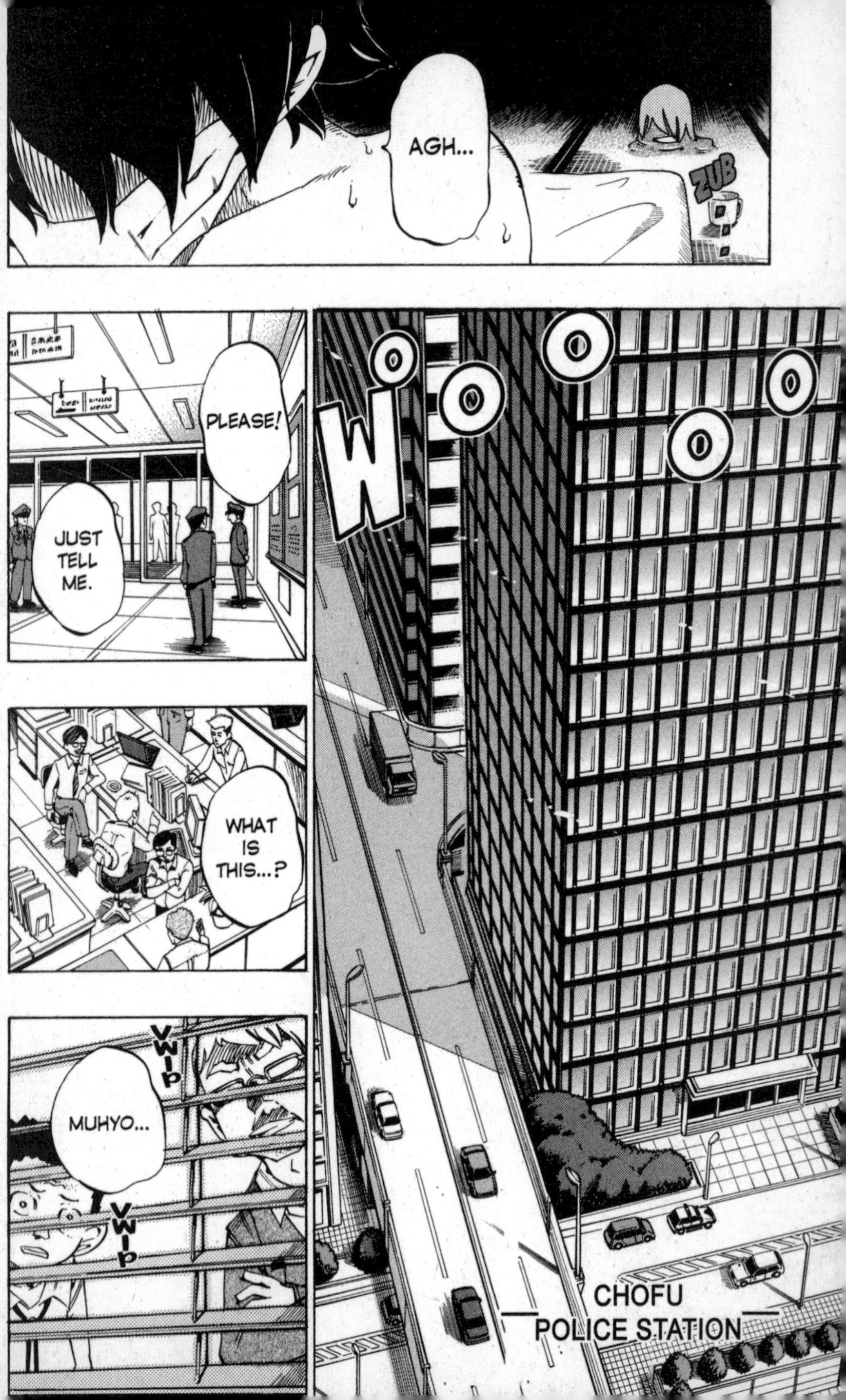
AGH...
ZUB
WOOOOO
CHOFU
POLICE STATION
PLEASE!
JUST TELL ME.
WHAT IS THIS...?
VWIP
MUHYO...
VWIP

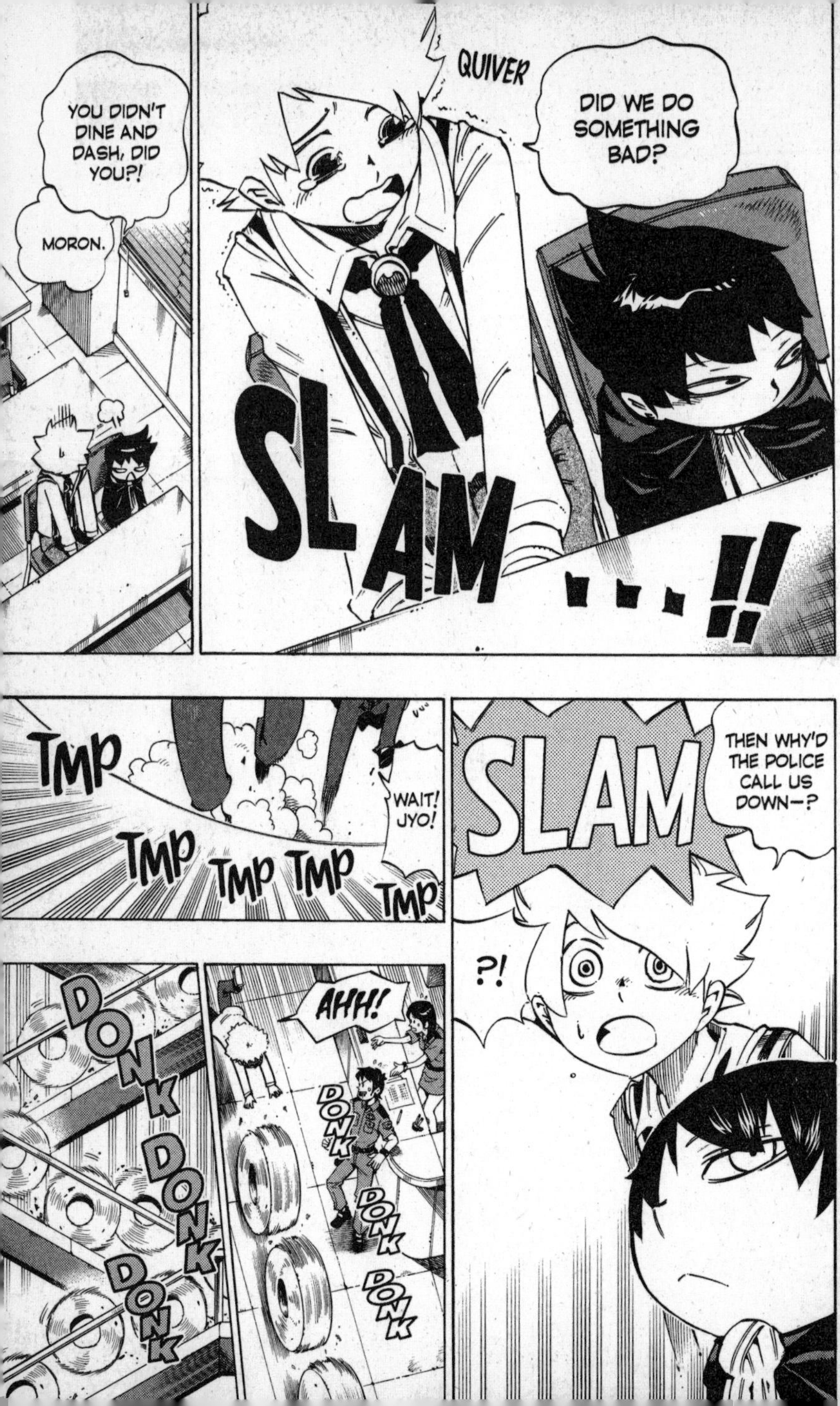
DID WE DO SOMETHING BAD?
QUIVER
SLAM...!!
YOU DIDN'T DINE AND DASH, DID YOU?!
MORON.
THEN WHY'D THE POLICE CALL US DOWN—?
SLAM
?!
WAIT! JYO!
TMP
TMP
TMP TMP
TMP
AHH!
DONK
DONK
DONK
DONK DONK
DONK

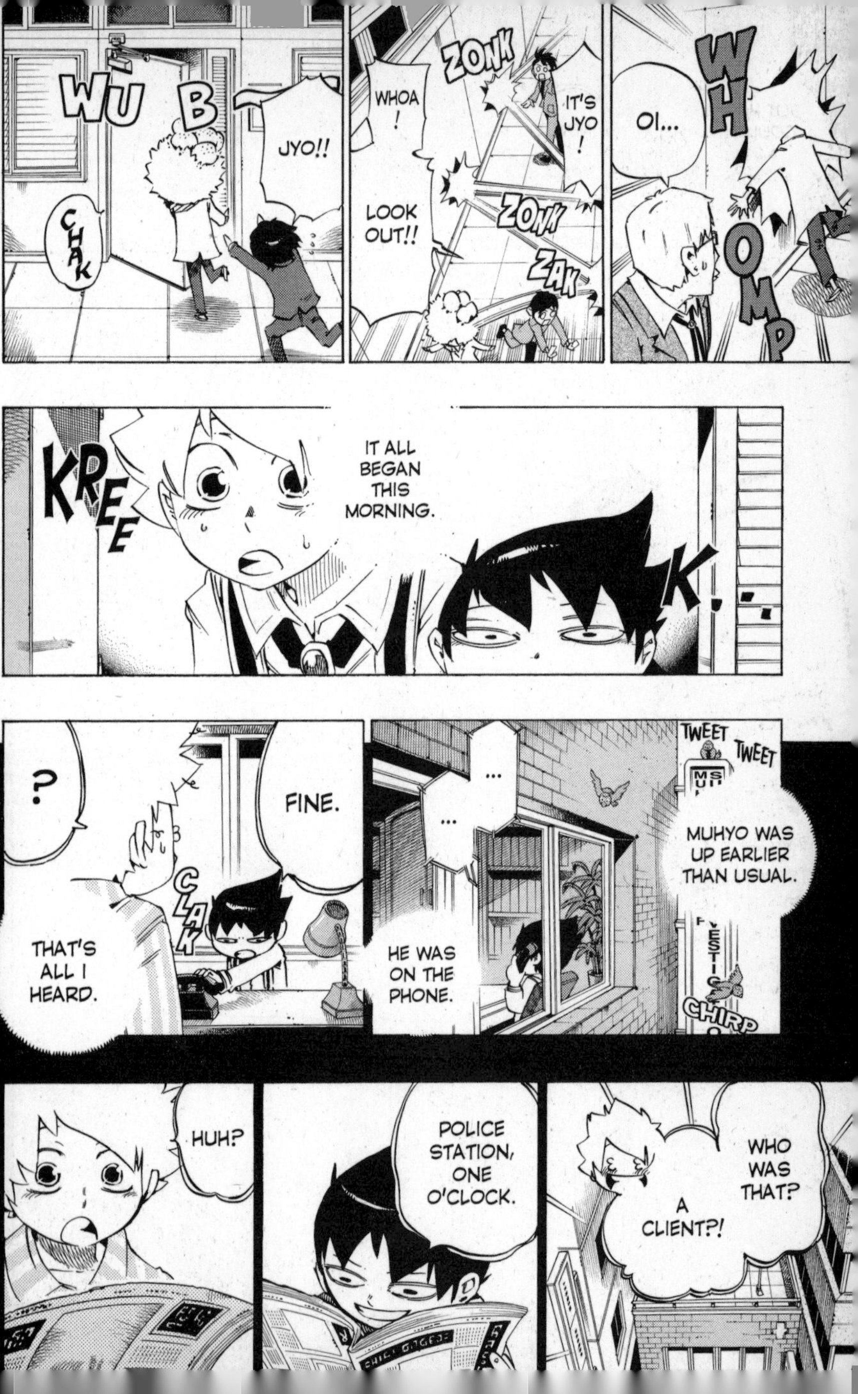
OI...
WHOMP
ZONK
IT'S JYO!
WHOA!
LOOK OUT!!
ZONK
ZAK
WU B
JYO!!
CHAK
IT ALL BEGAN THIS MORNING.
KREE
K.
TWEET TWEET
MUHYO WAS UP EARLIER THAN USUAL.
...
...
HE WAS ON THE PHONE.
CHIRP
FINE.
?
CLAK
THAT'S ALL I HEARD.
WHO WAS THAT?
A CLIENT?!
POLICE STATION, ONE O'CLOCK.
HUH?

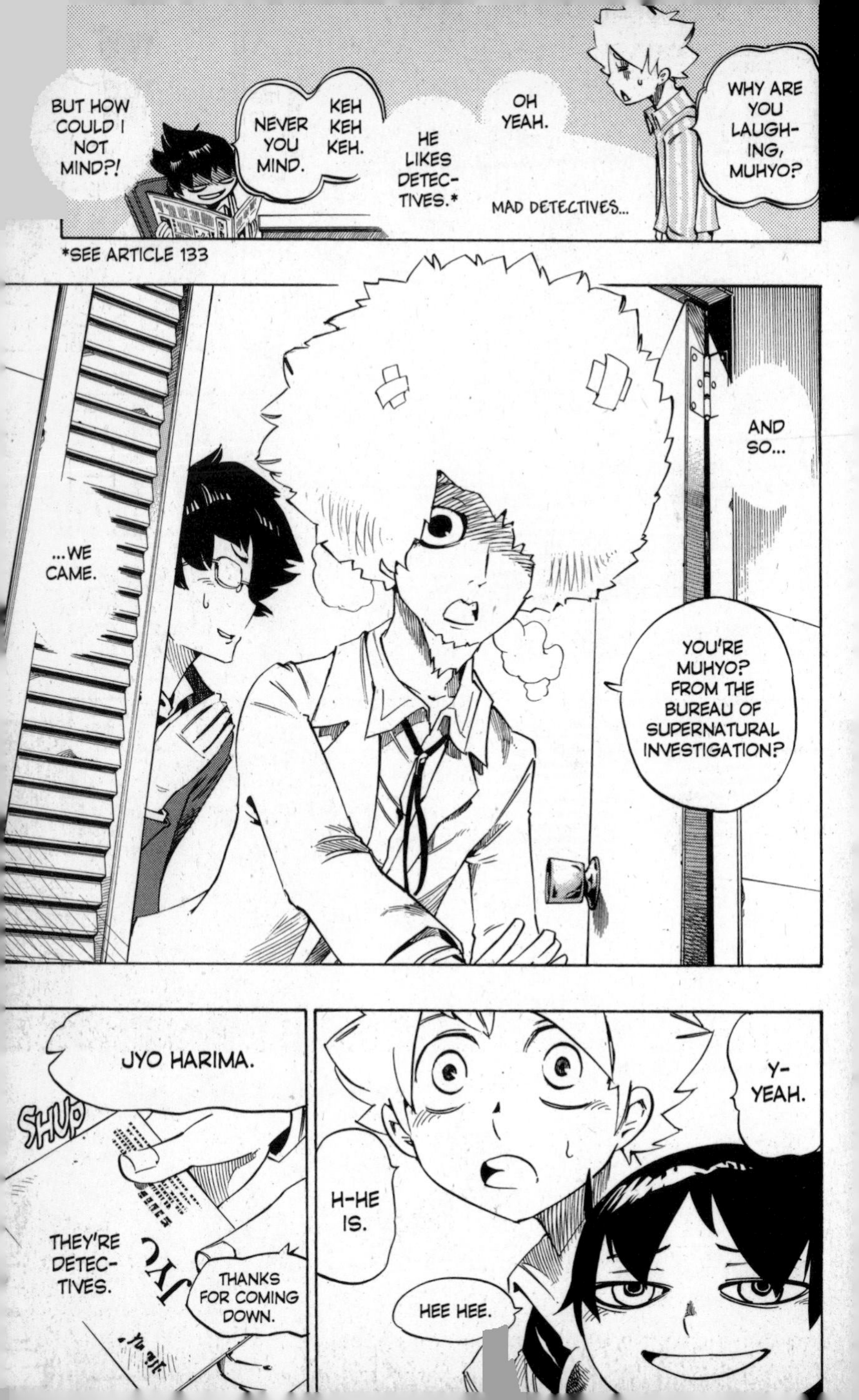
WHY ARE YOU LAUGHING, MUHYO?
OH YEAH.
MAD DETECTIVES...
HE LIKES DETECTIVES.*
KEH KEH KEH.
NEVER YOU MIND.
BUT HOW COULD I NOT MIND?!
*SEE ARTICLE 133
AND SO...
...WE CAME.
YOU'RE MUHYO? FROM THE BUREAU OF SUPERNATURAL INVESTIGATION?
Y-YEAH.
H-HE IS.
HEE HEE.
JYO HARIMA.
SHUP
THANKS FOR COMING DOWN.
THEY'RE DETECTIVES.

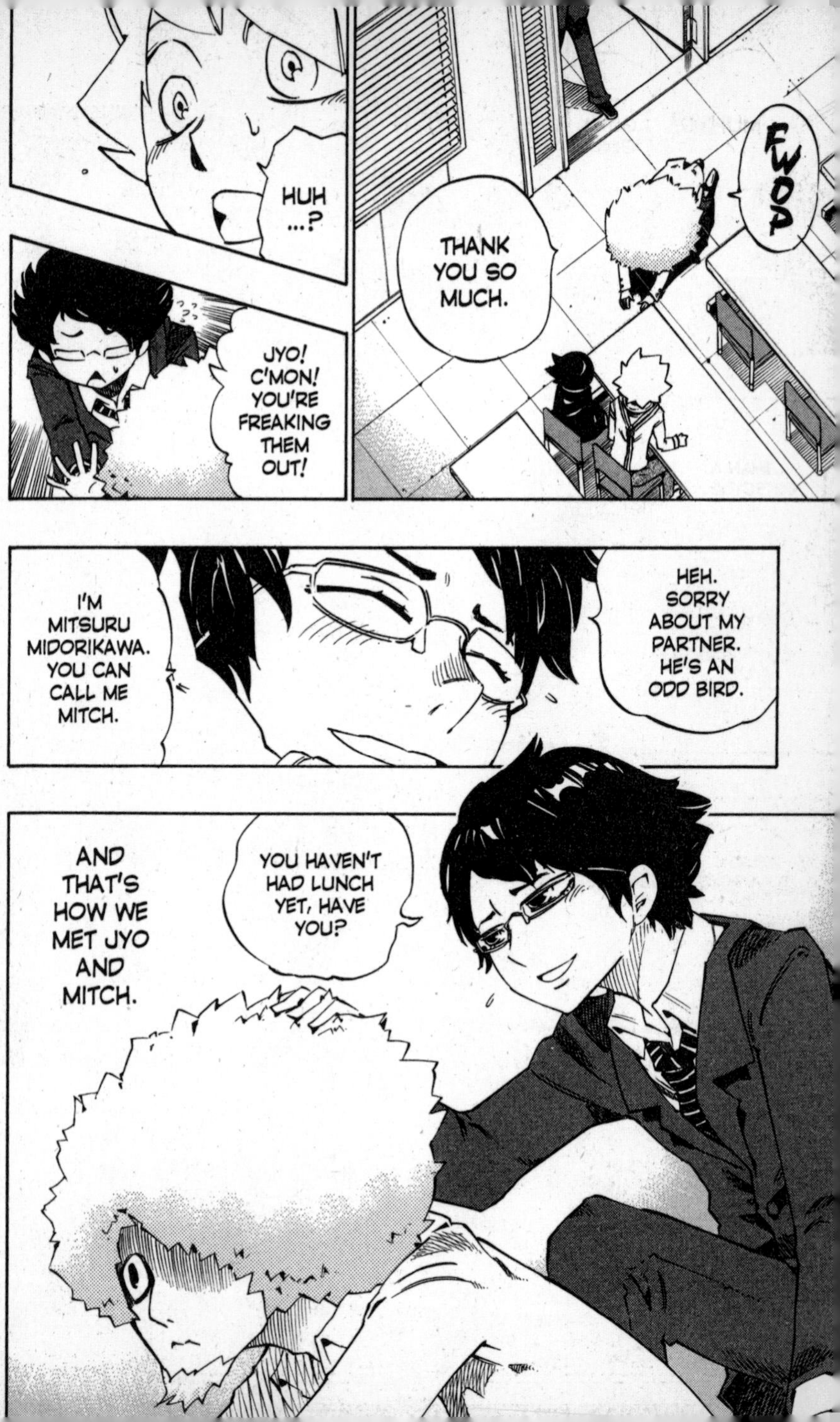
FWOP
THANK YOU SO MUCH.
HUH ...?
JYO! C'MON! YOU'RE FREAKING THEM OUT!
HEH. SORRY ABOUT MY PARTNER. HE'S AN ODD BIRD.
I'M MITSURU MIDORIKAWA. YOU CAN CALL ME MITCH.
YOU HAVEN'T HAD LUNCH YET, HAVE YOU?
AND THAT'S HOW WE MET JYO AND MITCH.

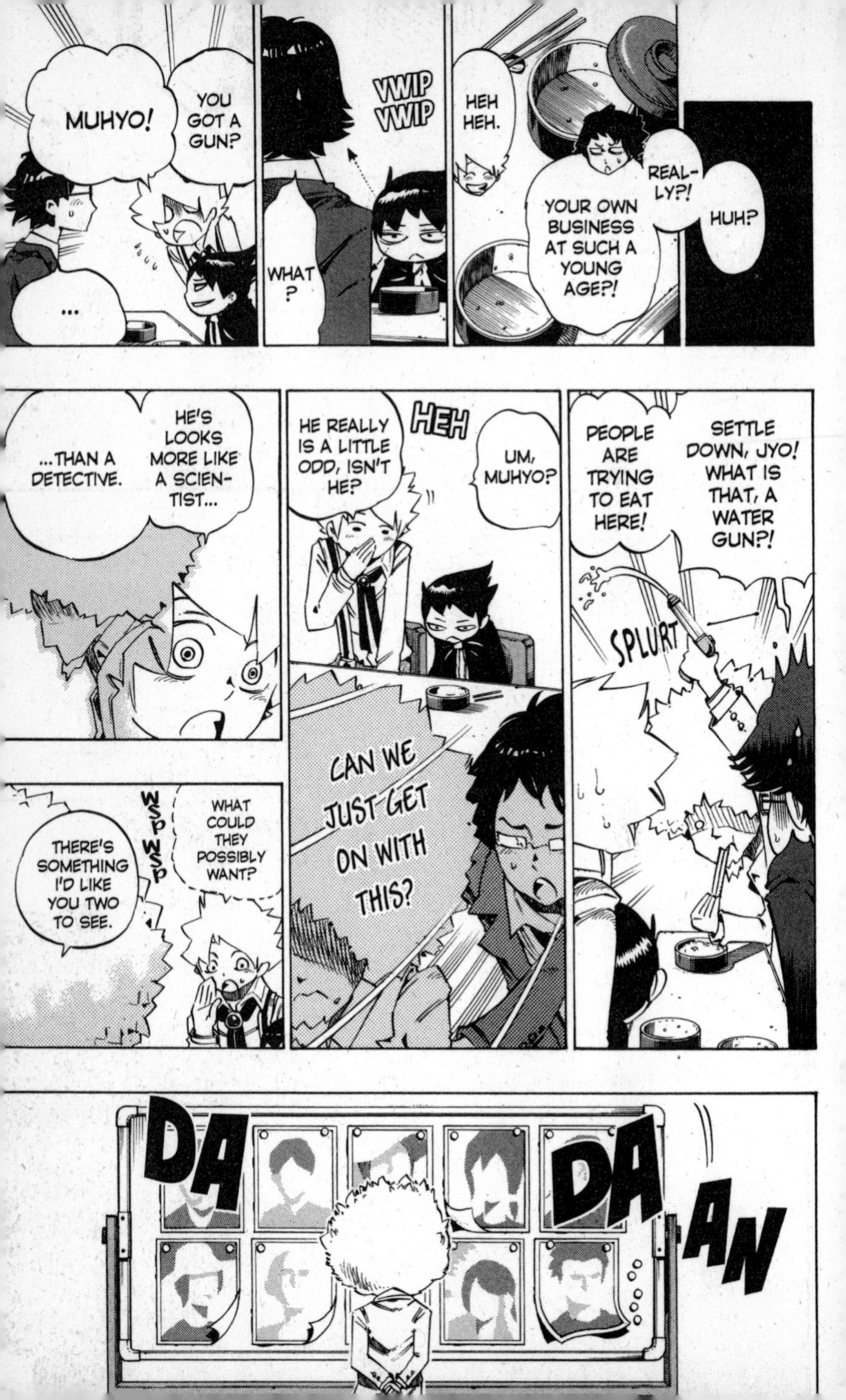
HUH?
REAL-LY?!
HEH HEH.
YOUR OWN BUSINESS AT SUCH A YOUNG AGE?!
VWIP VWIP
WHAT?
YOU GOT A GUN?
MUHYO!
...
SETTLE DOWN, JYO! WHAT IS THAT, A WATER GUN?!
PEOPLE ARE TRYING TO EAT HERE!
SPLURT
UM, MUHYO?
HEH
HE REALLY IS A LITTLE ODD, ISN'T HE?
CAN WE JUST GET ON WITH THIS?
HE'S LOOKS MORE LIKE A SCIEN-TIST...
...THAN A DETECTIVE.
WHAT COULD THEY POSSIBLY WANT?
WSP WSP
THERE'S SOMETHING I'D LIKE YOU TWO TO SEE.
DA
DA
AN

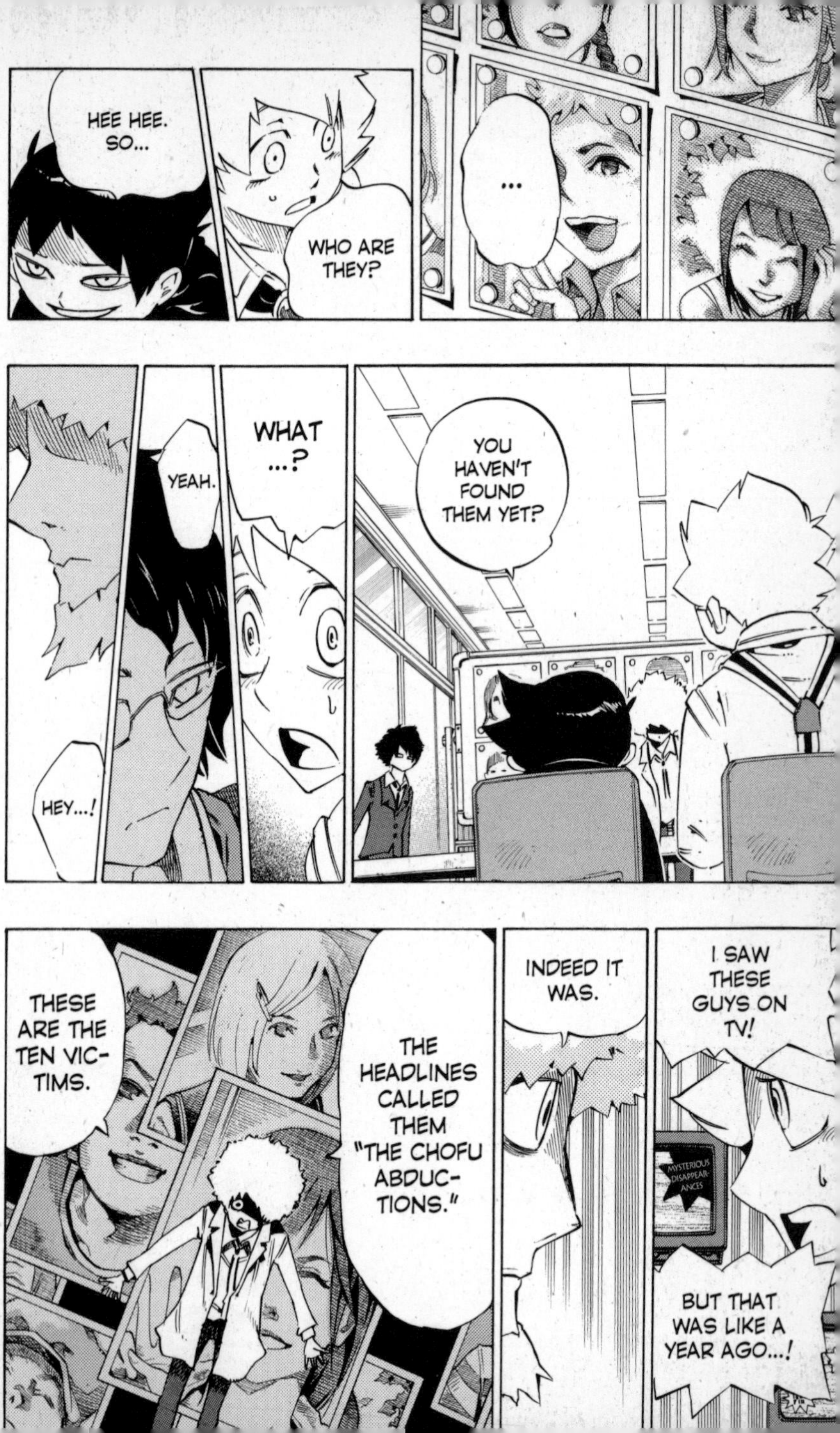
...
WHO ARE THEY?
HEE HEE. SO...
YOU HAVEN'T FOUND THEM YET?
WHAT ...?
YEAH.
HEY...!
I SAW THESE GUYS ON TV!
MYSTERIOUS DISAPPEARANCES
BUT THAT WAS LIKE A YEAR AGO...!
INDEED IT WAS.
THE HEADLINES CALLED THEM "THE CHOFU ABDUCTIONS."
THESE ARE THE TEN VICTIMS.

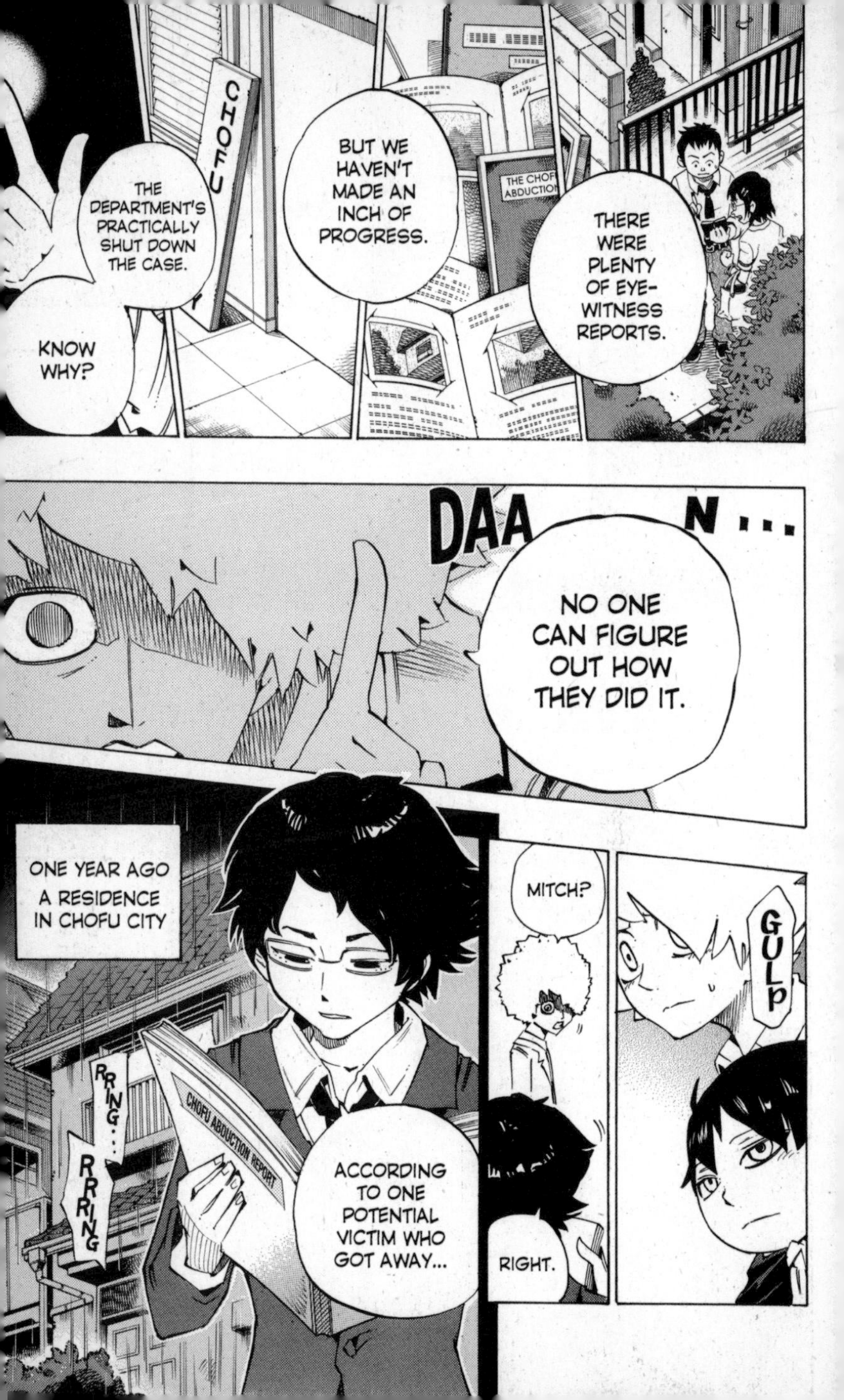
THE CHOFU ABDUCTION
THERE WERE PLENTY OF EYE-WITNESS REPORTS.
BUT WE HAVEN'T MADE AN INCH OF PROGRESS.
CHOFU
THE DEPARTMENT'S PRACTICALLY SHUT DOWN THE CASE.
KNOW WHY?
DAA N...
NO ONE CAN FIGURE OUT HOW THEY DID IT.
GULP
MITCH?
RIGHT.
ONE YEAR AGO A RESIDENCE IN CHOFU CITY
CHOFU ABDUCTION REPORT
ACCORDING TO ONE POTENTIAL VICTIM WHO GOT AWAY...
RRING...
RRRING

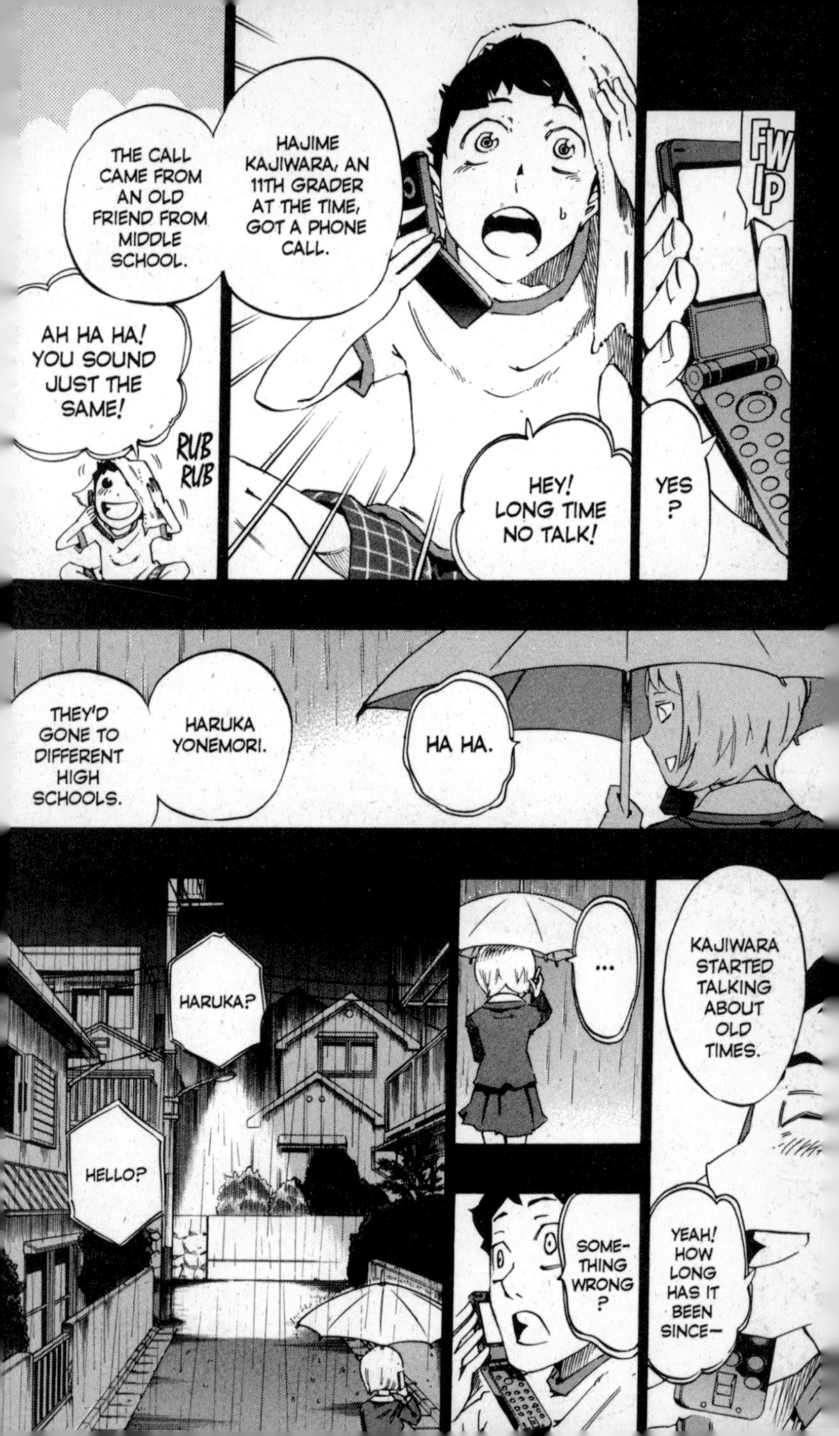
FWIP
YES?
HAJIME KAJIWARA, AN 11TH GRADER AT THE TIME, GOT A PHONE CALL.
HEY! LONG TIME NO TALK!
THE CALL CAME FROM AN OLD FRIEND FROM MIDDLE SCHOOL.
AH HA HA! YOU SOUND JUST THE SAME!
RUB RUB
HA HA.
HARUKA YONEMORI.
THEY'D GONE TO DIFFERENT HIGH SCHOOLS.
KAJIWARA STARTED TALKING ABOUT OLD TIMES.
YEAH! HOW LONG HAS IT BEEN SINCE—
...
SOME-THING WRONG?
HARUKA?
HELLO?

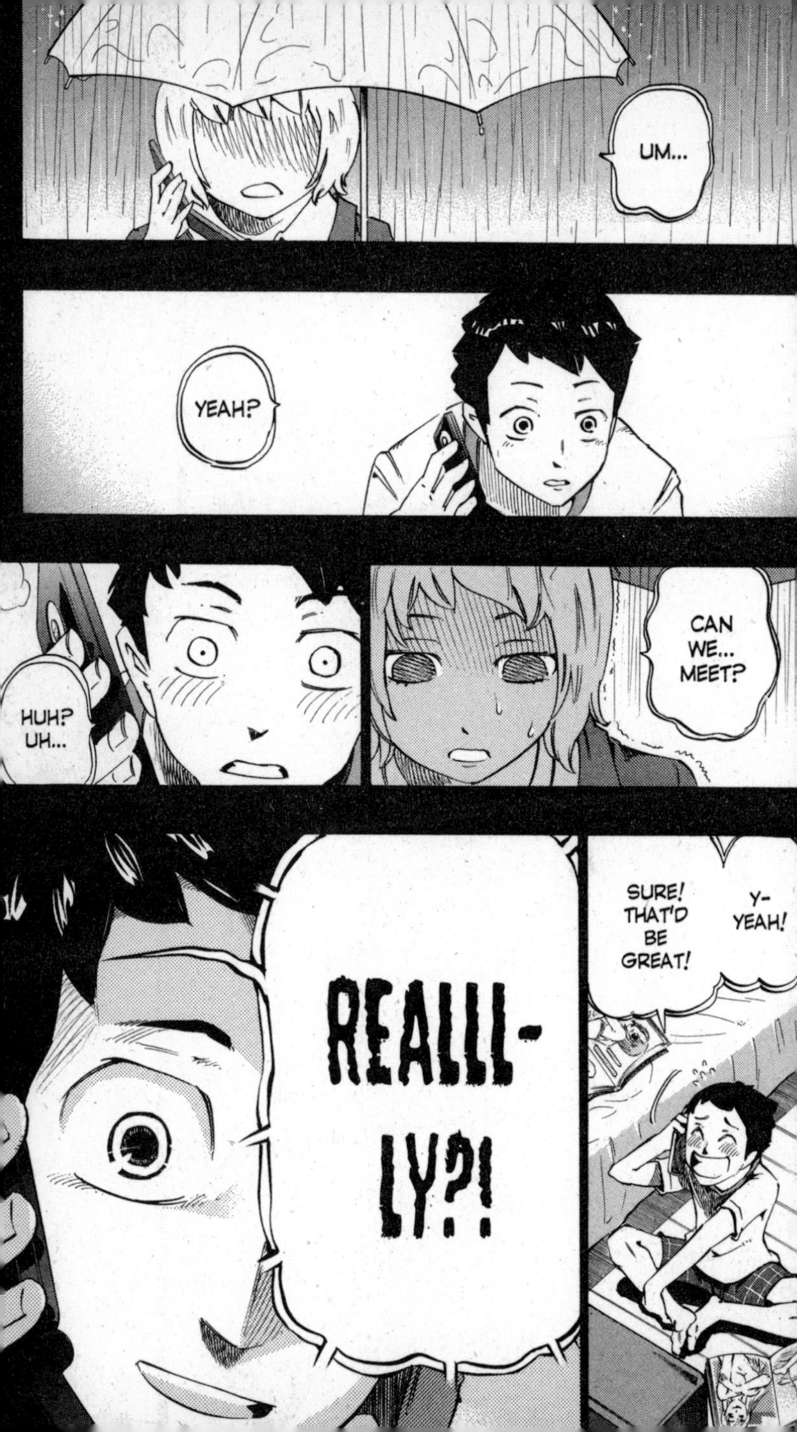
UM...
YEAH?
CAN WE... MEET?
HUH? UH...
Y-YEAH!
SURE! THAT'D BE GREAT!
REALL-LY?!

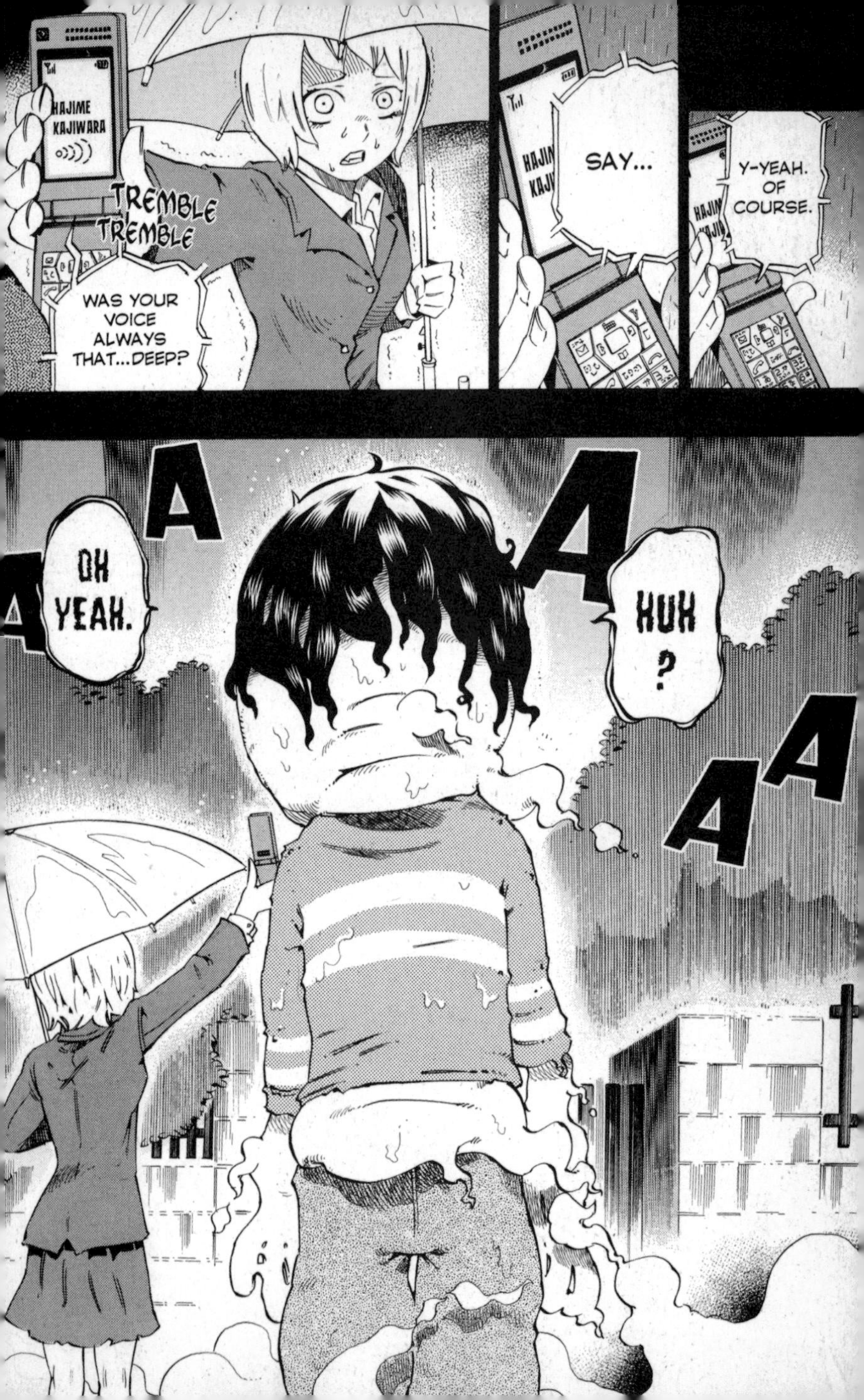
HAJIN KAJIW
Y-YEAH. OF COURSE.
HAJIM KAJI
SAY...
HAJIME KAJIWARA
TREMBLE TREMBLE
WAS YOUR VOICE ALWAYS THAT...DEEP?
A
HUH ?
AAA
A
OH YEAH.
A

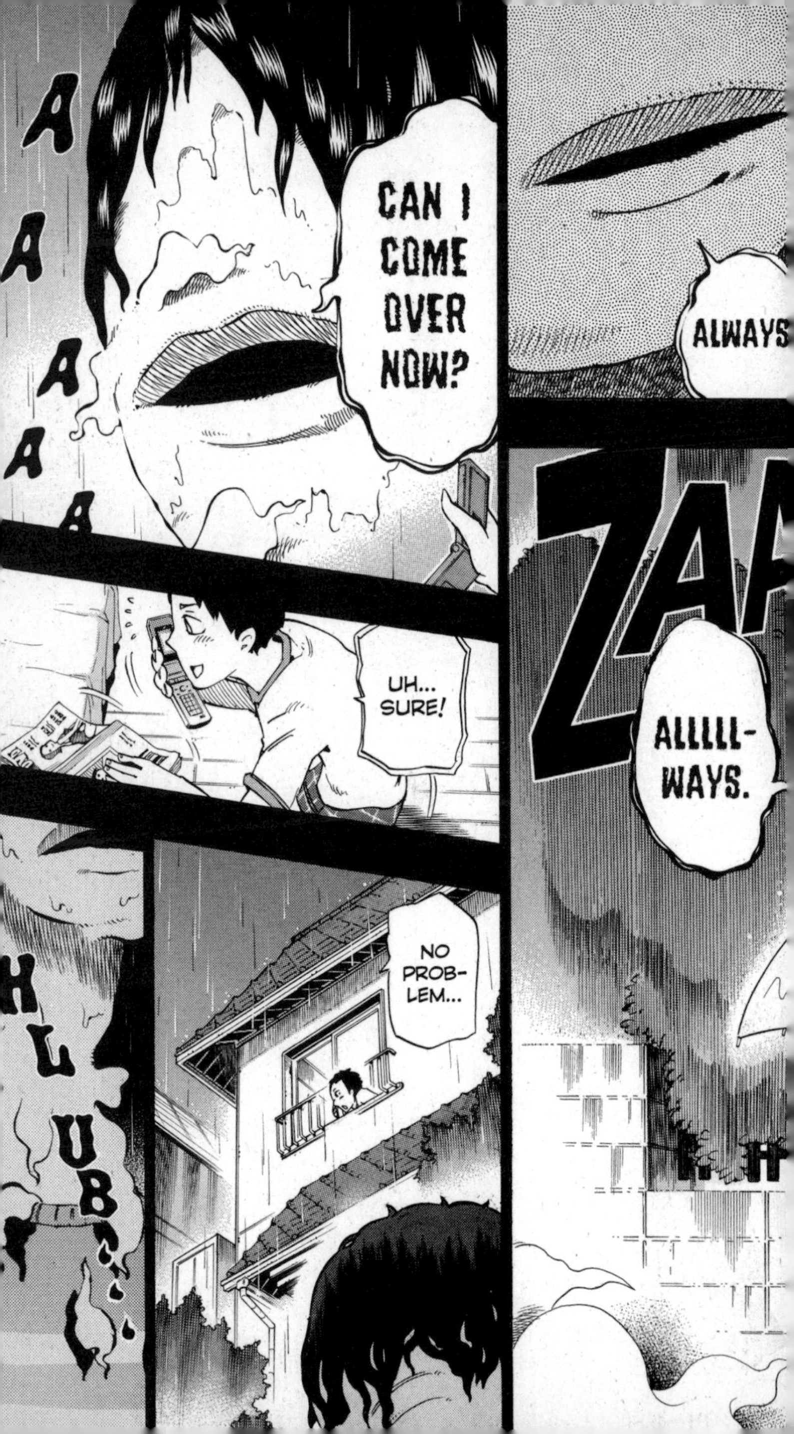
ALWAYS
ALLLLL-WAYS.
AAAAA
CAN I COME OVER NOW?
UH... SURE!
NO PROB-LEM...
HLUB

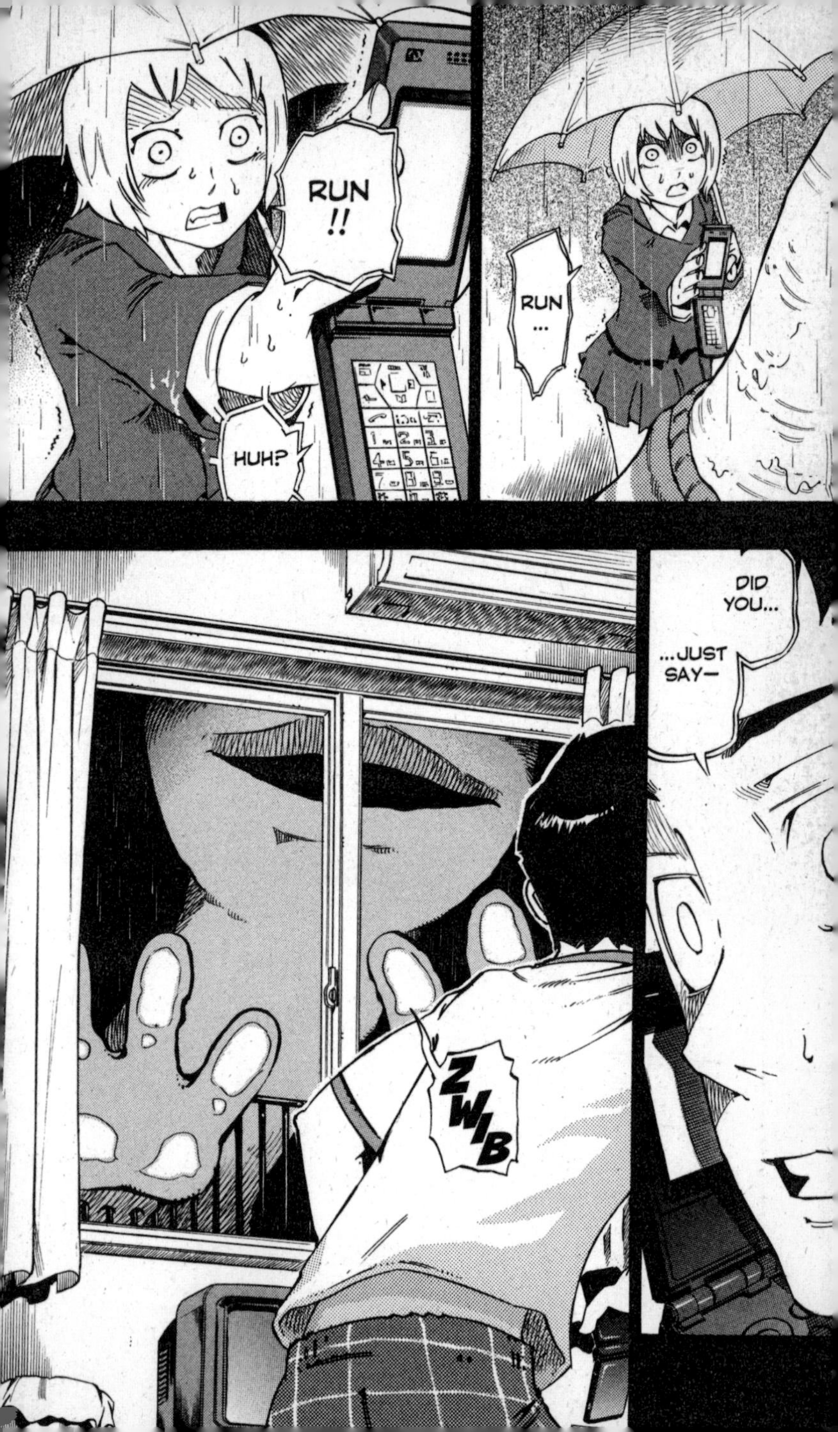
RUN ...
RUN !!
HUH?
DID YOU...
...JUST SAY—
ZWIB

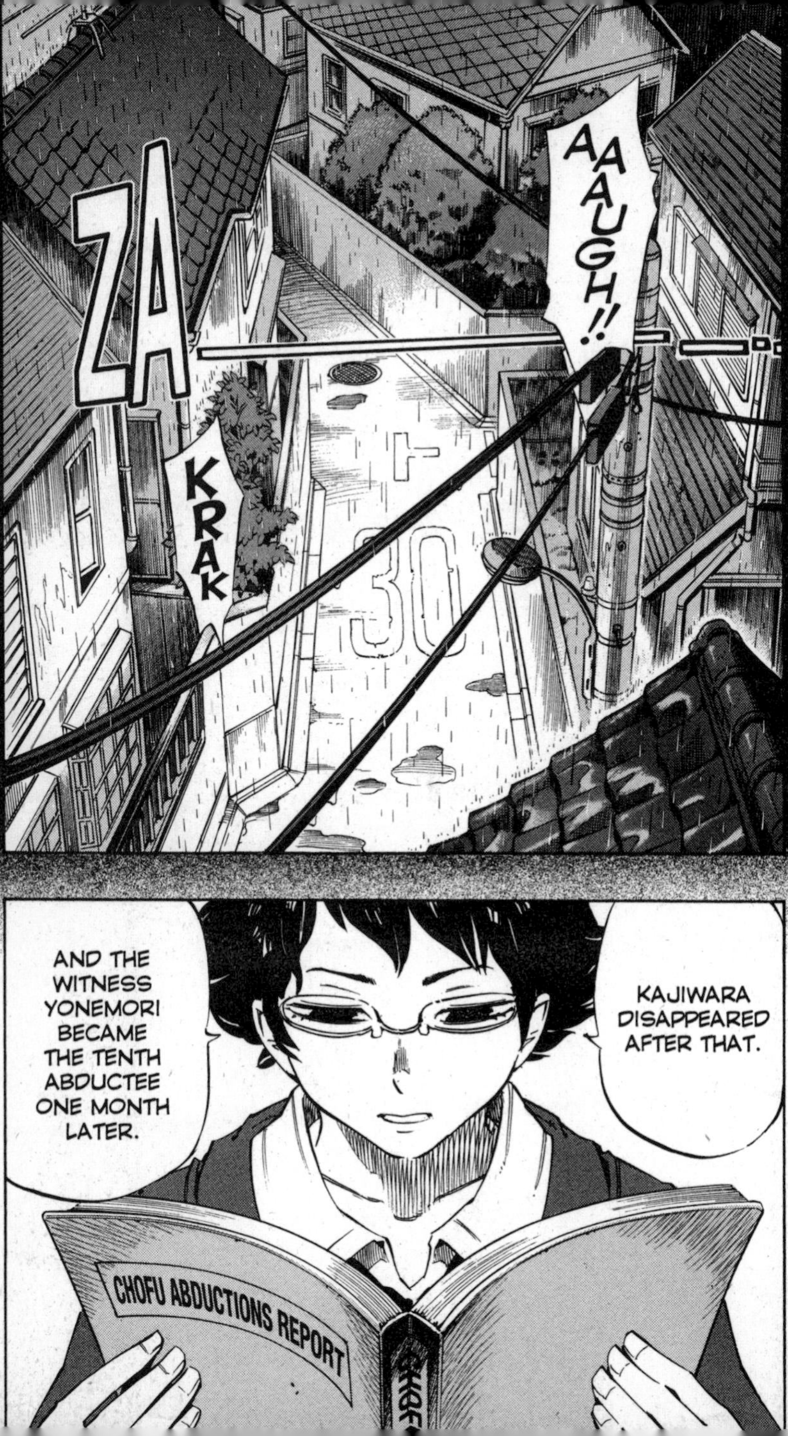
AAAUGH!!
ZA
KRAK
KAJIWARA DISAPPEARED AFTER THAT.
AND THE WITNESS YONEMORI BECAME THE TENTH ABDUCTEE ONE MONTH LATER.
CHOFU ABDUCTIONS REPORT

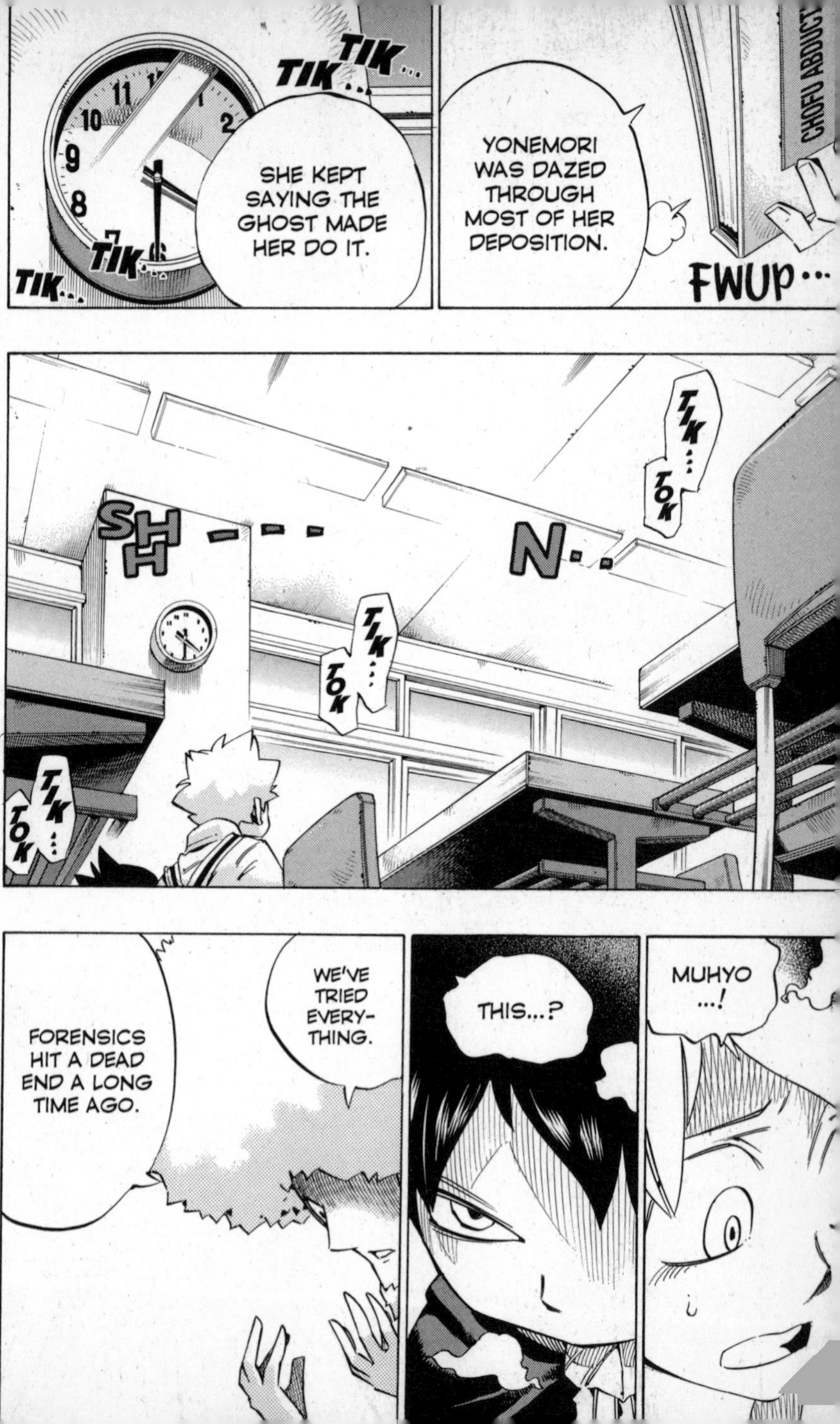
CHOFU ABDUCT
FWUP...
YONEMORI WAS DAZED THROUGH MOST OF HER DEPOSITION.
TIK TIK...
SHE KEPT SAYING THE GHOST MADE HER DO IT.
TIK... TIK...
TIK... TOK
SHH---N..
TIK... TOK
TIK... TOK
MUHYO ...!
THIS...?
WE'VE TRIED EVERY-THING.
FORENSICS HIT A DEAD END A LONG TIME AGO.

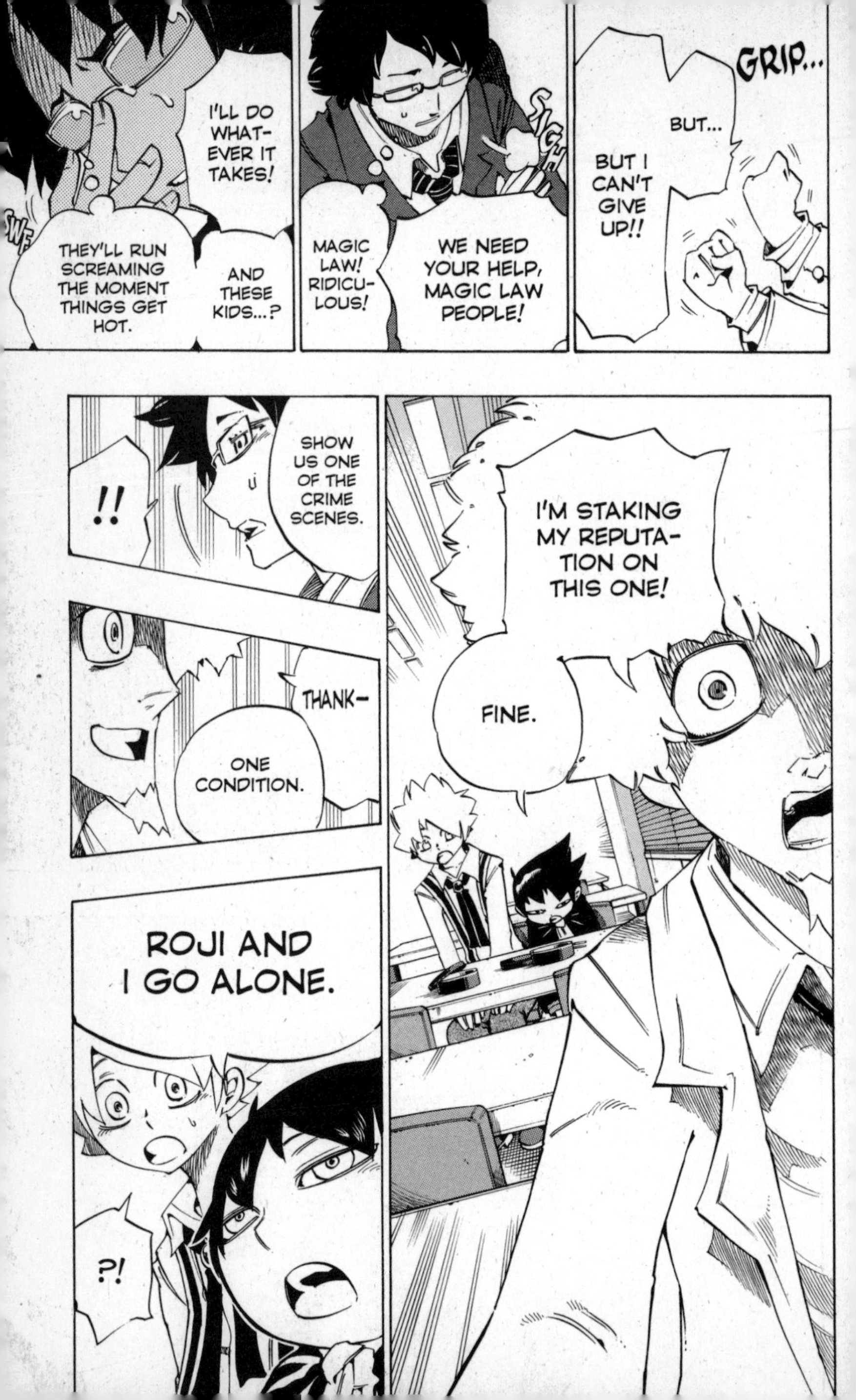
GRIP...
BUT...
BUT I CAN'T GIVE UP!!
SIGH
WE NEED YOUR HELP, MAGIC LAW PEOPLE!
MAGIC LAW! RIDICULOUS!
I'LL DO WHATEVER IT TAKES!
AND THESE KIDS...?
THEY'LL RUN SCREAMING THE MOMENT THINGS GET HOT.
SWF
I'M STAKING MY REPUTATION ON THIS ONE!
FINE.
SHOW US ONE OF THE CRIME SCENES.
!!
THANK-
ONE CONDITION.
ROJI AND I GO ALONE.
?!

Q1: (FROM P. IN HYOGO PREFECTURE)
SORRY IF THIS IS AN ANNOYING QUESTION, BUT WAY BACK WHEN SEVEN-FACED DOG FIRST SHOWED UP, MUHYO SAID HE WAS ONLY ABOUT AS BIG AS ROJI BECAUSE THE BOOK HE WAS USING WAS WEAK. THE DOG WAS FOUR TIMES AS BIG IN REALITY. BUT WHEN MUHYO GOT HIMSELF A NEW BOOK, SEVEN-FACED DOG WAS THE SAME QUARTER SIZE IN ARTICLES 138-140. HOW CAN THIS BE? WAS THERE SOME PROBLEM WITH THE SUMMONING?

Q2: (FROM F.M. IN HOKKAIDO)
WHICH CHARACTER SETS OFF KIRIKO'S HOTNESS SENSORS?

Q3: IS MUHYO INTO GIRLS? I MEAN, WHEN BUSUJIMA'S RUNNING AROUND NEAR-NAKED, HE'S WATCHING, RIGHT? WELL, IS HE?

A1: AH HA HA. YOU'RE RIGHT. THAT IS STRANGE. WHY'S HE STILL SMALL...?

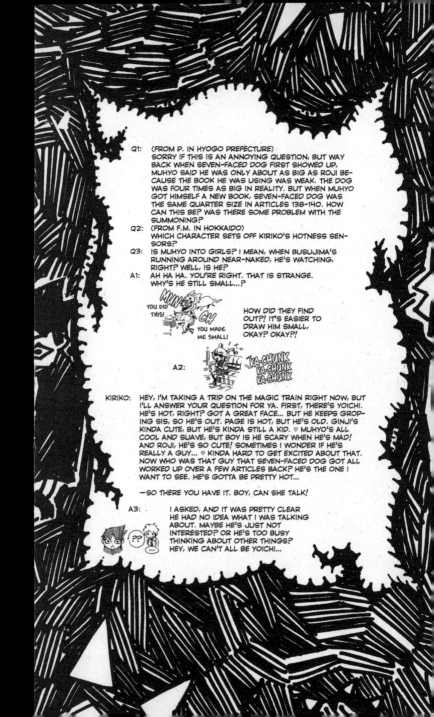

YOU DID THIS!
YOU MADE ME SMALL!

HOW DID THEY FIND OUT?! IT'S EASIER TO DRAW HIM SMALL, OKAY? OKAY?!

A2:

KA-CHUNK KA-CHUNK KA-CHUNK

KIRIKO: HEY, I'M TAKING A TRIP ON THE MAGIC TRAIN RIGHT NOW, BUT I'LL ANSWER YOUR QUESTION FOR YA. FIRST, THERE'S YOICHI. HE'S HOT, RIGHT? GOT A GREAT FACE... BUT HE KEEPS GROPING SIS, SO HE'S OUT. PAGE IS HOT, BUT HE'S OLD. GINJI'S KINDA CUTE, BUT HE'S KINDA STILL A KID. ♡ MUHYO'S ALL COOL AND SUAVE, BUT BOY IS HE SCARY WHEN HE'S MAD! AND ROJI, HE'S SO CUTE! SOMETIMES I WONDER IF HE'S REALLY A GUY... ♡ KINDA HARD TO GET EXCITED ABOUT THAT. NOW WHO WAS THAT GUY THAT SEVEN-FACED DOG GOT ALL WORKED UP OVER A FEW ARTICLES BACK? HE'S THE ONE I WANT TO SEE. HE'S GOTTA BE PRETTY HOT...

—SO THERE YOU HAVE IT. BOY, CAN SHE TALK!

A3: I ASKED, AND IT WAS PRETTY CLEAR HE HAD NO IDEA WHAT I WAS TALKING ABOUT. MAYBE HE'S JUST NOT INTERESTED? OR HE'S TOO BUSY THINKING ABOUT OTHER THINGS? HEY, WE CAN'T ALL BE YOICHI...

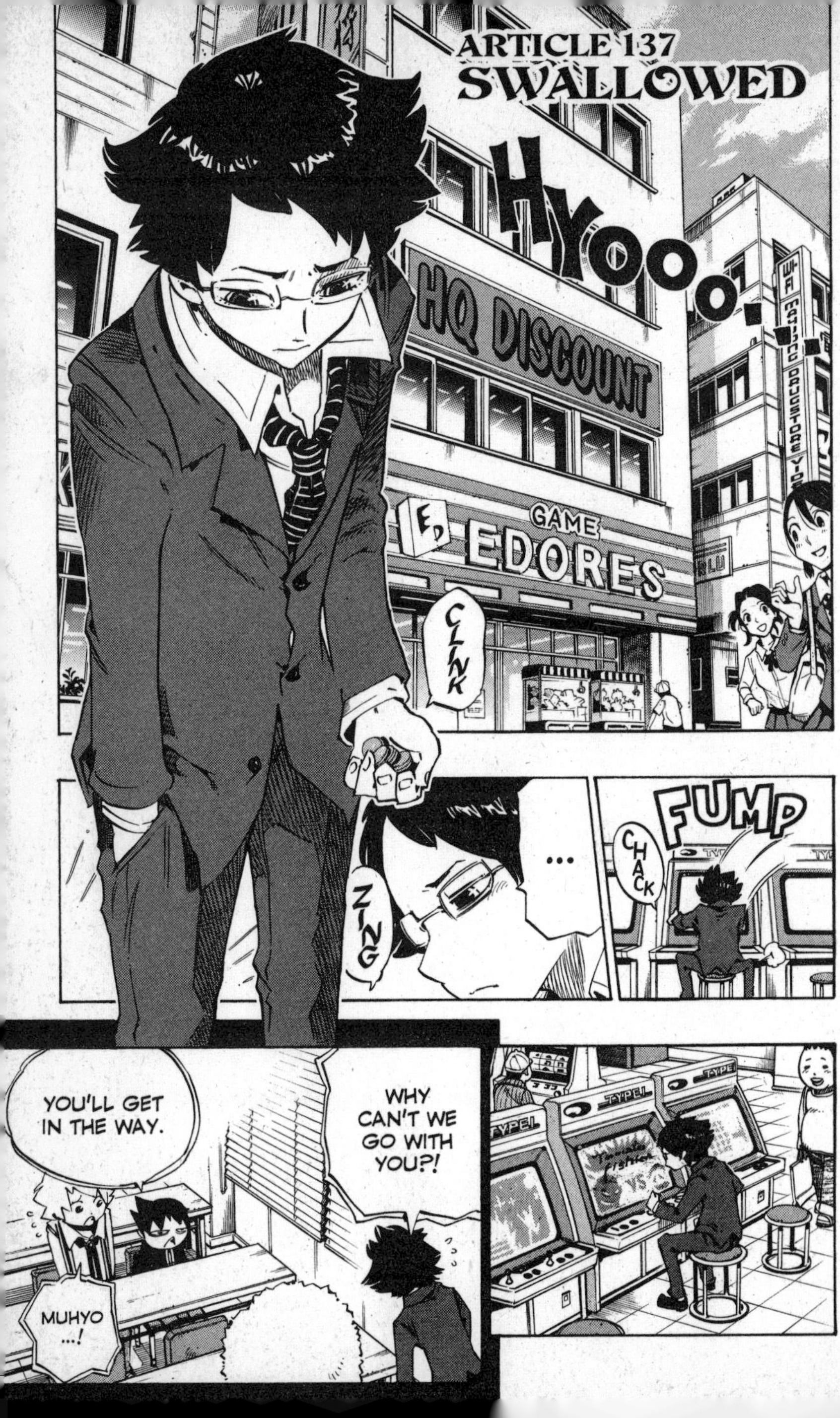
ARTICLE 137
SWALLOWED
HYOOO...
HQ DISCOUNT
GAME
EDORES
CLINK
FUMP
CHACK
...
ZING
WHY CAN'T WE GO WITH YOU?!
YOU'LL GET IN THE WAY.
MUHYO ...!

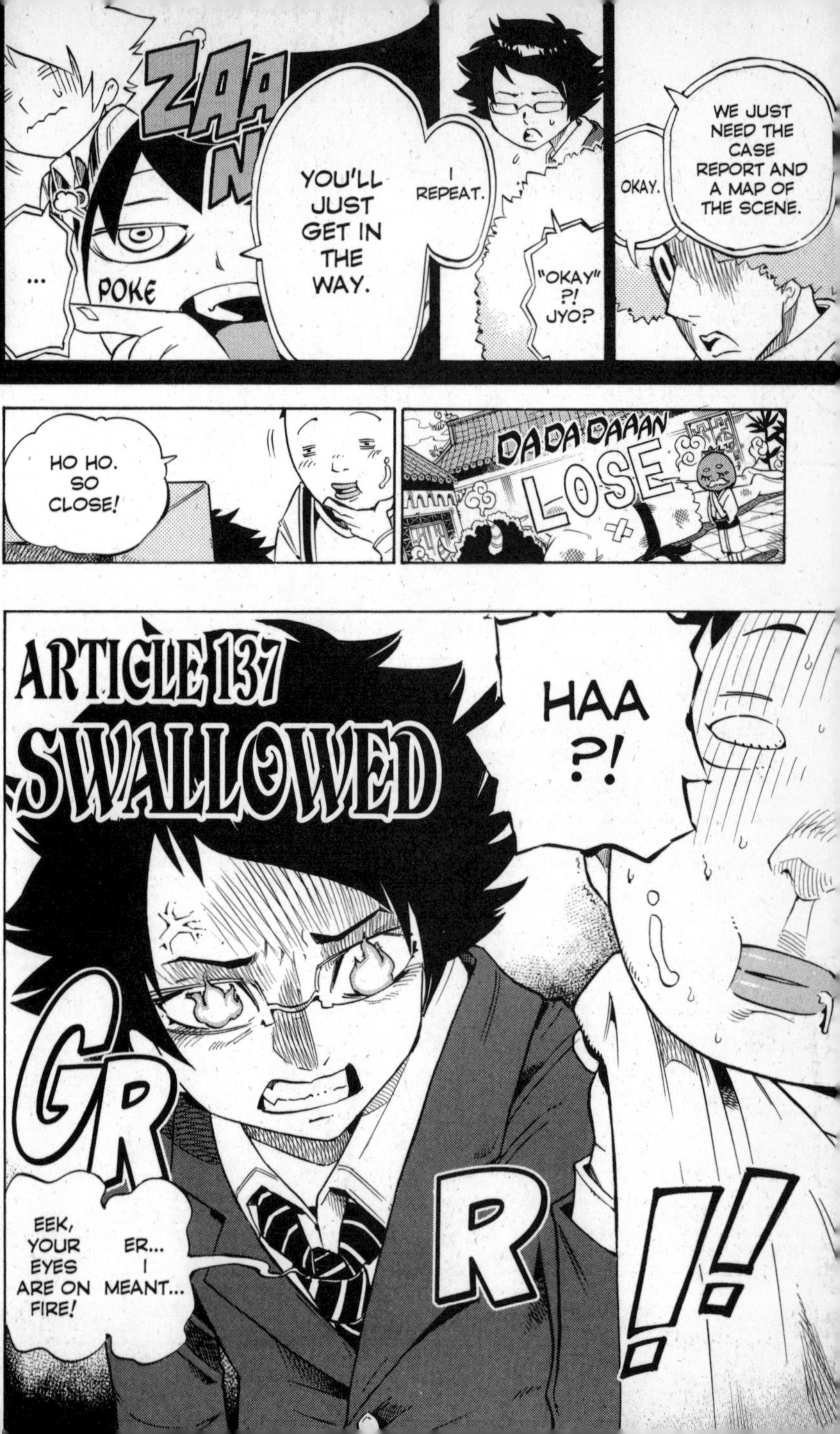
WE JUST NEED THE CASE REPORT AND A MAP OF THE SCENE.
OKAY.
"OKAY" ?! JYO?
I REPEAT.
ZAAN
YOU'LL JUST GET IN THE WAY.
POKE
...
DA DA DAAAN
LOSE
HO HO. SO CLOSE!
ARTICLE 137 SWALLOWED
HAA ?!
GRR!!
ER... I MEANT...
EEK, YOUR EYES ARE ON FIRE!

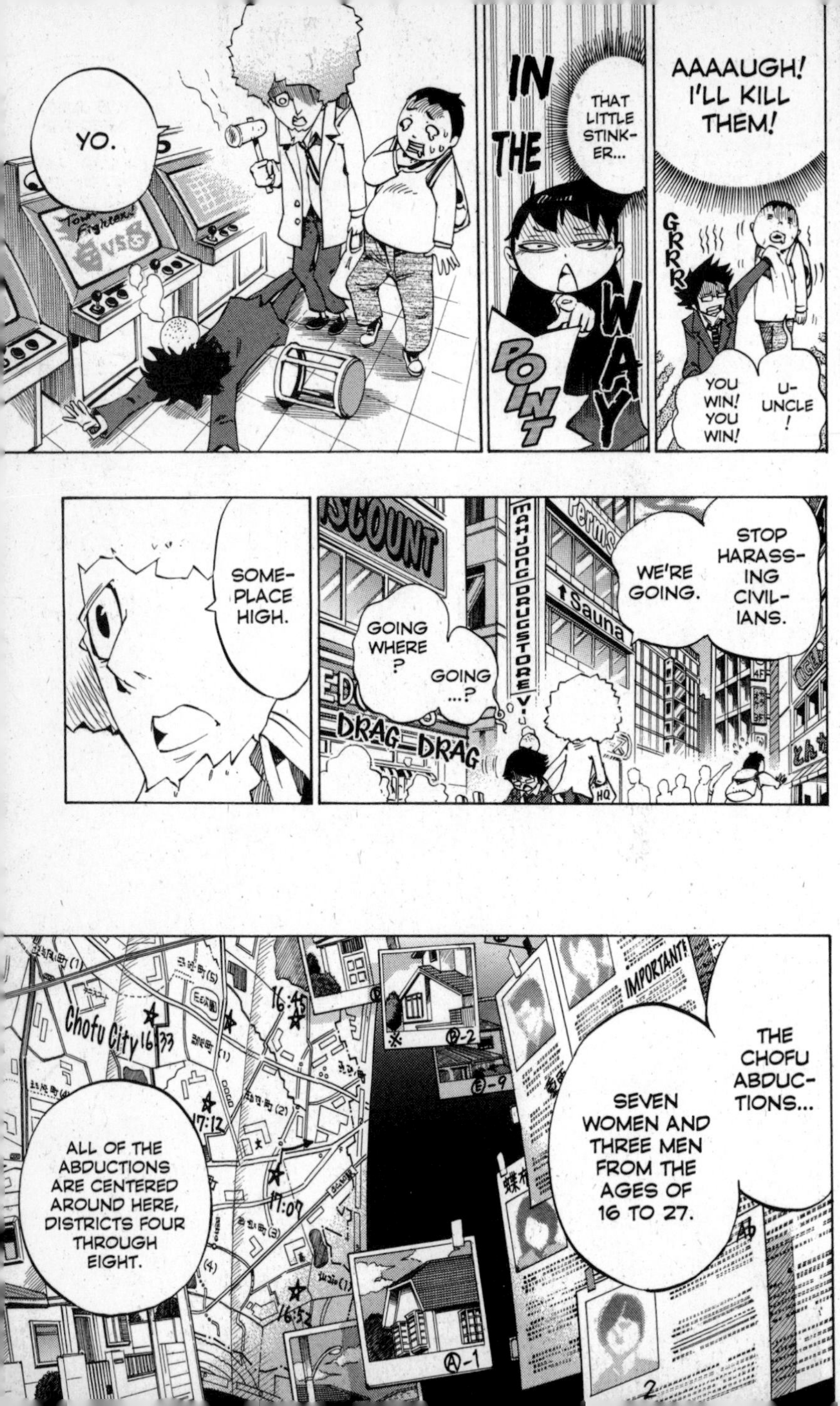
AAAAUGH! I'LL KILL THEM!
GRRR
U-UNCLE!
YOU WIN! YOU WIN!
IN THE WAY
THAT LITTLE STINK-ER...
POINT
YO.
STOP HARASS-ING CIVIL-IANS.
WE'RE GOING.
Perms
Sauna
MAHJONG DRUGSTORE V
GOING ...?
GOING WHERE ?
DRAG DRAG
SOME-PLACE HIGH.
THE CHOFU ABDUC-TIONS...
SEVEN WOMEN AND THREE MEN FROM THE AGES OF 16 TO 27.
IMPORTANT!
Chofu City
16:45
16:33
17:12
17:07
16:52
ALL OF THE ABDUCTIONS ARE CENTERED AROUND HERE, DISTRICTS FOUR THROUGH EIGHT.

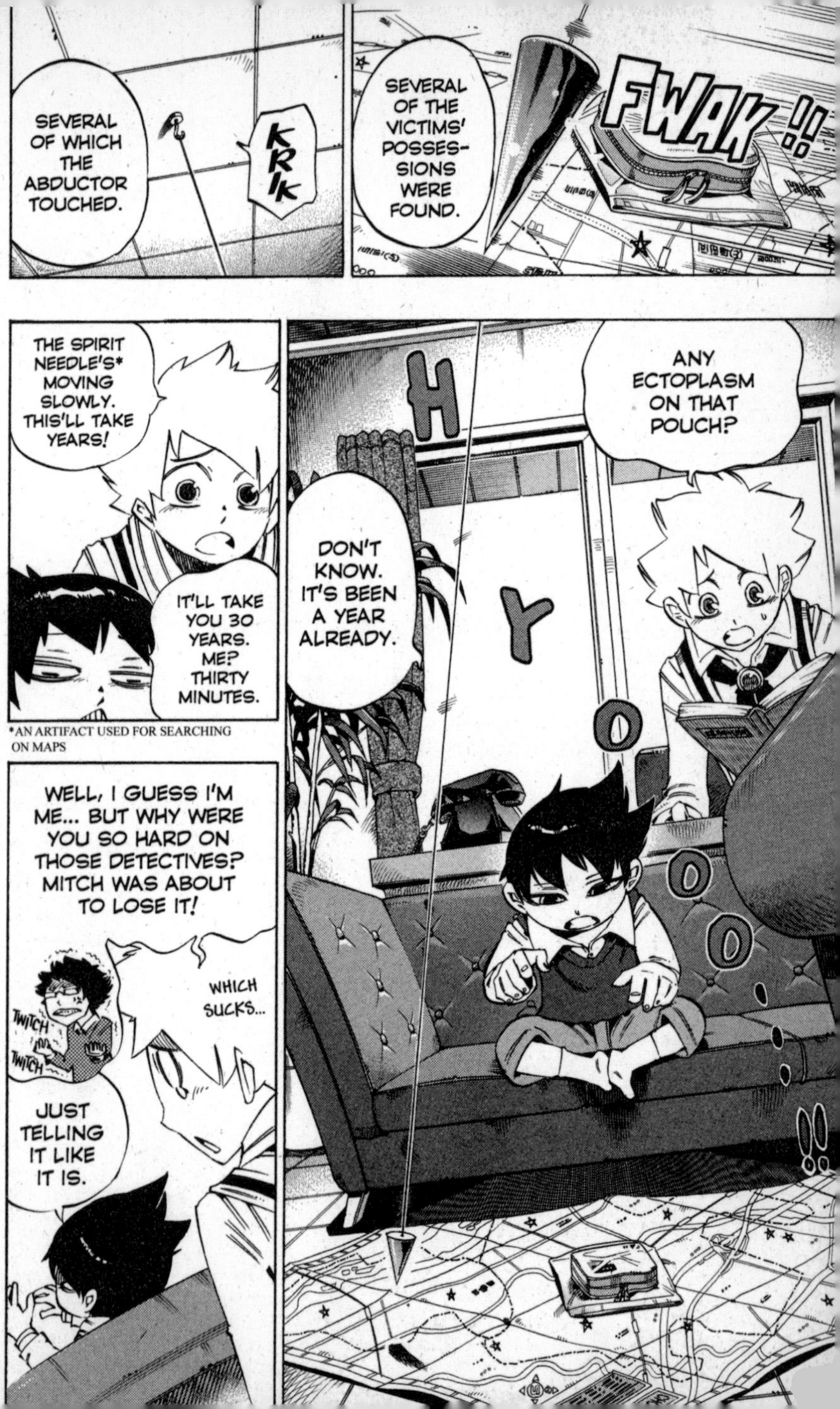
SEVERAL OF THE VICTIMS' POSSESSIONS WERE FOUND.
FWAK!!
SEVERAL OF WHICH THE ABDUCTOR TOUCHED.
KRIK
ANY ECTOPLASM ON THAT POUCH?
DON'T KNOW. IT'S BEEN A YEAR ALREADY.
HYOOOO...!!
THE SPIRIT NEEDLE'S* MOVING SLOWLY. THIS'LL TAKE YEARS!
IT'LL TAKE YOU 30 YEARS. ME? THIRTY MINUTES.
WELL, I GUESS I'M ME... BUT WHY WERE YOU SO HARD ON THOSE DETECTIVES? MITCH WAS ABOUT TO LOSE IT!
TWITCH
TWITCH
WHICH SUCKS...
JUST TELLING IT LIKE IT IS.
*AN ARTIFACT USED FOR SEARCHING ON MAPS

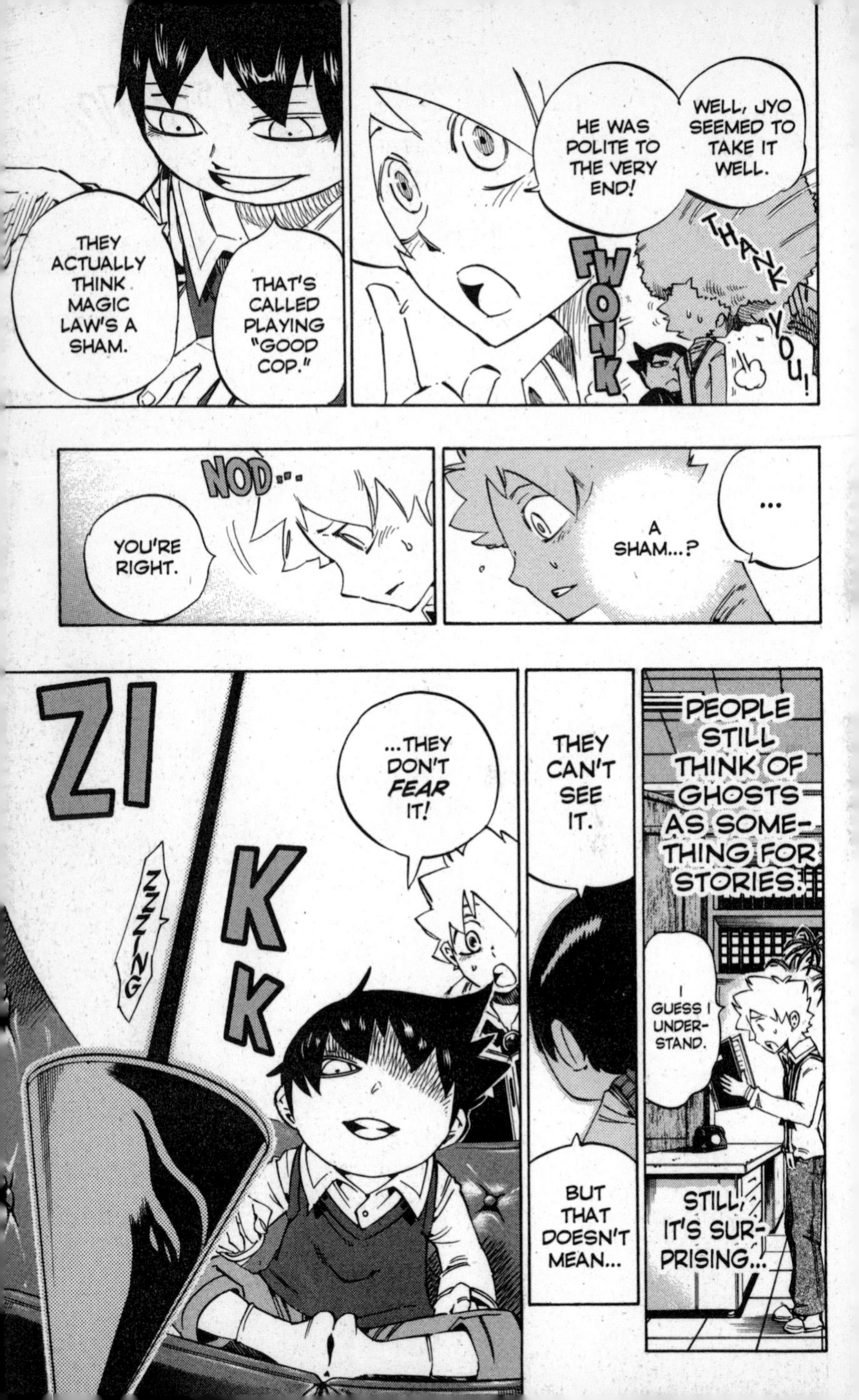
WELL, JYO SEEMED TO TAKE IT WELL.
HE WAS POLITE TO THE VERY END!
THANK YOU!
FWONK
THAT'S CALLED PLAYING "GOOD COP."
THEY ACTUALLY THINK MAGIC LAW'S A SHAM.
...
A SHAM...?
NOD...
YOU'RE RIGHT.
PEOPLE STILL THINK OF GHOSTS AS SOME-THING FOR STORIES.
I GUESS I UNDER-STAND.
STILL, IT'S SUR-PRISING...
THEY CAN'T SEE IT.
BUT THAT DOESN'T MEAN...
...THEY DON'T *FEAR* IT!
ZZZING
ZIKKK

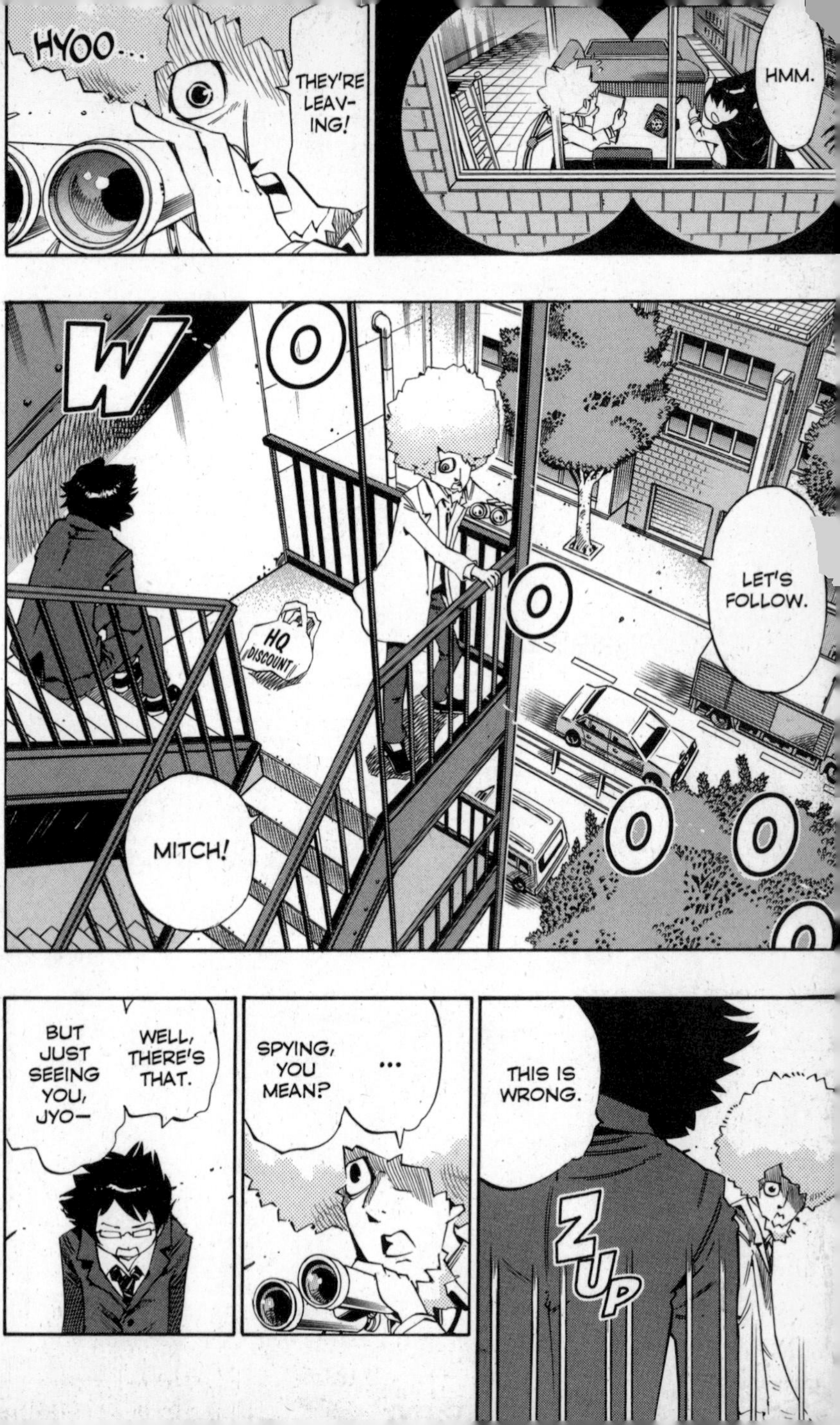
HMM.
HYOO...
THEY'RE LEAV-ING!
LET'S FOLLOW.
WOOOOOO
MITCH!
HQ DISCOUNT
THIS IS WRONG.
ZUP
...
SPYING, YOU MEAN?
WELL, THERE'S THAT.
BUT JUST SEEING YOU, JYO—

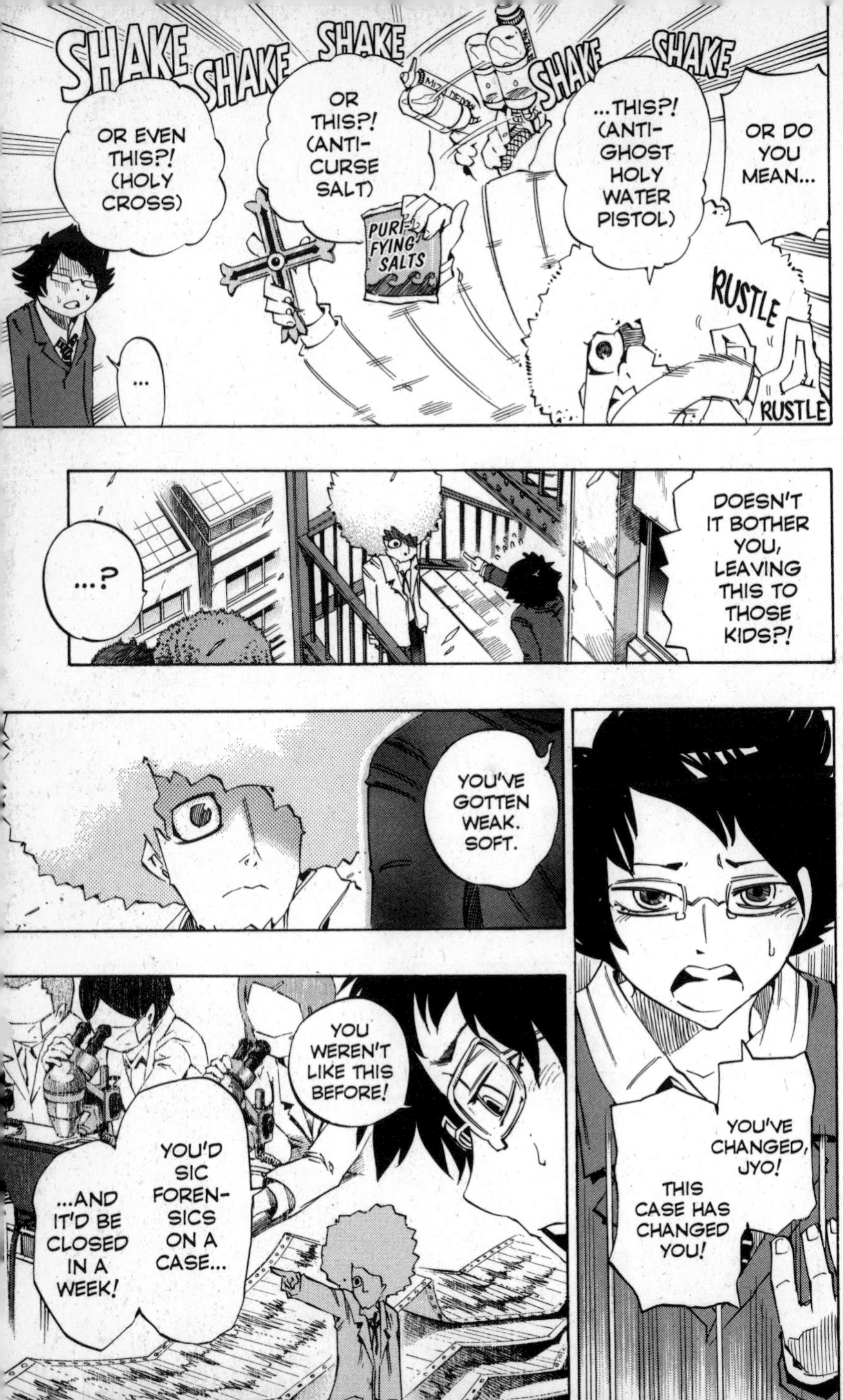
SHAKE
SHAKE
SHAKE
SHAKE
OR DO YOU MEAN...
...THIS?! (ANTI-GHOST HOLY WATER PISTOL)
OR THIS?! (ANTI-CURSE SALT)
PURI-FYING SALTS
OR EVEN THIS?! (HOLY CROSS)
RUSTLE
RUSTLE
...
DOESN'T IT BOTHER YOU, LEAVING THIS TO THOSE KIDS?!
...?
YOU'VE CHANGED, JYO!
THIS CASE HAS CHANGED YOU!
YOU'VE GOTTEN WEAK. SOFT.
YOU WEREN'T LIKE THIS BEFORE!
YOU'D SIC FORENSICS ON A CASE...
...AND IT'D BE CLOSED IN A WEEK!

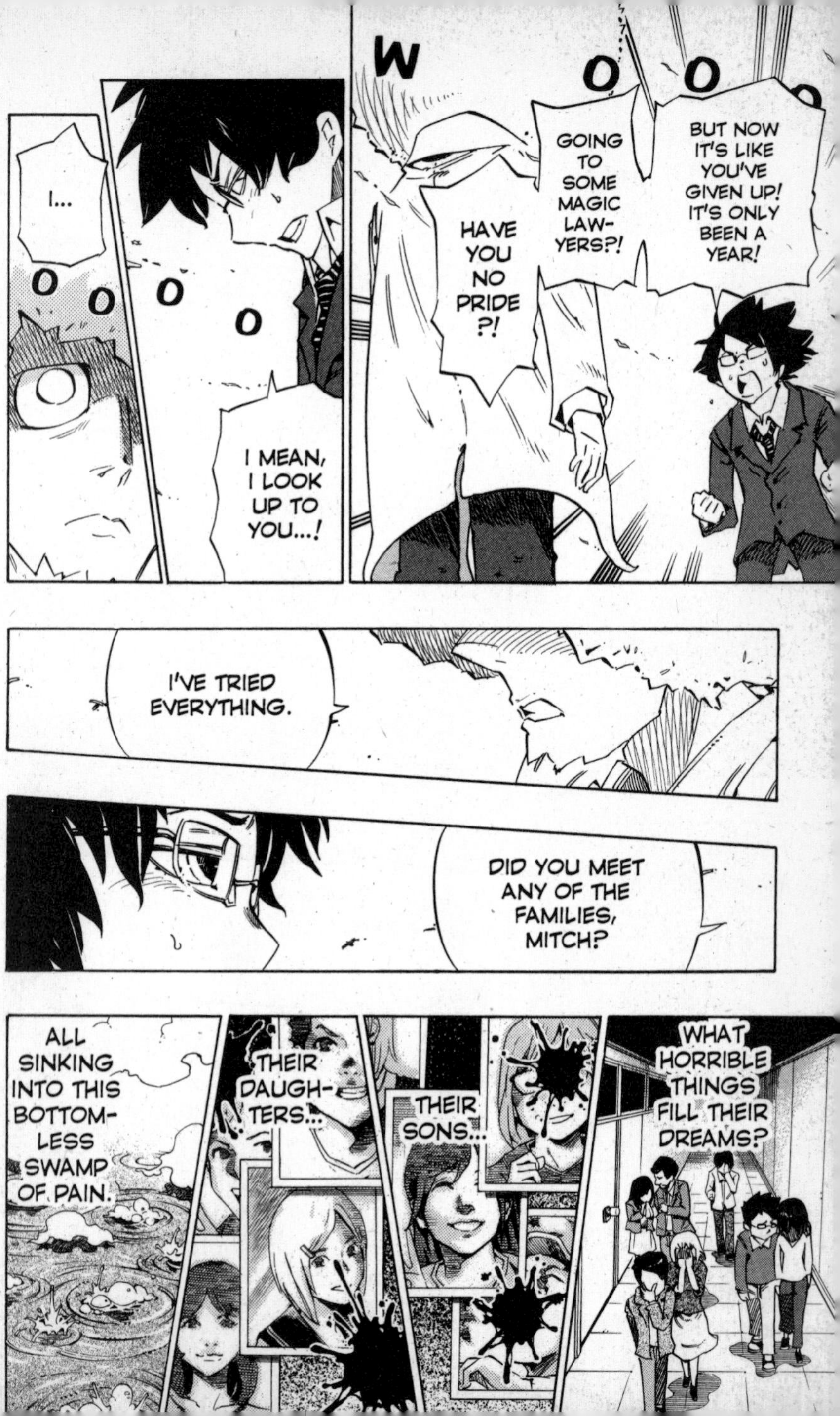
WOOOOOOOOO
BUT NOW IT'S LIKE YOU'VE GIVEN UP! IT'S ONLY BEEN A YEAR!
GOING TO SOME MAGIC LAW-YERS?!
HAVE YOU NO PRIDE?!
I MEAN, I LOOK UP TO YOU...!
I...
I'VE TRIED EVERYTHING.
DID YOU MEET ANY OF THE FAMILIES, MITCH?
WHAT HORRIBLE THINGS FILL THEIR DREAMS?
THEIR SONS...
THEIR DAUGH-TERS...
ALL SINKING INTO THIS BOTTOM-LESS SWAMP OF PAIN.

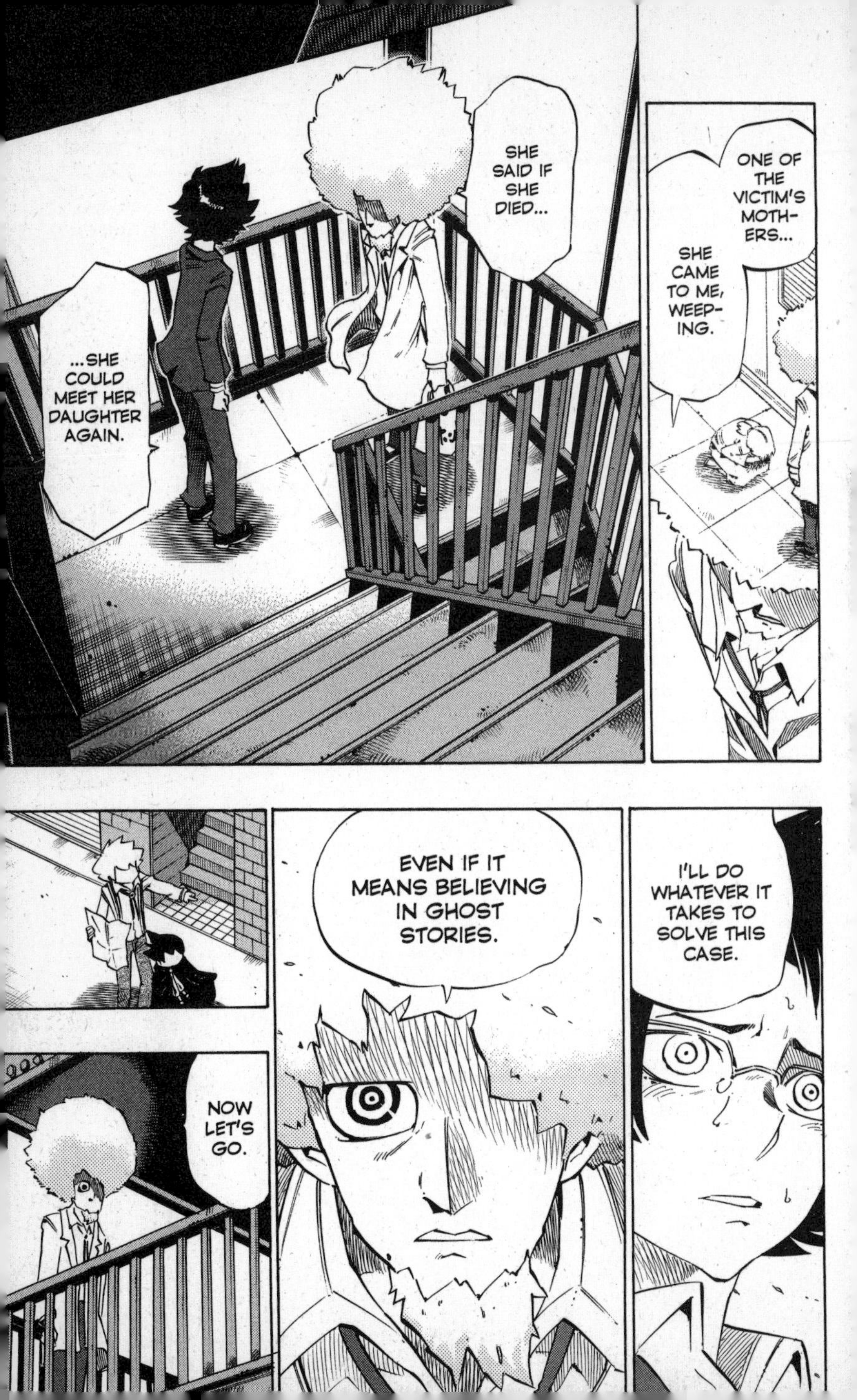
ONE OF THE VICTIM'S MOTHERS...
SHE CAME TO ME, WEEPING.
SHE SAID IF SHE DIED...
...SHE COULD MEET HER DAUGHTER AGAIN.
I'LL DO WHATEVER IT TAKES TO SOLVE THIS CASE.
EVEN IF IT MEANS BELIEVING IN GHOST STORIES.
NOW LET'S GO.

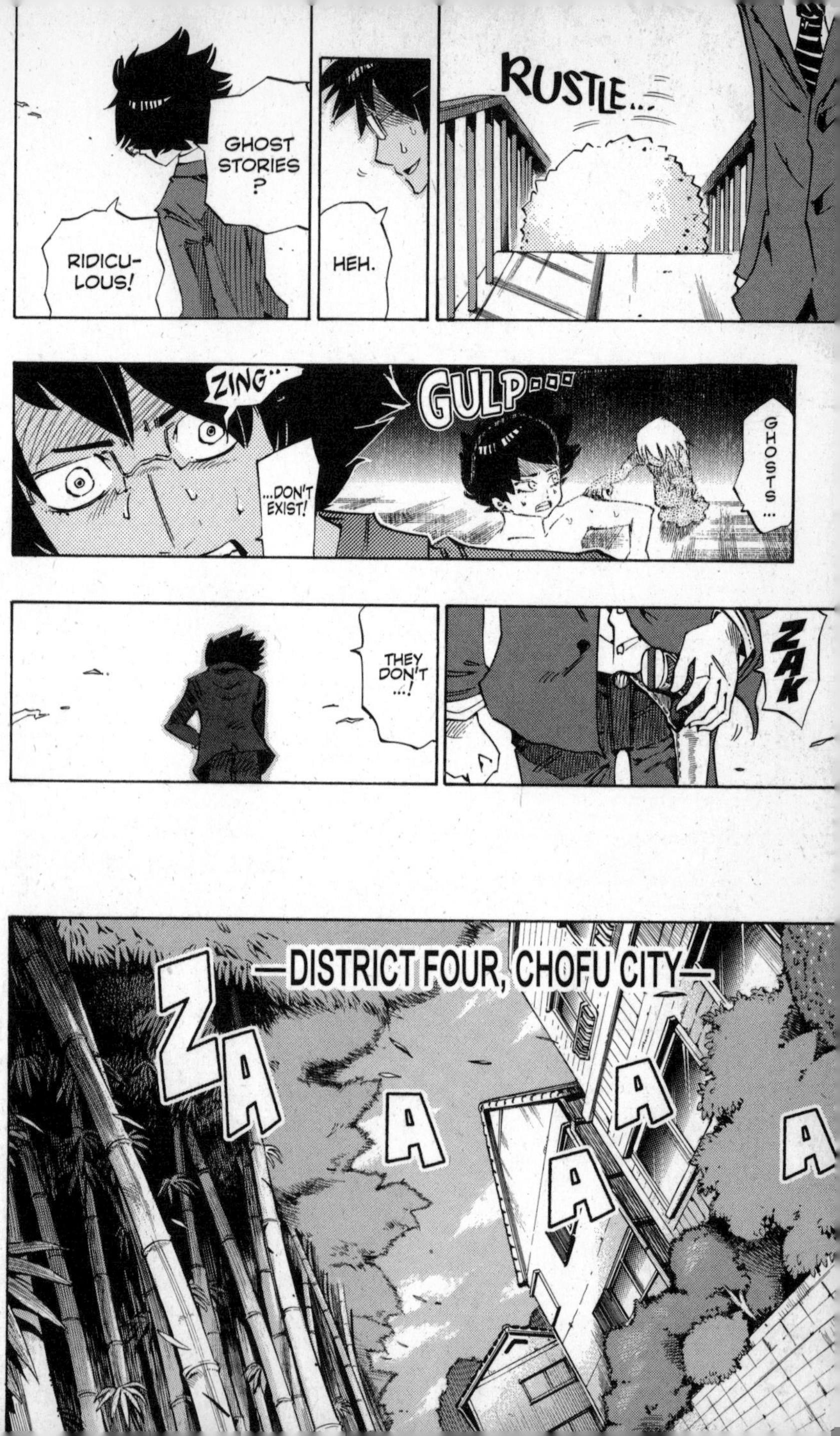
RUSTLE...
HEH.
GHOST STORIES?
RIDICULOUS!
GHOSTS...
GULP...
ZING...
...DON'T EXIST!
ZAK
THEY DON'T...!
—DISTRICT FOUR, CHOFU CITY—
ZAAAAAA

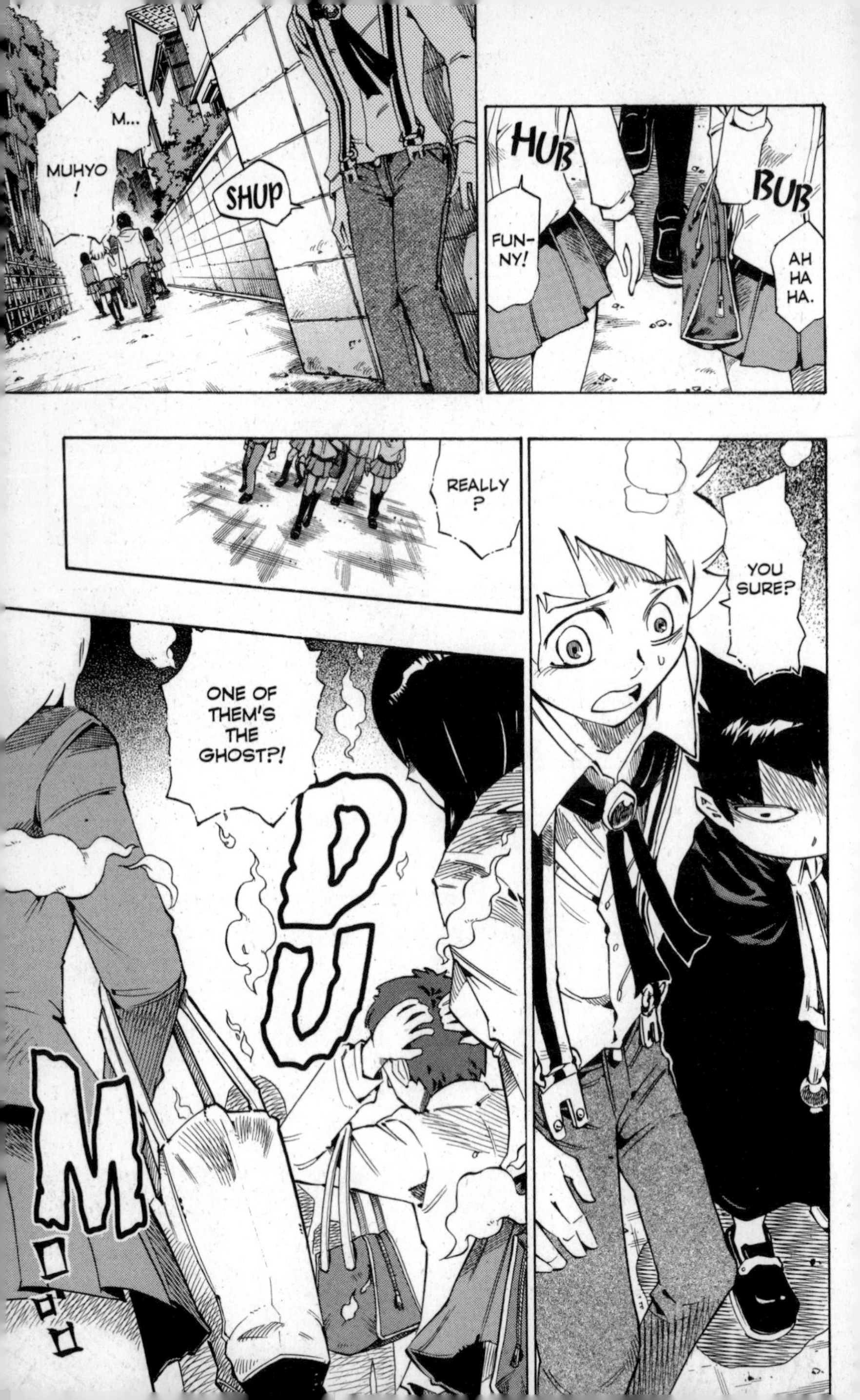

BUB
AH HA HA.
HUB
FUN-NY!
SHUP
M...
MUHYO!
YOU SURE?
REALLY?
ONE OF THEM'S THE GHOST?!
DUM

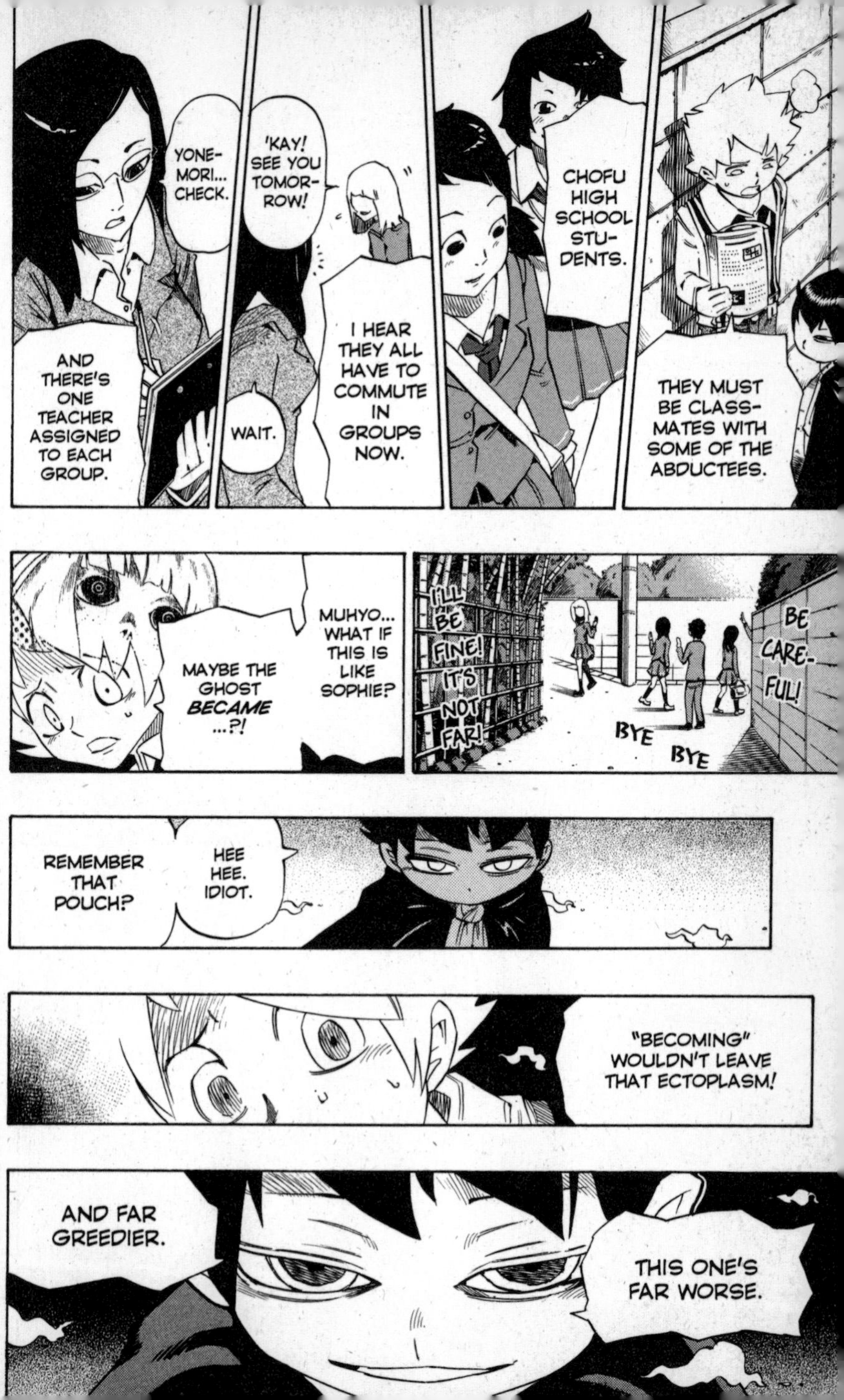
CHOFU HIGH SCHOOL STUDENTS.
THEY MUST BE CLASSMATES WITH SOME OF THE ABDUCTEES.
I HEAR THEY ALL HAVE TO COMMUTE IN GROUPS NOW.
'KAY! SEE YOU TOMORROW!
WAIT.
YONEMORI... CHECK.
AND THERE'S ONE TEACHER ASSIGNED TO EACH GROUP.
BE CAREFUL!
I'LL BE FINE! IT'S NOT FAR!
BYE BYE
MUHYO... WHAT IF THIS IS LIKE SOPHIE?
MAYBE THE GHOST *BECAME* ...?!
HEE HEE. IDIOT.
REMEMBER THAT POUCH?
"BECOMING" WOULDN'T LEAVE THAT ECTOPLASM!
THIS ONE'S FAR WORSE.
AND FAR GREEDIER.

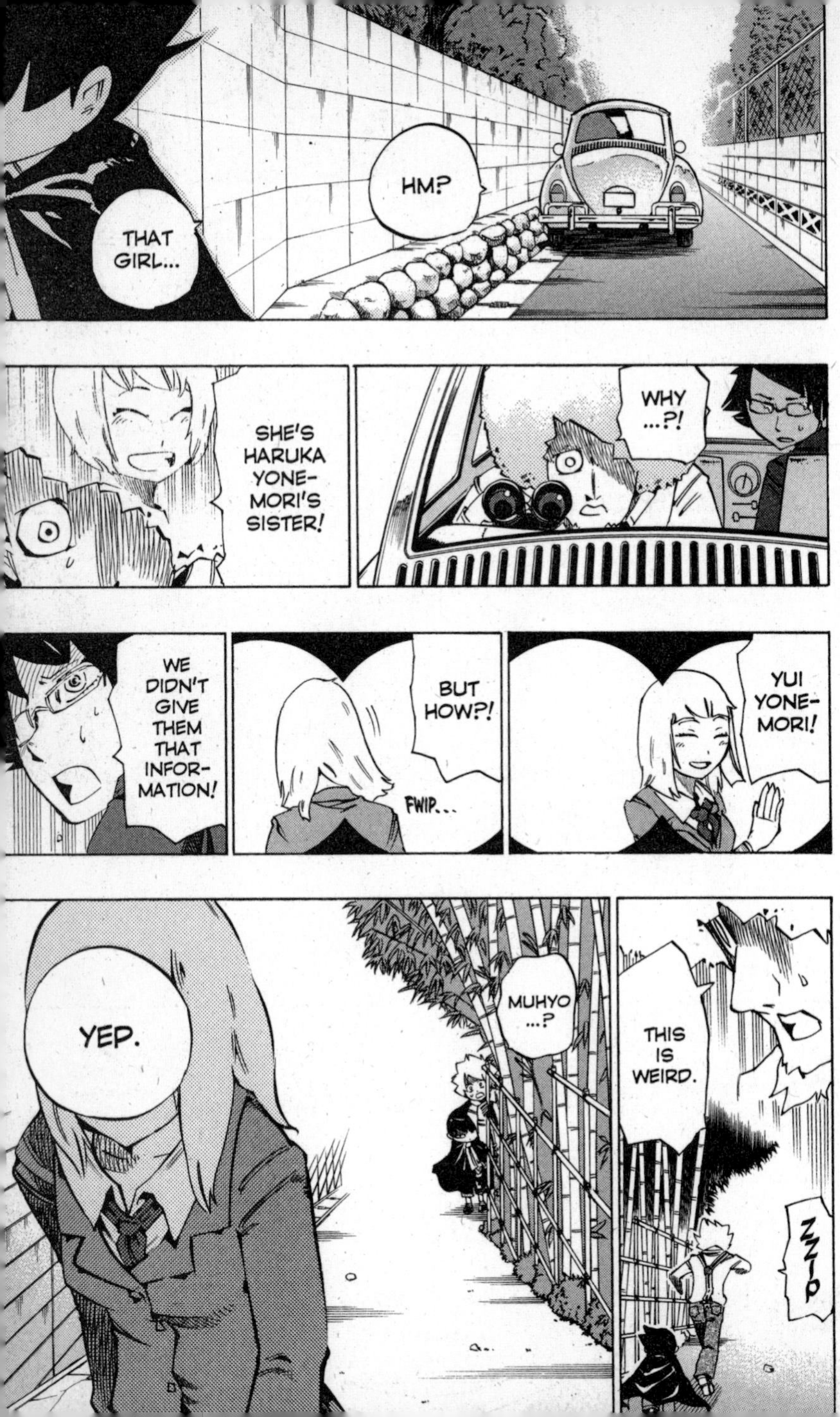
HM?
THAT GIRL...
WHY ...?!
SHE'S HARUKA YONE-MORI'S SISTER!
YUI YONE-MORI!
BUT HOW?!
FWIP...
WE DIDN'T GIVE THEM THAT INFOR-MATION!
THIS IS WEIRD.
ZZIP
MUHYO ...?
YEP.

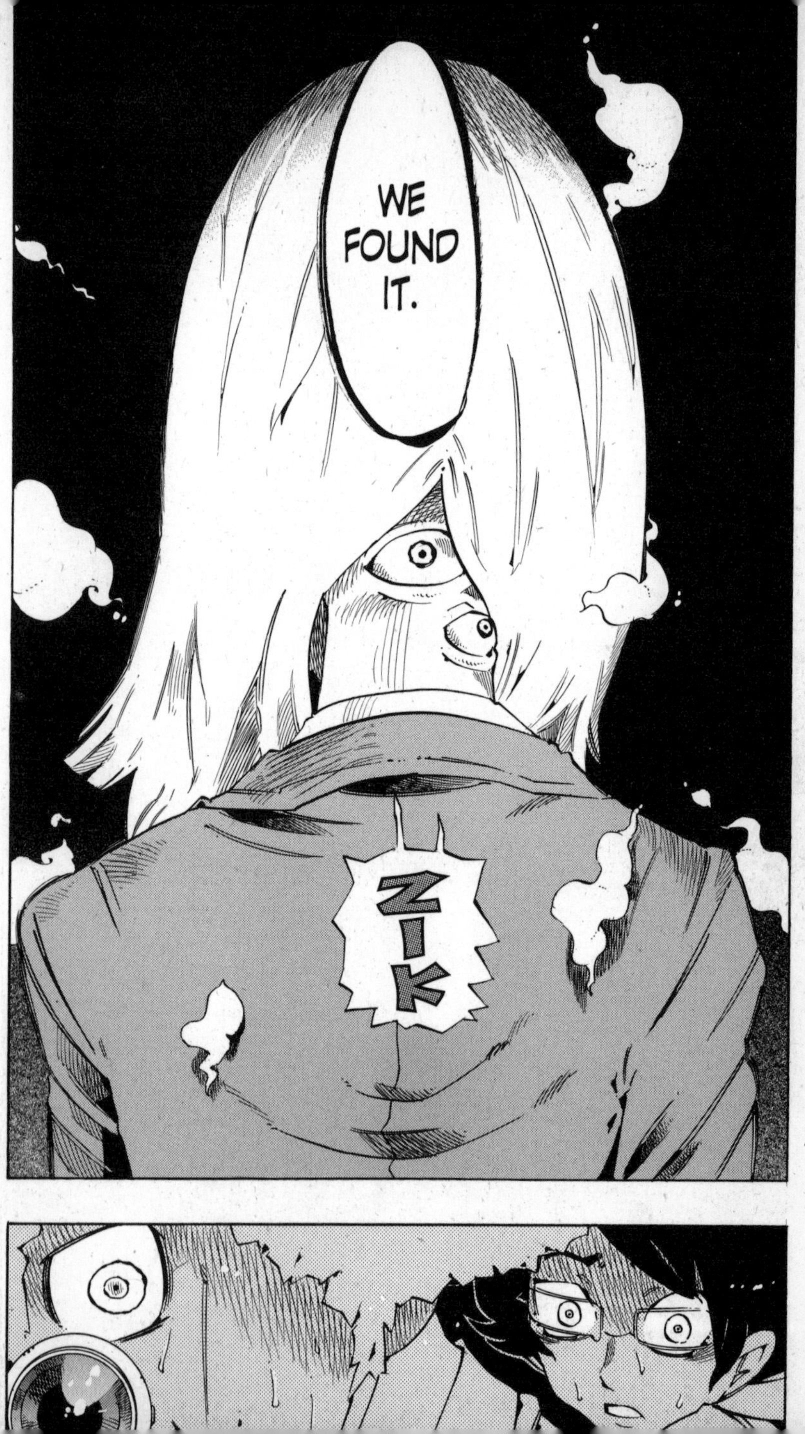
WE FOUND IT.
ZIK

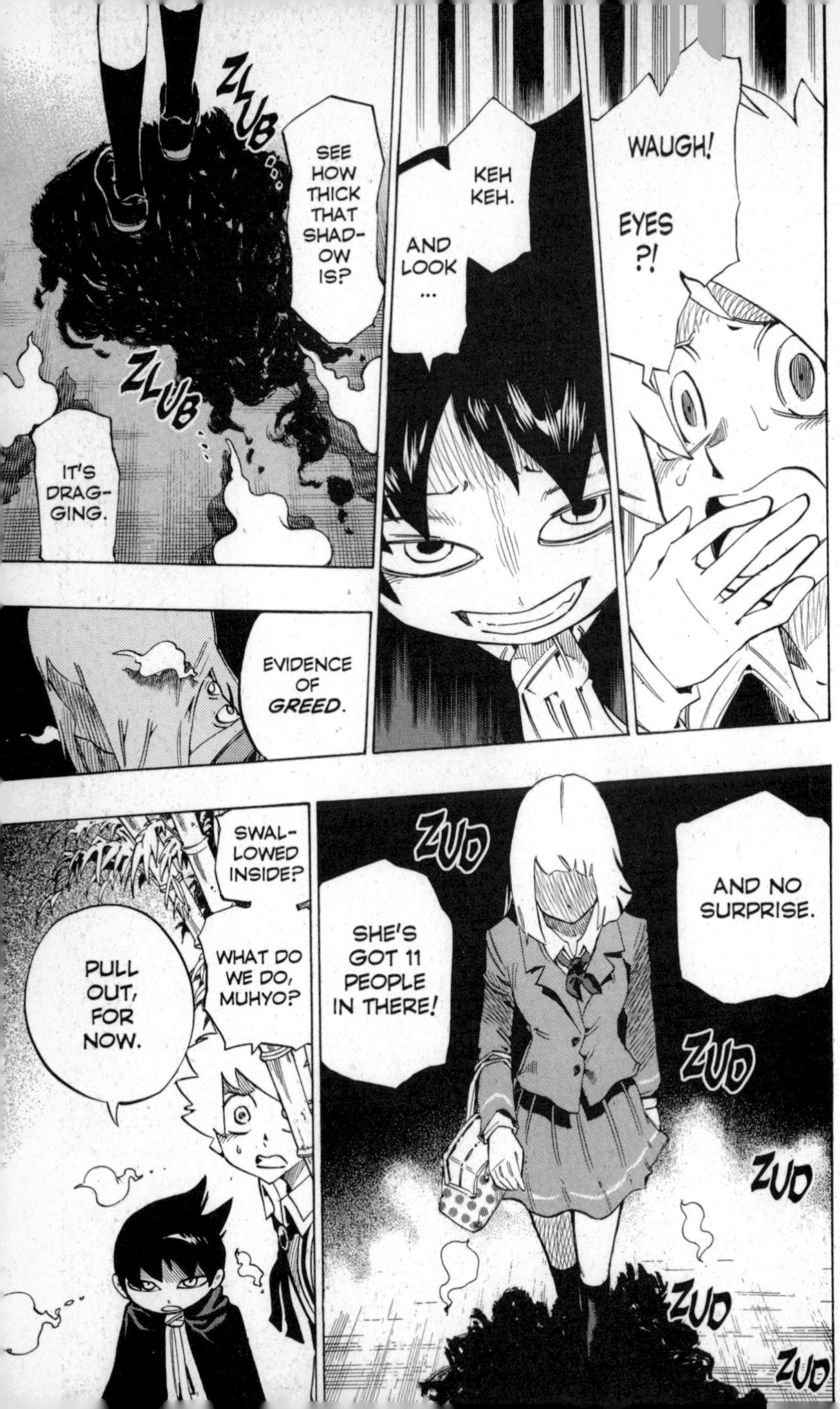
WAUGH!
EYES ?!
KEH KEH.
AND LOOK ...
ZLUB...
SEE HOW THICK THAT SHAD-OW IS?
ZLUB...
IT'S DRAG-GING.
EVIDENCE OF *GREED*.
ZUD
AND NO SURPRISE.
SHE'S GOT 11 PEOPLE IN THERE!
ZUD
ZUD
ZUD
ZUD
SWAL-LOWED INSIDE?
WHAT DO WE DO, MUHYO?
PULL OUT, FOR NOW.

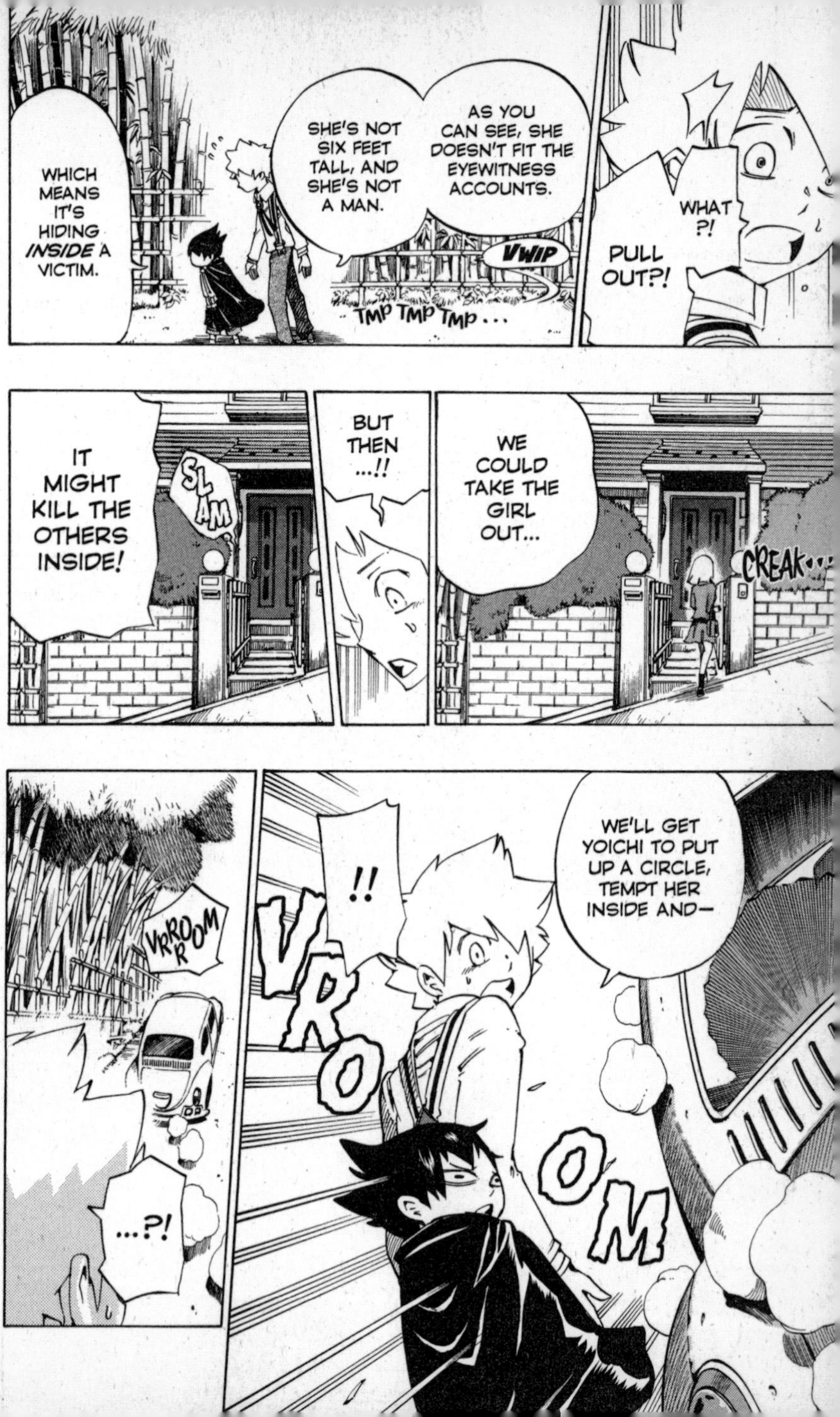
WHAT ?!
PULL OUT?!
AS YOU CAN SEE, SHE DOESN'T FIT THE EYEWITNESS ACCOUNTS.
SHE'S NOT SIX FEET TALL, AND SHE'S NOT A MAN.
VWIP
TMP TMP TMP...
WHICH MEANS IT'S HIDING *INSIDE* A VICTIM.
CREAK...
WE COULD TAKE THE GIRL OUT...
BUT THEN ...!!
SLAM
IT MIGHT KILL THE OTHERS INSIDE!
WE'LL GET YOICHI TO PUT UP A CIRCLE, TEMPT HER INSIDE AND—
!!
VROOOM
VRROOM
...?!

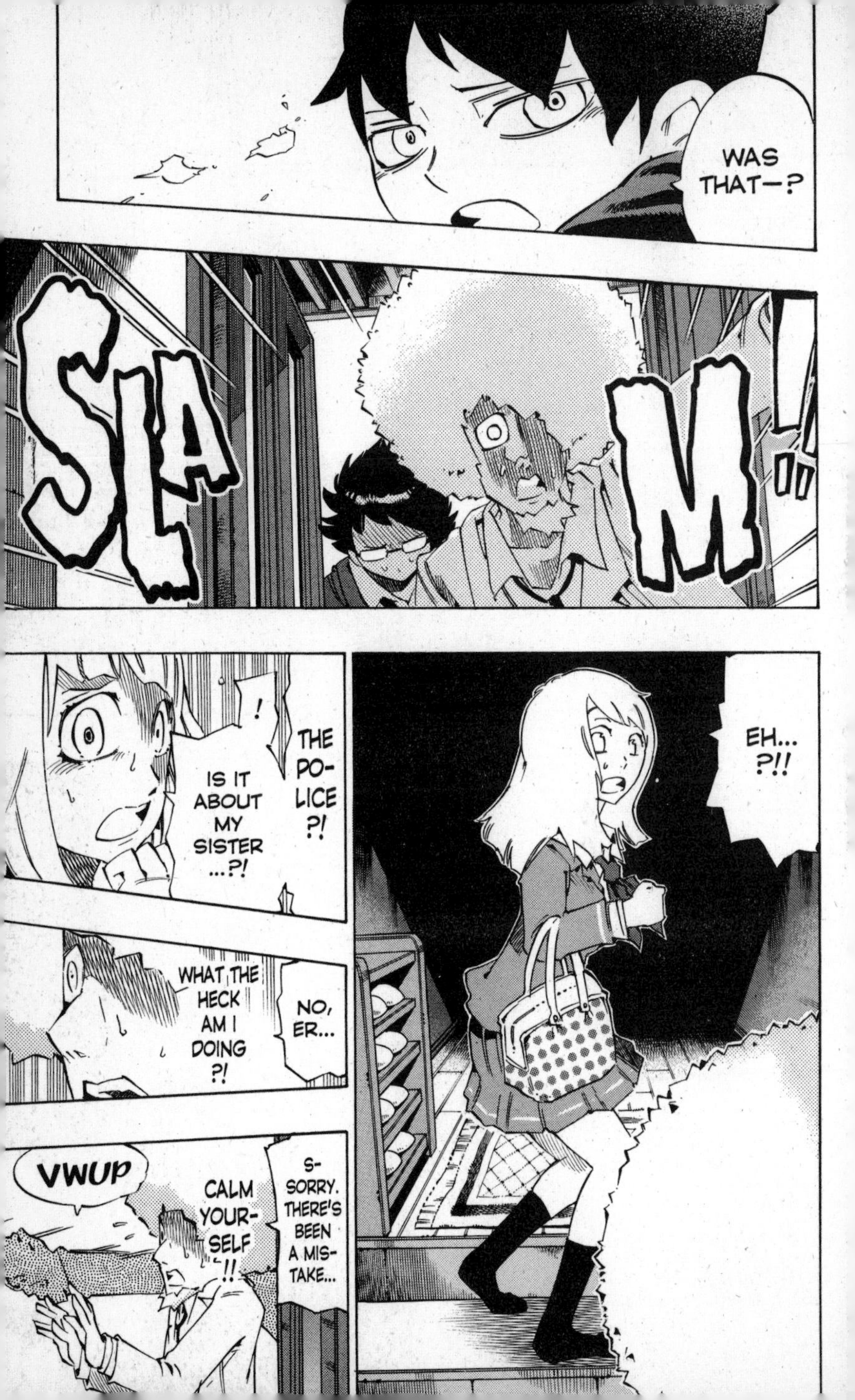
WAS THAT—?
SLAM!!
EH...?!!
THE PO-LICE?!
IS IT ABOUT MY SISTER...?!
NO, ER...
WHAT THE HECK AM I DOING?!
S-SORRY. THERE'S BEEN A MIS-TAKE...
CALM YOUR-SELF!!
VWUP

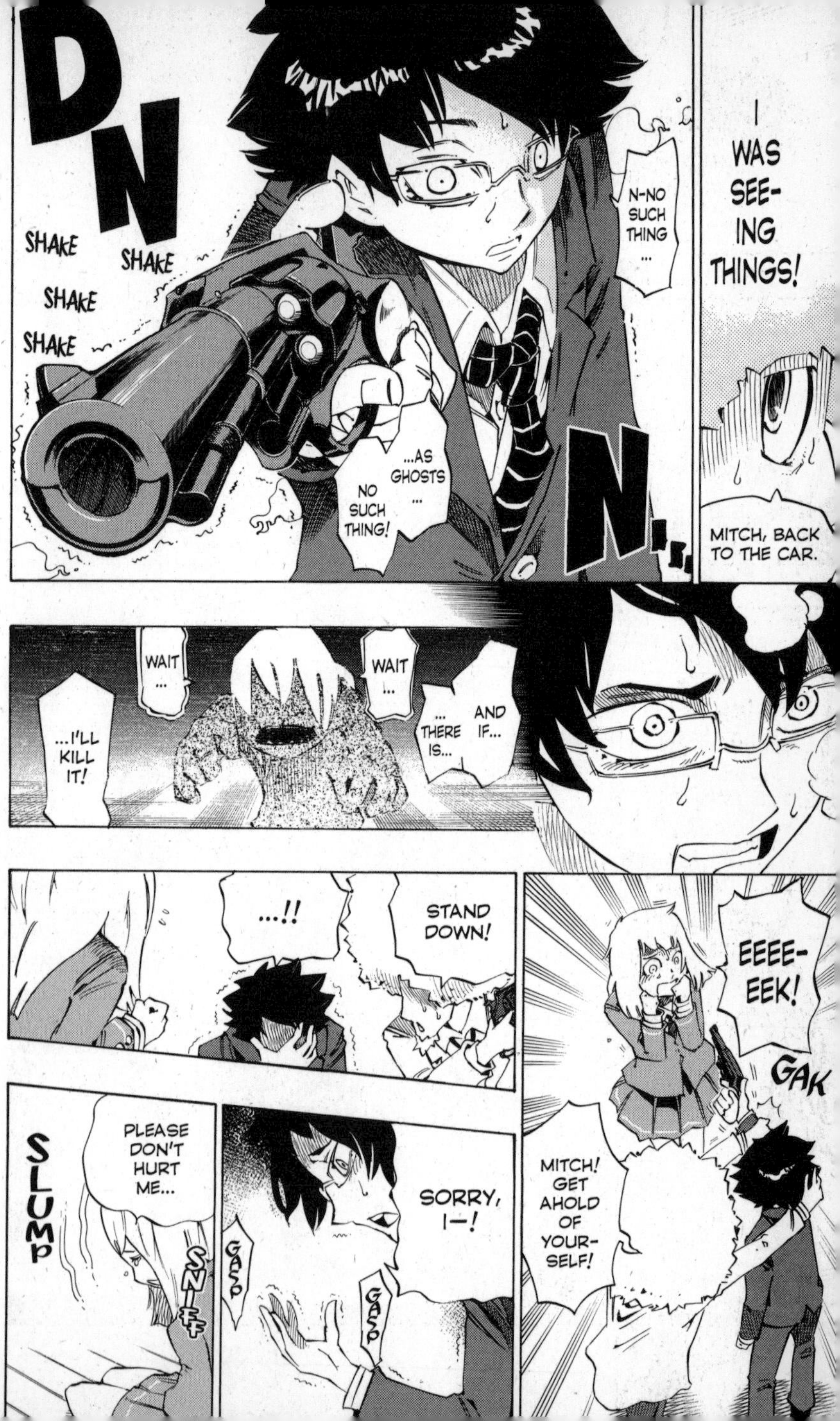
I WAS SEE-ING THINGS!
MITCH, BACK TO THE CAR.
N-NO SUCH THING ...
DN
SHAKE
SHAKE
SHAKE
SHAKE
...AS GHOSTS ...
NO SUCH THING!
N...
AND IF...
... THERE IS...
WAIT ...
WAIT ...
...I'LL KILL IT!
EEEE-EEK!
GAK
MITCH! GET AHOLD OF YOURSELF!
STAND DOWN!
...!!
SORRY, I—!
GASP
GASP
PLEASE DON'T HURT ME...
SNIFF
SLUMP

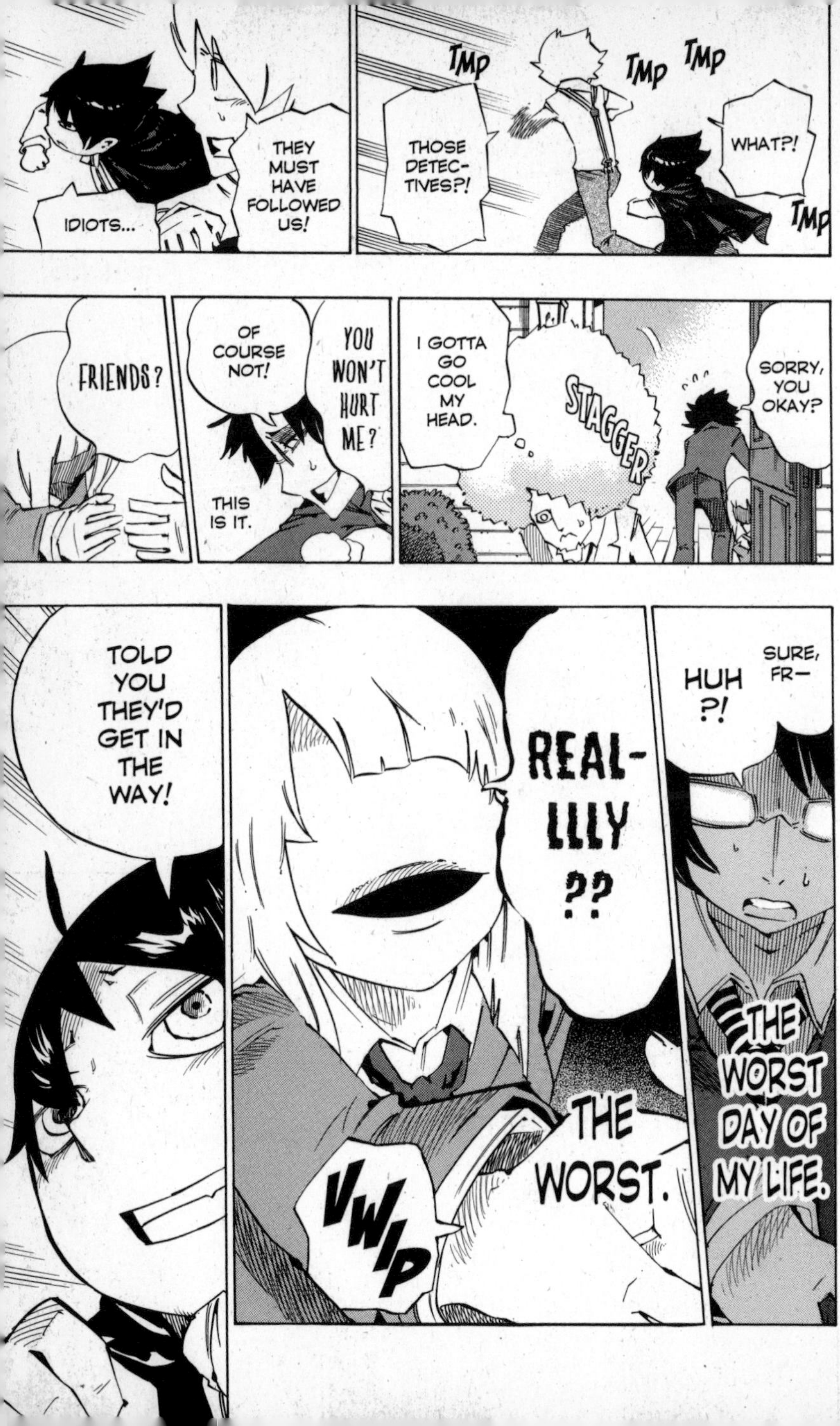
TMP
TMP
TMP
WHAT?!
THOSE DETEC-TIVES?!
TMP
THEY MUST HAVE FOLLOWED US!
IDIOTS...
SORRY, YOU OKAY?
STAGGER
I GOTTA GO COOL MY HEAD.
YOU WON'T HURT ME?
OF COURSE NOT!
THIS IS IT.
FRIENDS?
SURE, FR—
HUH?!
THE WORST DAY OF MY LIFE.
REAL-LLLY??
THE WORST.
VWIP
TOLD YOU THEY'D GET IN THE WAY!

MITSURU MIDORIKAWA

BIRTHDAY:
MARCH 3

HEIGHT:
175 CM

LIKES:
ARCADE GAMES
MANGA
COFFEE

TALENTS:
GOOD AT
FIGHTING GAMES
MARKSMANSHIP
REMEMBERING
MANGA TRIVIA
QUICK CUFFING

DISLIKES:
PAPERWORK
DIFFICULT
BOOKS/MOVIES
MILK
GHOSTS

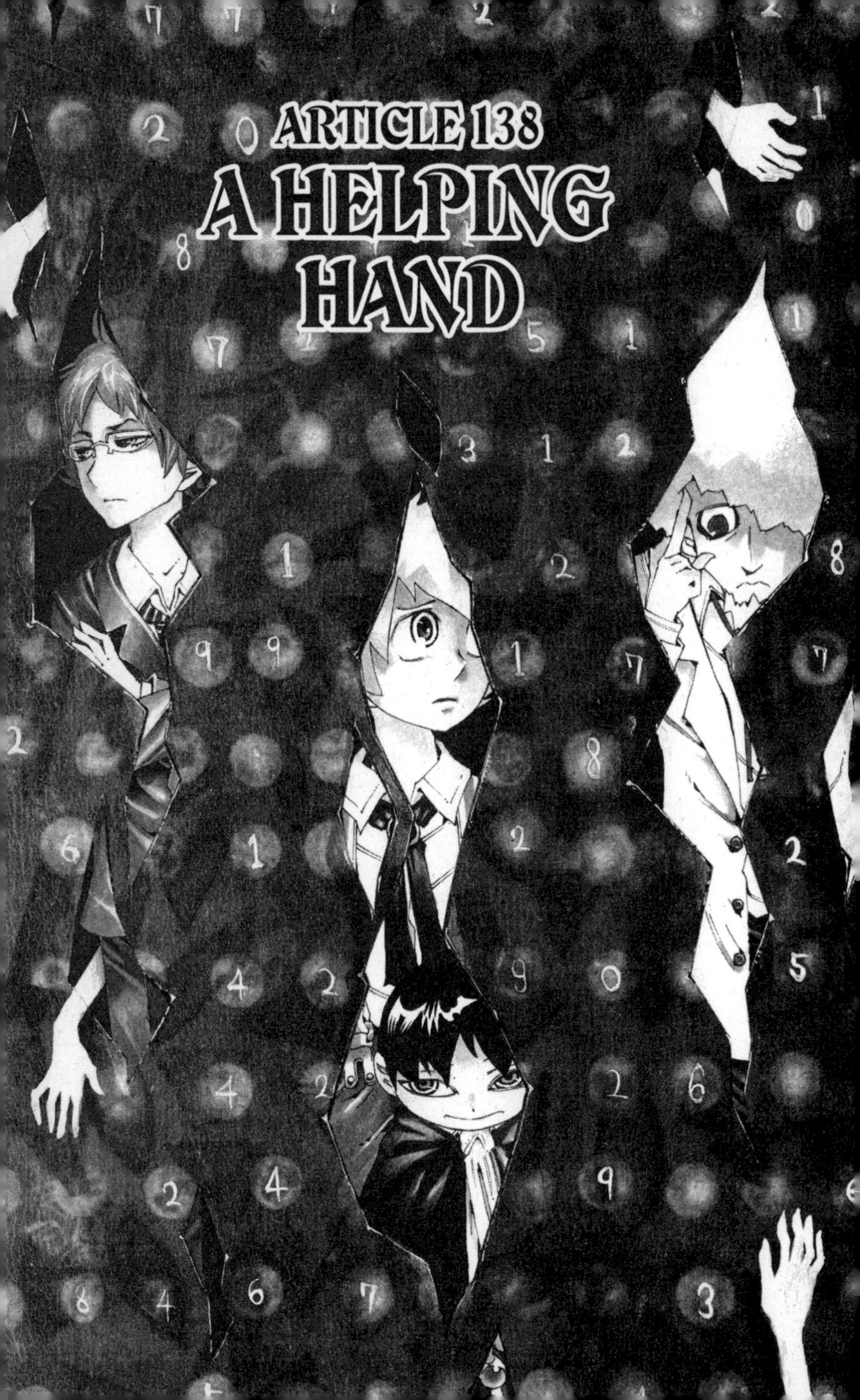
ARTICLE 138
A HELPING HAND

JYO HARIMA

BIRTHDAY:
SEPTEMBER 12

HEIGHT:
173 CM
(WITHOUT AFRO)

LIKES:
MECHANICAL
PARTS
SECRETS
MYSTERY
NOVELS

TALENTS:
BEING A MOD
SPEED READING
INFORMATION
ANALYSIS
JIGSAW
PUZZLES

DISLIKES:
PYSCHO-
ANALYSIS
TEARJERKERS
COMPUTERS

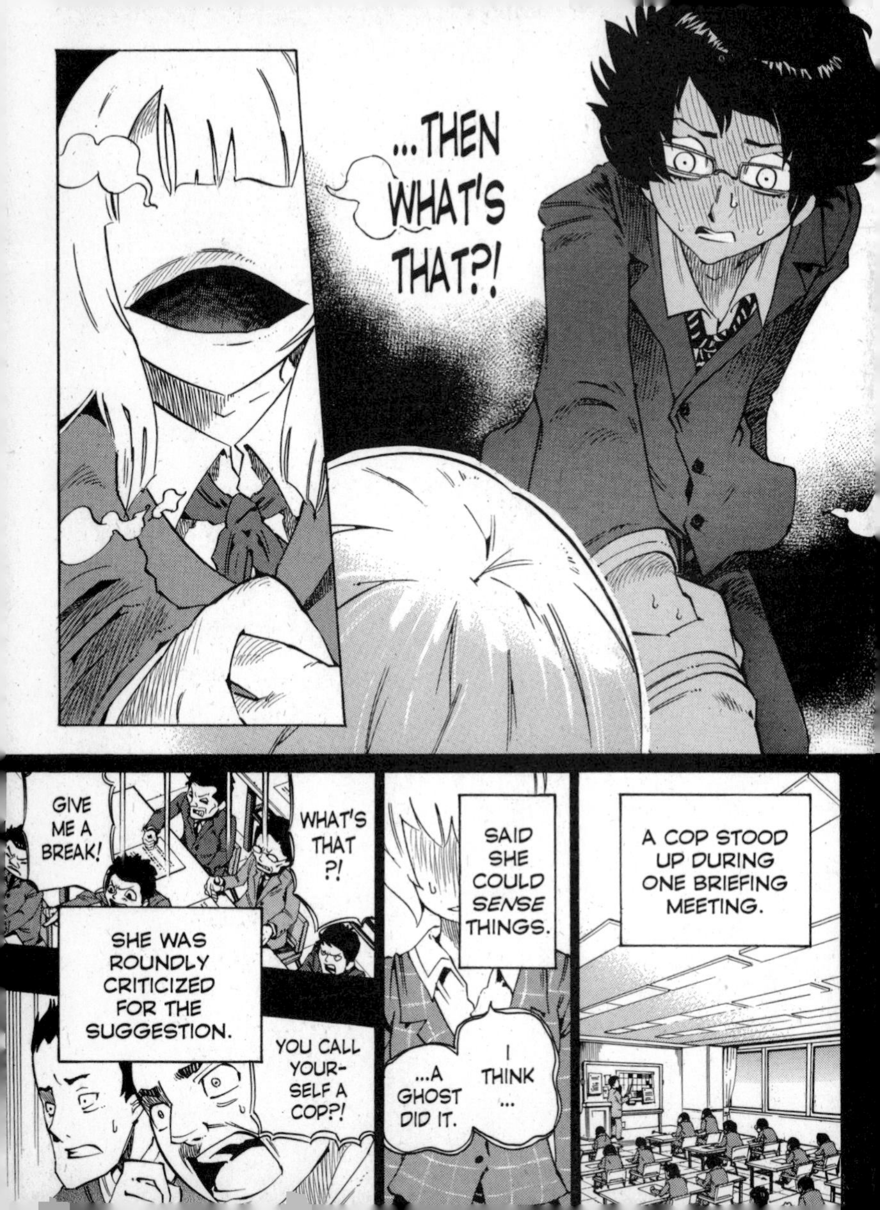
...THEN WHAT'S THAT?!
A COP STOOD UP DURING ONE BRIEFING MEETING.
SAID SHE COULD *SENSE* THINGS.
I THINK ...
...A GHOST DID IT.
WHAT'S THAT ?!
GIVE ME A BREAK!
SHE WAS ROUNDLY CRITICIZED FOR THE SUGGESTION.
YOU CALL YOUR-SELF A COP?!

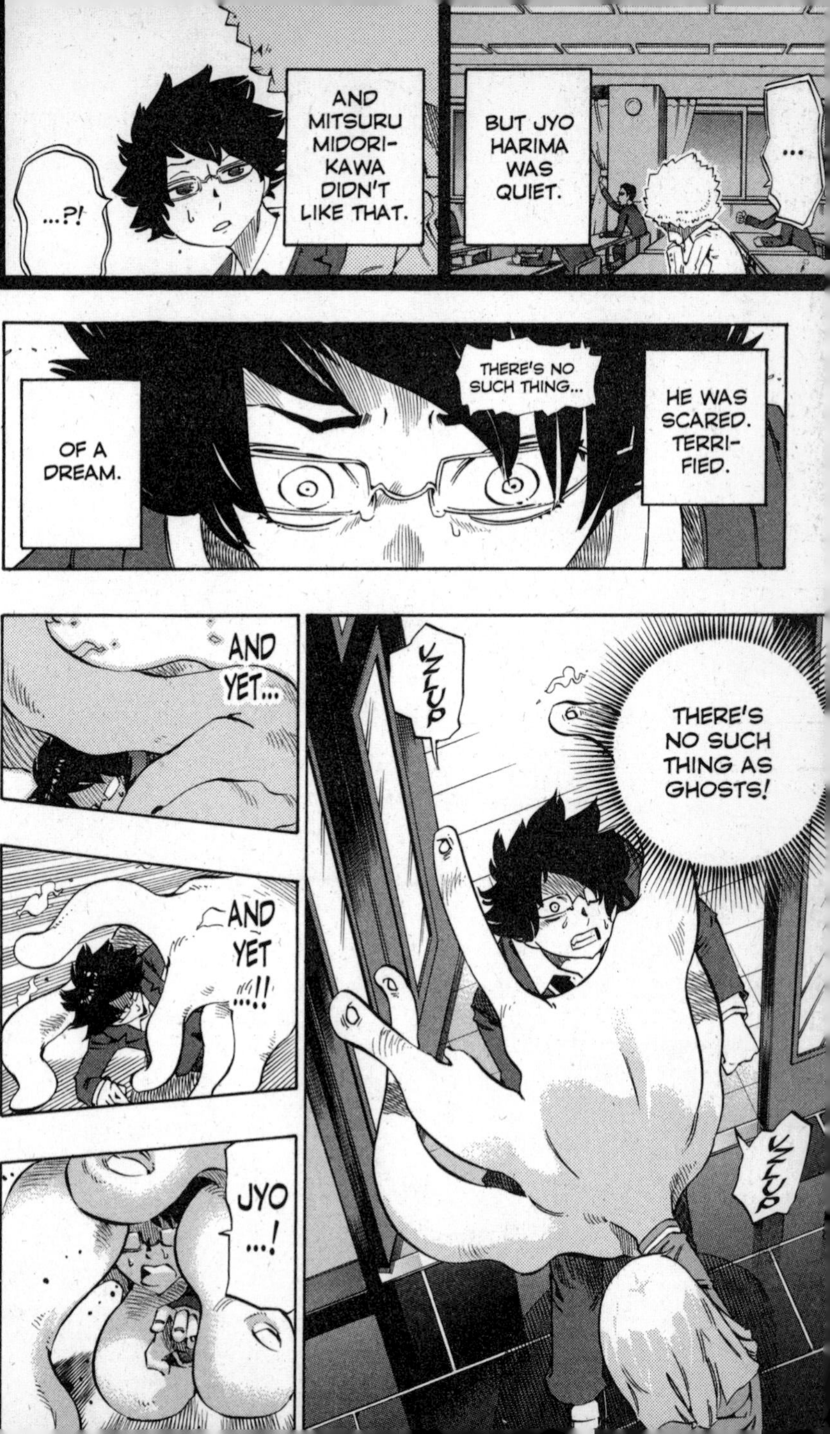
BUT JYO HARIMA WAS QUIET.
...
AND MITSURU MIDORI-KAWA DIDN'T LIKE THAT.
...?!
HE WAS SCARED. TERRI-FIED.
THERE'S NO SUCH THING...
OF A DREAM.
THERE'S NO SUCH THING AS GHOSTS!
AND YET...
AND YET...!!
JYO...!

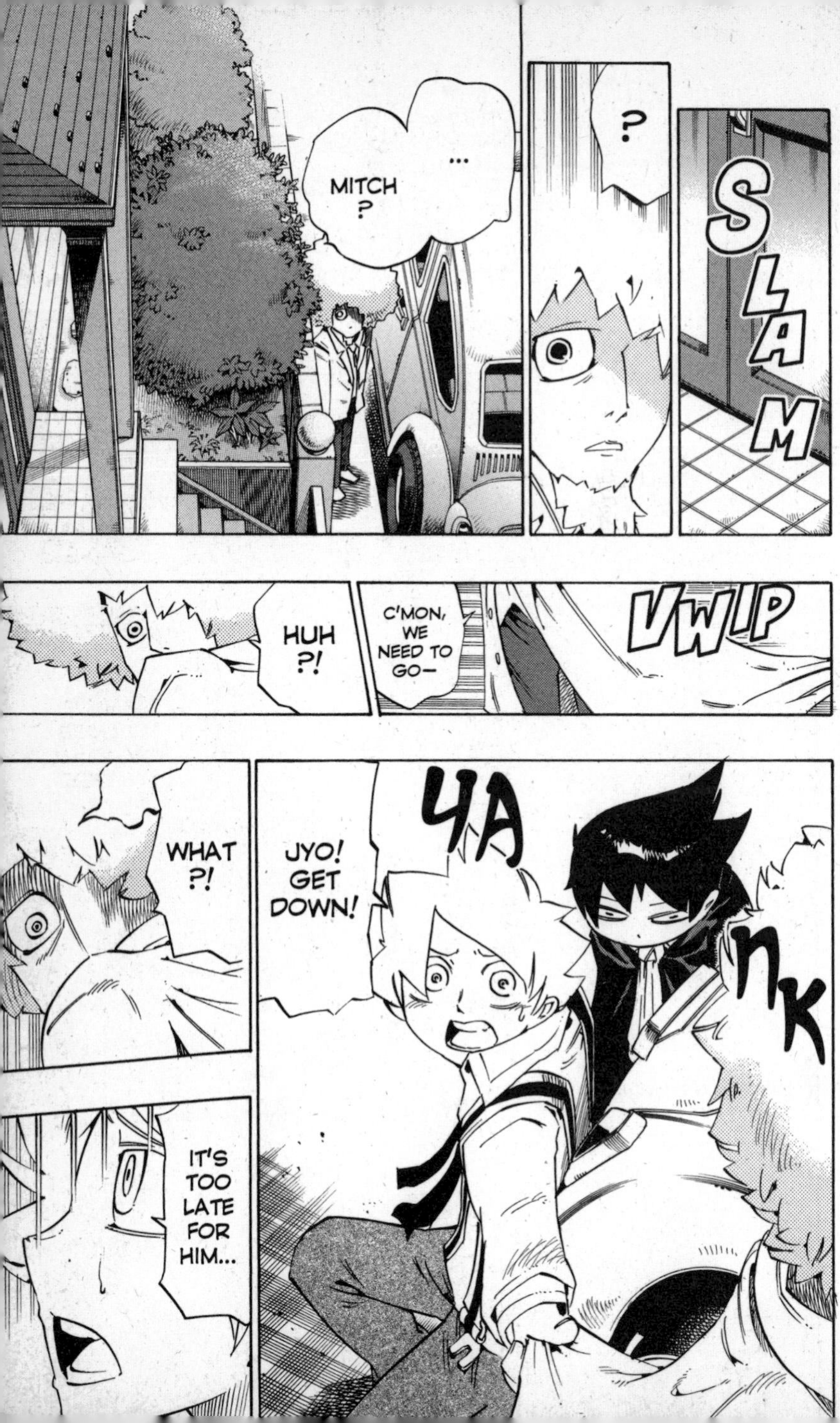
SLAM
?
... MITCH ?
VWIP
C'MON, WE NEED TO GO—
HUH ?!
...
YANK
JYO! GET DOWN!
WHAT ?!
IT'S TOO LATE FOR HIM...

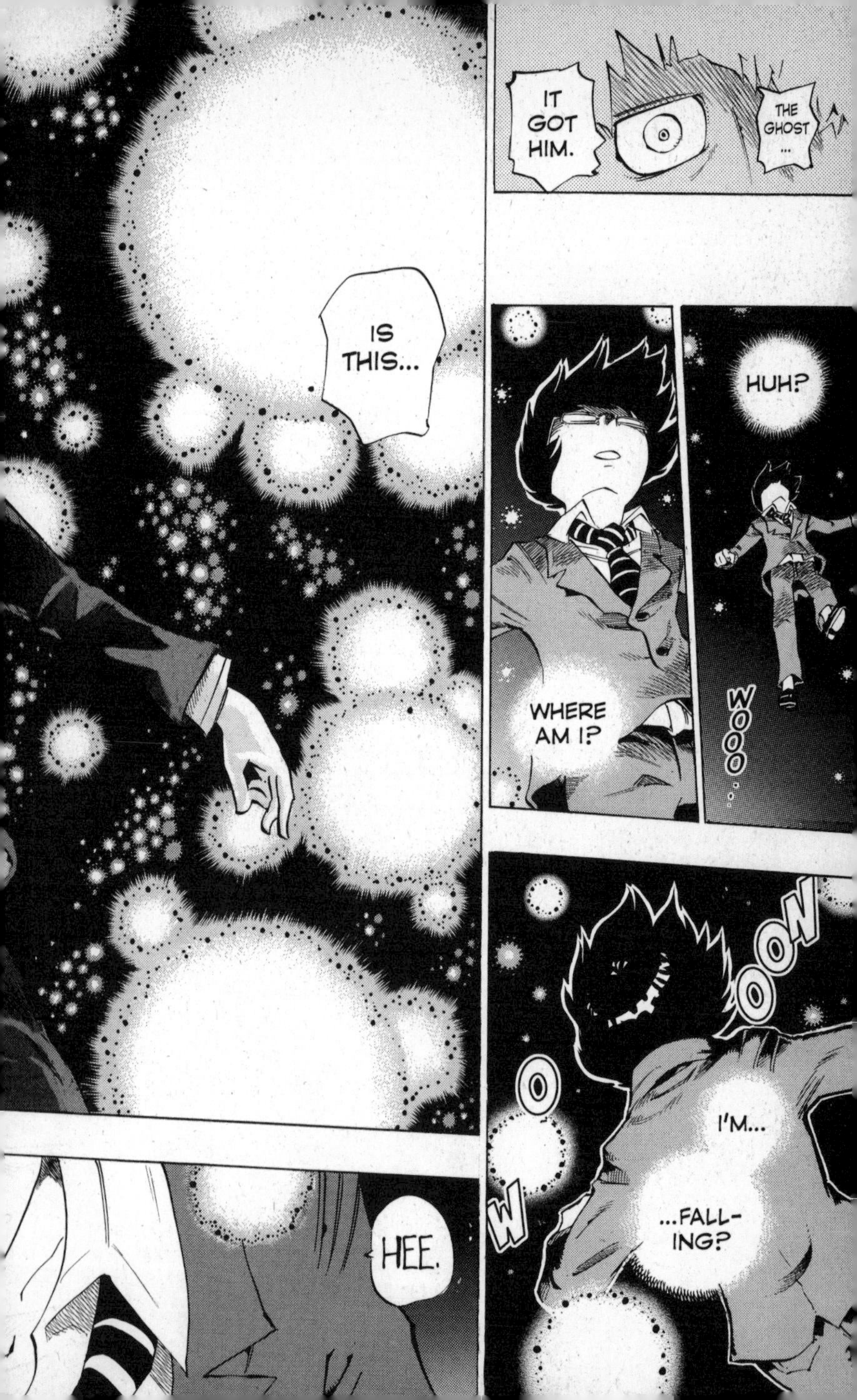
THE GHOST ...
IT GOT HIM.
HUH?
WOOO...
WHERE AM I?
WOOOON
I'M...
...FALL-ING?
IS THIS...
HEE.

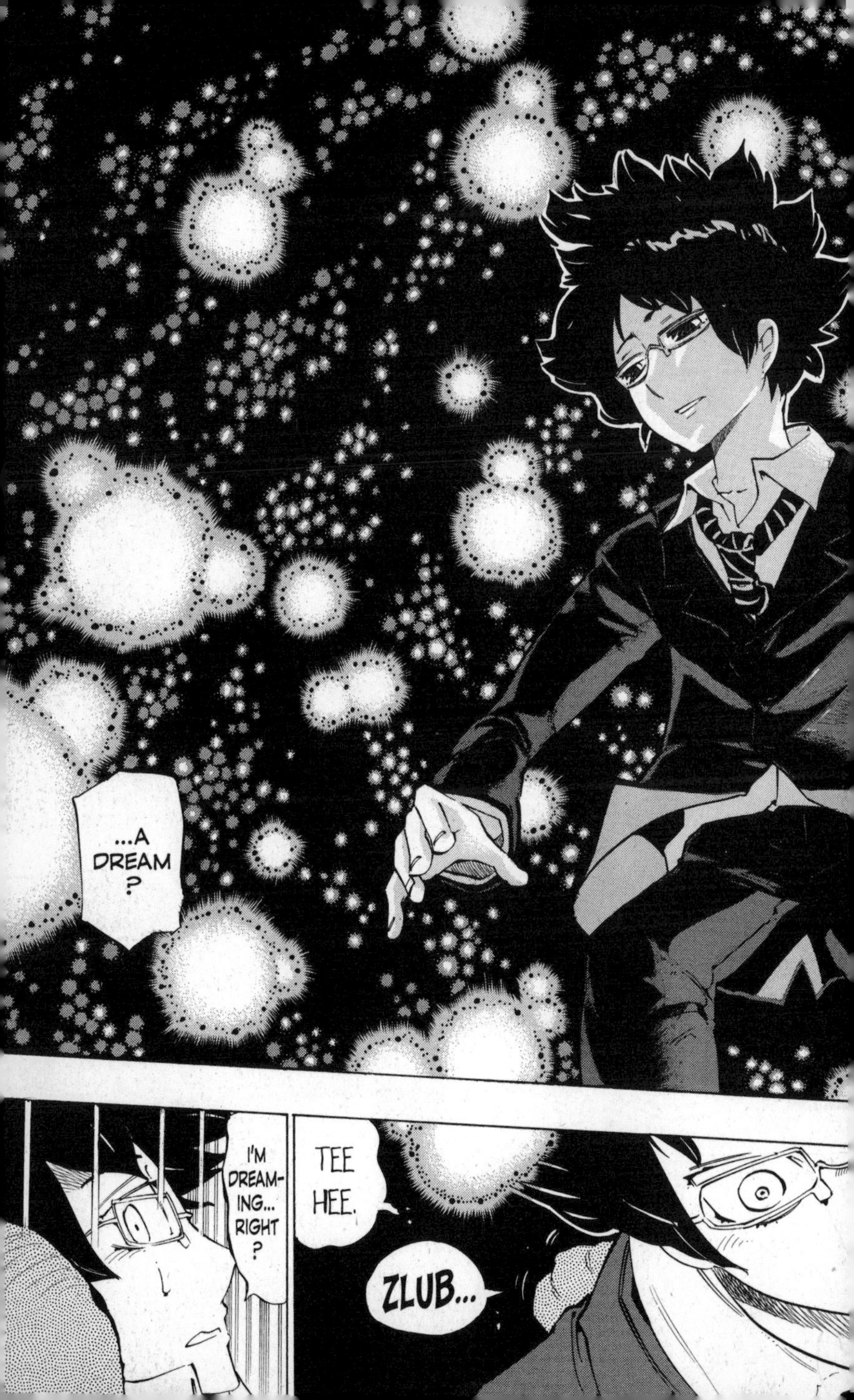
...A DREAM?
TEE HEE.
ZLUB...
I'M DREAMING... RIGHT?

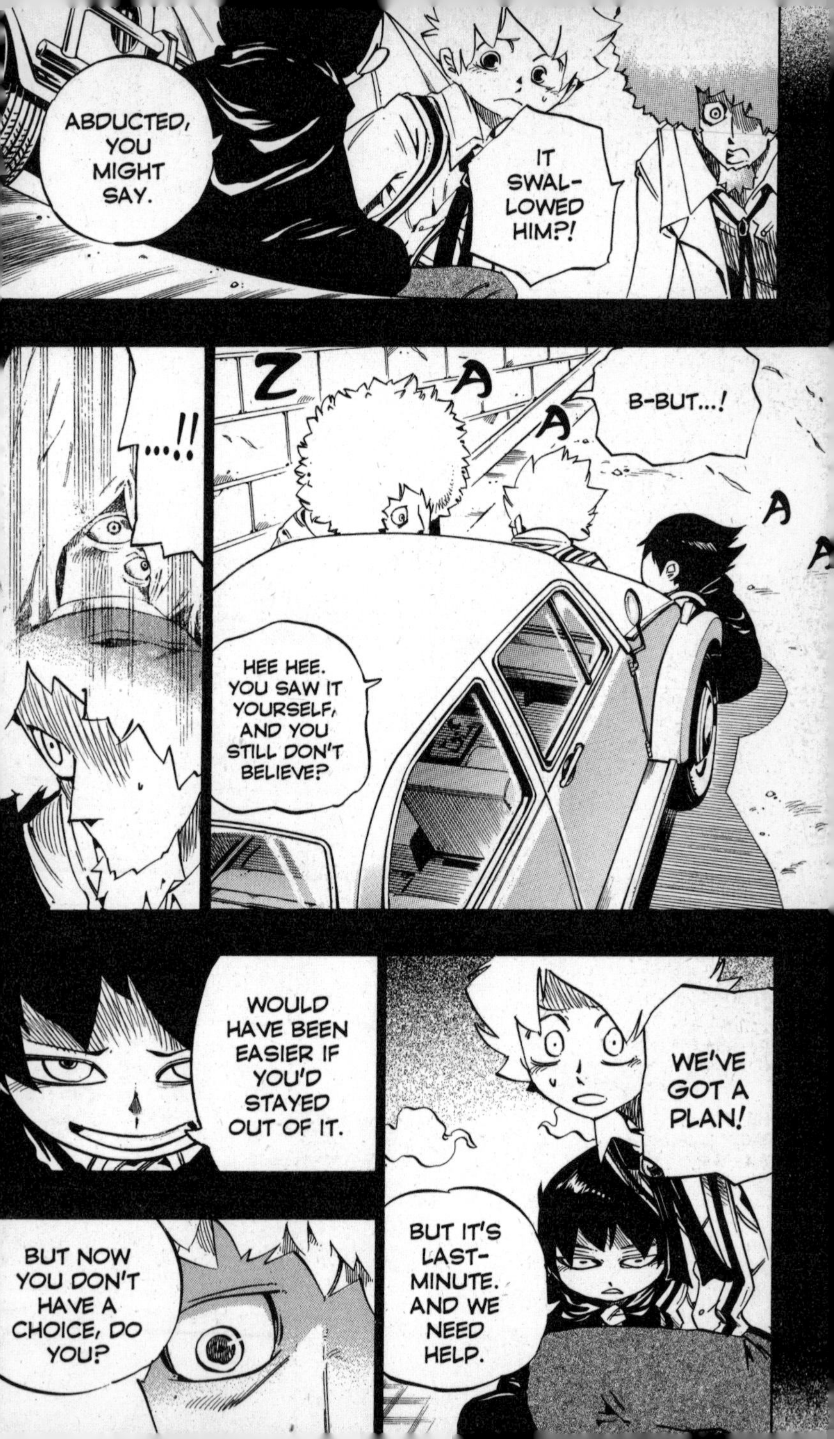
IT SWAL-LOWED HIM?!
ABDUCTED, YOU MIGHT SAY.
B-BUT...!
ZAAAAA
HEE HEE. YOU SAW IT YOURSELF, AND YOU STILL DON'T BELIEVE?
...!!
WE'VE GOT A PLAN!
BUT IT'S LAST-MINUTE. AND WE NEED HELP.
WOULD HAVE BEEN EASIER IF YOU'D STAYED OUT OF IT.
BUT NOW YOU DON'T HAVE A CHOICE, DO YOU?

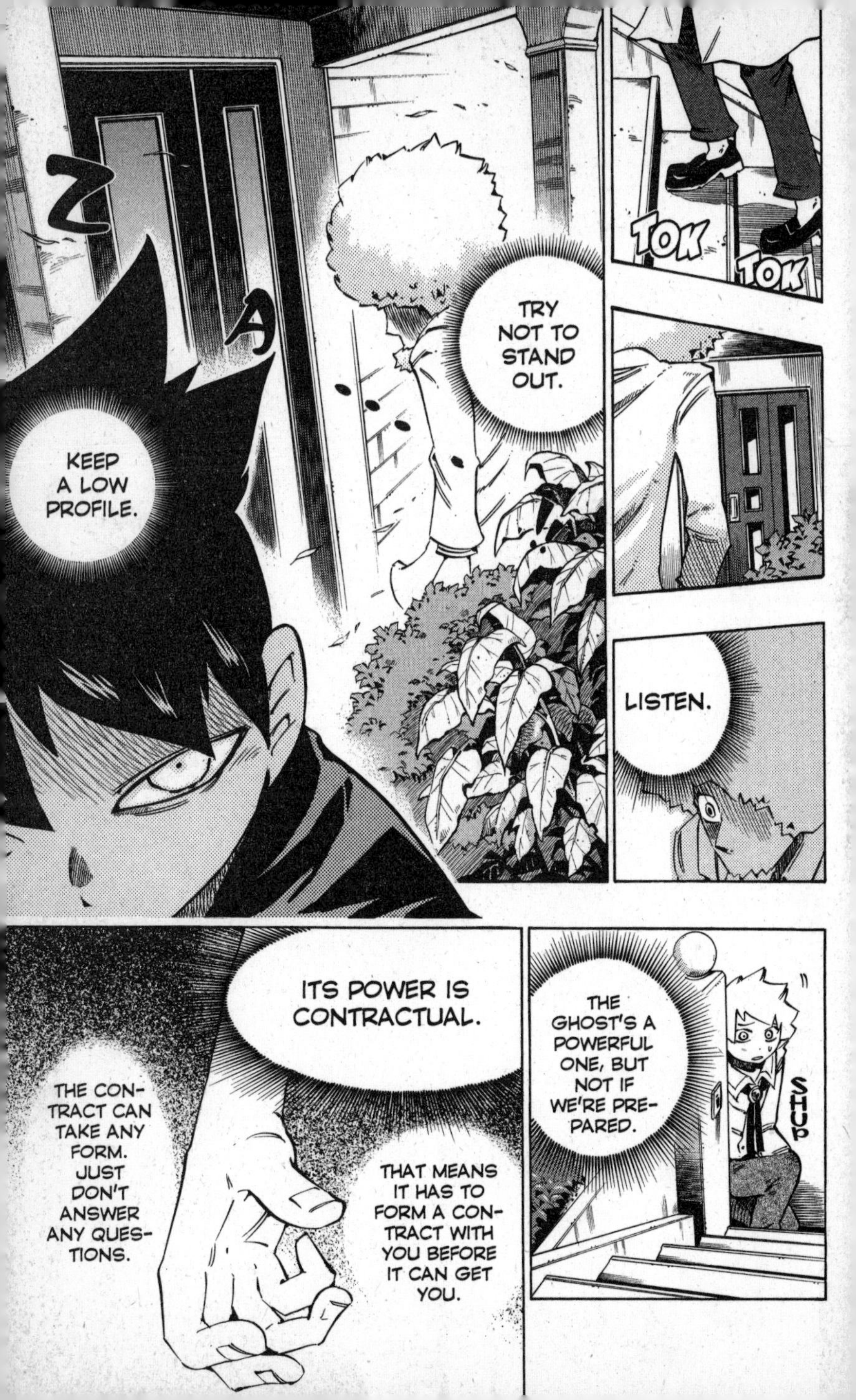
TOK
TOK
LISTEN.
TRY NOT TO STAND OUT.
KEEP A LOW PROFILE.
ZA
THE GHOST'S A POWERFUL ONE, BUT NOT IF WE'RE PREPARED.
SHUP
ITS POWER IS CONTRACTUAL.
THAT MEANS IT HAS TO FORM A CONTRACT WITH YOU BEFORE IT CAN GET YOU.
THE CONTRACT CAN TAKE ANY FORM. JUST DON'T ANSWER ANY QUESTIONS.

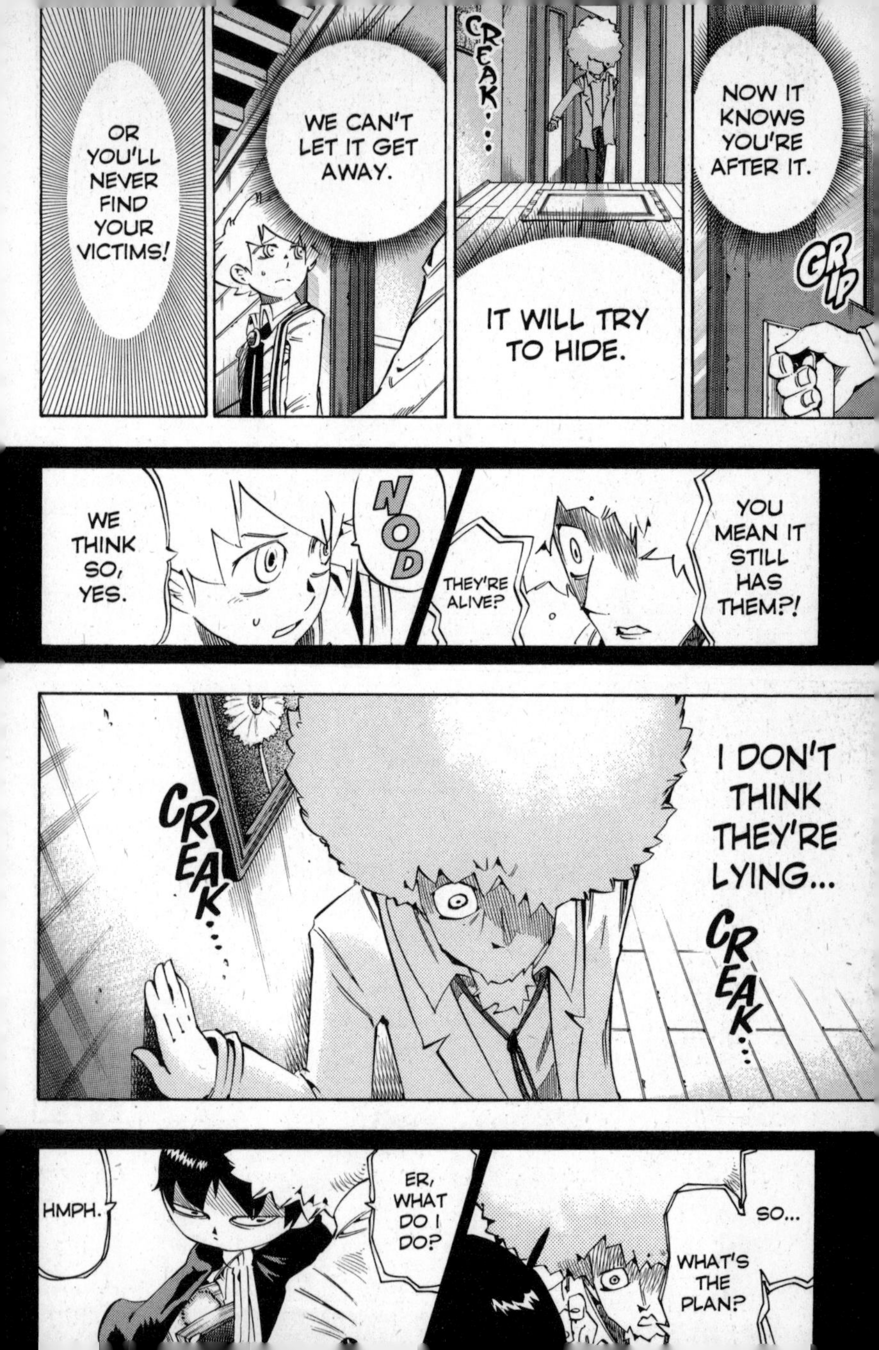
NOW IT KNOWS YOU'RE AFTER IT.
GRIP
CREAK...
IT WILL TRY TO HIDE.
WE CAN'T LET IT GET AWAY.
OR YOU'LL NEVER FIND YOUR VICTIMS!
YOU MEAN IT STILL HAS THEM?!
THEY'RE ALIVE?
NOD
WE THINK SO, YES.
I DON'T THINK THEY'RE LYING...
CREAK...
CREAK...
SO...
WHAT'S THE PLAN?
ER, WHAT DO I DO?
HMPH.

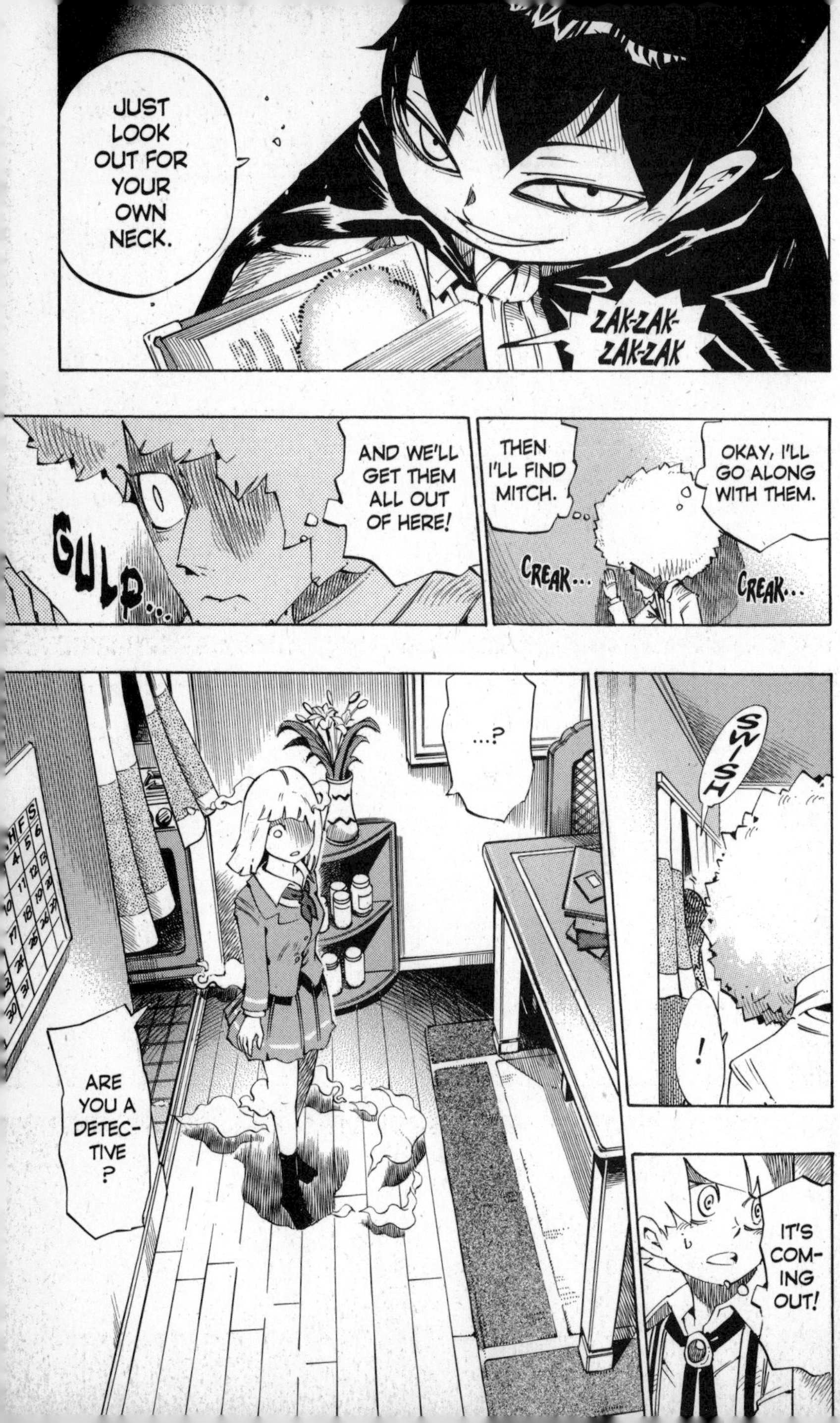
JUST LOOK OUT FOR YOUR OWN NECK.
ZAK-ZAK-ZAK-ZAK
OKAY, I'LL GO ALONG WITH THEM.
THEN I'LL FIND MITCH.
CREAK...
CREAK...
AND WE'LL GET THEM ALL OUT OF HERE!
GULP...
SWISH
!
IT'S COMING OUT!
...?
ARE YOU A DETECTIVE?

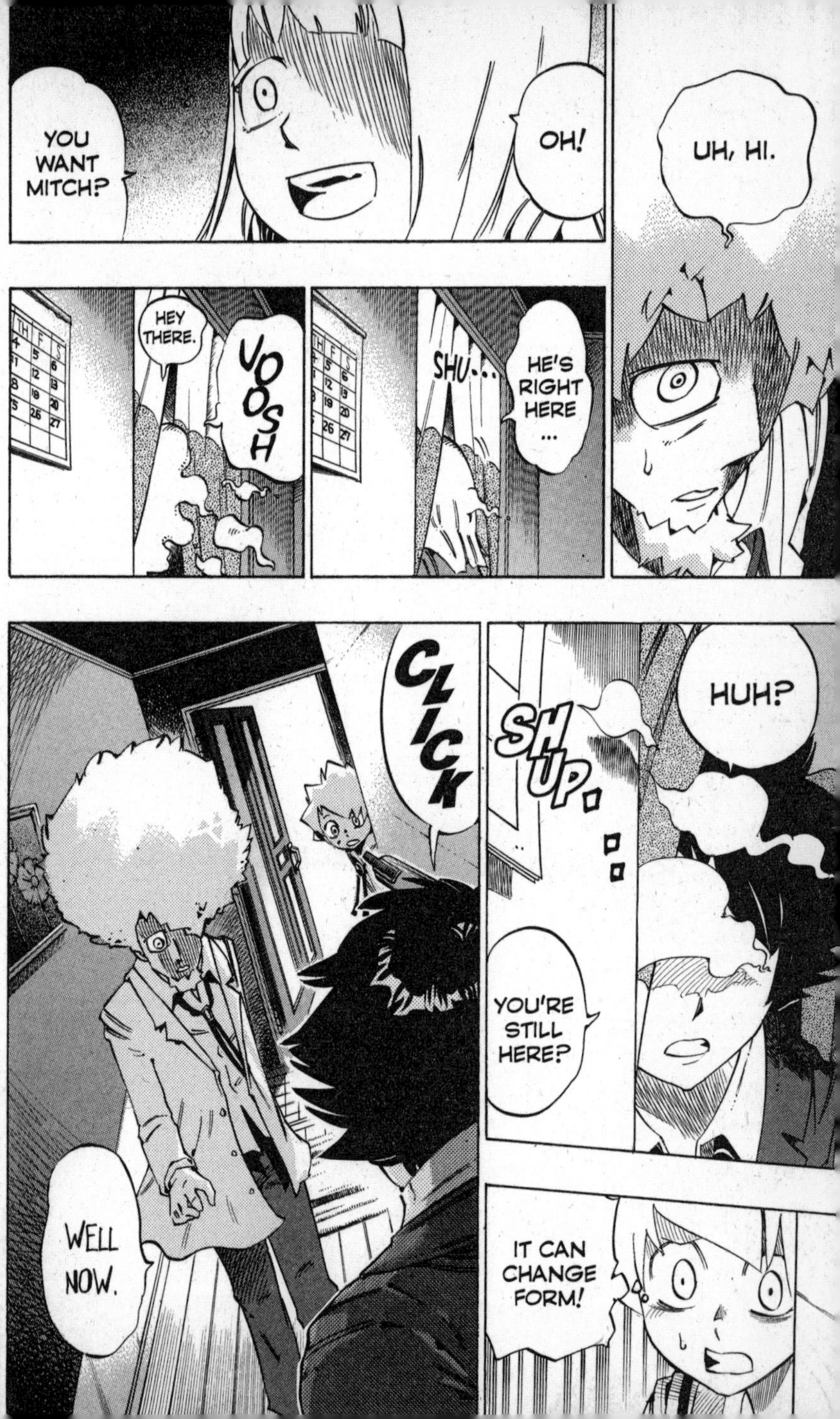
UH, HI.
OH!
YOU WANT MITCH?
HE'S RIGHT HERE ...
SHU...
VOOSH
HEY THERE.
HUH?
SHUP...
YOU'RE STILL HERE?
IT CAN CHANGE FORM!
CLICK
WELL NOW.

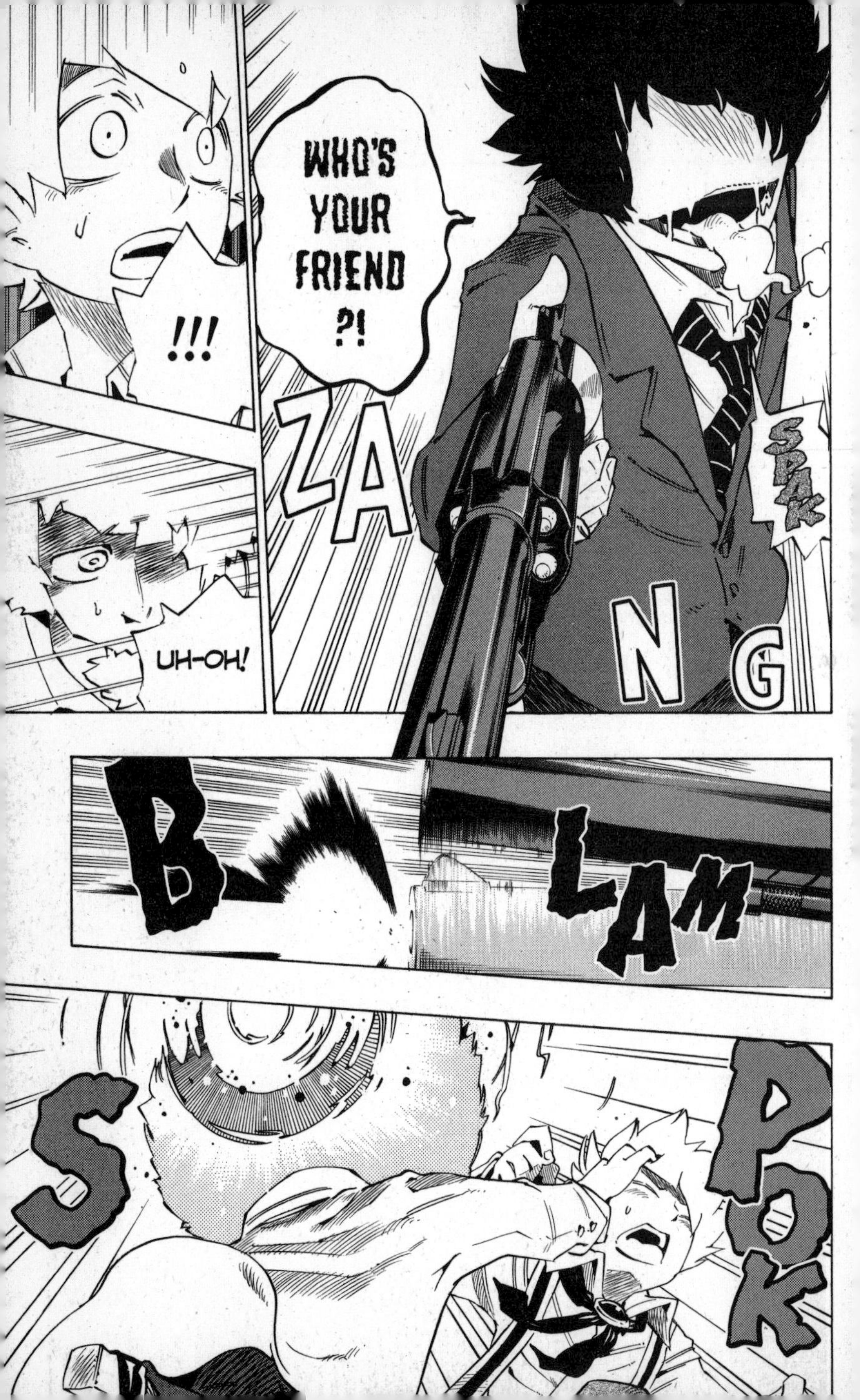
WHO'S YOUR FRIEND ?!
SPAK
ZANG
!!!
UH-OH!
BLAM
SPOK

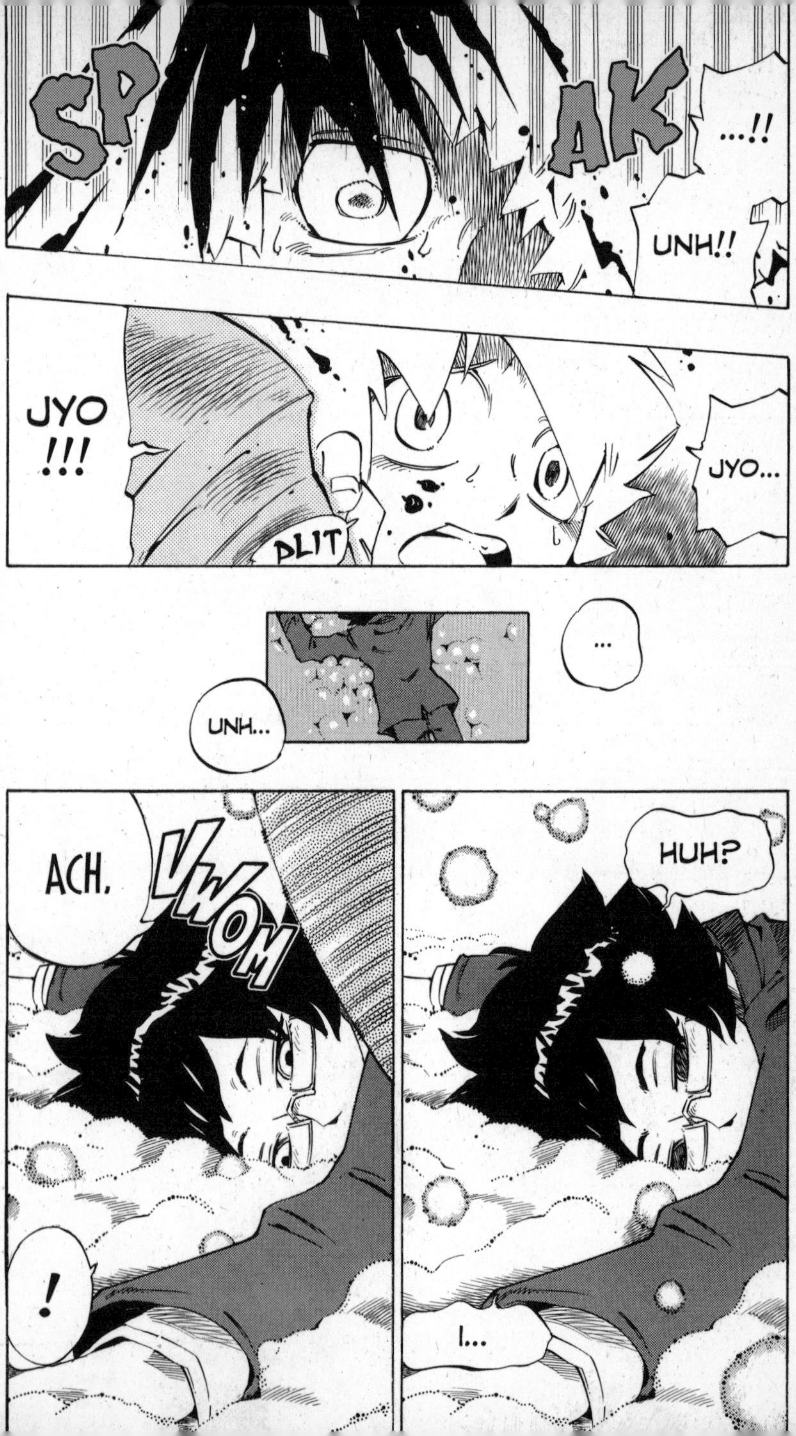
SPAK
...!!
UNH!!
JYO...
PLIT
JYO !!!
...
UNH...
HUH?
I...
VWOM
ACH.
!

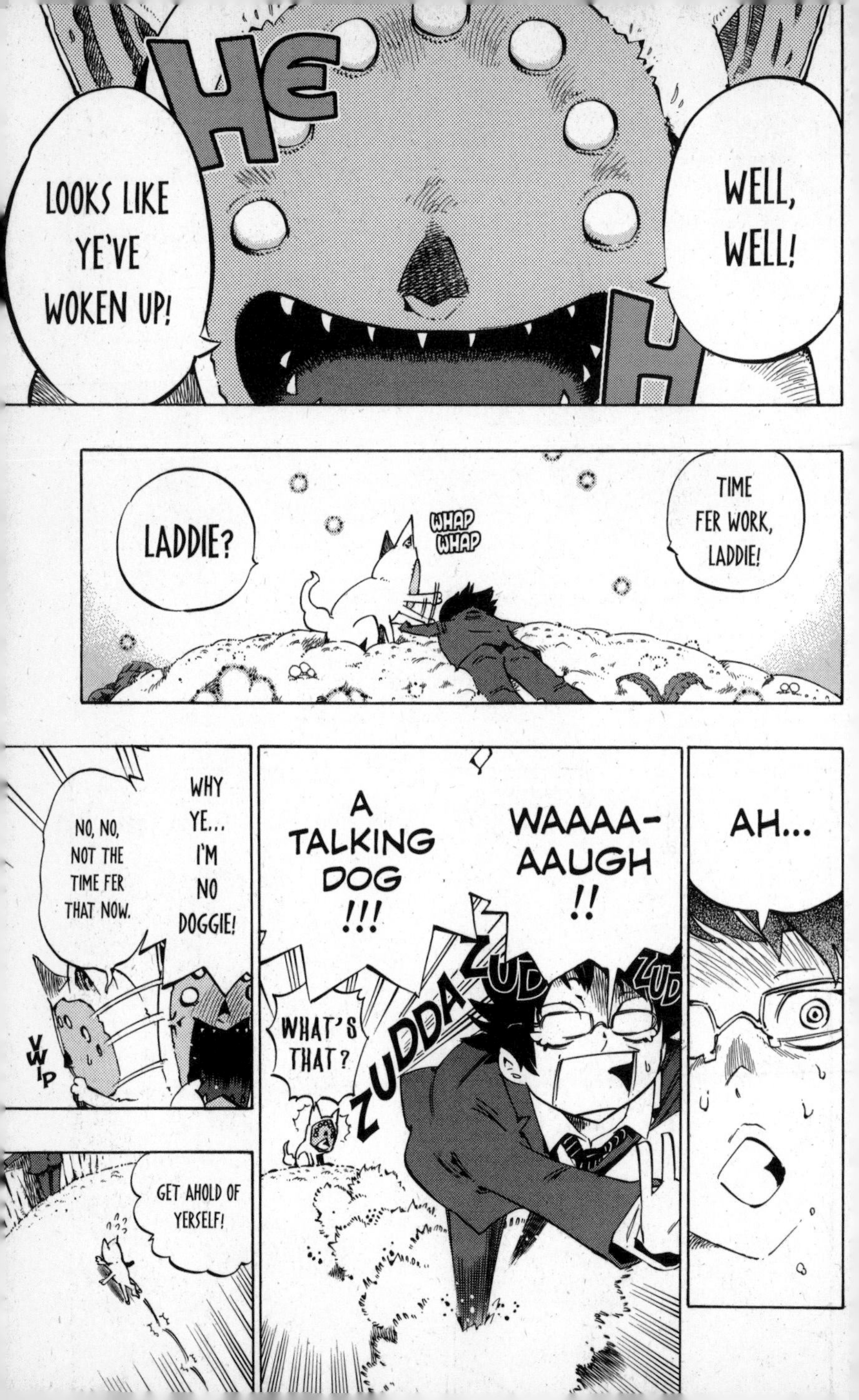
WELL, WELL!
LOOKS LIKE YE'VE WOKEN UP!
HEH
TIME FER WORK, LADDIE!
WHAP WHAP
LADDIE?
AH...
WAAAA-AAUGH!!
A TALKING DOG!!!
ZUD ZUD
ZUDDA
WHAT'S THAT?
WHY YE... I'M NO DOGGIE!
NO, NO, NOT THE TIME FER THAT NOW.
VWIP
GET AHOLD OF YERSELF!

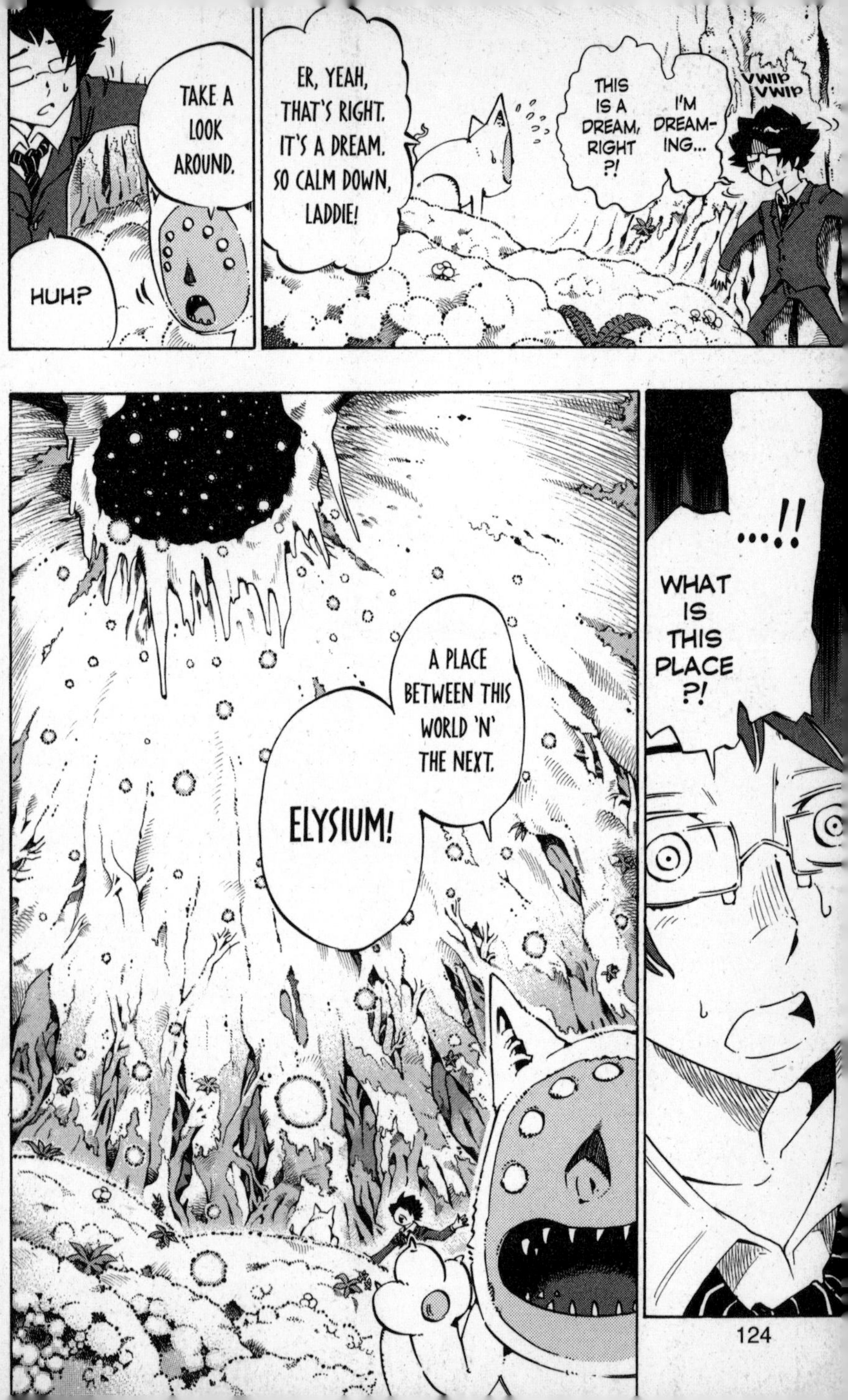
VWIP VWIP
I'M DREAMING...
THIS IS A DREAM, RIGHT?!
ER, YEAH, THAT'S RIGHT. IT'S A DREAM. SO CALM DOWN, LADDIE!
TAKE A LOOK AROUND.
HUH?
...!!
WHAT IS THIS PLACE?!
A PLACE BETWEEN THIS WORLD 'N' THE NEXT.
ELYSIUM!

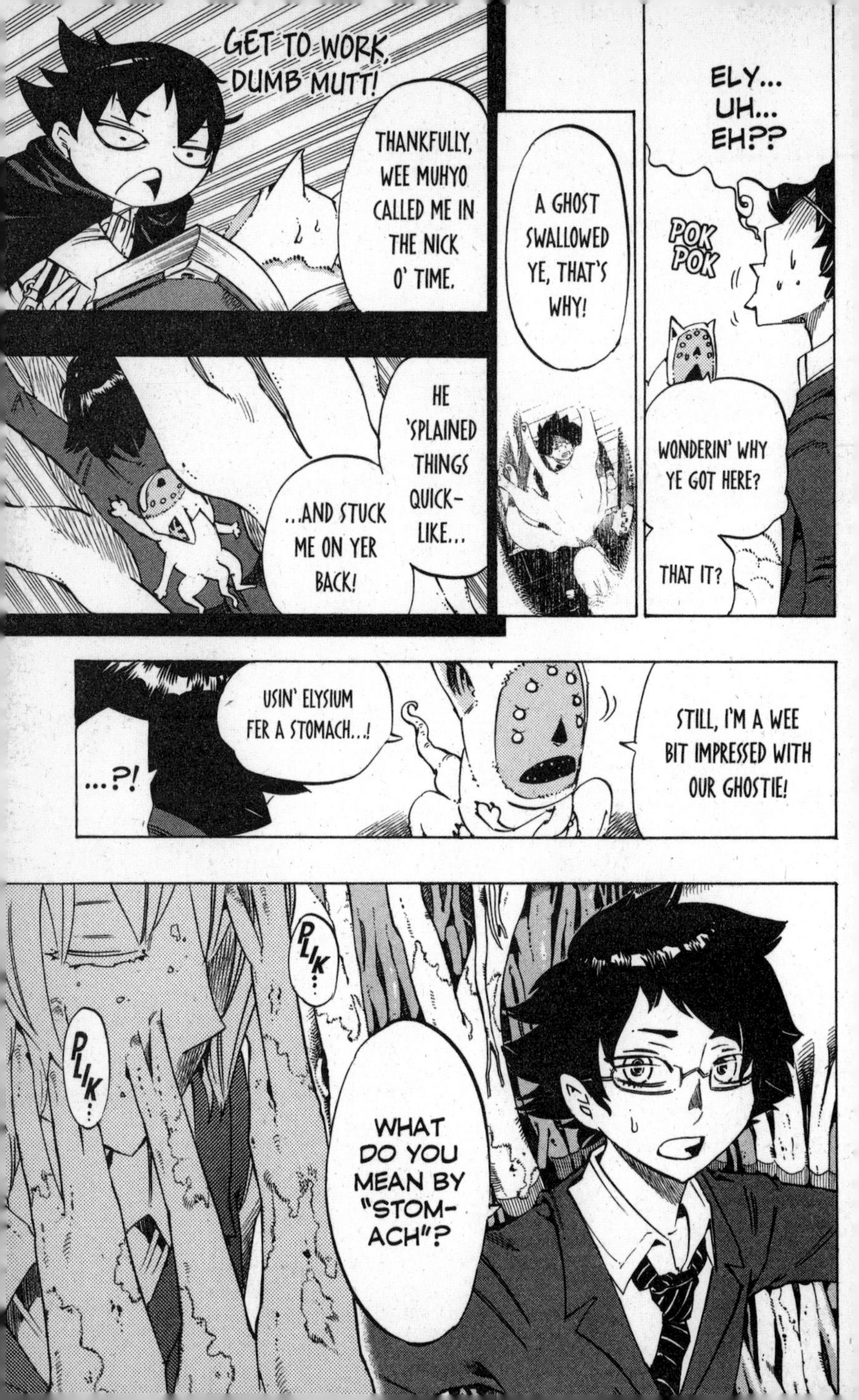
ELY... UH... EH??
POK POK
WONDERIN' WHY YE GOT HERE?
THAT IT?
A GHOST SWALLOWED YE, THAT'S WHY!
THANKFULLY, WEE MUHYO CALLED ME IN THE NICK O' TIME.
GET TO WORK, DUMB MUTT!
HE 'SPLAINED THINGS QUICK-LIKE...
...AND STUCK ME ON YER BACK!
STILL, I'M A WEE BIT IMPRESSED WITH OUR GHOSTIE!
USIN' ELYSIUM FER A STOMACH...!
...?!
PLIK...
WHAT DO YOU MEAN BY "STOMACH"?
PLIK...

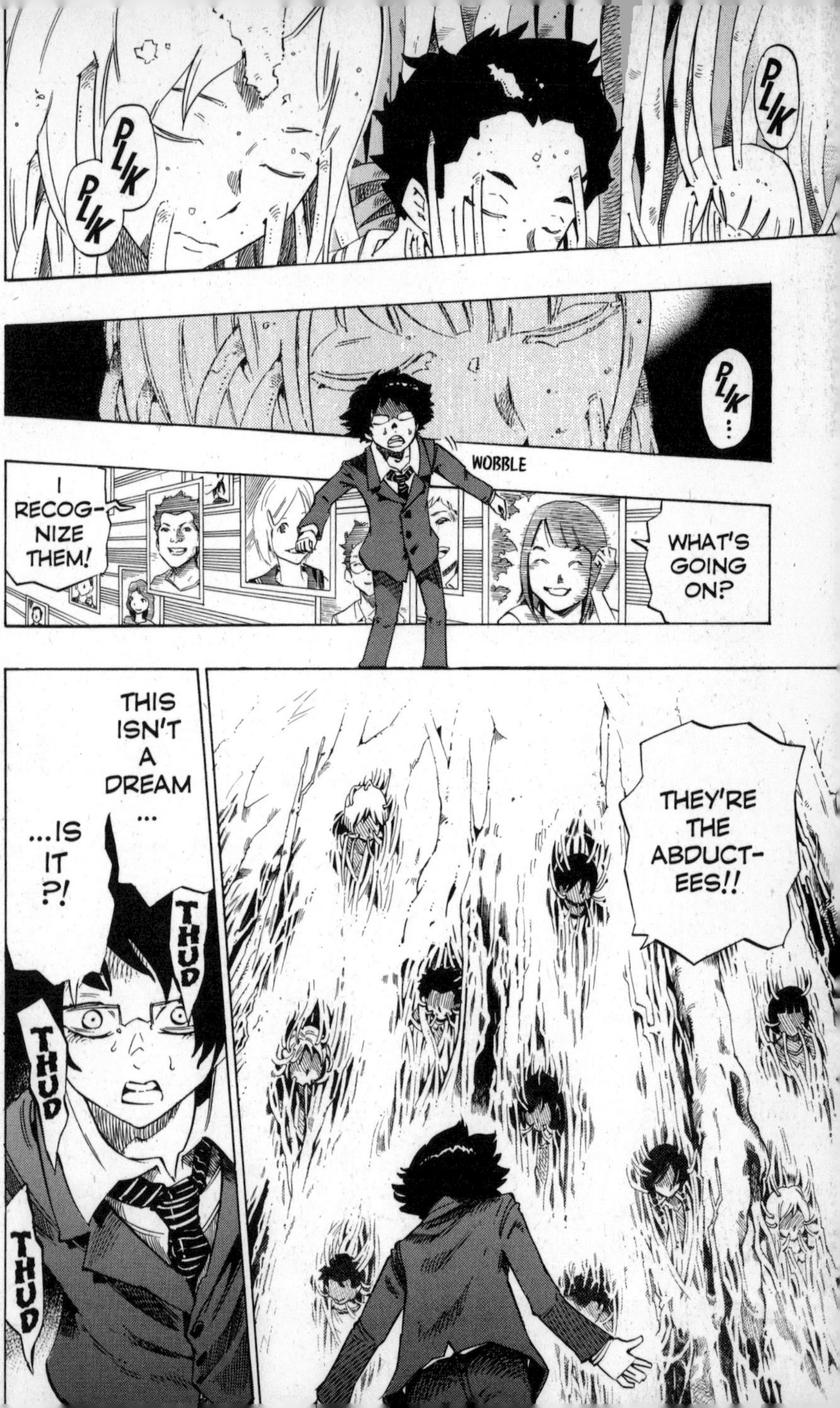
PLIK
PLIK
PLIK
PLIK...
WHAT'S GOING ON?
WOBBLE
I RECOGNIZE THEM!
THEY'RE THE ABDUCTEES!!
THIS ISN'T A DREAM...
...IS IT?!
THUD
THUD
THUD

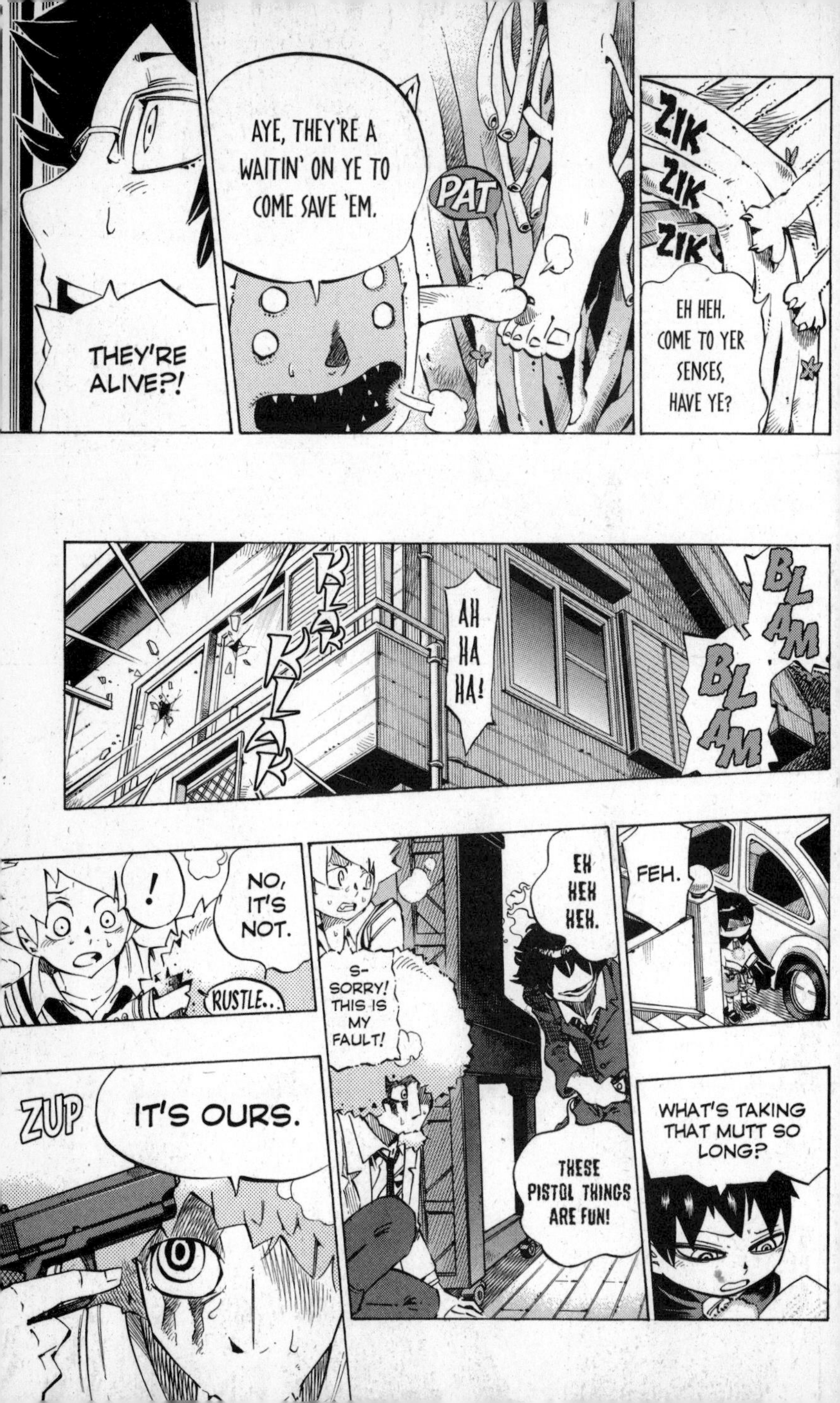
ZIK
ZIK
ZIK
EH HEH. COME TO YER SENSES, HAVE YE?
PAT
AYE, THEY'RE A WAITIN' ON YE TO COME SAVE 'EM.
THEY'RE ALIVE?!
BLAM
BLAM
AH HA HA!
KLAK
KLAK
FEH.
WHAT'S TAKING THAT MUTT SO LONG?
EH HEH HEH.
THESE PISTOL THINGS ARE FUN!
S-SORRY! THIS IS MY FAULT!
!
NO, IT'S NOT.
RUSTLE...
ZUP
IT'S OURS.

Muhyo & Roji's
Bureau of Supernatural Investigation
BSI

ARTICLE 139 MEMORIES

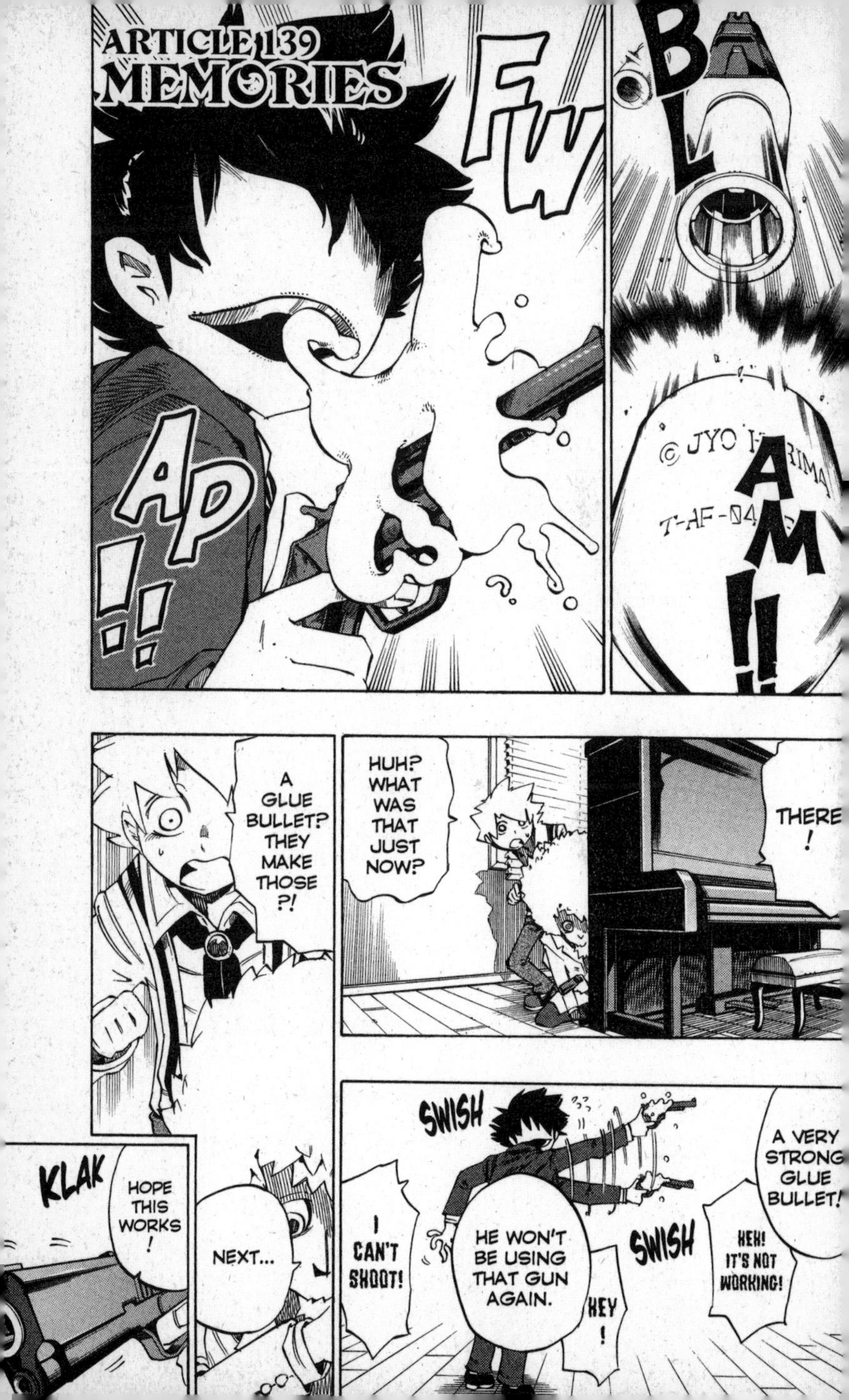
BLAM!!
FWAP!!
THERE!
HUH? WHAT WAS THAT JUST NOW?
A GLUE BULLET? THEY MAKE THOSE?!
A VERY STRONG GLUE BULLET!
HEH! IT'S NOT WORKING!
SWISH
HEY!
HE WON'T BE USING THAT GUN AGAIN.
I CAN'T SHOOT!
SWISH
NEXT...
HOPE THIS WORKS!
KLAK

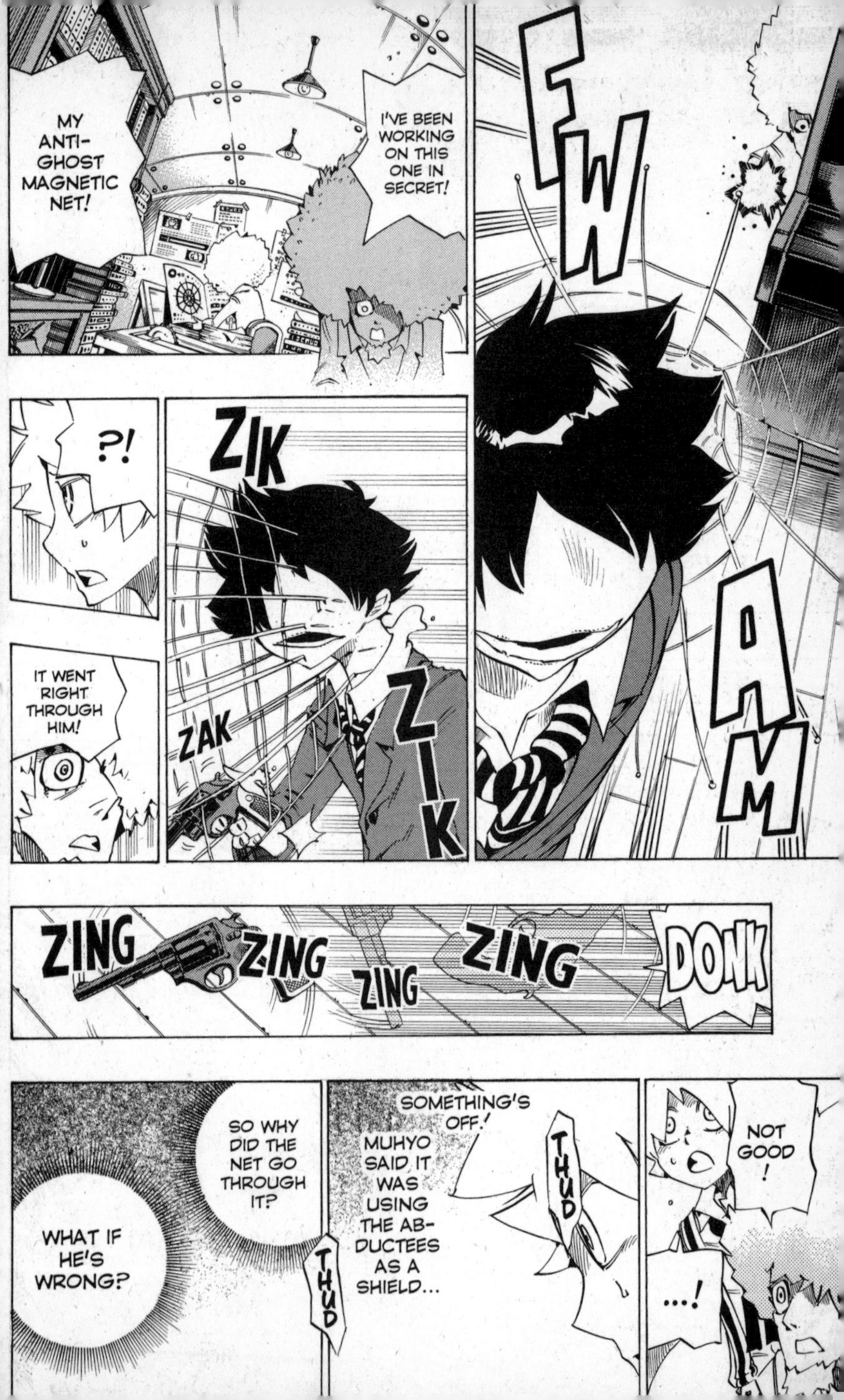
FW
AM
I'VE BEEN WORKING ON THIS ONE IN SECRET!
MY ANTI-GHOST MAGNETIC NET!
ZIK
ZAK
ZIK
?!
IT WENT RIGHT THROUGH HIM!
DONK
ZING
ZING
ZING
ZING
NOT GOOD!
...!
SOMETHING'S OFF!
THUD
MUHYO SAID IT WAS USING THE ABDUCTEES AS A SHIELD...
SO WHY DID THE NET GO THROUGH IT?
THUD
WHAT IF HE'S WRONG?

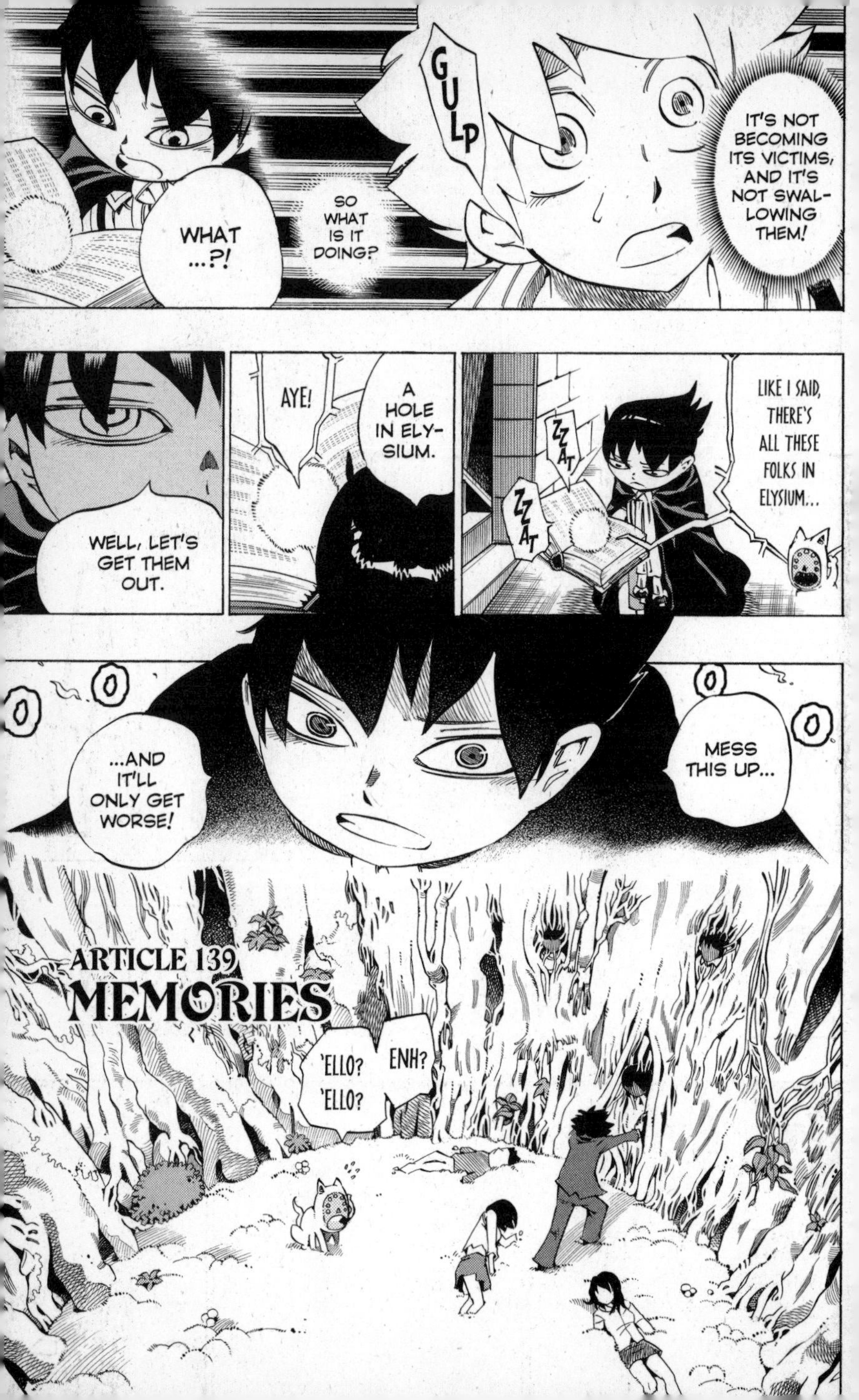
IT'S NOT BECOMING ITS VICTIMS, AND IT'S NOT SWAL-LOWING THEM!
GULP
SO WHAT IS IT DOING?
WHAT ...?!
LIKE I SAID, THERE'S ALL THESE FOLKS IN ELYSIUM...
ZZAT
ZZAT
A HOLE IN ELY-SIUM.
AYE!
WELL, LET'S GET THEM OUT.
MESS THIS UP...
...AND IT'LL ONLY GET WORSE!
ARTICLE 139
MEMORIES
ENH?
'ELLO? 'ELLO?

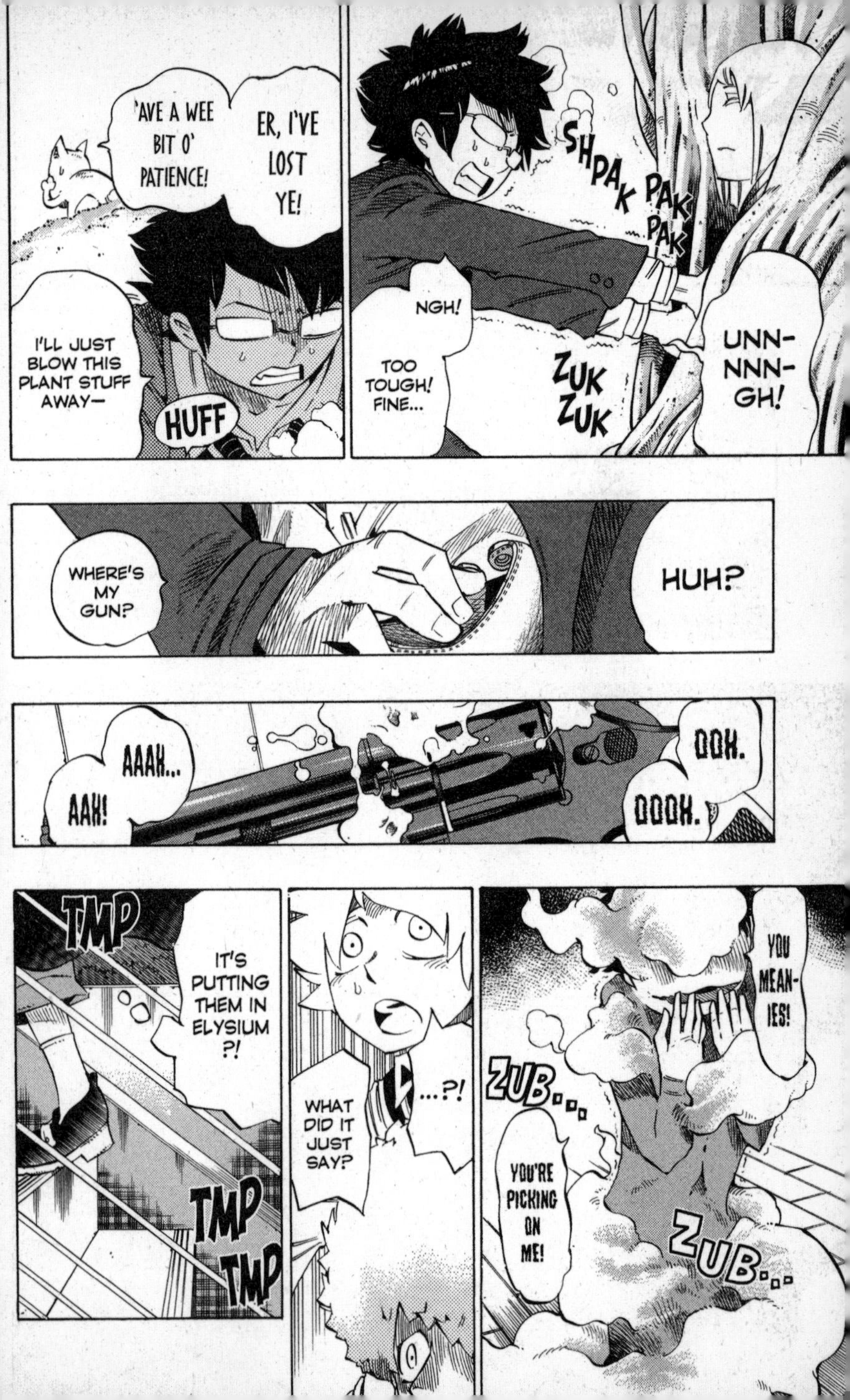
SHPAK PAK PAK
UNN-NNN-GH!
NGH!
TOO TOUGH! FINE...
ZUK ZUK
ER, I'VE LOST YE!
'AVE A WEE BIT O' PATIENCE!
I'LL JUST BLOW THIS PLANT STUFF AWAY—
HUFF
HUH?
WHERE'S MY GUN?
OOH.
OOOH.
AAAH...
AAH!
YOU MEAN-IES!
ZUB...
YOU'RE PICKING ON ME!
ZUB...
...?!
WHAT DID IT JUST SAY?
TMP
IT'S PUTTING THEM IN ELYSIUM ?!
TMP
TMP

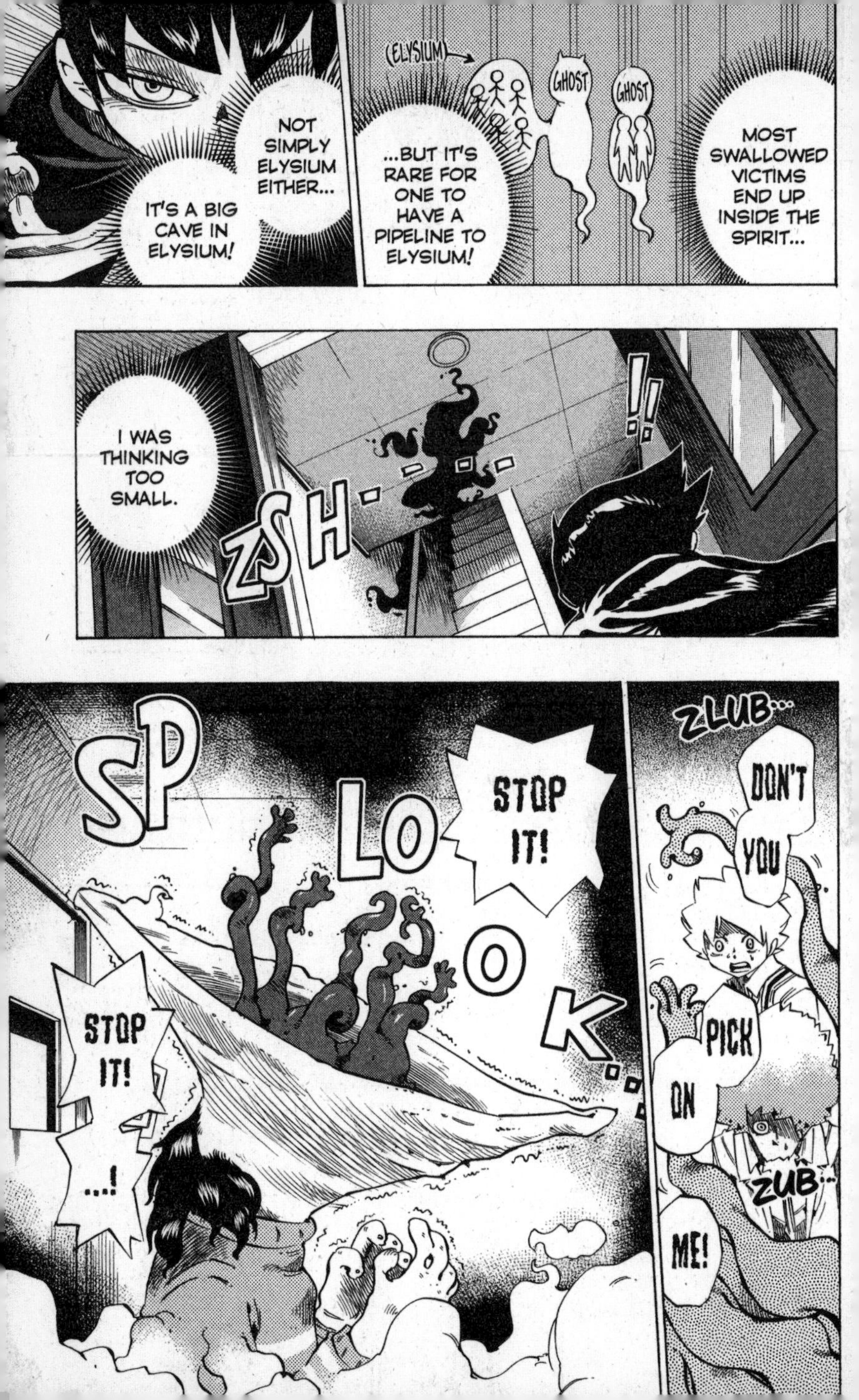
MOST SWALLOWED VICTIMS END UP INSIDE THE SPIRIT...
(ELYSIUM)
GHOST
GHOST
...BUT IT'S RARE FOR ONE TO HAVE A PIPELINE TO ELYSIUM!
NOT SIMPLY ELYSIUM EITHER...
IT'S A BIG CAVE IN ELYSIUM!
!!
ZSH-
I WAS THINKING TOO SMALL.
ZLUB...
DON'T YOU PICK ON ME!
ZUB...
SPLOOK...
STOP IT!
STOP IT!
...!

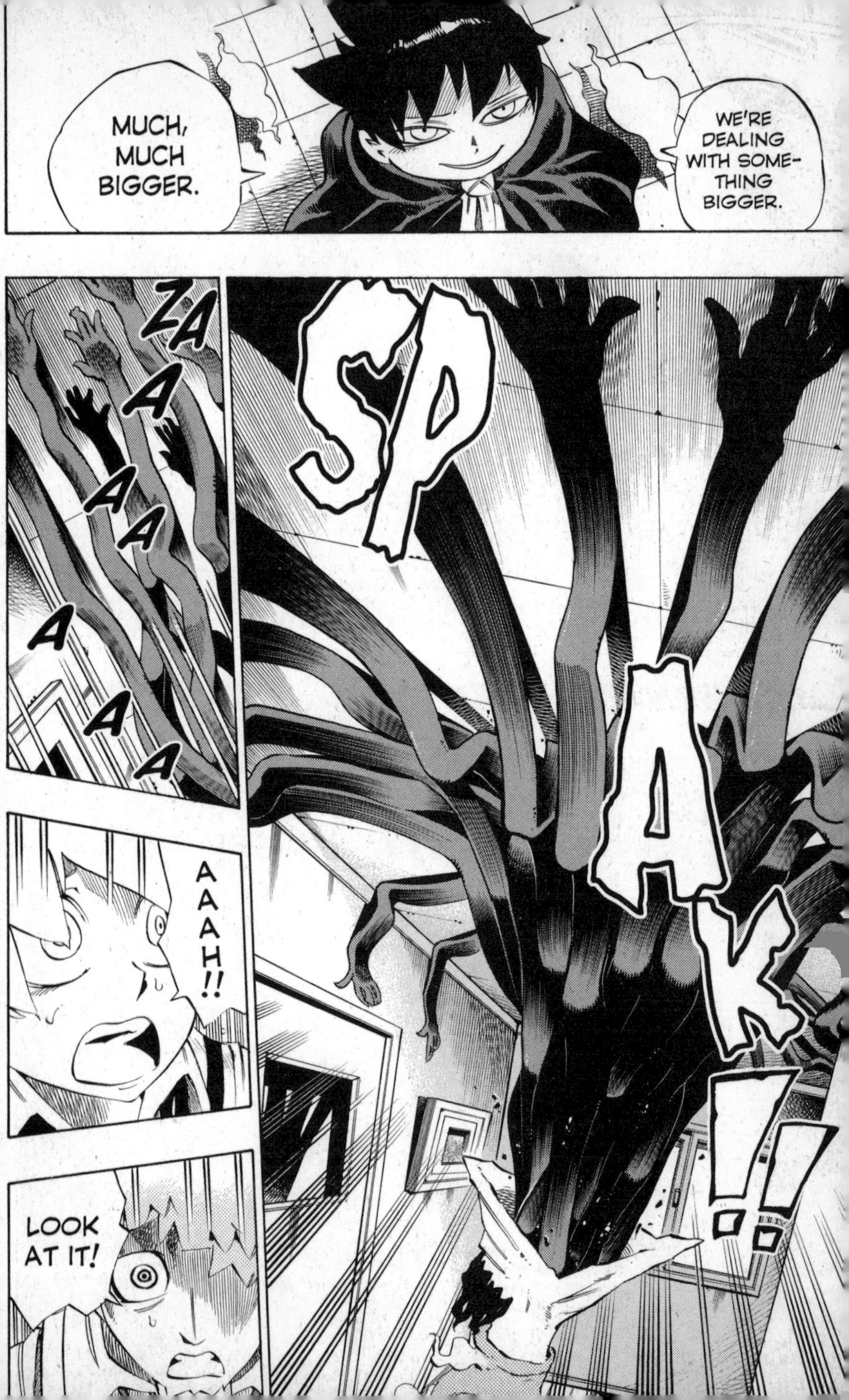
WE'RE DEALING WITH SOME-THING BIGGER.
MUCH, MUCH BIGGER.
SPAAK!!
ZAAAAAAA
AAAAH!!
LOOK AT IT!

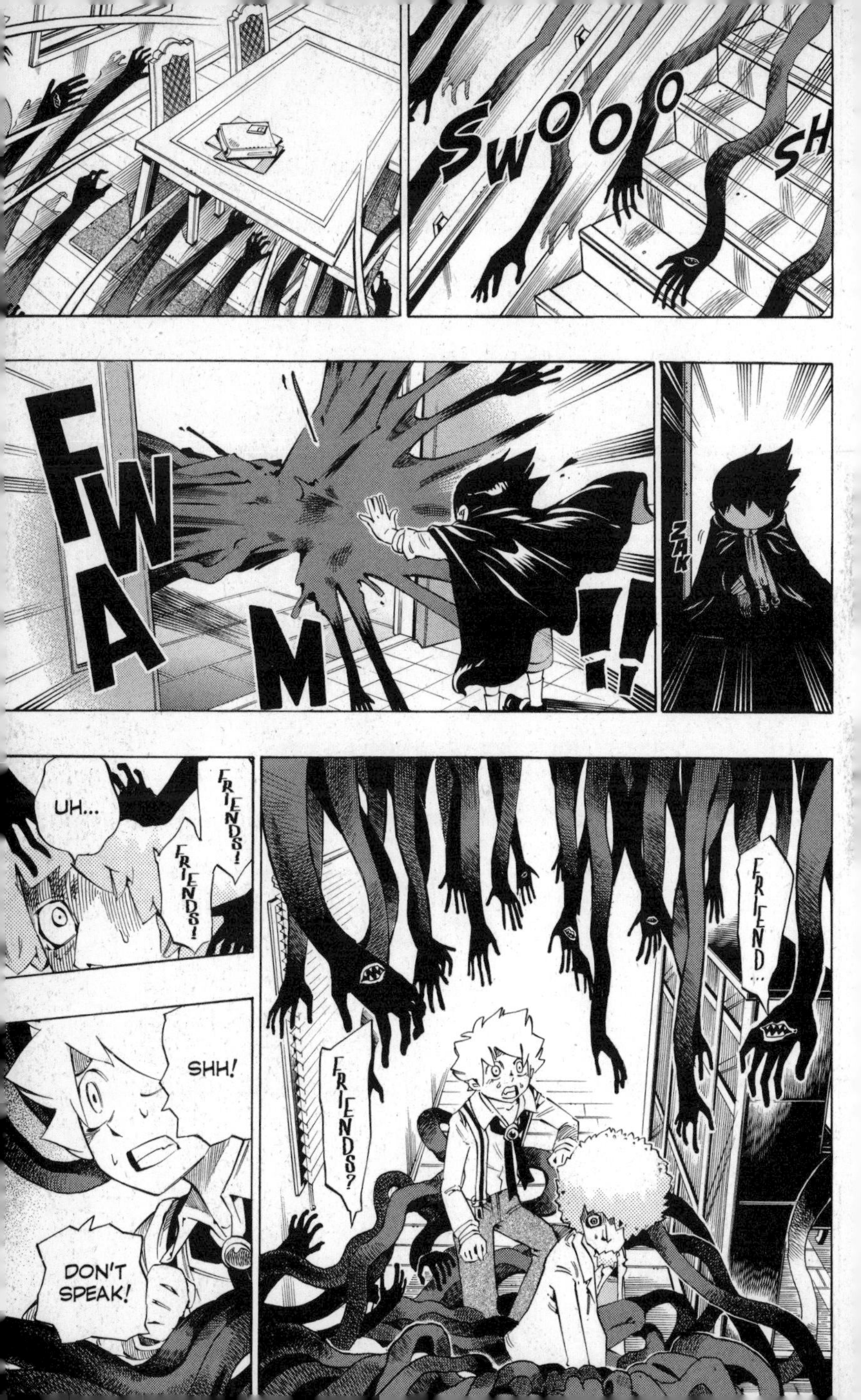
SWOOOSH
ZAK
FWAM!!
FRIEND...
FRIENDS?
FRIENDS!
FRIENDS!
UH...
SHH!
DON'T SPEAK!

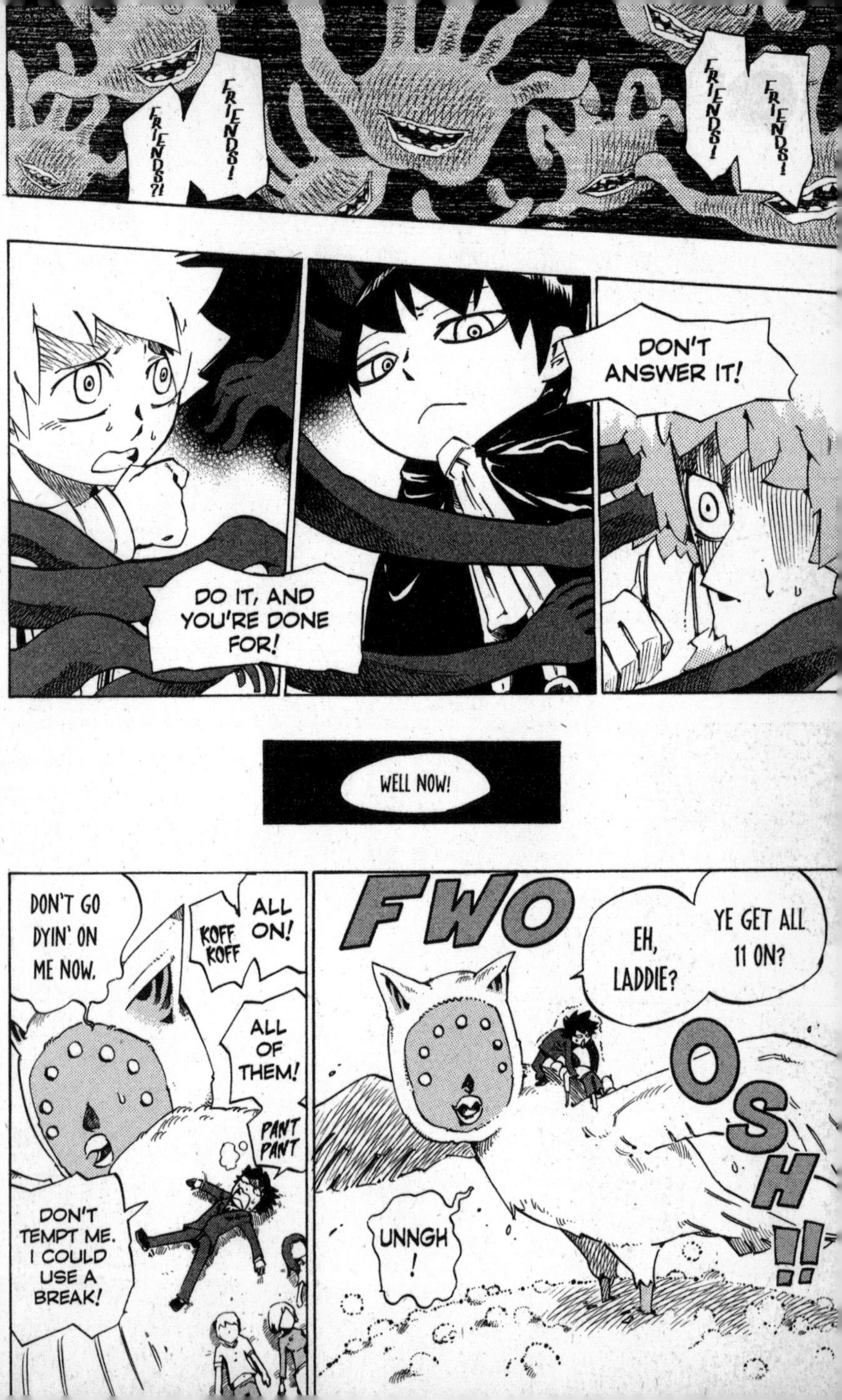
FRIENDS!
FRIENDS!
FRIENDS!
FRIENDS?!
DON'T ANSWER IT!
DO IT, AND YOU'RE DONE FOR!
WELL NOW!
YE GET ALL 11 ON?
EH, LADDIE?
FWOOSH!!
UNNGH!
ALL ON!
KOFF KOFF
DON'T GO DYIN' ON ME NOW.
ALL OF THEM!
PANT PANT
DON'T TEMPT ME. I COULD USE A BREAK!

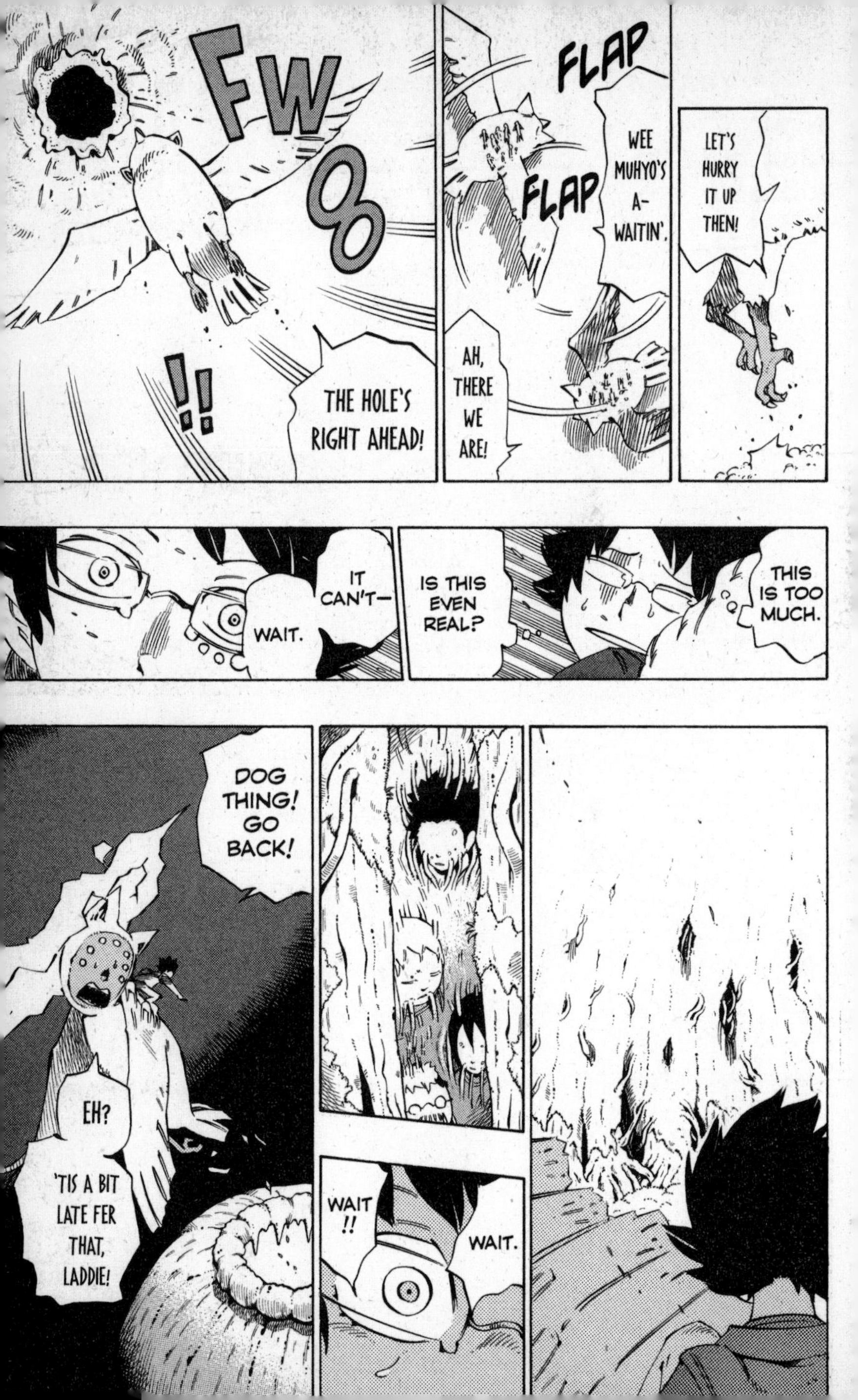
LET'S HURRY IT UP THEN!
FLAP
WEE MUHYO'S A-WAITIN'.
FLAP
AH, THERE WE ARE!
FWOO
!!
THE HOLE'S RIGHT AHEAD!
THIS IS TOO MUCH.
IS THIS EVEN REAL?
IT CAN'T—
WAIT.
WAIT.
WAIT !!
DOG THING! GO BACK!
EH?
'TIS A BIT LATE FER THAT, LADDIE!

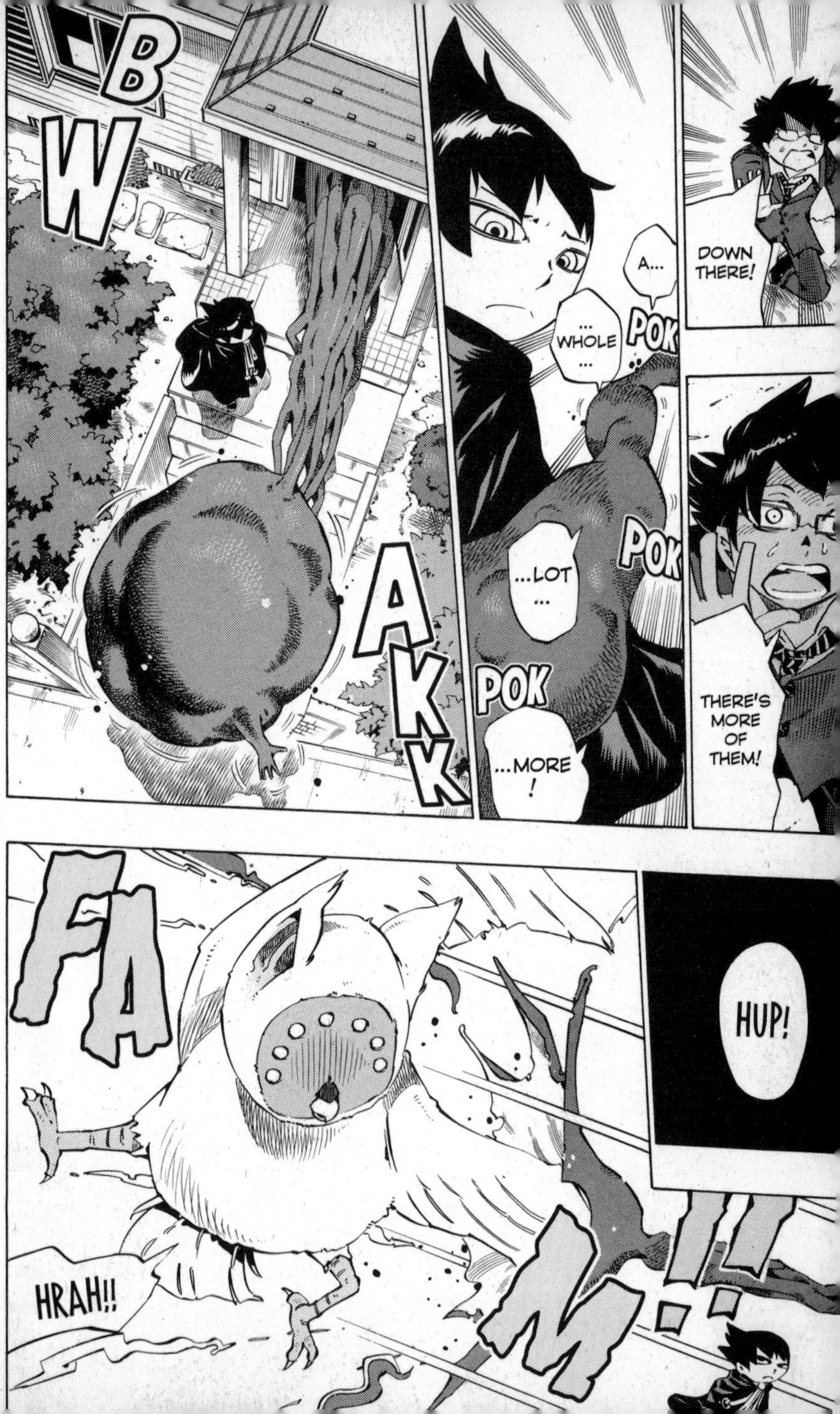
DOWN THERE!
THERE'S MORE OF THEM!
A...
POK
...WHOLE...
POK
...LOT...
POK
...MORE!
BWAKK
HUP!
FA
M!
HRAH!!

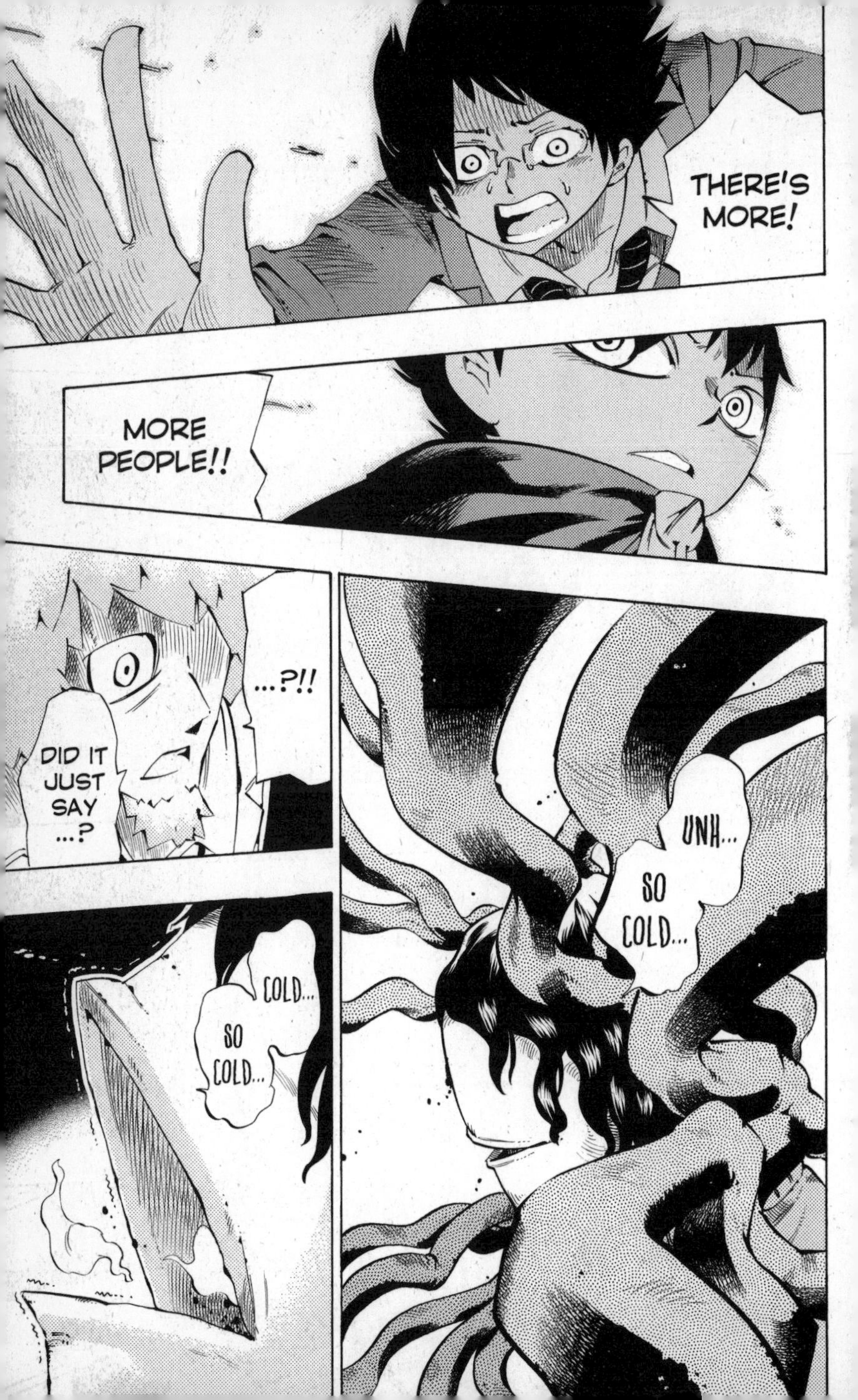
THERE'S MORE!
MORE PEOPLE!!
UNH... SO COLD...
...?!!
DID IT JUST SAY ...?
COLD...
SO COLD...

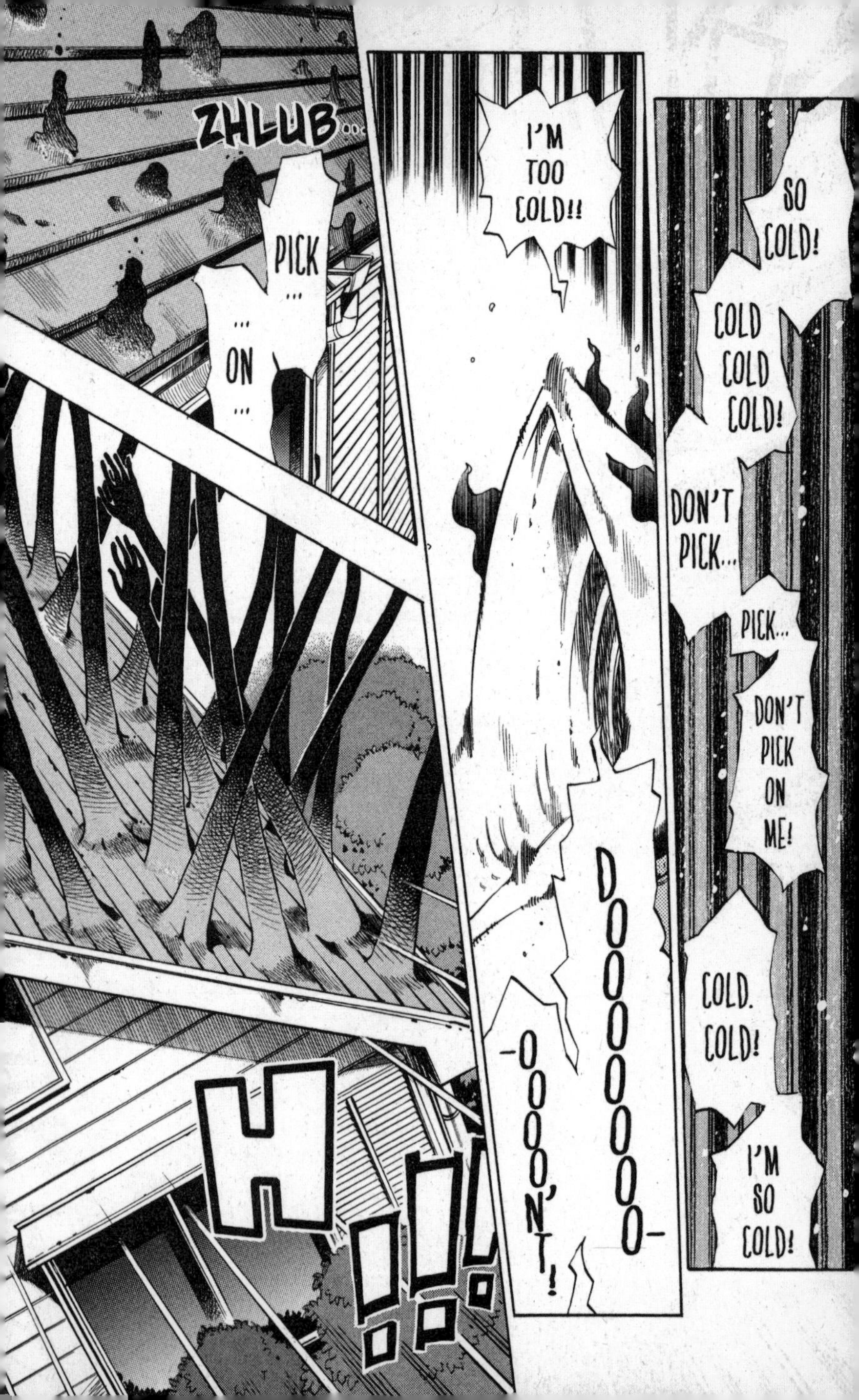
SO COLD!
COLD COLD COLD!
DON'T PICK...
PICK...
DON'T PICK ON ME!
COLD. COLD!
I'M SO COLD!
I'M TOO COLD!!
DOOOOOOOOO-
-OOOON'T!
ZHLUB...
PICK...
...ON...
H!!!

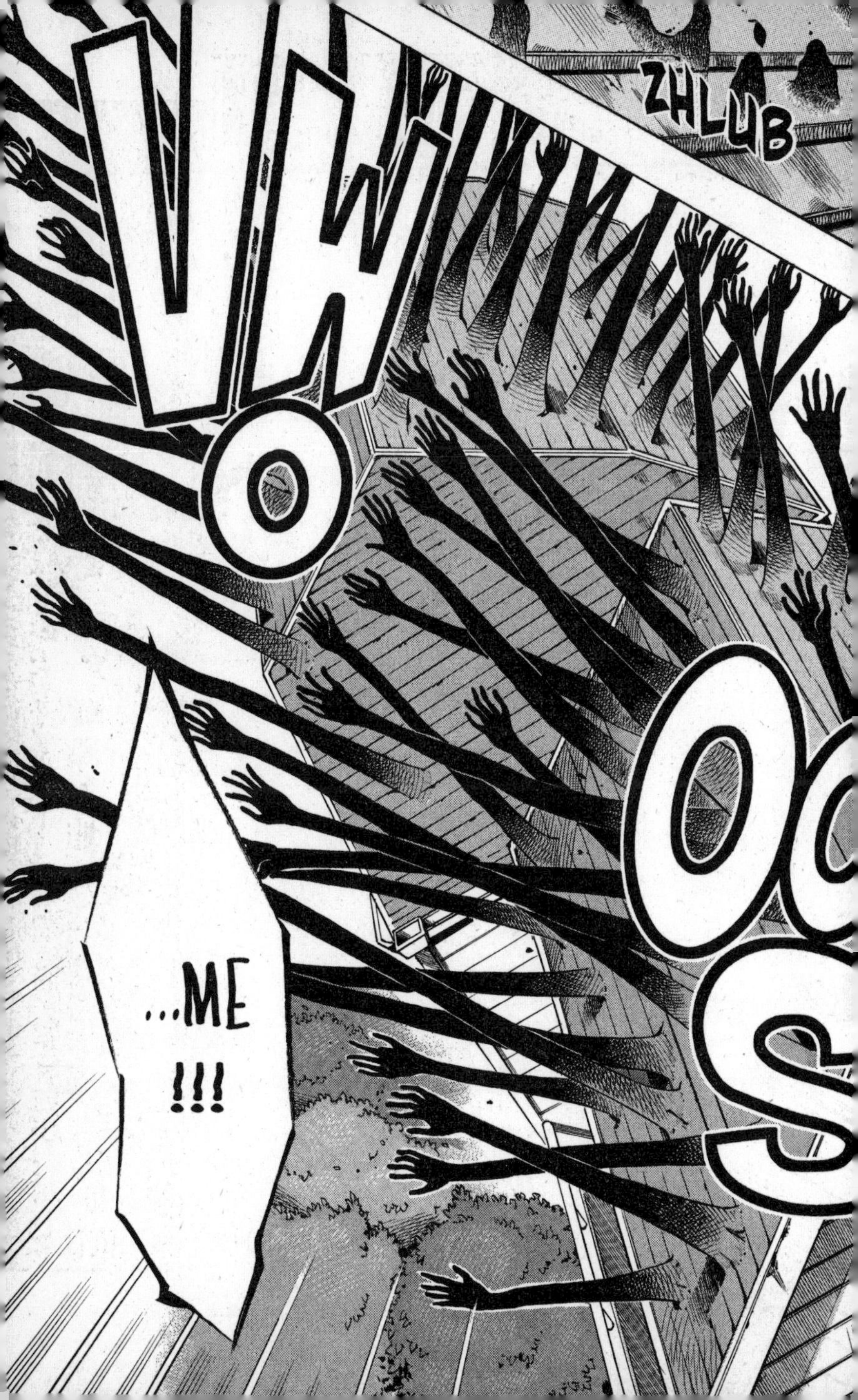
ZHLUB
VWOOOS
...ME
!!!

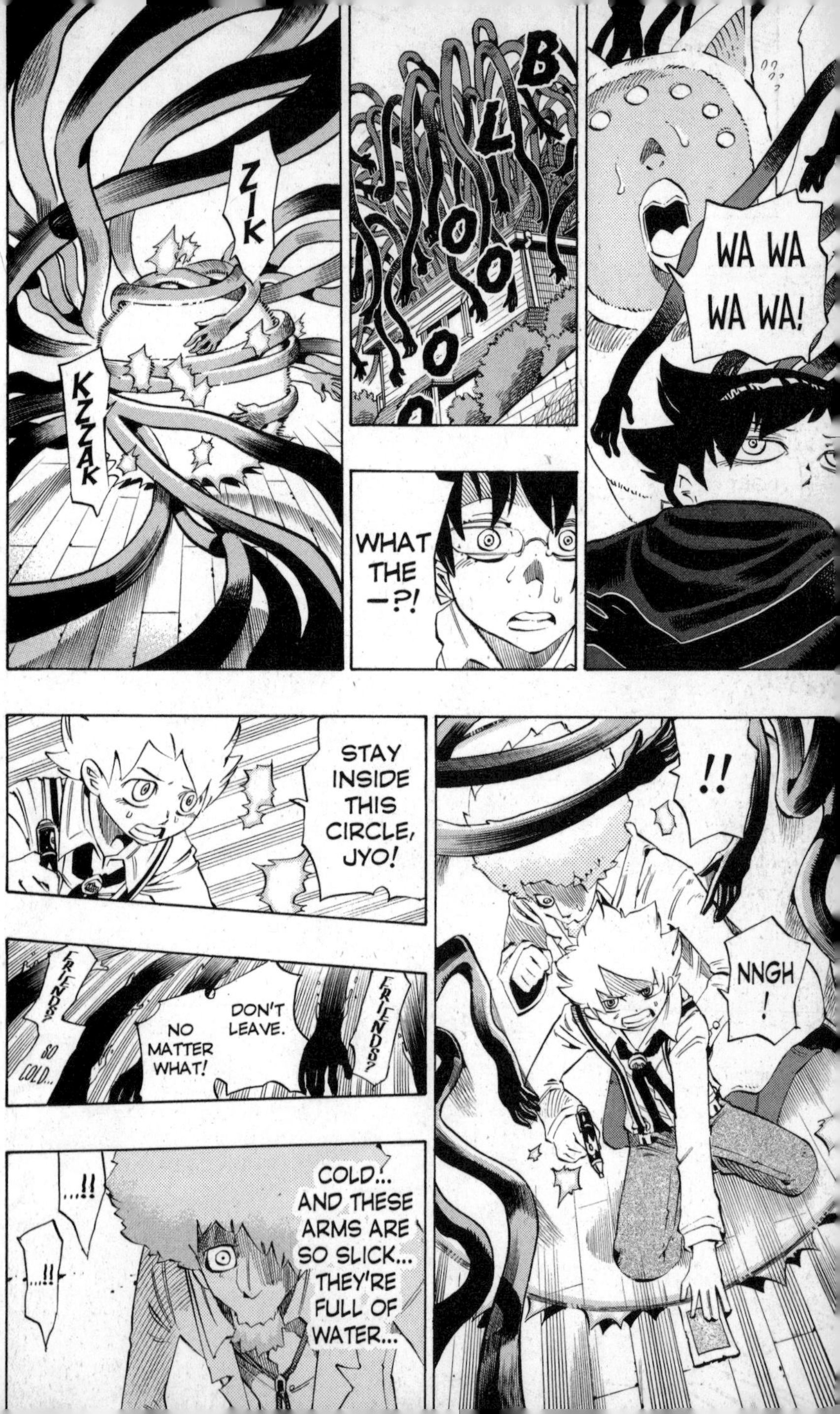
WA WA WA WA!
BLOOOO
WHAT THE—?!
ZIK
KZZAK
!!
NNGH!
STAY INSIDE THIS CIRCLE, JYO!
FRIENDS?
DON'T LEAVE.
NO MATTER WHAT!
FRIENDS?
SO COLD...
COLD... AND THESE ARMS ARE SO SLICK... THEY'RE FULL OF WATER...
...!!
...!!

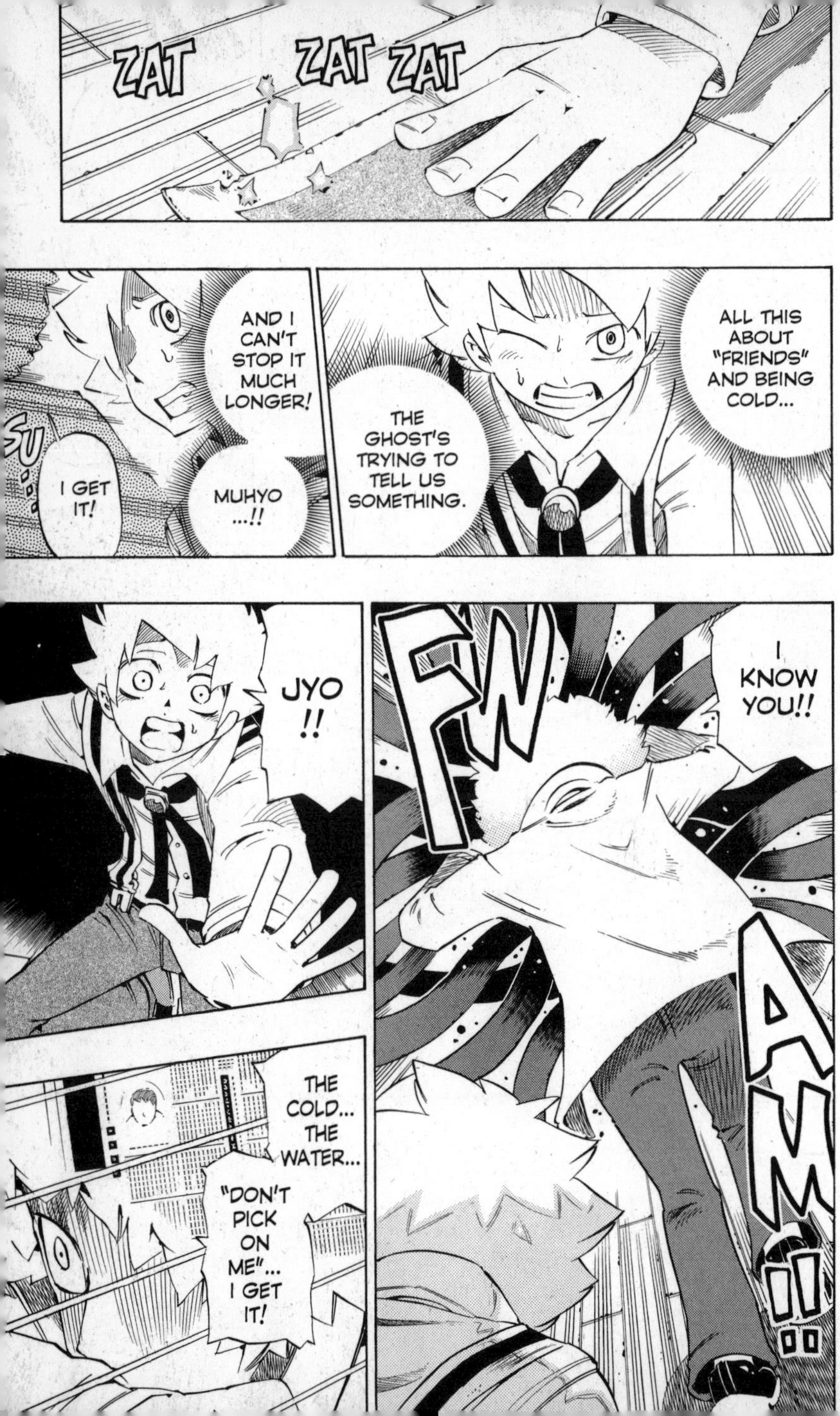
ZAT
ZAT ZAT
ALL THIS ABOUT "FRIENDS" AND BEING COLD...
THE GHOST'S TRYING TO TELL US SOMETHING.
AND I CAN'T STOP IT MUCH LONGER!
MUHYO ...!!
SU...
I GET IT!
I KNOW YOU!!
FW
AM!!
JYO !!
THE COLD... THE WATER...
"DON'T PICK ON ME"... I GET IT!

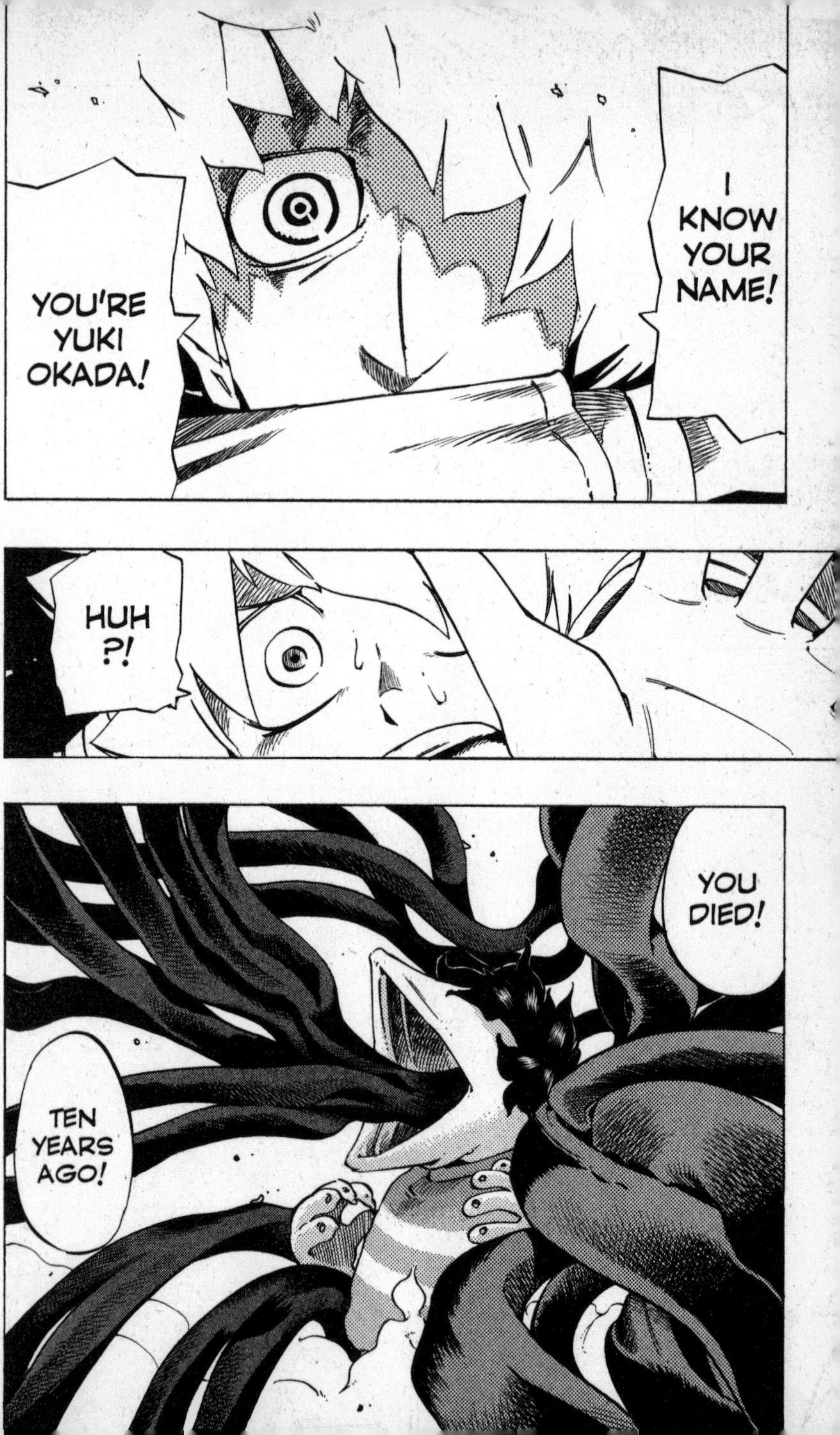
I KNOW YOUR NAME!
YOU'RE YUKI OKADA!
HUH ?!
YOU DIED!
TEN YEARS AGO!

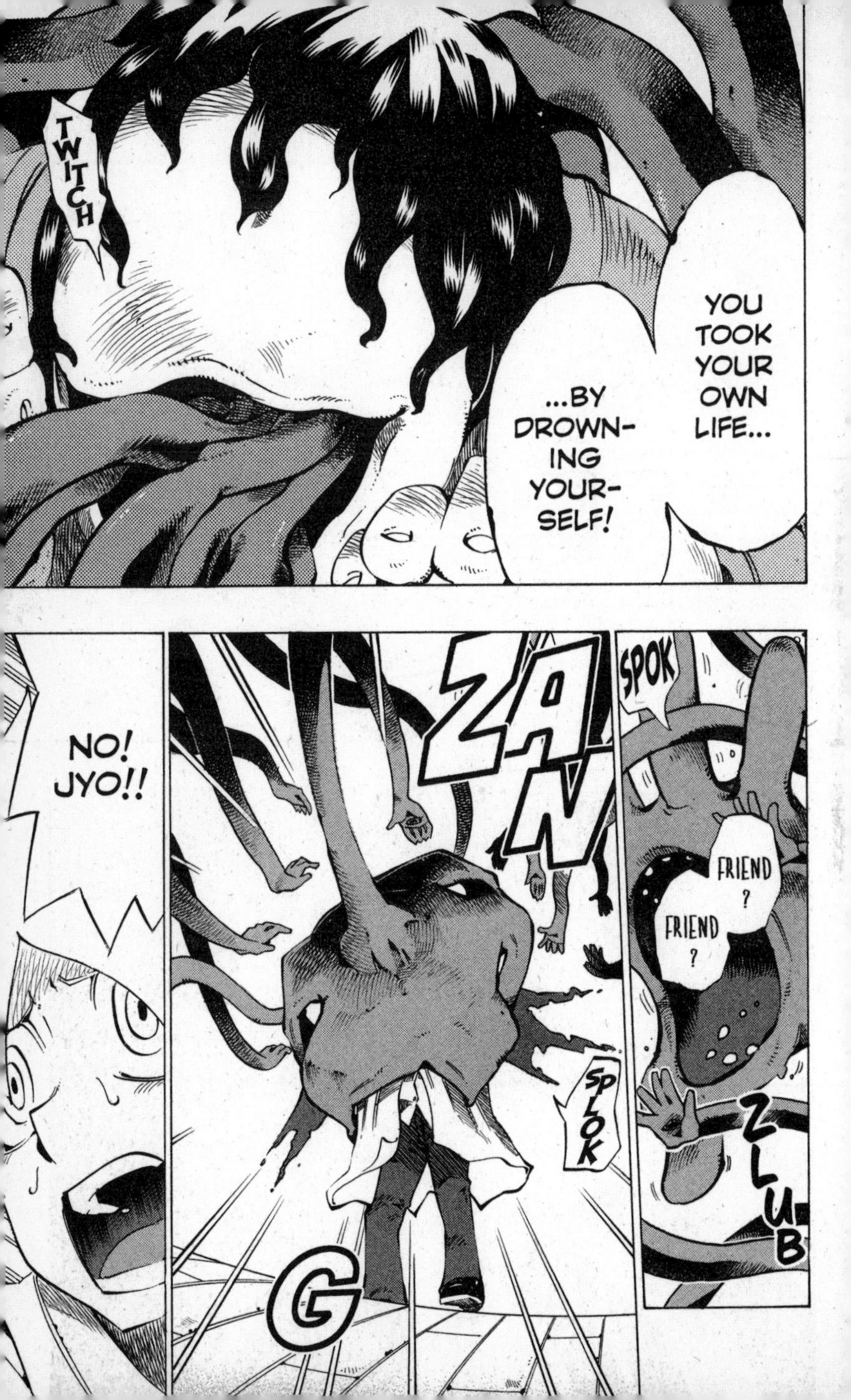
TWITCH
YOU TOOK YOUR OWN LIFE...
...BY DROWNING YOURSELF!
SPOK
FRIEND?
FRIEND?
ZLLUB
ZAN
SPLOK
G
NO! JYO!!

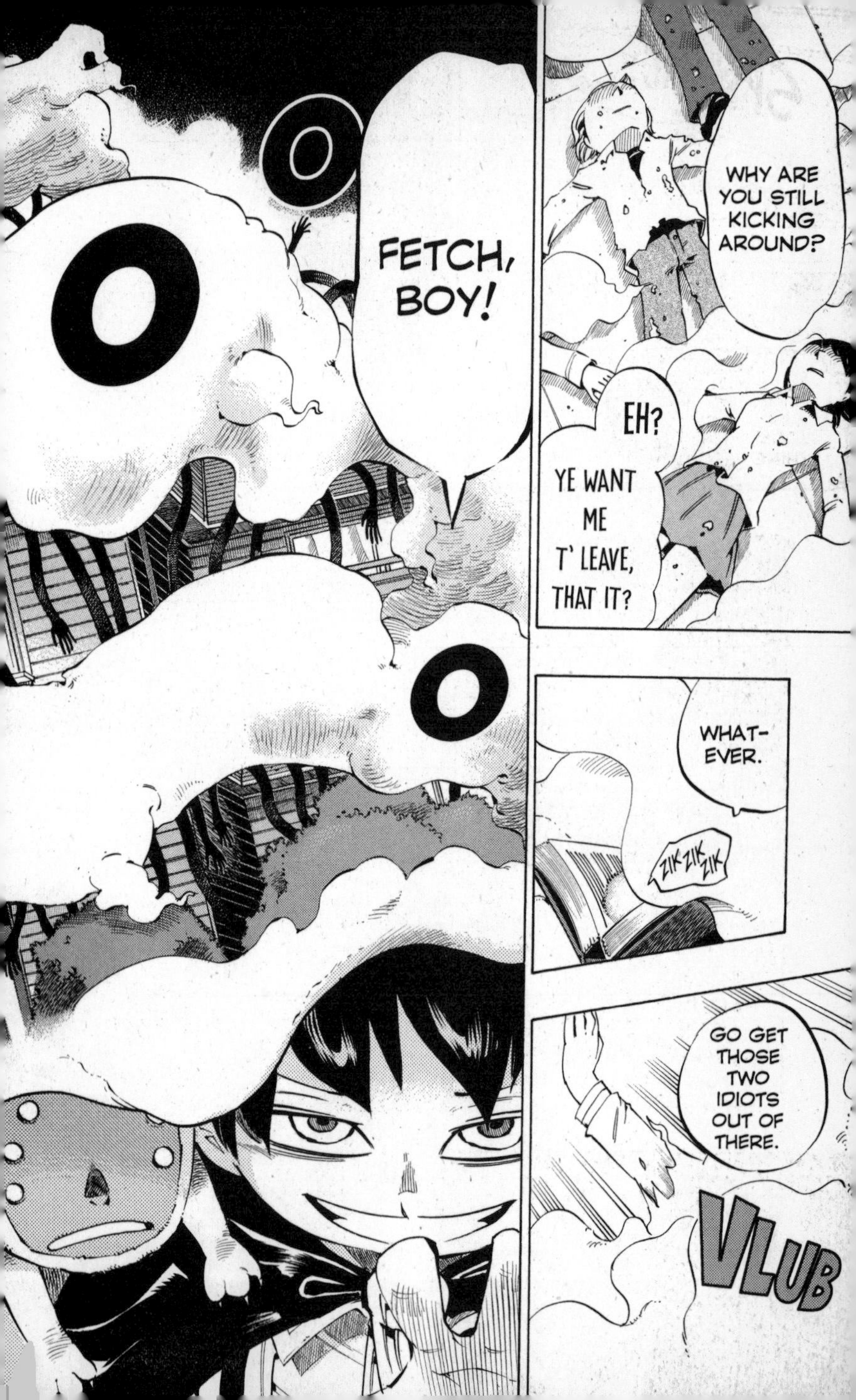
WHY ARE YOU STILL KICKING AROUND?
EH?
YE WANT ME T' LEAVE, THAT IT?
WHAT-EVER.
ZIK ZIK ZIK
GO GET THOSE TWO IDIOTS OUT OF THERE.
VLUB
FETCH, BOY!

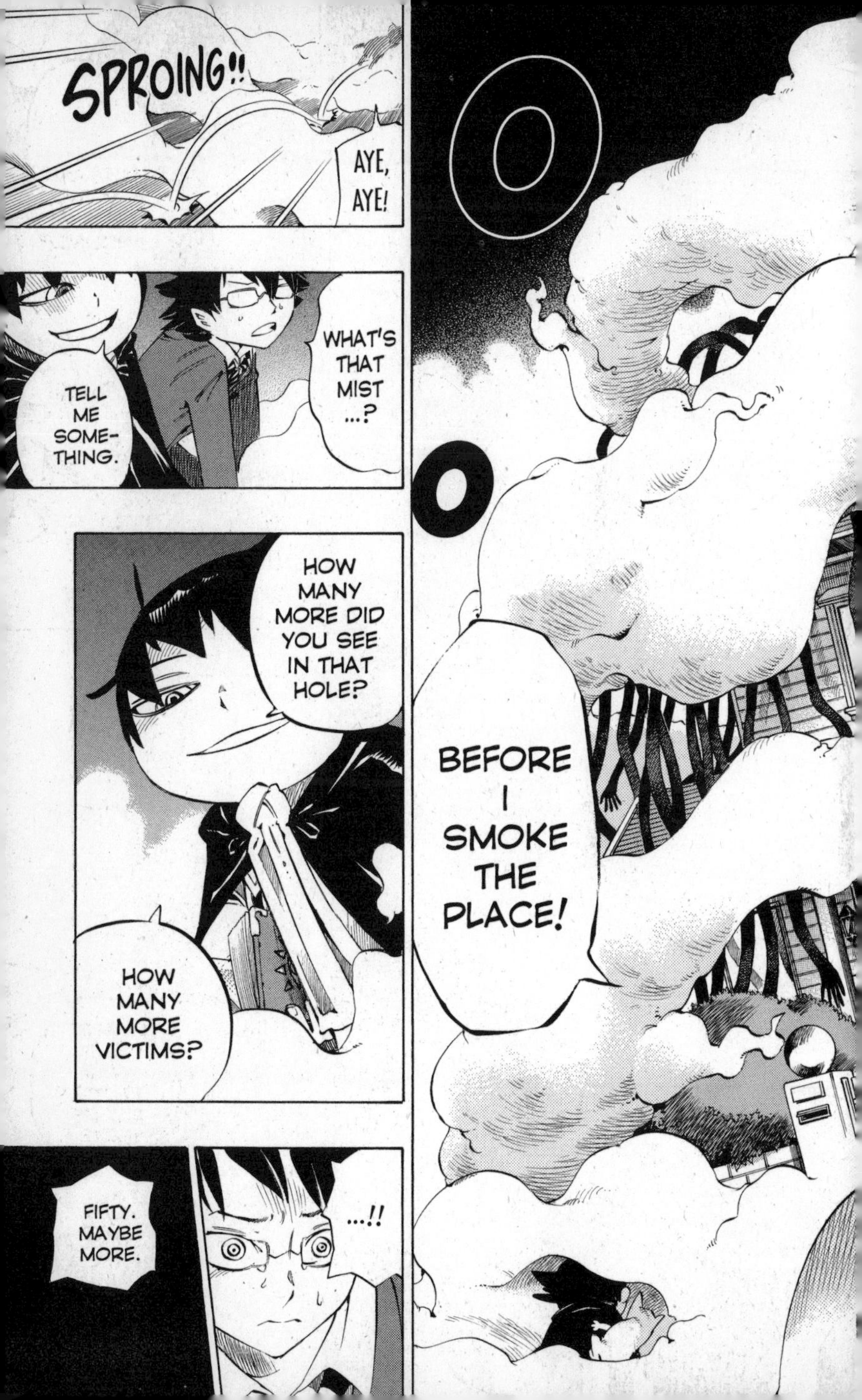
SPROING!!
AYE, AYE!
WHAT'S THAT MIST ...?
TELL ME SOME-THING.
HOW MANY MORE DID YOU SEE IN THAT HOLE?
HOW MANY MORE VICTIMS?
FIFTY. MAYBE MORE.
...!!
BEFORE I SMOKE THE PLACE!

Muhyo & Roji's
Bureau of Supernatural Investigation
BSI

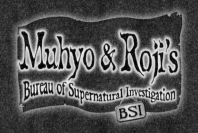

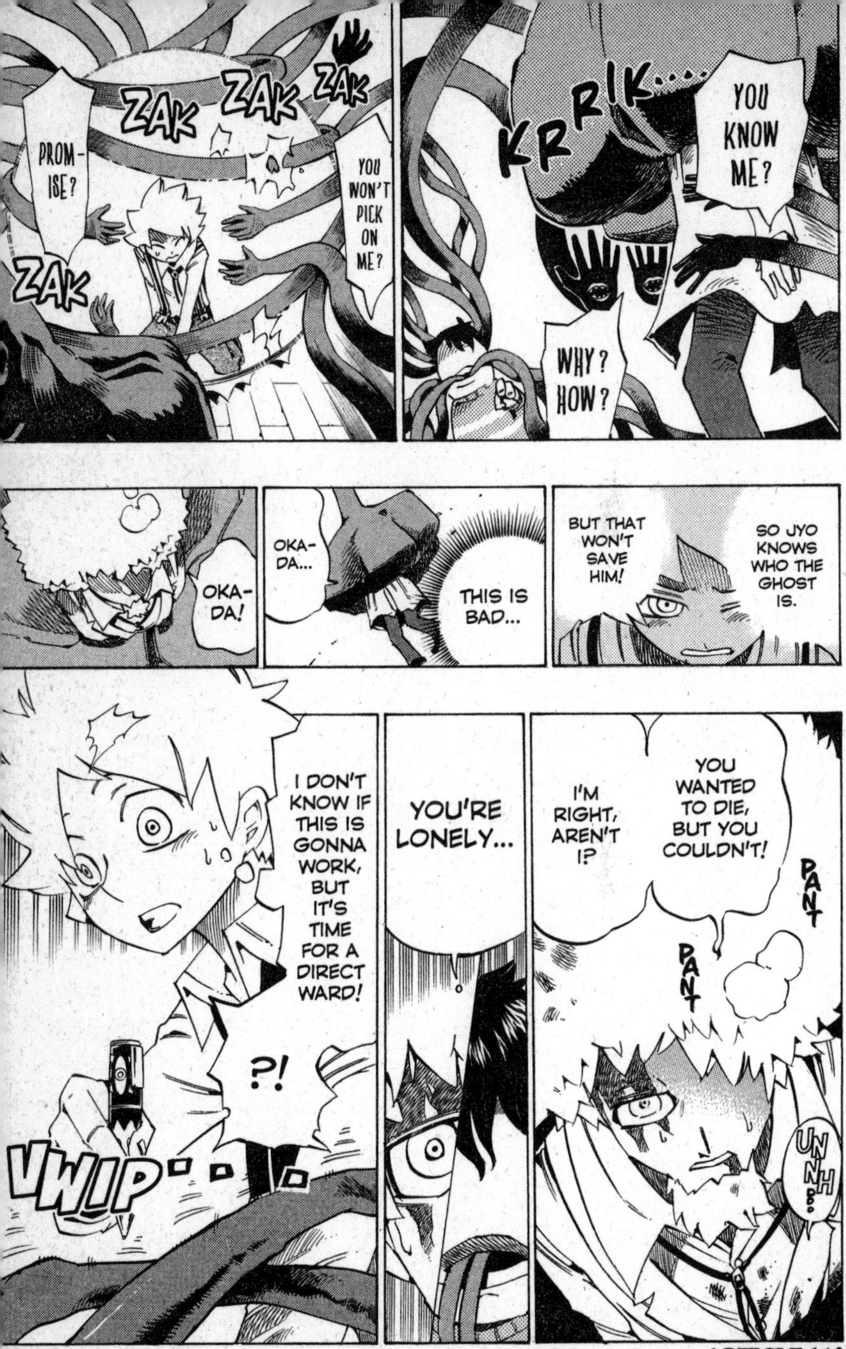
KRRIK....
YOU KNOW ME?
WHY? HOW?
ZAK
YOU WON'T PICK ON ME?
ZAK
ZAK
PROM-ISE?
ZAK
SO JYO KNOWS WHO THE GHOST IS.
BUT THAT WON'T SAVE HIM!
OKA-DA...
THIS IS BAD...
OKA-DA!
YOU WANTED TO DIE, BUT YOU COULDN'T!
I'M RIGHT, AREN'T I?
PANT
PANT
UNNH
YOU'RE LONELY...
I DON'T KNOW IF THIS IS GONNA WORK, BUT IT'S TIME FOR A DIRECT WARD!
?!
VWIP

ARTICLE 140

WHAT CANNOT BE SEEN

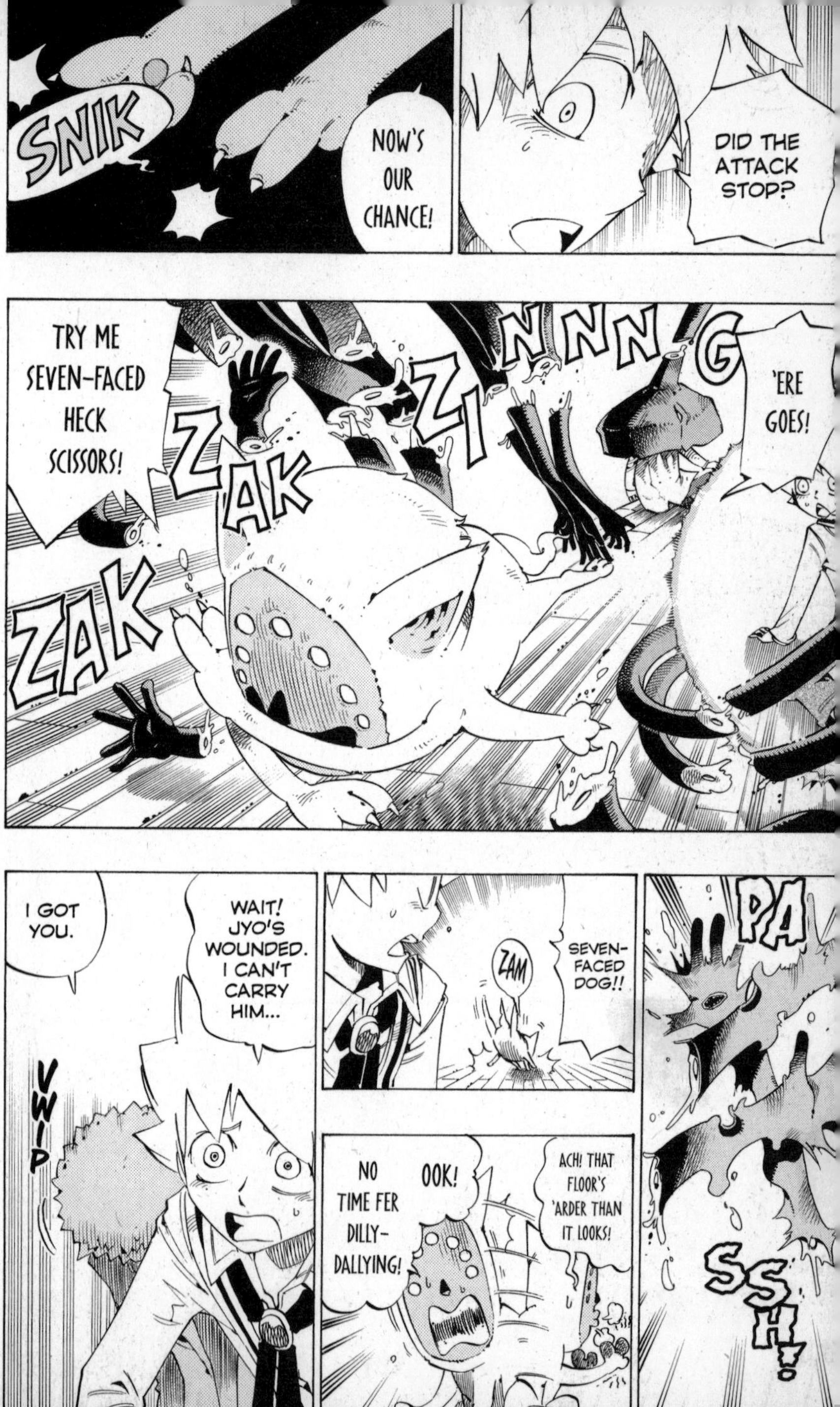
DID THE ATTACK STOP?
NOW'S OUR CHANCE!
SNIK
'ERE GOES!
ZINNNNG
TRY ME SEVEN-FACED HECK SCISSORS!
ZAK
ZAK
PA
SSH!
SEVEN-FACED DOG!!
ZAM
ACH! THAT FLOOR'S 'ARDER THAN IT LOOKS!
OOK!
NO TIME FER DILLY-DALLYING!
WAIT! JYO'S WOUNDED. I CAN'T CARRY HIM...
I GOT YOU.
VWIP

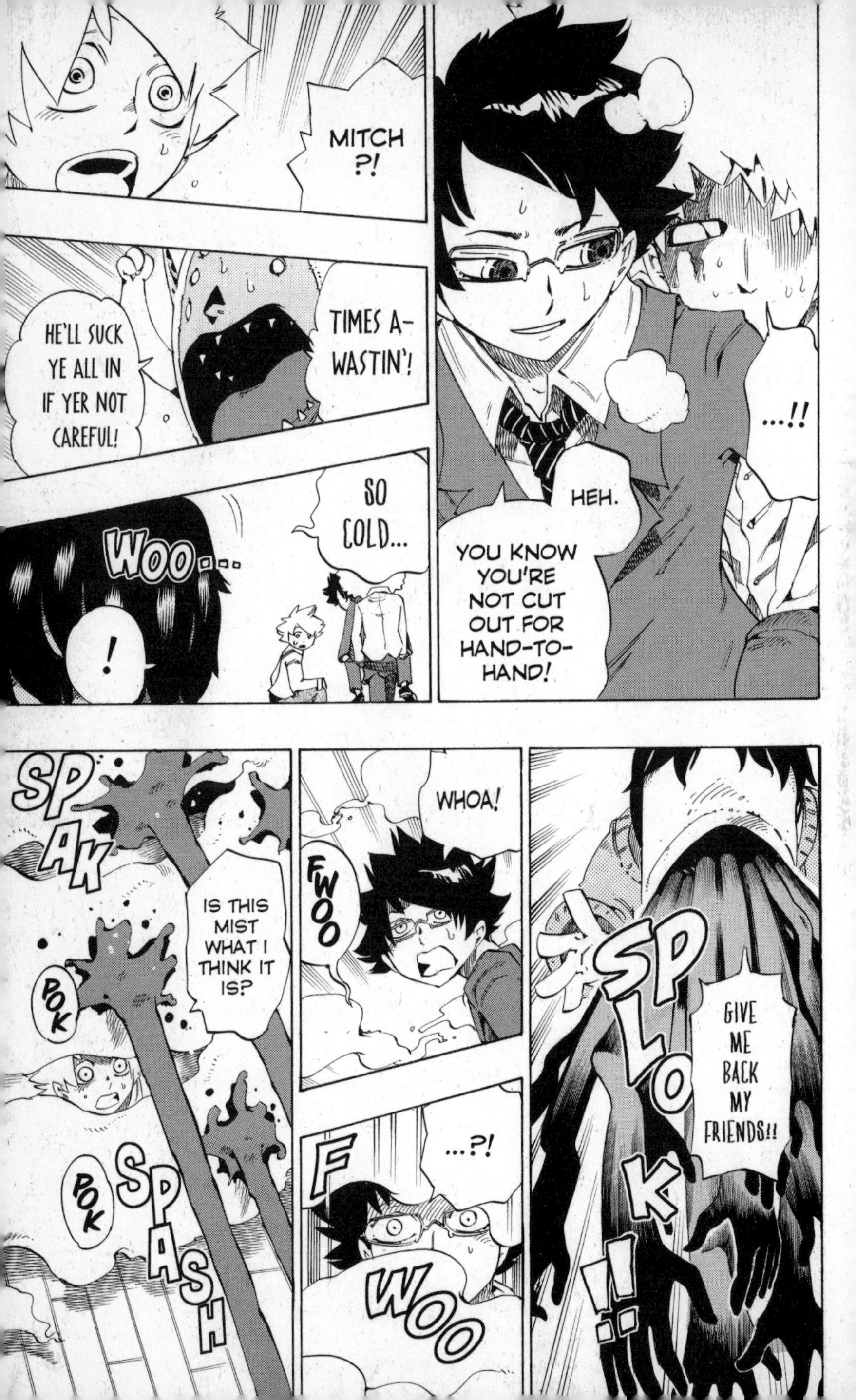
...!!
HEH.
YOU KNOW YOU'RE NOT CUT OUT FOR HAND-TO-HAND!
MITCH ?!
TIMES A-WASTIN'!
HE'LL SUCK YE ALL IN IF YER NOT CAREFUL!
SO COLD...
WOO...
!
SPLOK
GIVE ME BACK MY FRIENDS!!
!!
WHOA!
FWOO
...?!
F
WOO
SPAK
IS THIS MIST WHAT I THINK IT IS?
POK
POK
SPASH

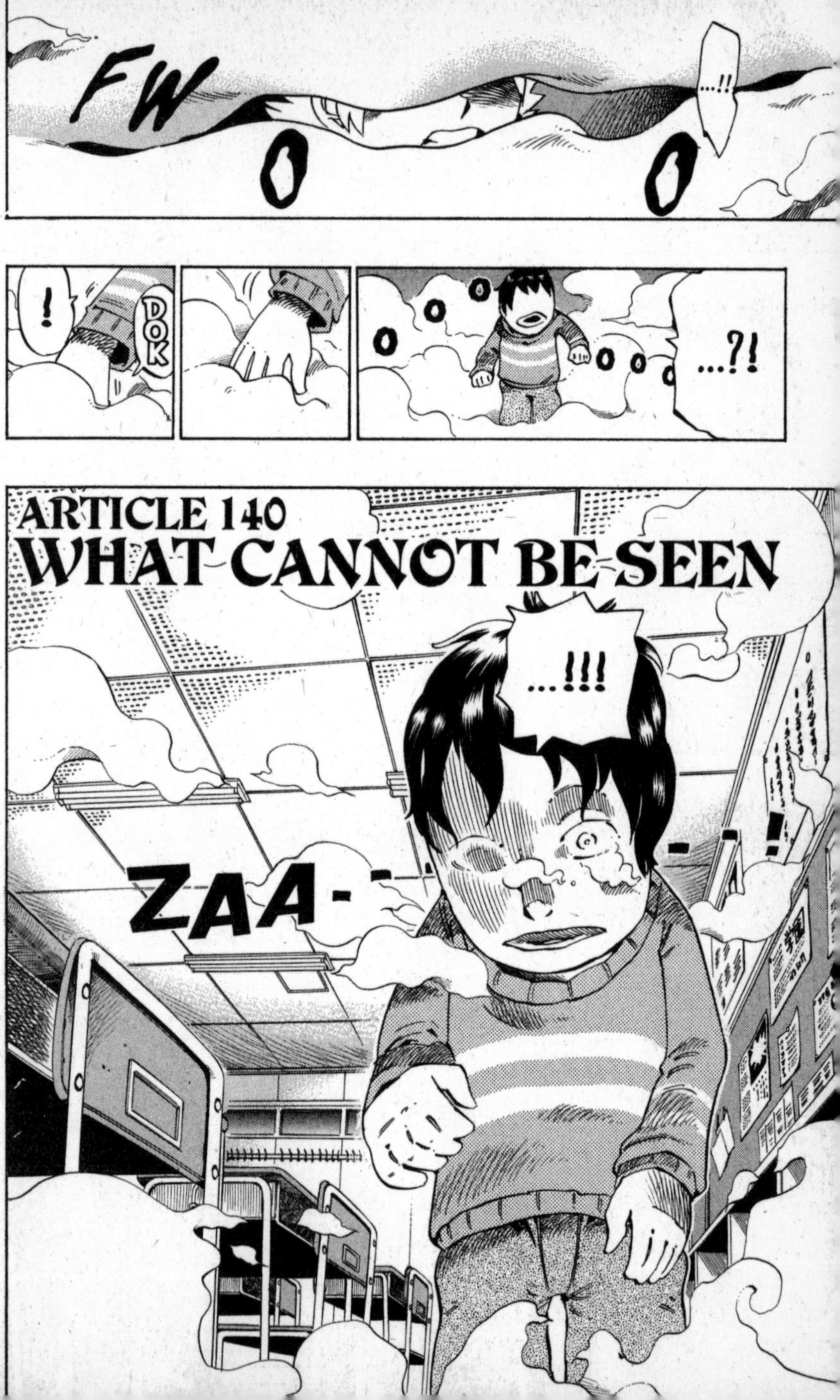
FWOO
...!!
OOOOOOO
...?!
!
DOK
ARTICLE 140
WHAT CANNOT BE SEEN
...!!!
ZAA---!

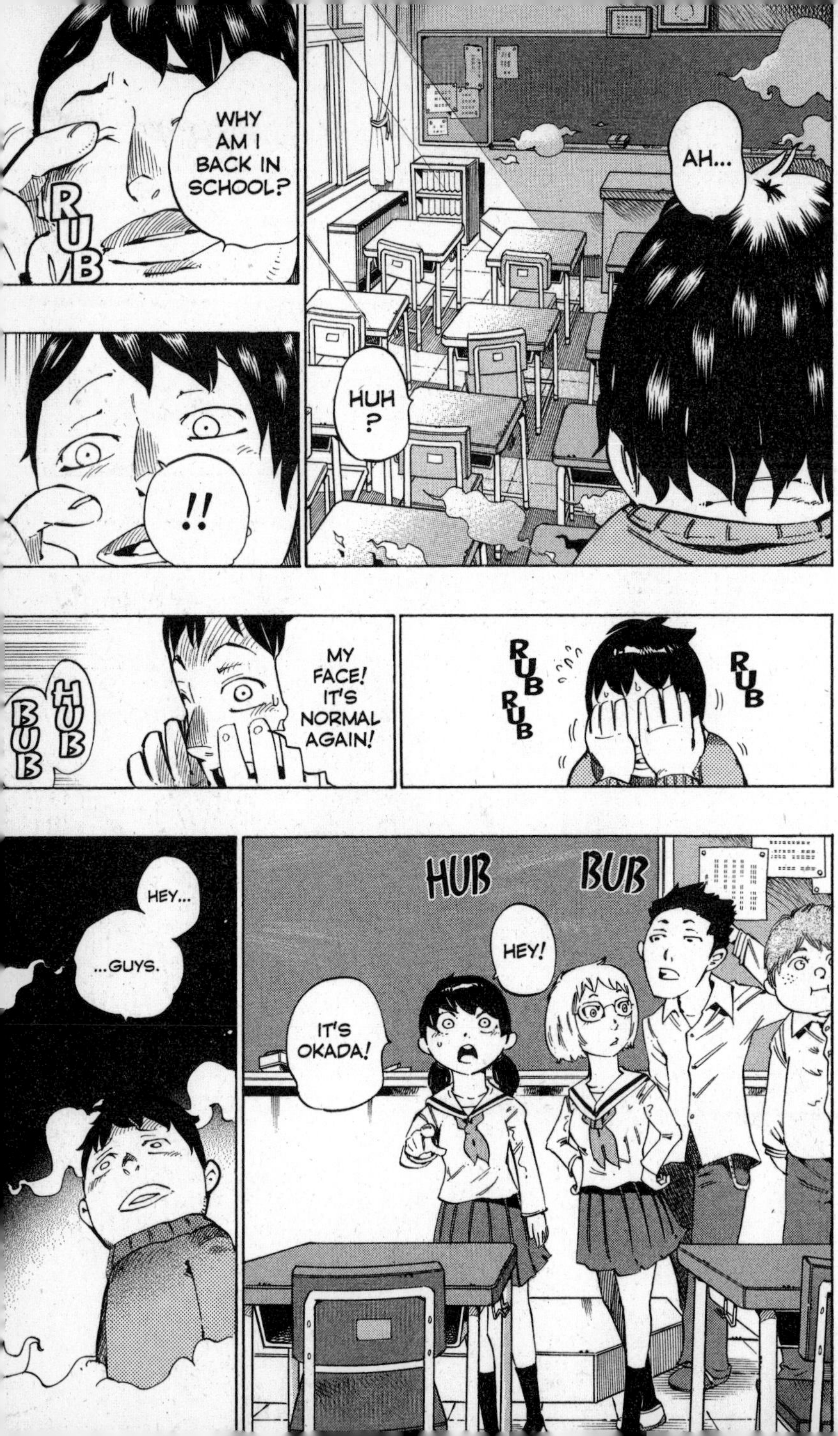
AH...
HUH?
RUB
WHY AM I BACK IN SCHOOL?
!!
RUB RUB
RUB
MY FACE! IT'S NORMAL AGAIN!
HUB BUB
HUB BUB
HEY!
IT'S OKADA!
HEY...
...GUYS.

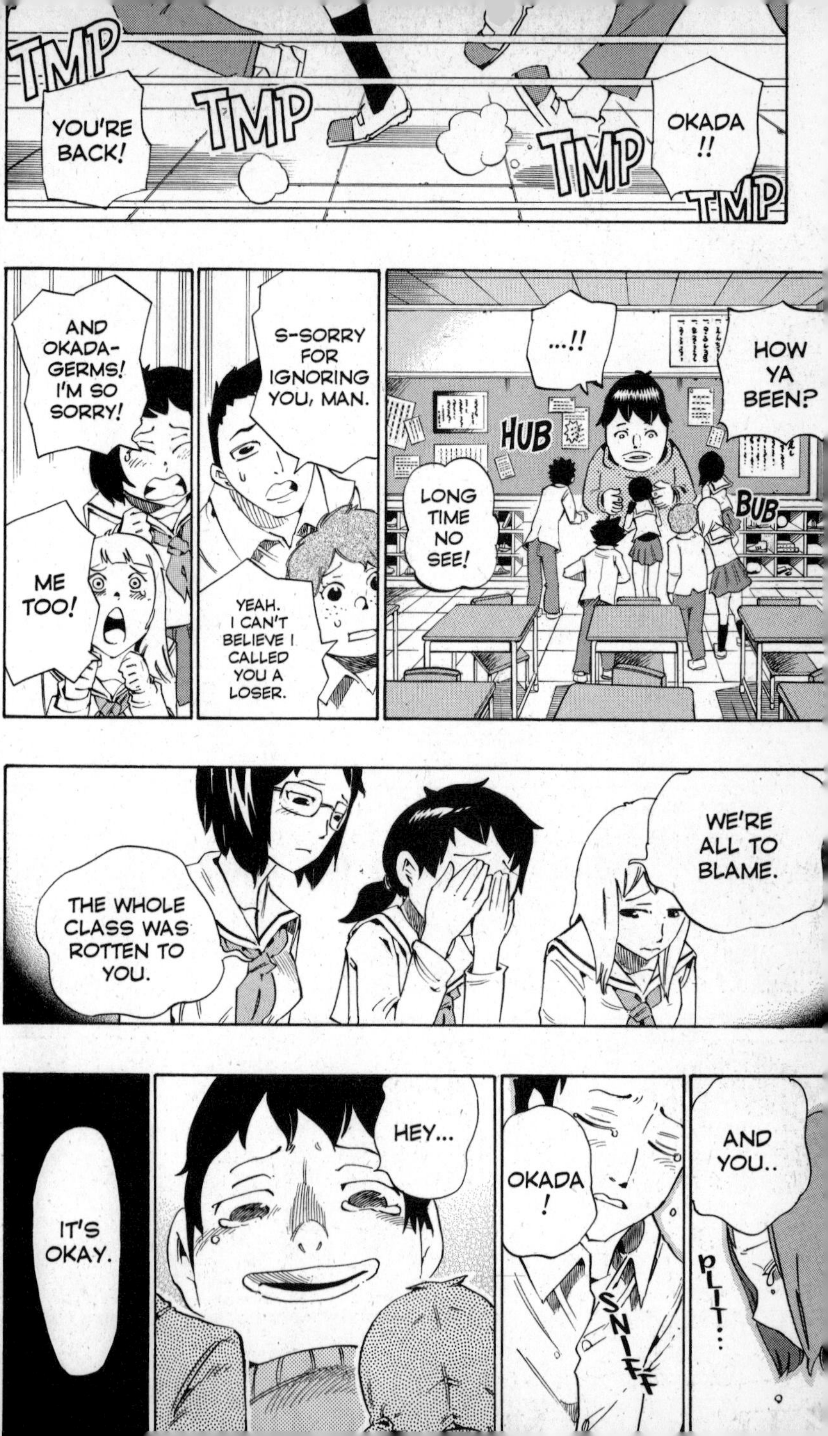
OKADA !!
TMP
TMP
TMP
YOU'RE BACK!
TMP
HOW YA BEEN?
...!!
HUB
BUB
LONG TIME NO SEE!
S-SORRY FOR IGNORING YOU, MAN.
YEAH. I CAN'T BELIEVE I CALLED YOU A LOSER.
AND OKADA-GERMS! I'M SO SORRY!
ME TOO!
WE'RE ALL TO BLAME.
THE WHOLE CLASS WAS ROTTEN TO YOU.
AND YOU..
PLIT...
OKADA !
SNIFF
HEY...
IT'S OKAY.

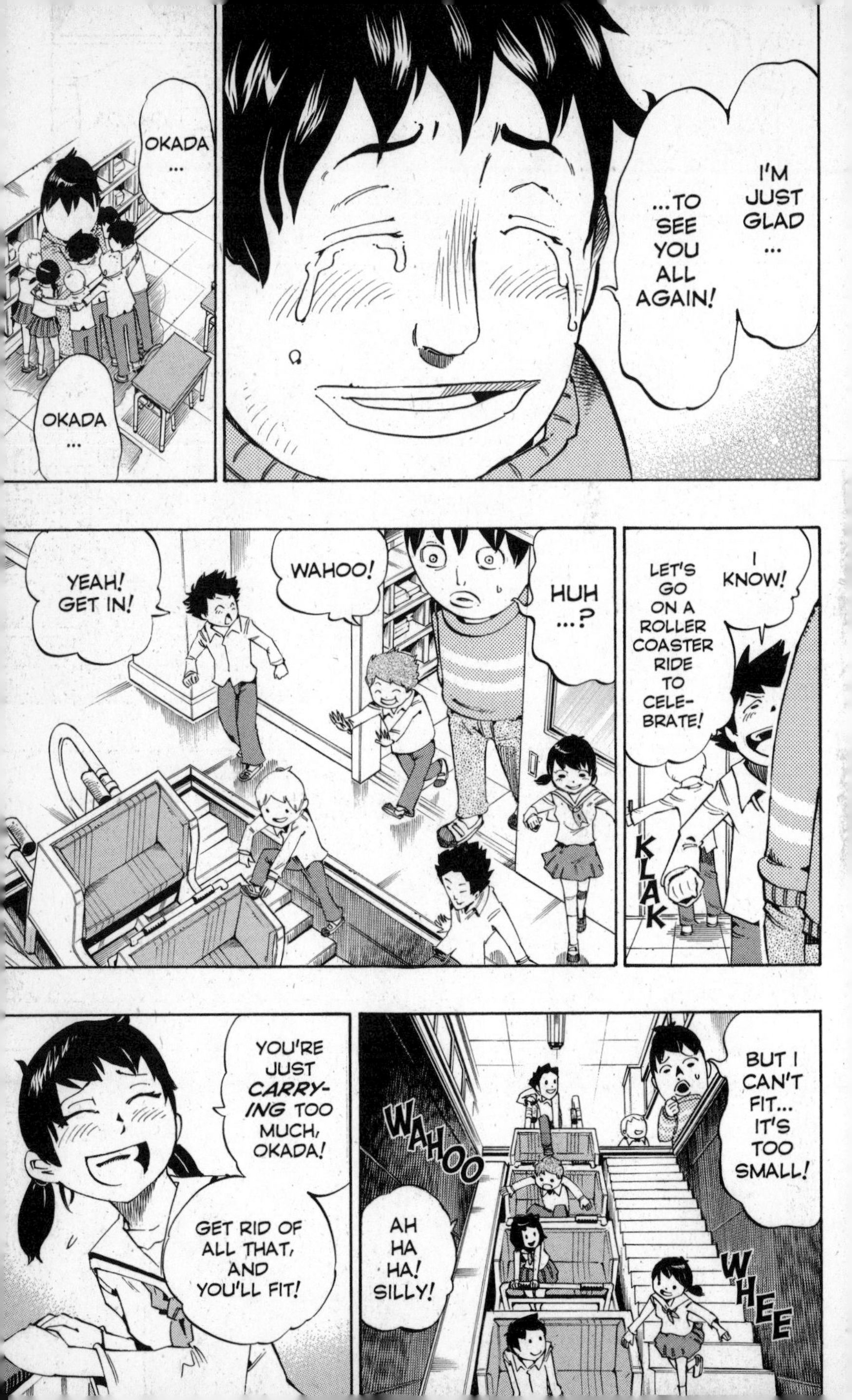
I'M JUST GLAD...
...TO SEE YOU ALL AGAIN!
OKADA...
OKADA...
I KNOW!
LET'S GO ON A ROLLER COASTER RIDE TO CELEBRATE!
KLAK
HUH...?
WAHOO!
YEAH! GET IN!
BUT I CAN'T FIT... IT'S TOO SMALL!
WAHOO
WHEE
AH HA HA! SILLY!
YOU'RE JUST *CARRYING* TOO MUCH, OKADA!
GET RID OF ALL THAT, AND YOU'LL FIT!

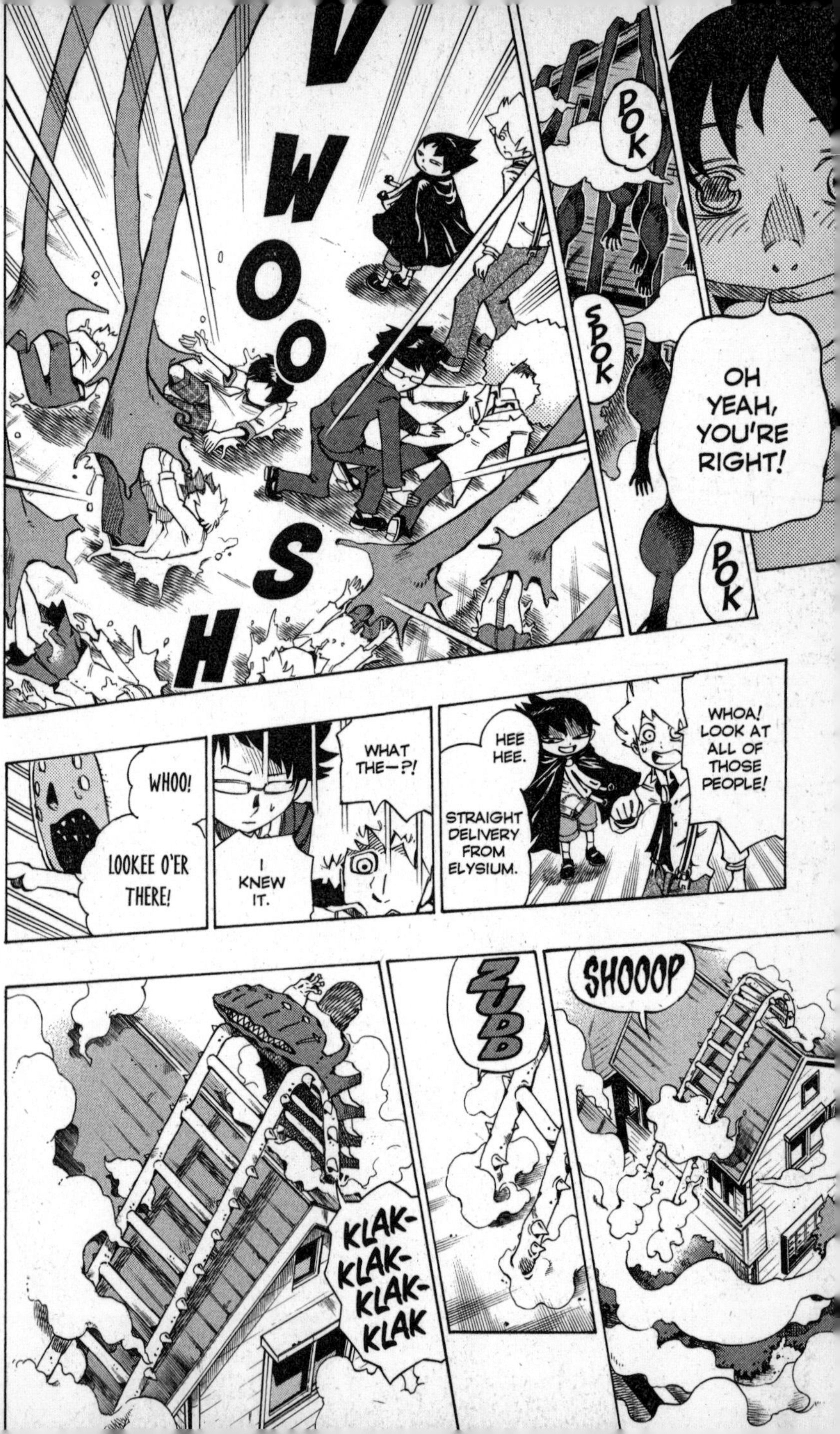
OH YEAH, YOU'RE RIGHT!
POK
SPOK
POK
VWOOSH
WHOA! LOOK AT ALL OF THOSE PEOPLE!
HEE HEE.
STRAIGHT DELIVERY FROM ELYSIUM.
WHAT THE—?!
I KNEW IT.
WHOO!
LOOKEE O'ER THERE!
SHOOOP
ZUDD
KLAK-KLAK-KLAK-KLAK

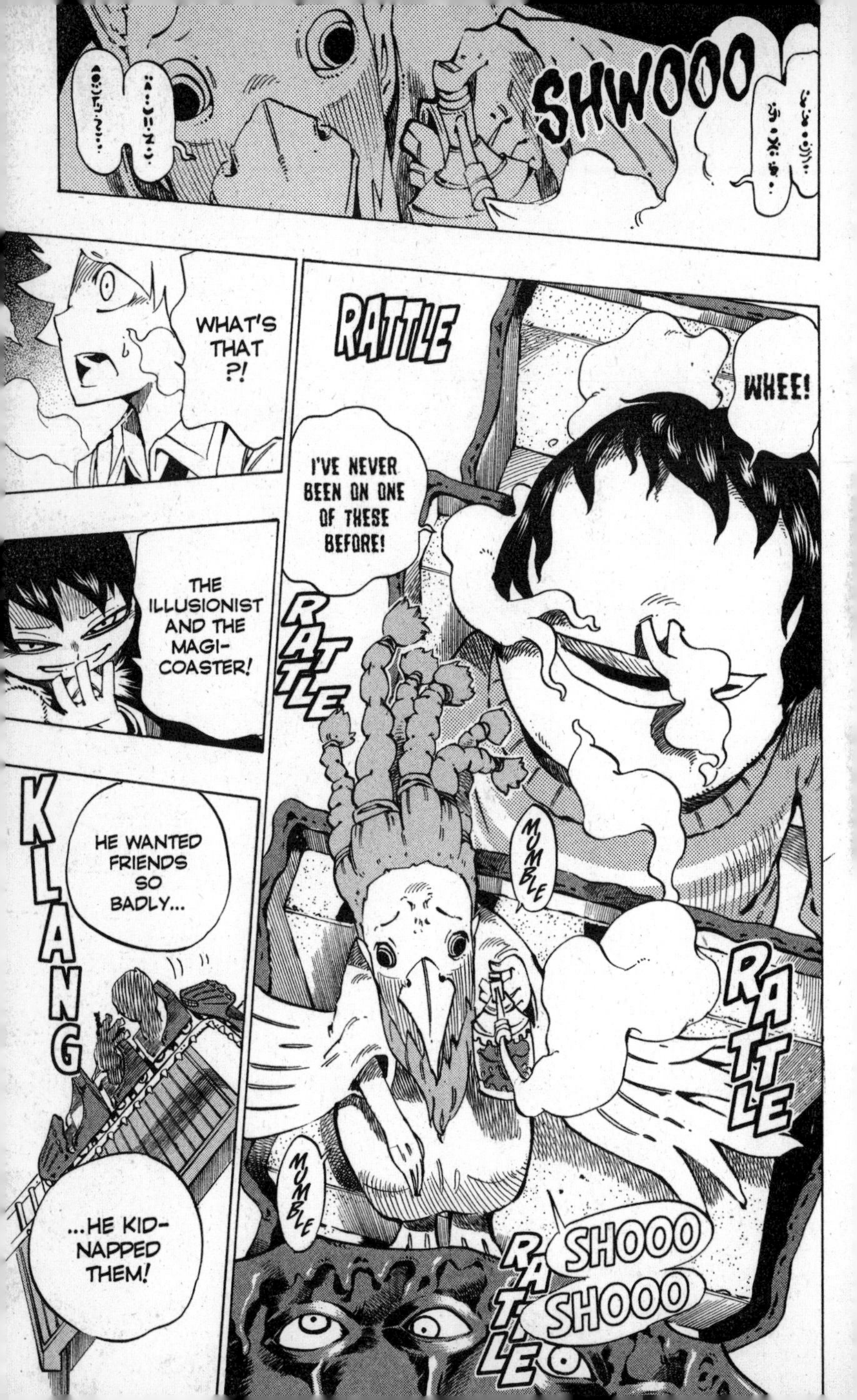
SHWOOO
RATTLE
WHEE!
I'VE NEVER BEEN ON ONE OF THESE BEFORE!
RATTLE
MUMBLE
RATTLE
MUMBLE
RATTLE
SHOOO
SHOOO
WHAT'S THAT?!
THE ILLUSIONIST AND THE MAGI-COASTER!
KLLANG
HE WANTED FRIENDS SO BADLY...
...HE KID-NAPPED THEM!

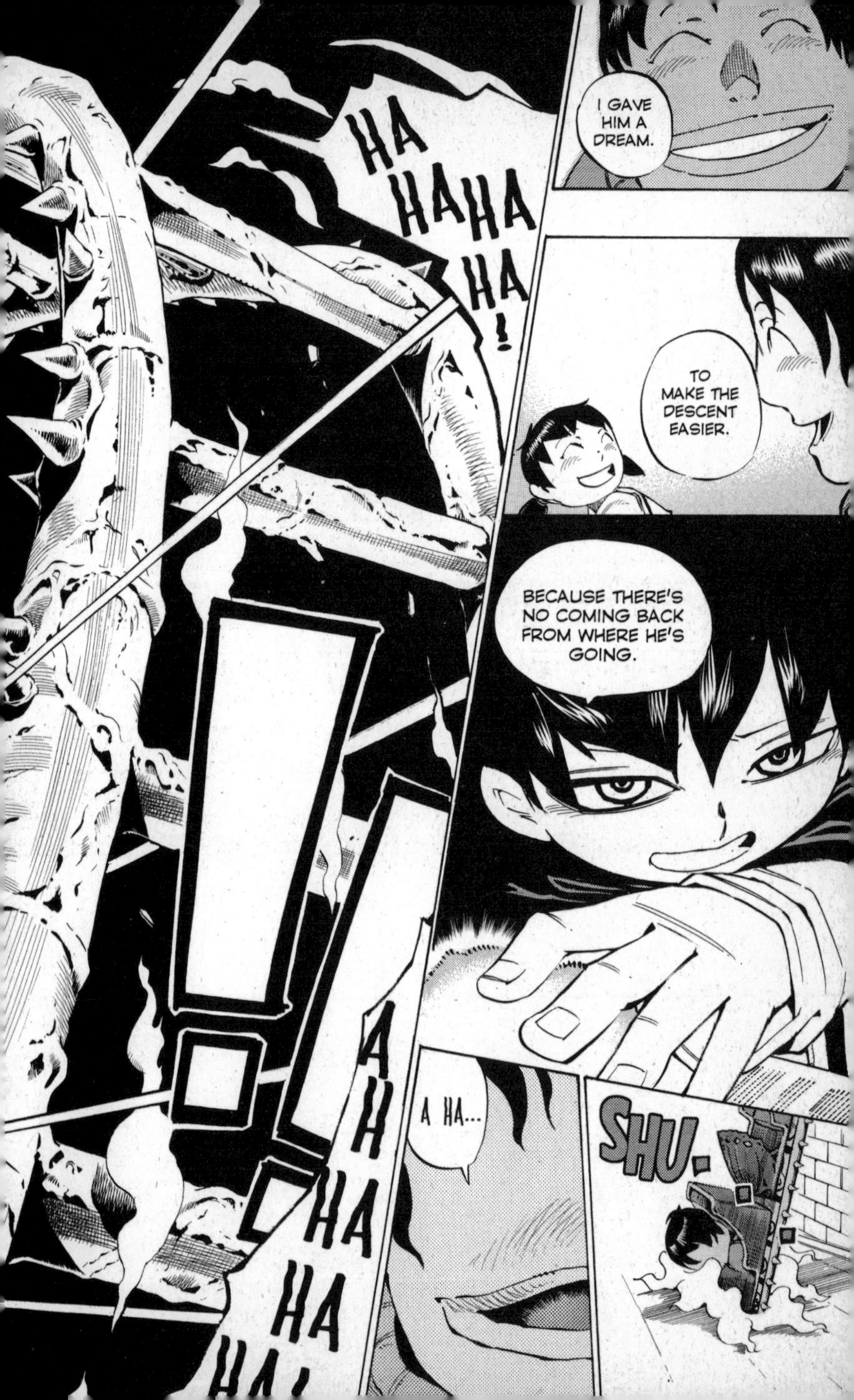
I GAVE HIM A DREAM.
TO MAKE THE DESCENT EASIER.
BECAUSE THERE'S NO COMING BACK FROM WHERE HE'S GOING.
SHU.
A HA...
HA HAHA HA HA!
AHH HA HA HA HA

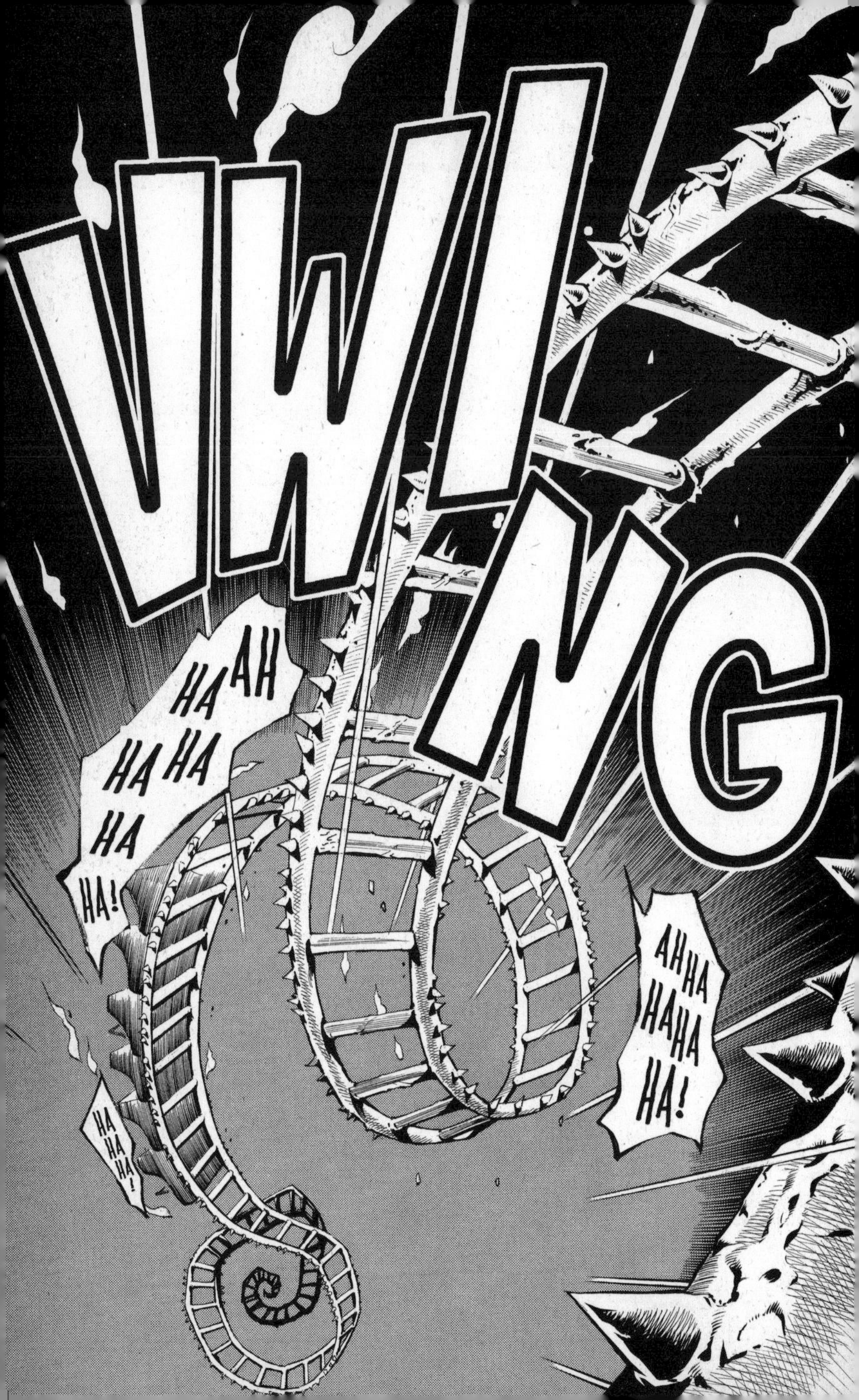
VWING
AH HA HA HA HA HA!
AH HA HA HA HA HA!
HA HA HA!

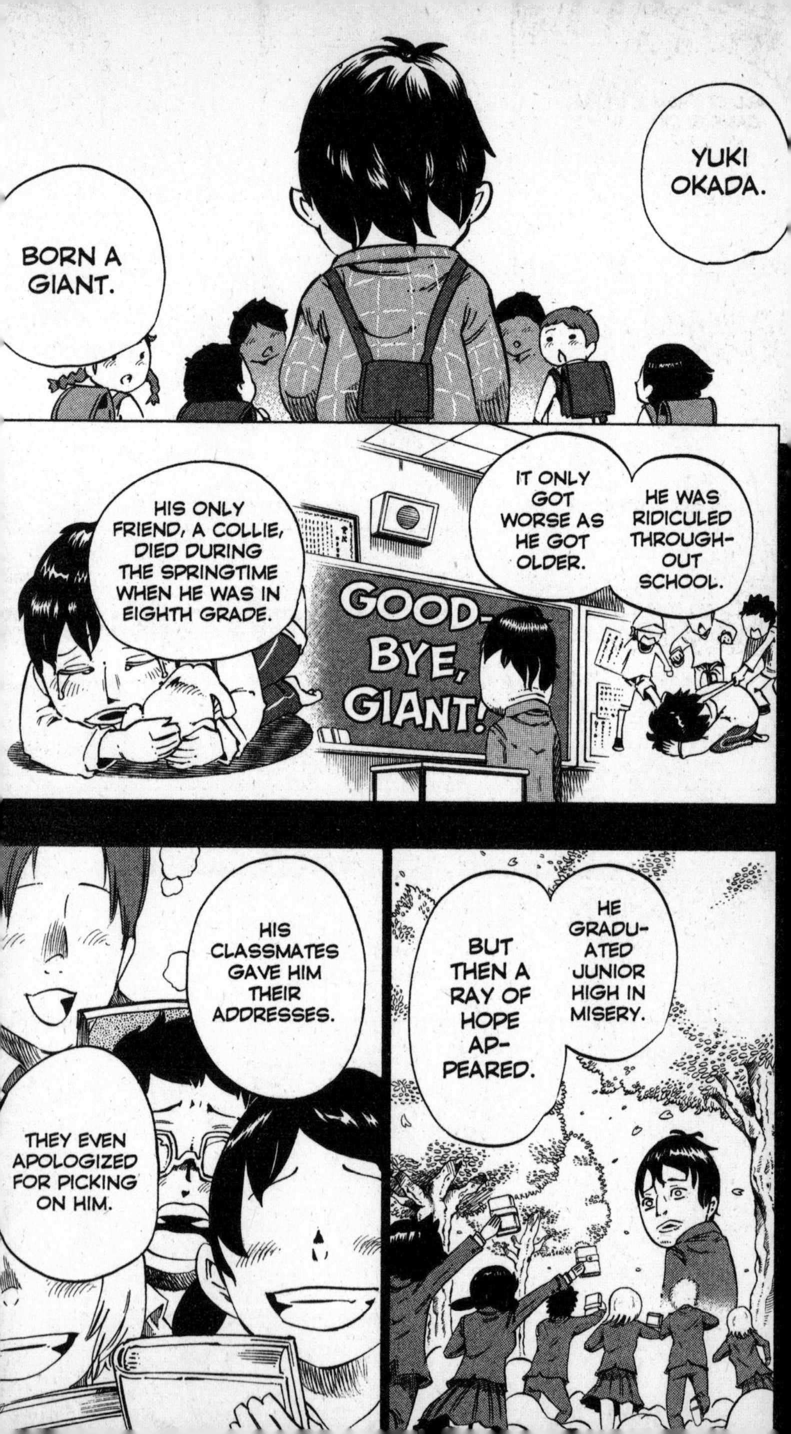
YUKI OKADA.
BORN A GIANT.
HE WAS RIDICULED THROUGHOUT SCHOOL.
IT ONLY GOT WORSE AS HE GOT OLDER.
HIS ONLY FRIEND, A COLLIE, DIED DURING THE SPRINGTIME WHEN HE WAS IN EIGHTH GRADE.
GOOD-BYE, GIANT!
HE GRADUATED JUNIOR HIGH IN MISERY.
BUT THEN A RAY OF HOPE APPEARED.
HIS CLASSMATES GAVE HIM THEIR ADDRESSES.
THEY EVEN APOLOGIZED FOR PICKING ON HIM.

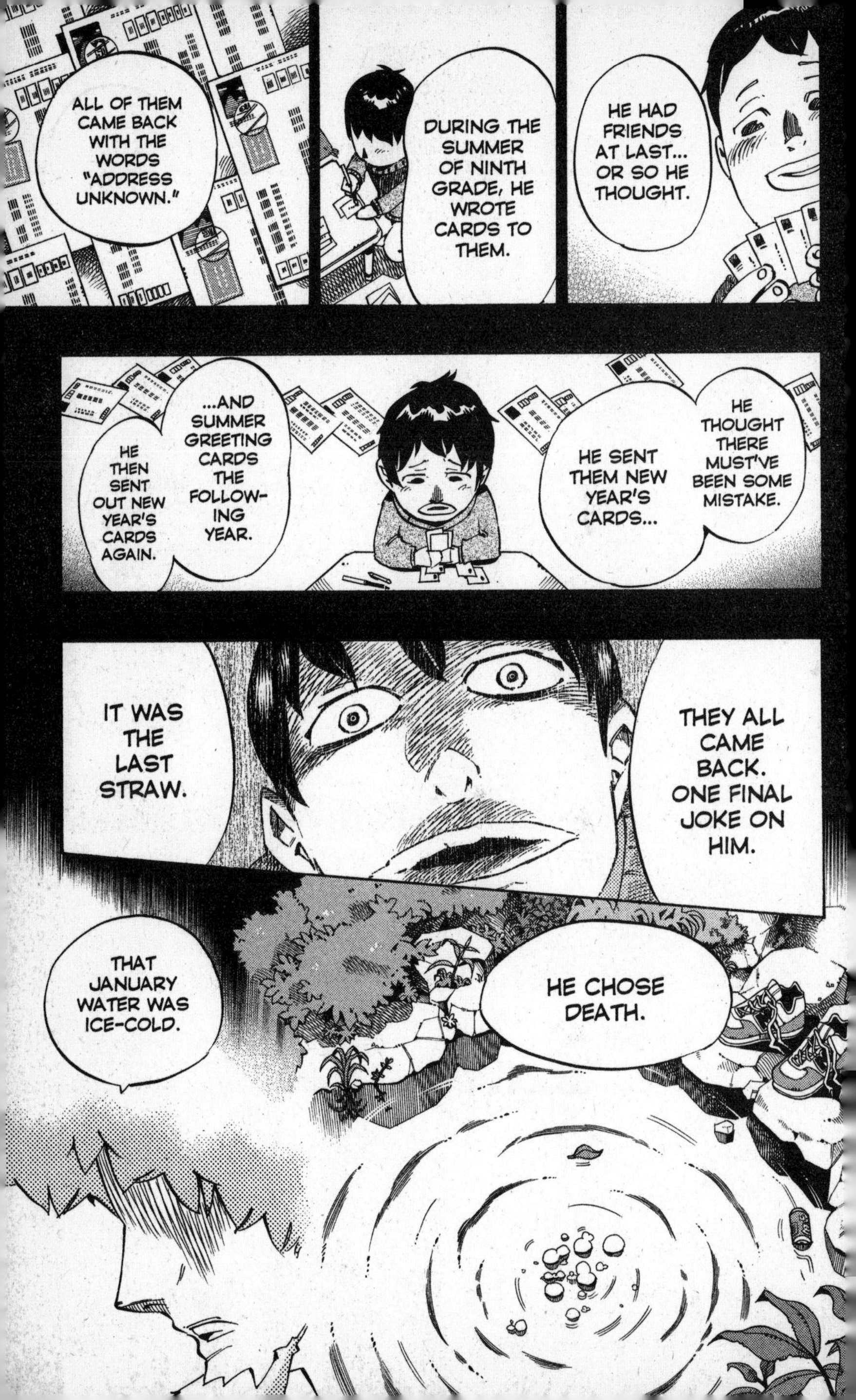
HE HAD FRIENDS AT LAST... OR SO HE THOUGHT.
DURING THE SUMMER OF NINTH GRADE, HE WROTE CARDS TO THEM.
ALL OF THEM CAME BACK WITH THE WORDS "ADDRESS UNKNOWN."
HE THOUGHT THERE MUST'VE BEEN SOME MISTAKE.
HE SENT THEM NEW YEAR'S CARDS...
...AND SUMMER GREETING CARDS THE FOLLOW-ING YEAR.
HE THEN SENT OUT NEW YEAR'S CARDS AGAIN.
THEY ALL CAME BACK. ONE FINAL JOKE ON HIM.
IT WAS THE LAST STRAW.
HE CHOSE DEATH.
THAT JANUARY WATER WAS ICE-COLD.

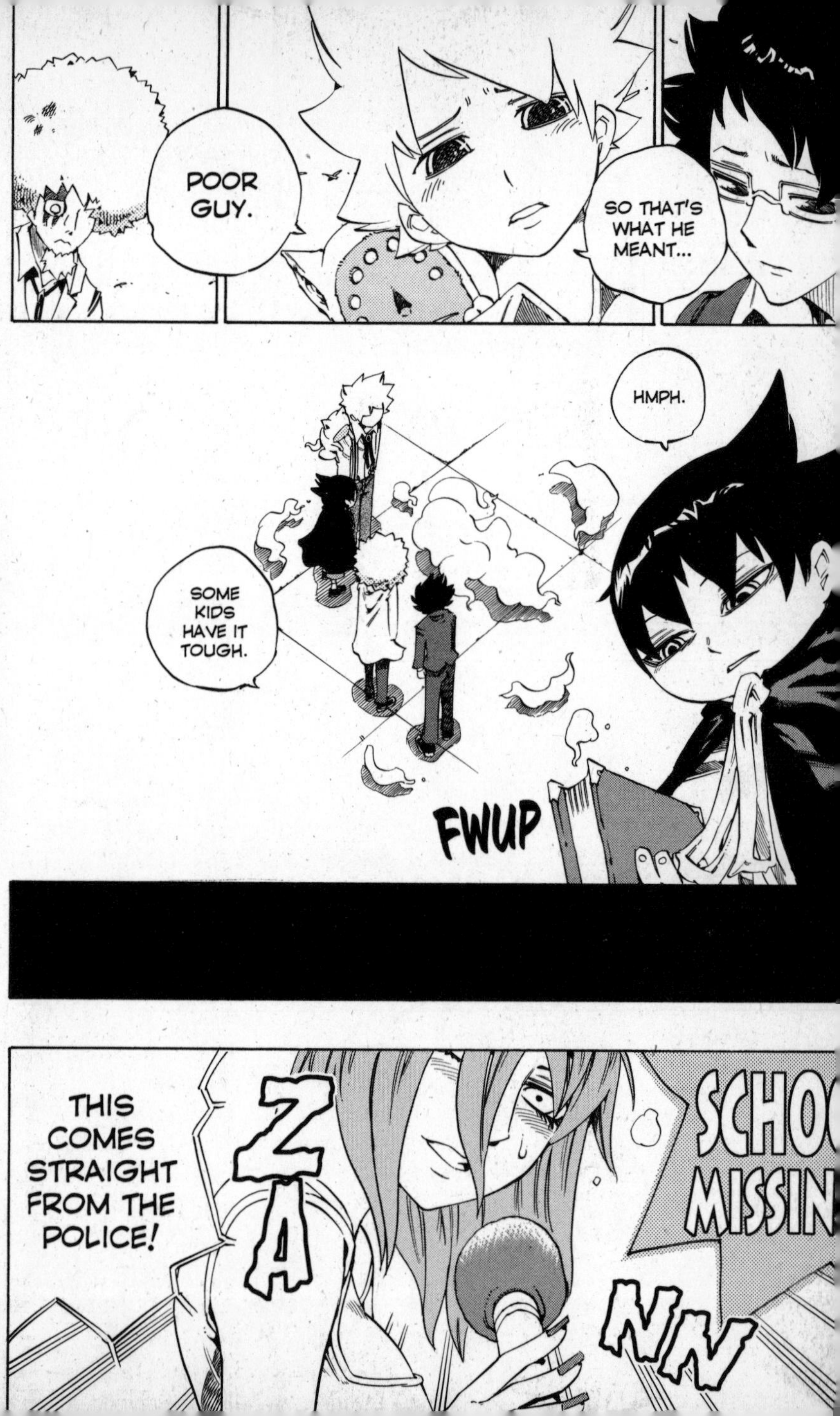
SO THAT'S WHAT HE MEANT...
POOR GUY.
HMPH.
SOME KIDS HAVE IT TOUGH.
FWUP
SCHO
MISSIN
ZA
NN
THIS COMES STRAIGHT FROM THE POLICE!

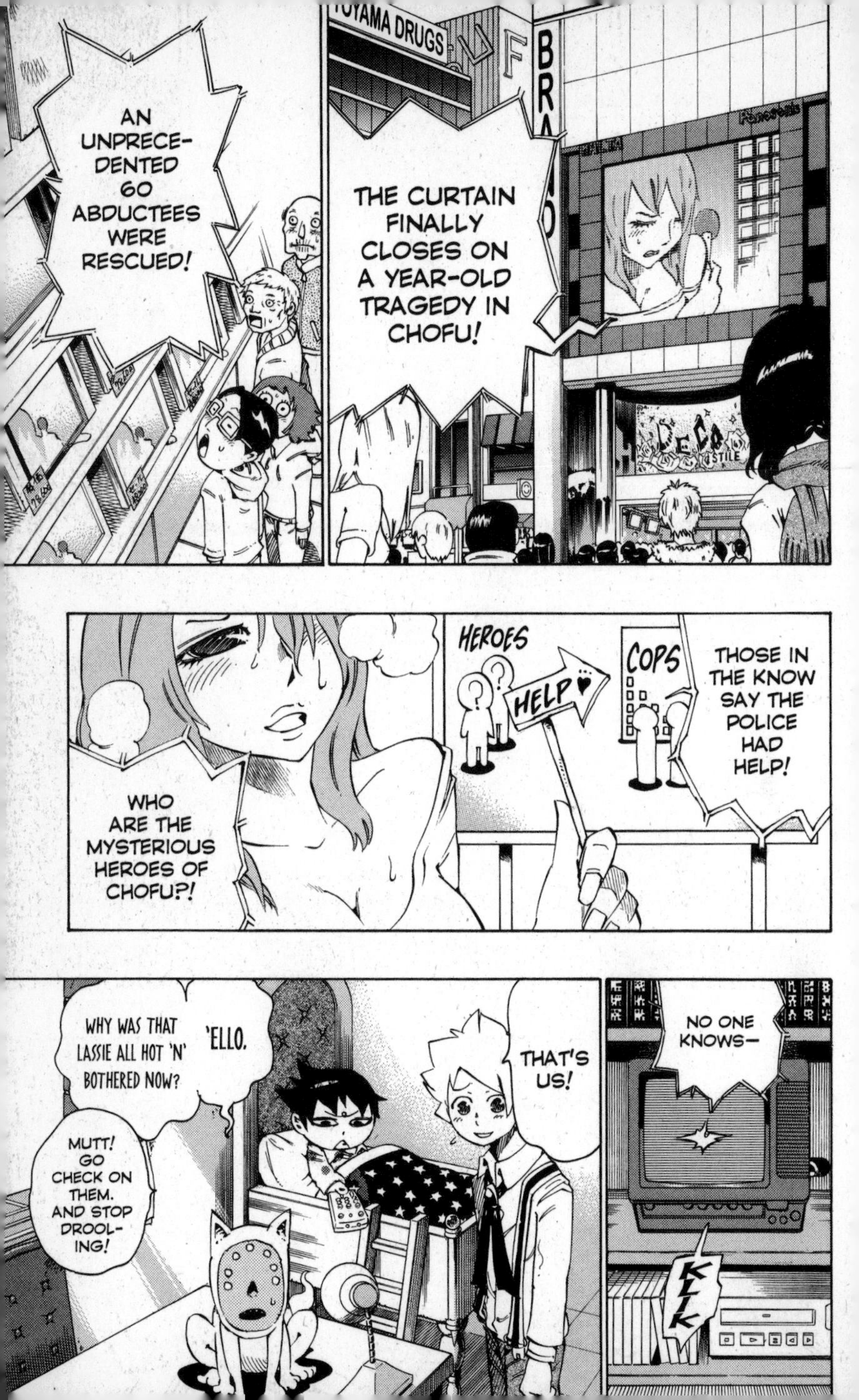
THE CURTAIN FINALLY CLOSES ON A YEAR-OLD TRAGEDY IN CHOFU!
AN UNPRECEDENTED 60 ABDUCTEES WERE RESCUED!
THOSE IN THE KNOW SAY THE POLICE HAD HELP!
COPS
HELP
HEROES
WHO ARE THE MYSTERIOUS HEROES OF CHOFU?!
NO ONE KNOWS—
KLIK
THAT'S US!
'ELLO.
WHY WAS THAT LASSIE ALL HOT 'N' BOTHERED NOW?
MUTT! GO CHECK ON THEM. AND STOP DROOL-ING!

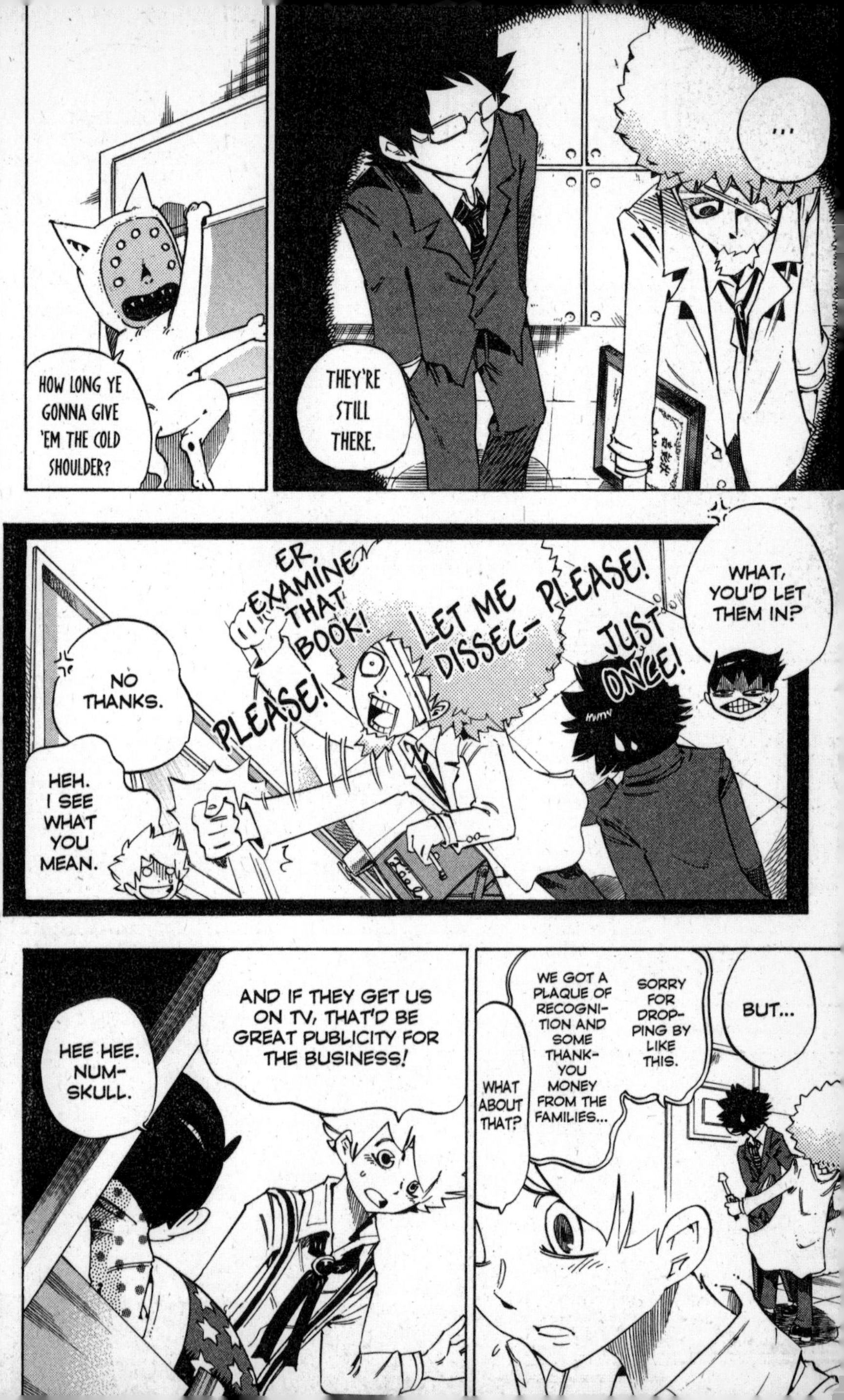
...
THEY'RE STILL THERE.
HOW LONG YE GONNA GIVE 'EM THE COLD SHOULDER?
WHAT, YOU'D LET THEM IN?
JUST ONCE!
LET ME DISSEC- PLEASE!
ER, EXAMINE THAT BOOK! PLEASE!
NO THANKS.
HEH. I SEE WHAT YOU MEAN.
BUT...
SORRY FOR DROP-PING BY LIKE THIS.
WE GOT A PLAQUE OF RECOGNI-TION AND SOME THANK-YOU MONEY FROM THE FAMILIES...
WHAT ABOUT THAT?
AND IF THEY GET US ON TV, THAT'D BE GREAT PUBLICITY FOR THE BUSINESS!
HEE HEE. NUM-SKULL.

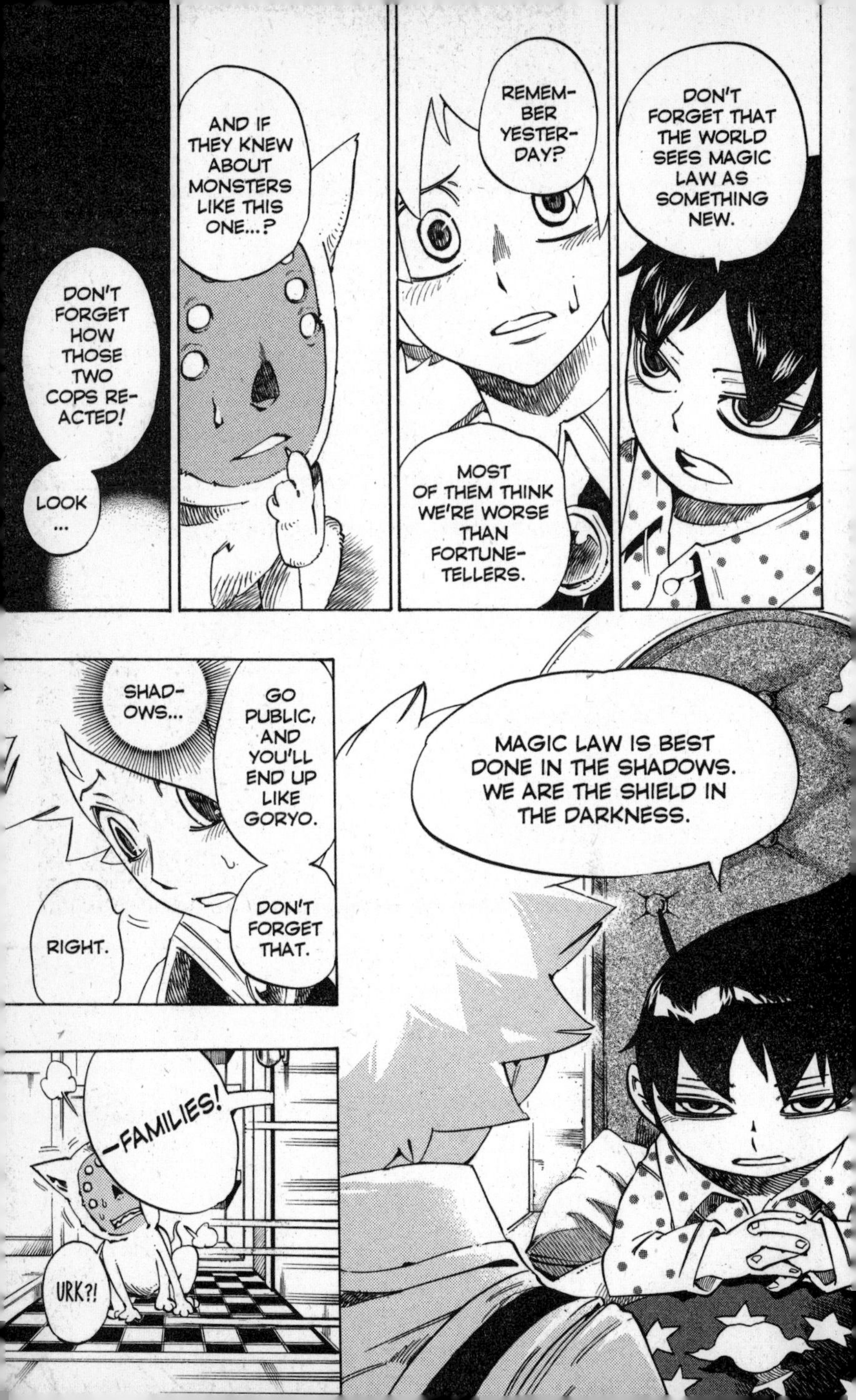
DON'T FORGET THAT THE WORLD SEES MAGIC LAW AS SOMETHING NEW.
REMEMBER YESTERDAY?
MOST OF THEM THINK WE'RE WORSE THAN FORTUNE-TELLERS.
AND IF THEY KNEW ABOUT MONSTERS LIKE THIS ONE...?
DON'T FORGET HOW THOSE TWO COPS REACTED!
LOOK...
MAGIC LAW IS BEST DONE IN THE SHADOWS. WE ARE THE SHIELD IN THE DARKNESS.
GO PUBLIC, AND YOU'LL END UP LIKE GORYO.
SHADOWS...
DON'T FORGET THAT.
RIGHT.
—FAMILIES!
URK?!

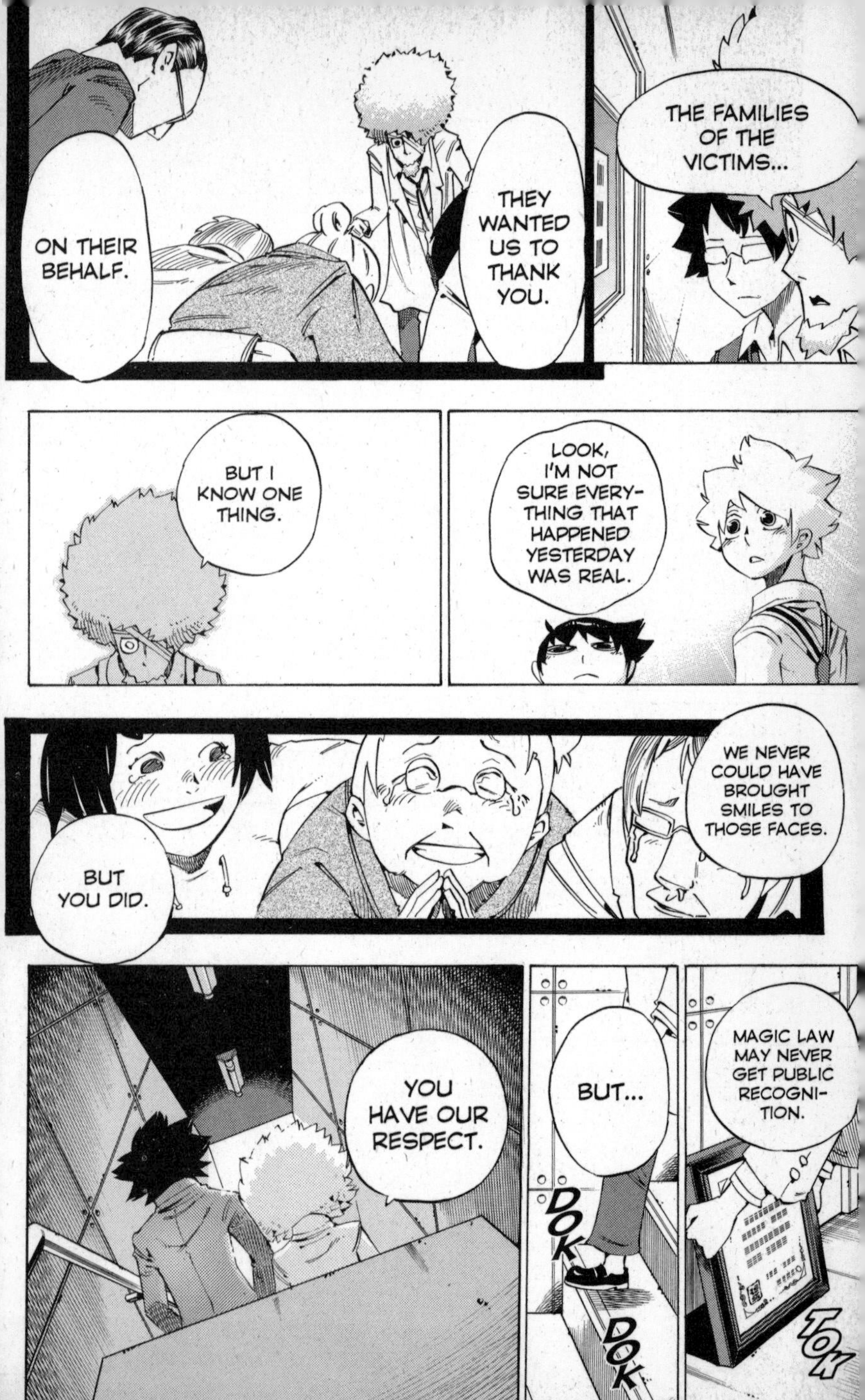
THE FAMILIES OF THE VICTIMS...
THEY WANTED US TO THANK YOU.
ON THEIR BEHALF.
LOOK, I'M NOT SURE EVERYTHING THAT HAPPENED YESTERDAY WAS REAL.
BUT I KNOW ONE THING.
WE NEVER COULD HAVE BROUGHT SMILES TO THOSE FACES.
BUT YOU DID.
MAGIC LAW MAY NEVER GET PUBLIC RECOGNITION.
TOK
BUT...
DOK
DOK
YOU HAVE OUR RESPECT.

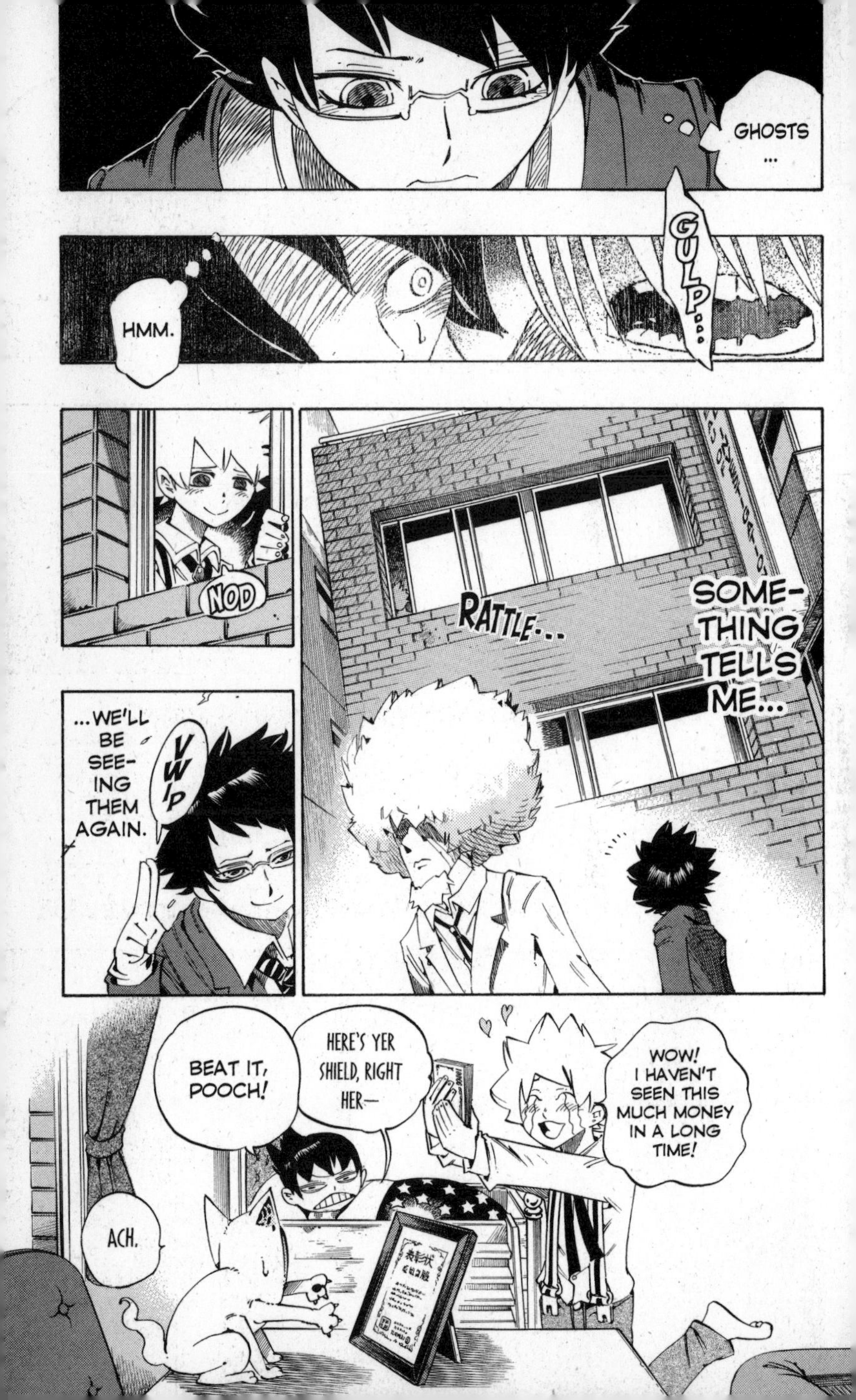
GHOSTS ...
GULP...
HMM.
SOME-THING TELLS ME...
RATTLE...
NOD
...WE'LL BE SEE-ING THEM AGAIN.
VWIP
WOW! I HAVEN'T SEEN THIS MUCH MONEY IN A LONG TIME!
HERE'S YER SHIELD, RIGHT HER—
BEAT IT, POOCH!
ACH.

MEDIUM

A ~~SHORT~~ EXPLANATION

WHEW. HONESTLY, I HAD NO IDEA THIS SERIES WOULD GET QUITE SO HEAVY. I KIND OF WANTED IT MORE ACTION PACKED LIKE A CRIME THRILLER. A LOT OF STORIES HAVE BEEN ABOUT BULLYING THOUGH, HAVEN'T THEY? KIND OF HARD TO TAKE THAT LIGHTLY. I'VE HEARD SOME AMAZING THINGS IN YOUR FAN LETTERS TOO. OF COURSE I'M GLAD I DREW THE STORIES I DID IN THE END.

INCIDENTALLY, THE NEWSCASTER THAT SHOWS UP AT THE END OF LAST CHAPTER GOT LOTS OF RESPONSES LIKE "WHY?" AND "WAS THAT REALLY NECESSARY?" AND "MORE PLEASE!" (HAHA.)

WAS IT NECESSARY? MAYBE NOT. BUT MY HAND JUST DREW THAT ON ITS OWN, HONEST! HEH HEH.

NEXT UP: A PROLOGUE TO A NEW STORY ARC CALLED "DISTANT THUNDER." BUT BEFORE WE GET ON WITH THAT...

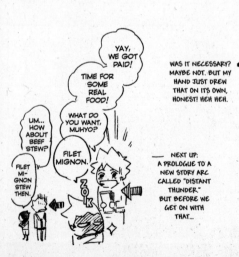

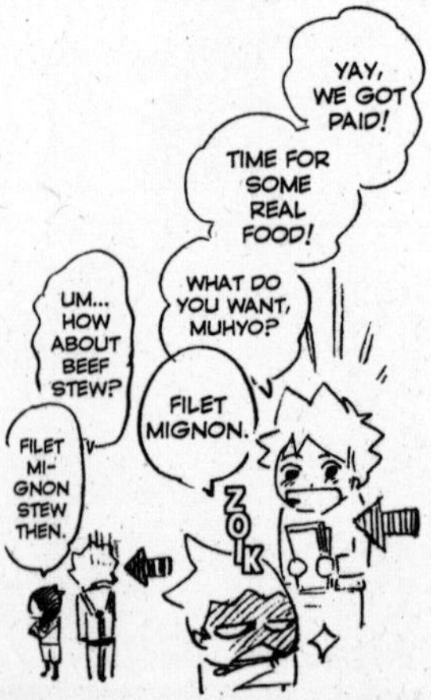
YAY, WE GOT PAID!
TIME FOR SOME REAL FOOD!
WHAT DO YOU WANT, MUHYO?
FILET MIGNON.
UM... HOW ABOUT BEEF STEW?
FILET MI-GNON STEW THEN.
ZOK

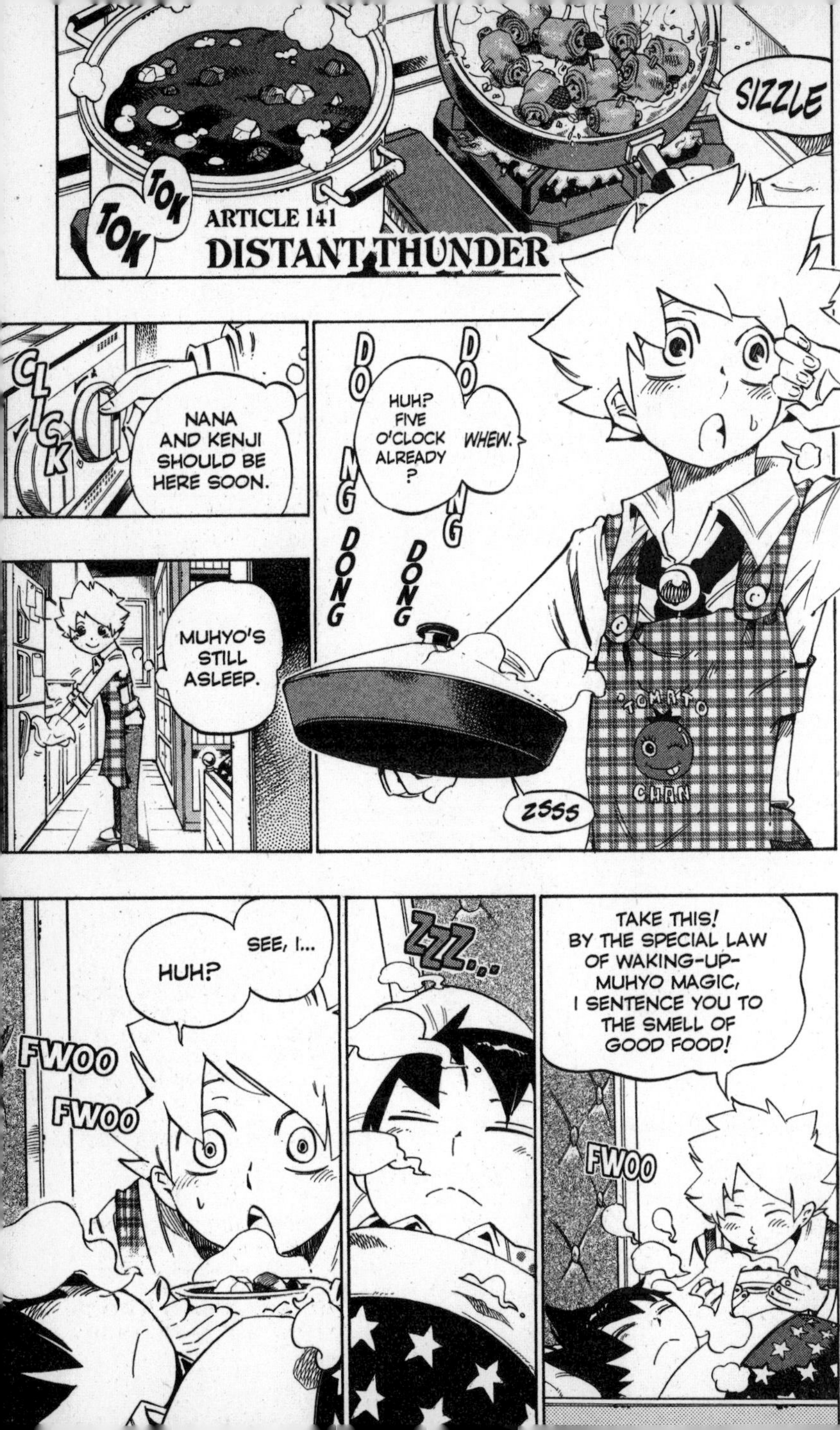
SIZZLE
ARTICLE 141
DISTANT THUNDER
TOK TOK
WHEW.
DONG
HUH? FIVE O'CLOCK ALREADY?
DONG DONG
ZSSS
NANA AND KENJI SHOULD BE HERE SOON.
CLICK
MUHYO'S STILL ASLEEP.
TAKE THIS! BY THE SPECIAL LAW OF WAKING-UP-MUHYO MAGIC, I SENTENCE YOU TO THE SMELL OF GOOD FOOD!
FWOO
ZZZ...
SEE, I...
HUH?
FWOO
FWOO

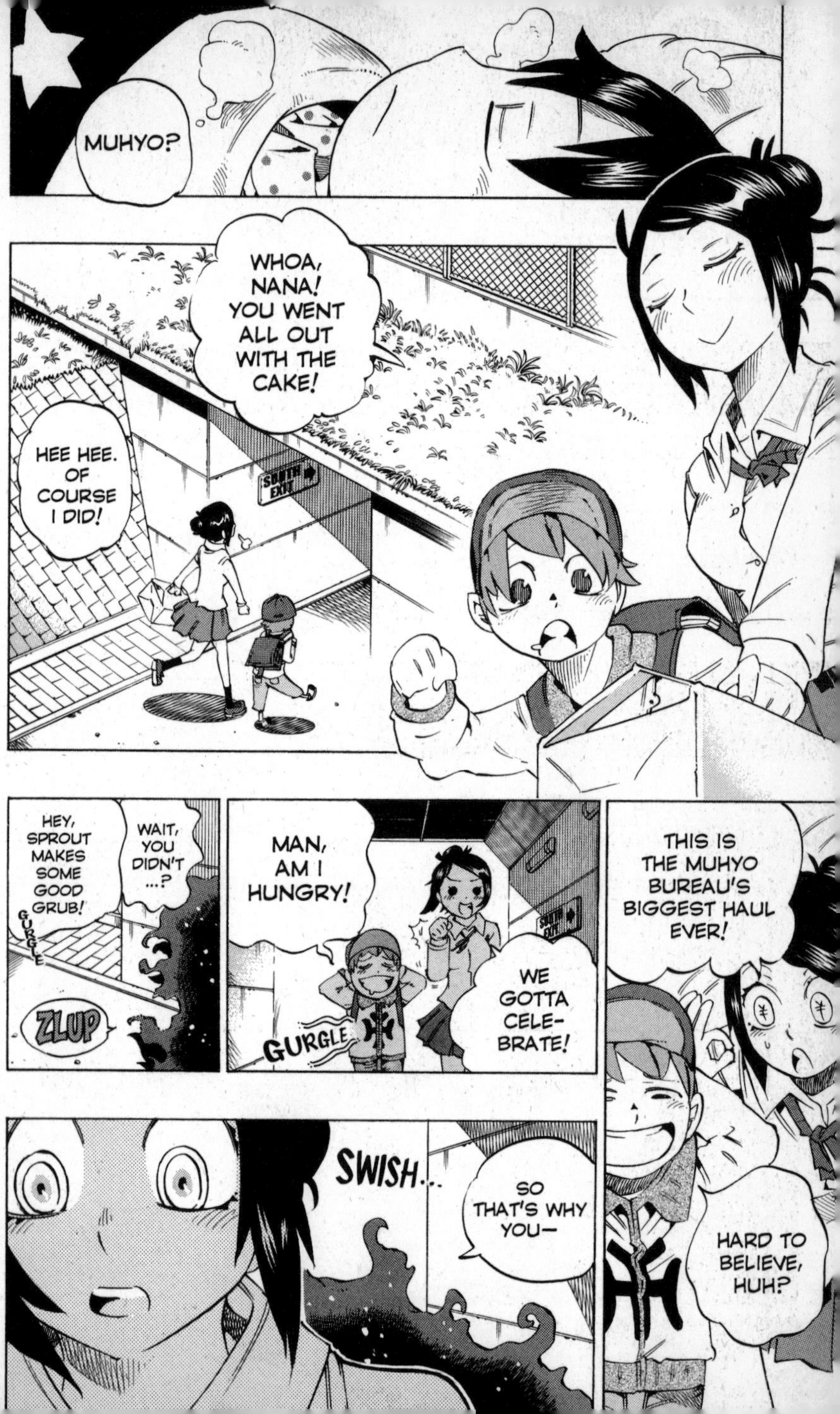

MUHYO?
WHOA, NANA! YOU WENT ALL OUT WITH THE CAKE!
SOUTH EXIT
HEE HEE. OF COURSE I DID!
THIS IS THE MUHYO BUREAU'S BIGGEST HAUL EVER!
HARD TO BELIEVE, HUH?
MAN, AM I HUNGRY!
WE GOTTA CELE-BRATE!
GURGLE
WAIT, YOU DIDN'T ...?
HEY, SPROUT MAKES SOME GOOD GRUB!
GURGLE
ZLUP
SO THAT'S WHY YOU—
SWISH...

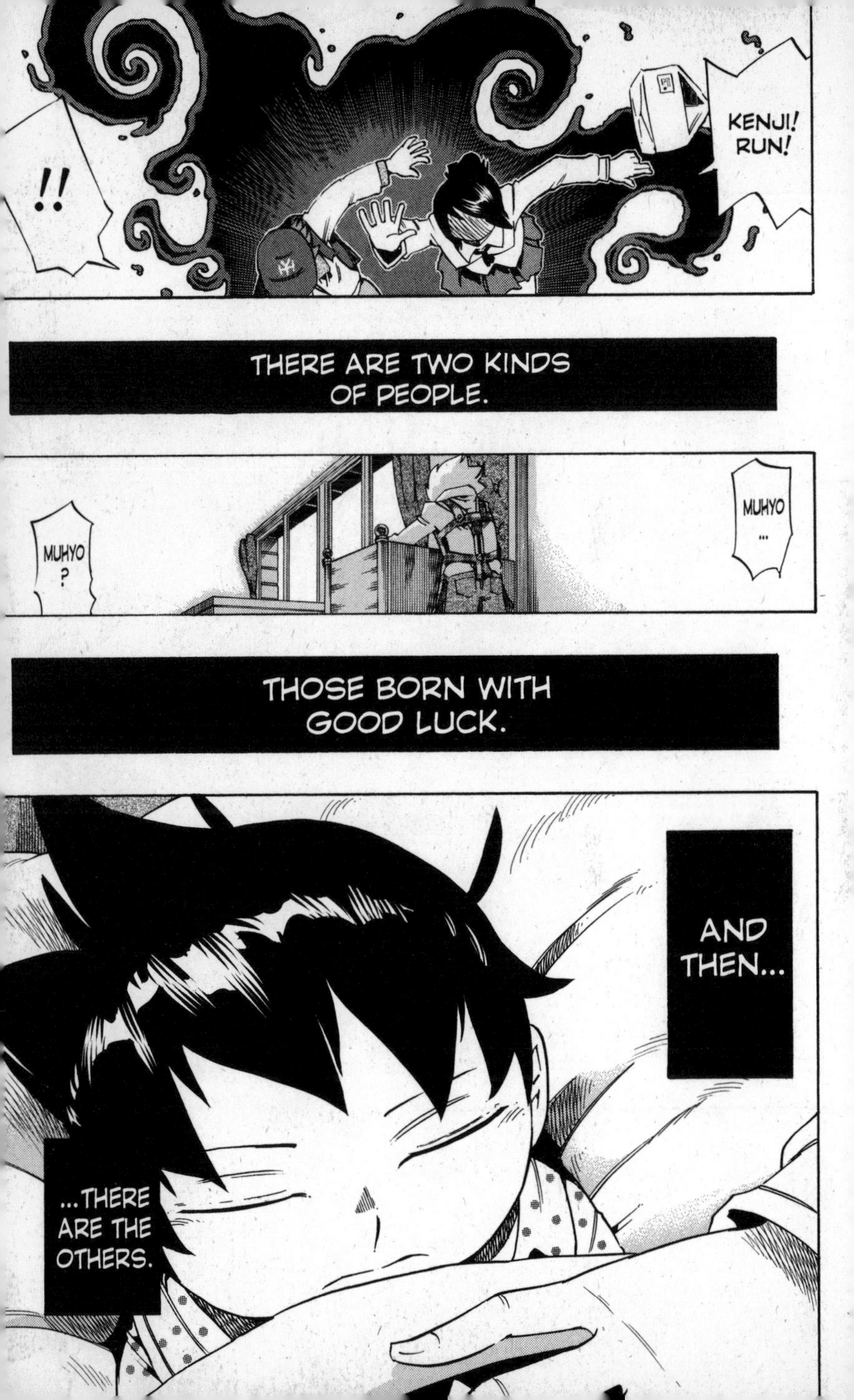
KENJI! RUN!
!!
THERE ARE TWO KINDS OF PEOPLE.
MUHYO ...
MUHYO ?
THOSE BORN WITH GOOD LUCK.
AND THEN...
...THERE ARE THE OTHERS.

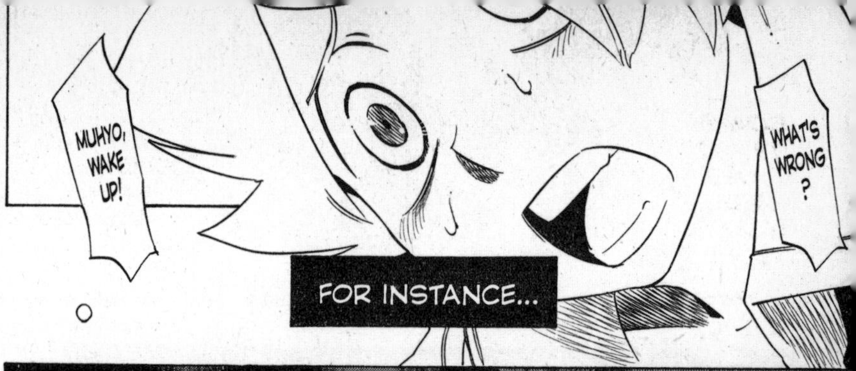
WHAT'S WRONG ?
MUHYO, WAKE UP!
FOR INSTANCE...

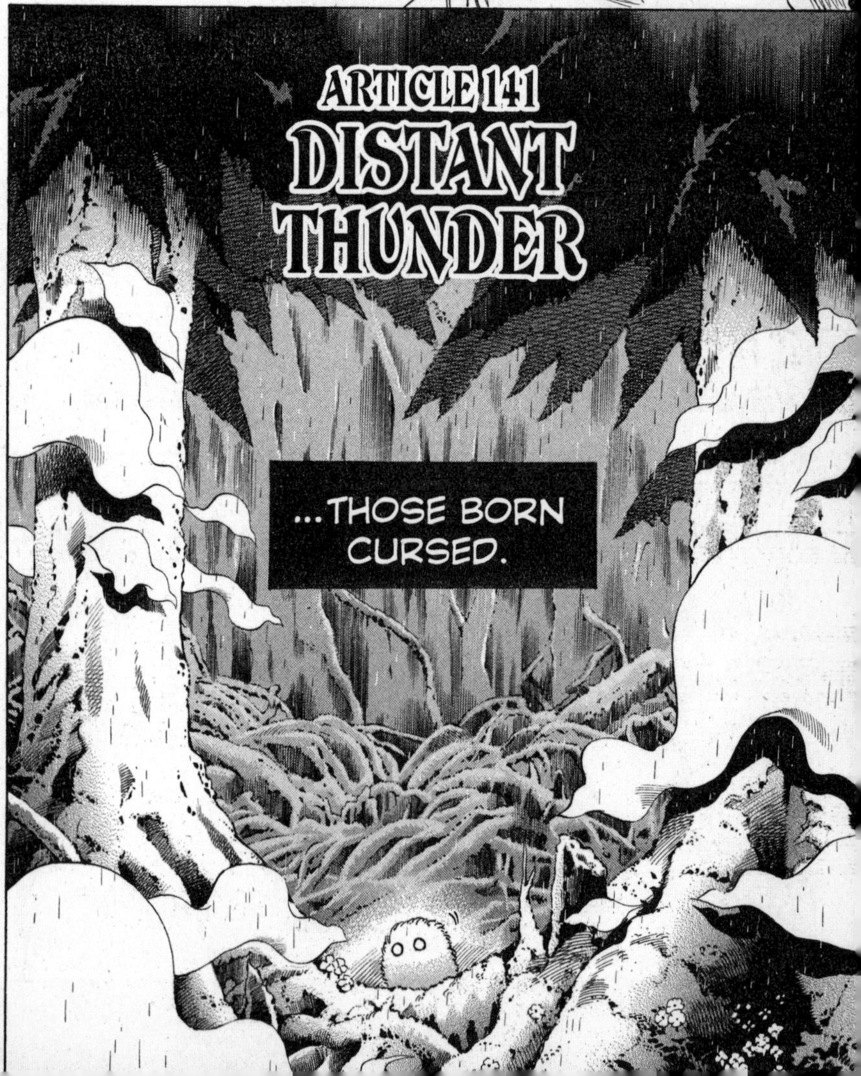
ARTICLE 141
DISTANT THUNDER
...THOSE BORN CURSED.

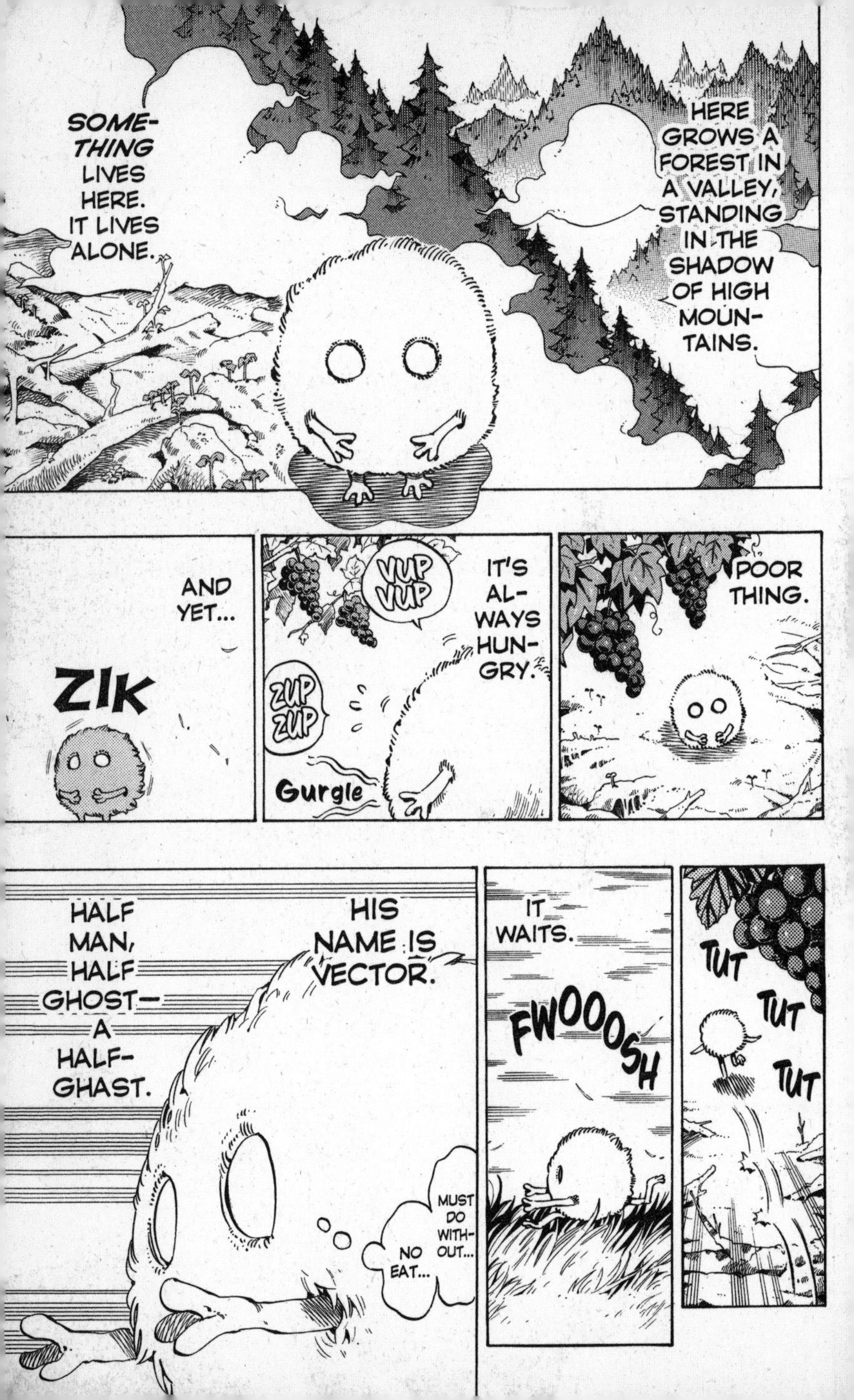
HERE GROWS A FOREST IN A VALLEY, STANDING IN THE SHADOW OF HIGH MOUNTAINS.
SOMETHING LIVES HERE. IT LIVES ALONE.
AND YET...
ZIK
IT'S ALWAYS HUNGRY.
VUP VUP
ZUP ZUP
Gurgle
POOR THING.
HALF MAN, HALF GHOST— A HALF-GHAST.
HIS NAME IS VECTOR.
MUST DO WITHOUT...
NO EAT...
IT WAITS.
FWOOOSH
TUT
TUT
TUT

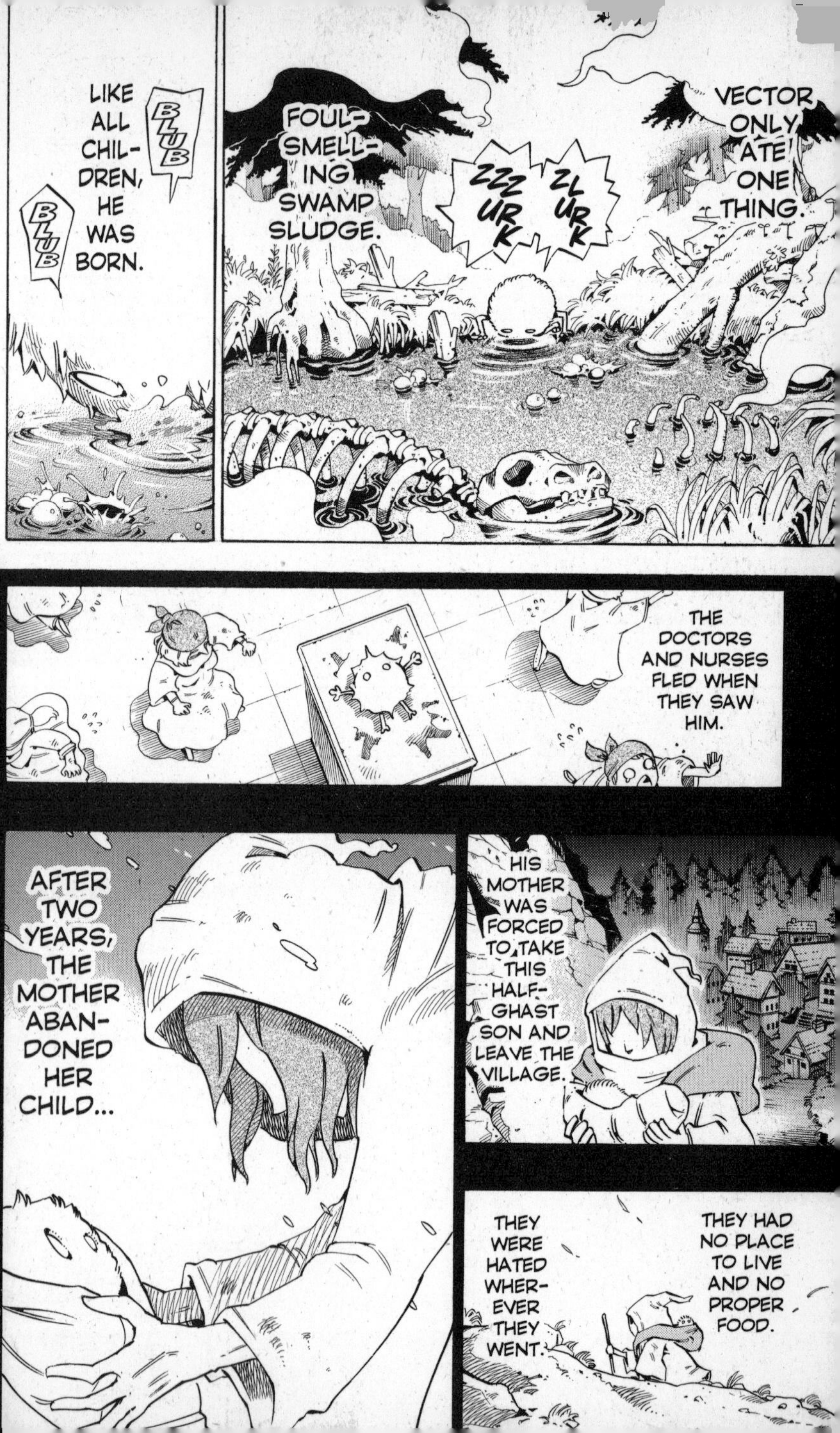

VECTOR ONLY ATE ONE THING.
ZLURK
ZZZURK
FOUL-SMELLING SWAMP SLUDGE.
BLUB
LIKE ALL CHILDREN, HE WAS BORN.
BLUB
THE DOCTORS AND NURSES FLED WHEN THEY SAW HIM.
HIS MOTHER WAS FORCED TO TAKE THIS HALF-GHAST SON AND LEAVE THE VILLAGE.
THEY HAD NO PLACE TO LIVE AND NO PROPER FOOD.
THEY WERE HATED WHEREVER THEY WENT.
AFTER TWO YEARS, THE MOTHER ABANDONED HER CHILD...

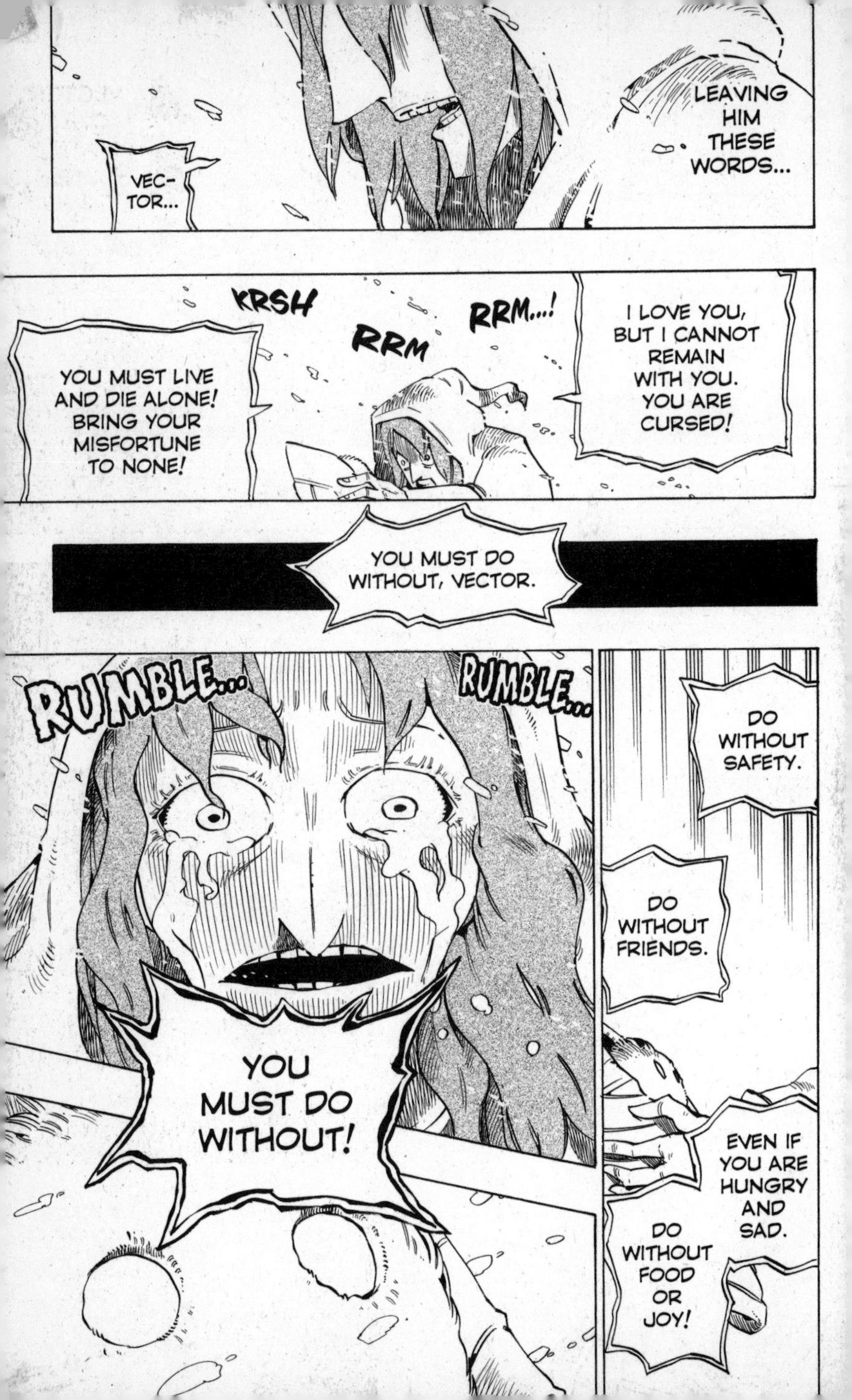
LEAVING HIM THESE WORDS...
VEC-TOR...
I LOVE YOU, BUT I CANNOT REMAIN WITH YOU. YOU ARE CURSED!
RRM...!
KRSH
RRM
YOU MUST LIVE AND DIE ALONE! BRING YOUR MISFORTUNE TO NONE!
YOU MUST DO WITHOUT, VECTOR.
DO WITHOUT SAFETY.
DO WITHOUT FRIENDS.
EVEN IF YOU ARE HUNGRY AND SAD.
DO WITHOUT FOOD OR JOY!
RUMBLE...
RUMBLE...
YOU MUST DO WITHOUT!

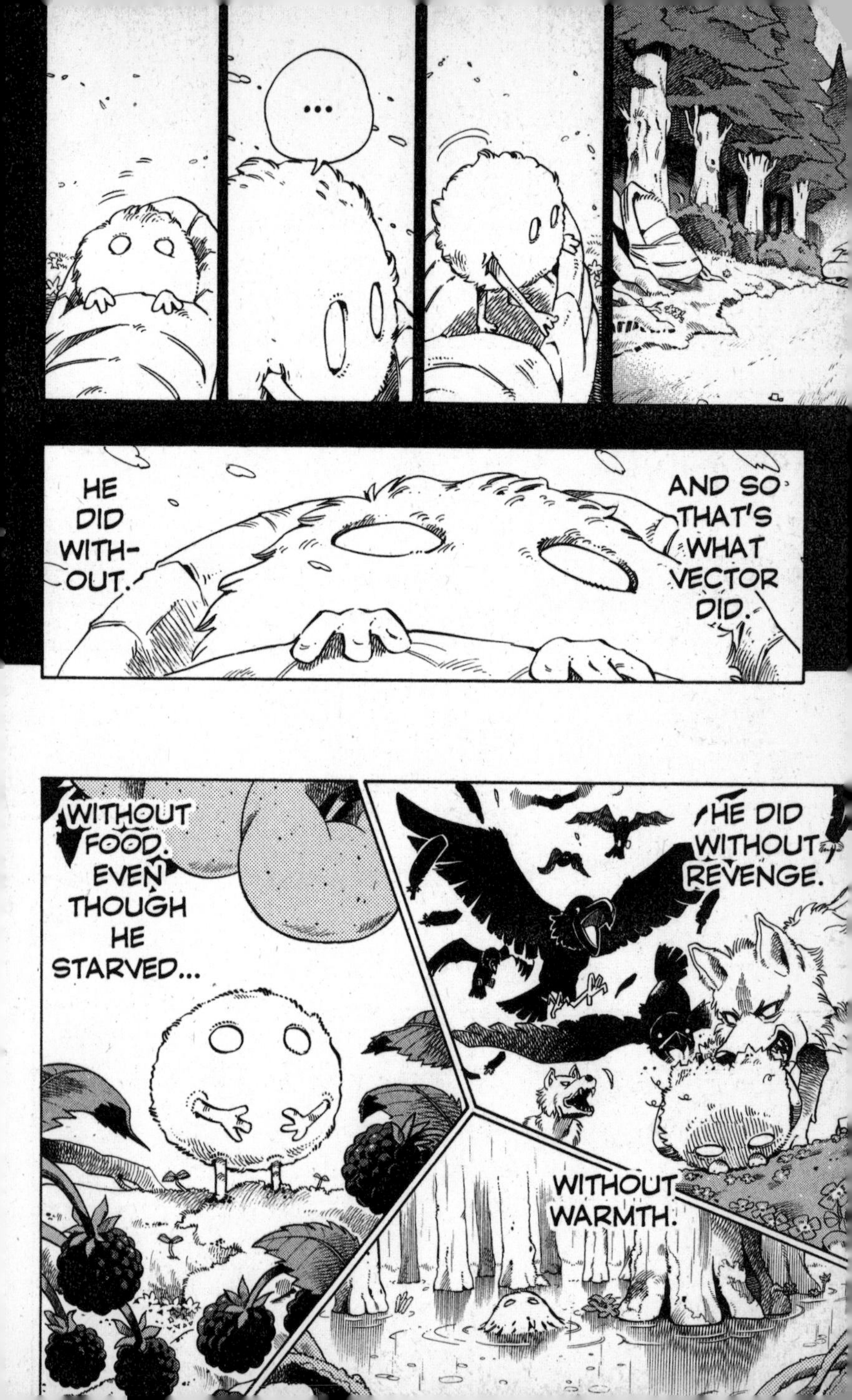
...
AND SO THAT'S WHAT VECTOR DID.
HE DID WITH-OUT.
HE DID WITHOUT REVENGE.
WITHOUT WARMTH.
WITHOUT FOOD. EVEN THOUGH HE STARVED...

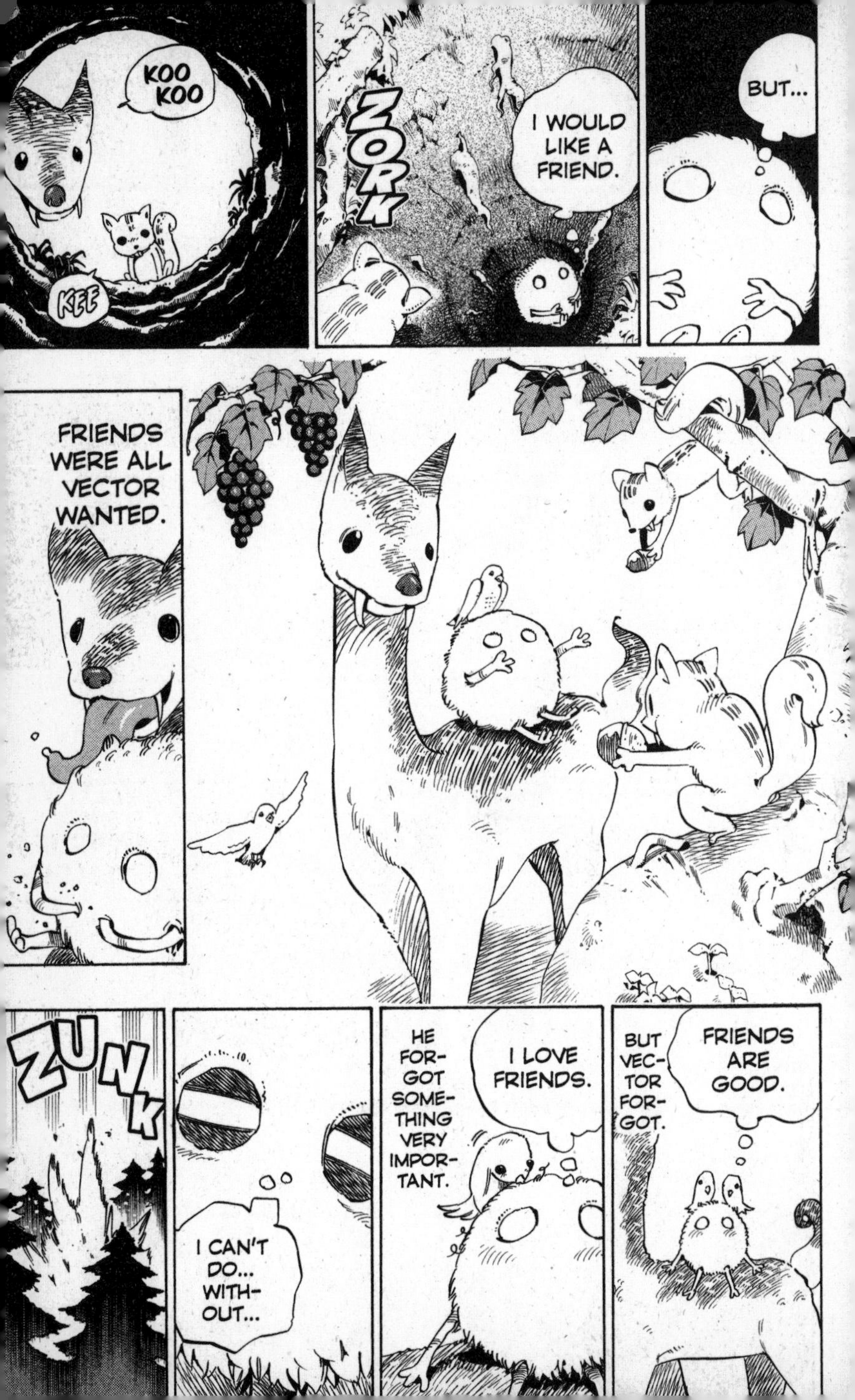
BUT...
ZORK
I WOULD LIKE A FRIEND.
KOO KOO
KEE
FRIENDS WERE ALL VECTOR WANTED.
FRIENDS ARE GOOD.
BUT VECTOR FORGOT.
I LOVE FRIENDS.
HE FORGOT SOMETHING VERY IMPORTANT.
I CAN'T DO... WITHOUT...
ZUNK

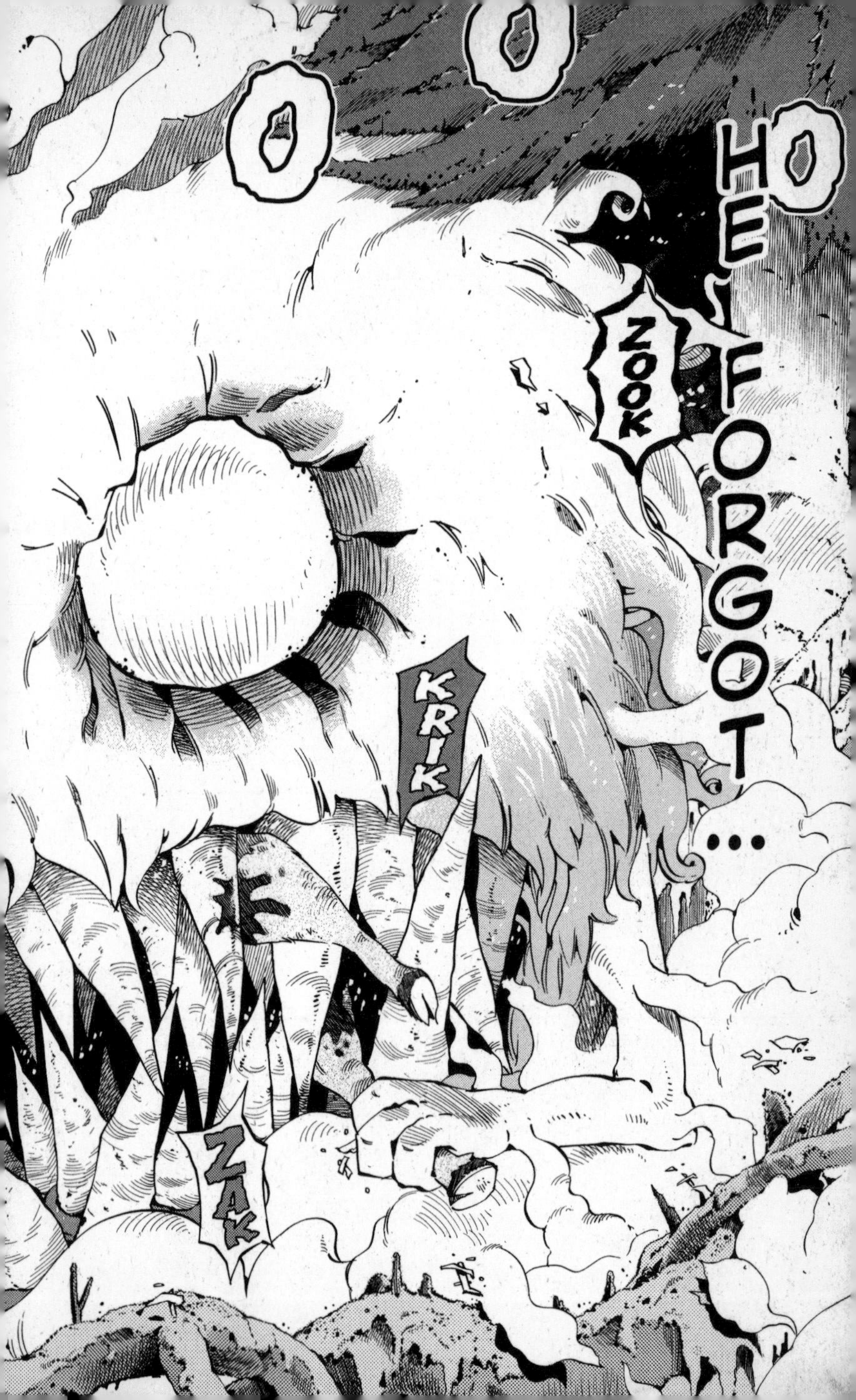
HOOO
HE FORGOT...
ZOOK
KRIK
ZAK

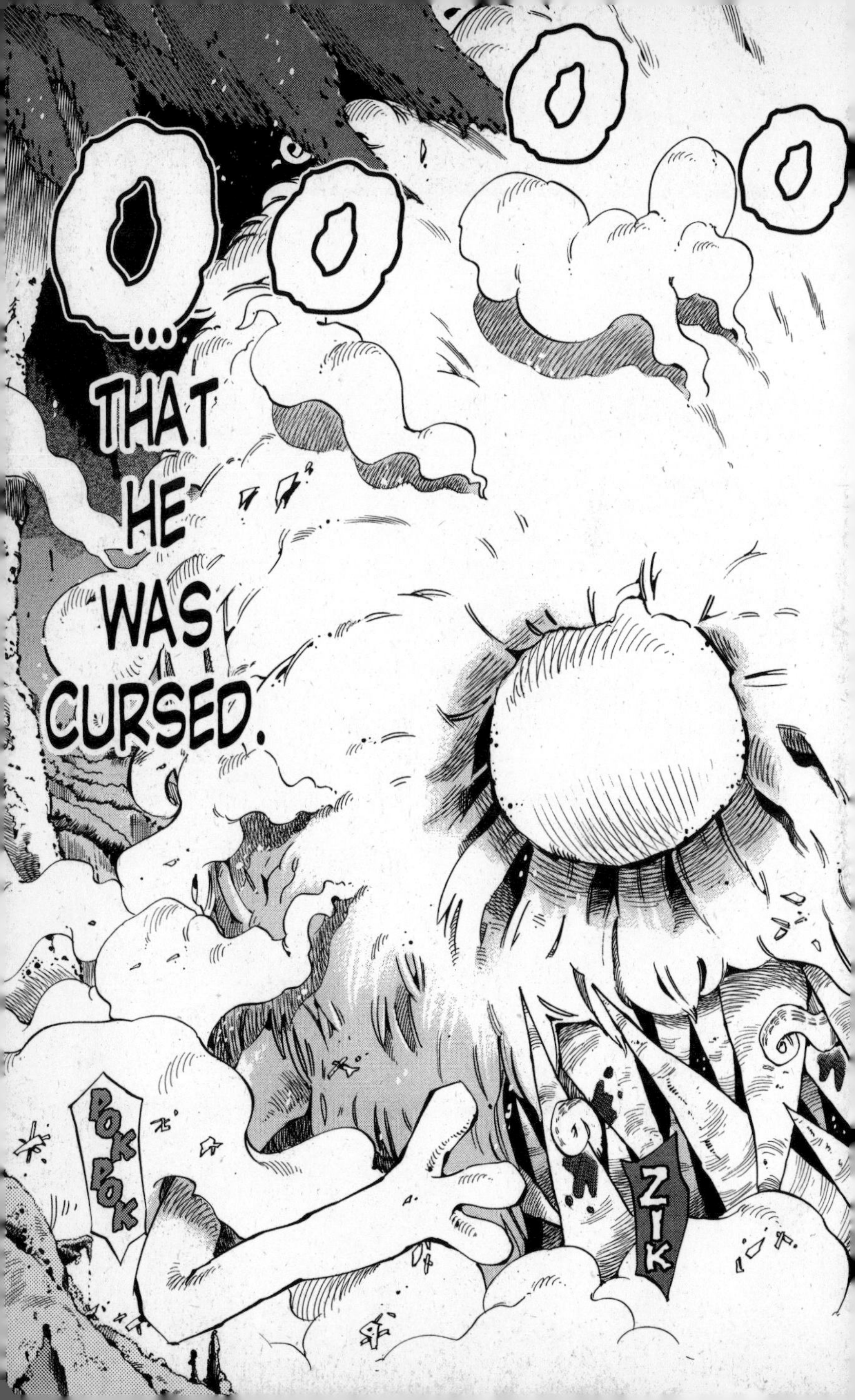

OOOO
...THAT HE WAS CURSED.
POK POK
ZIK

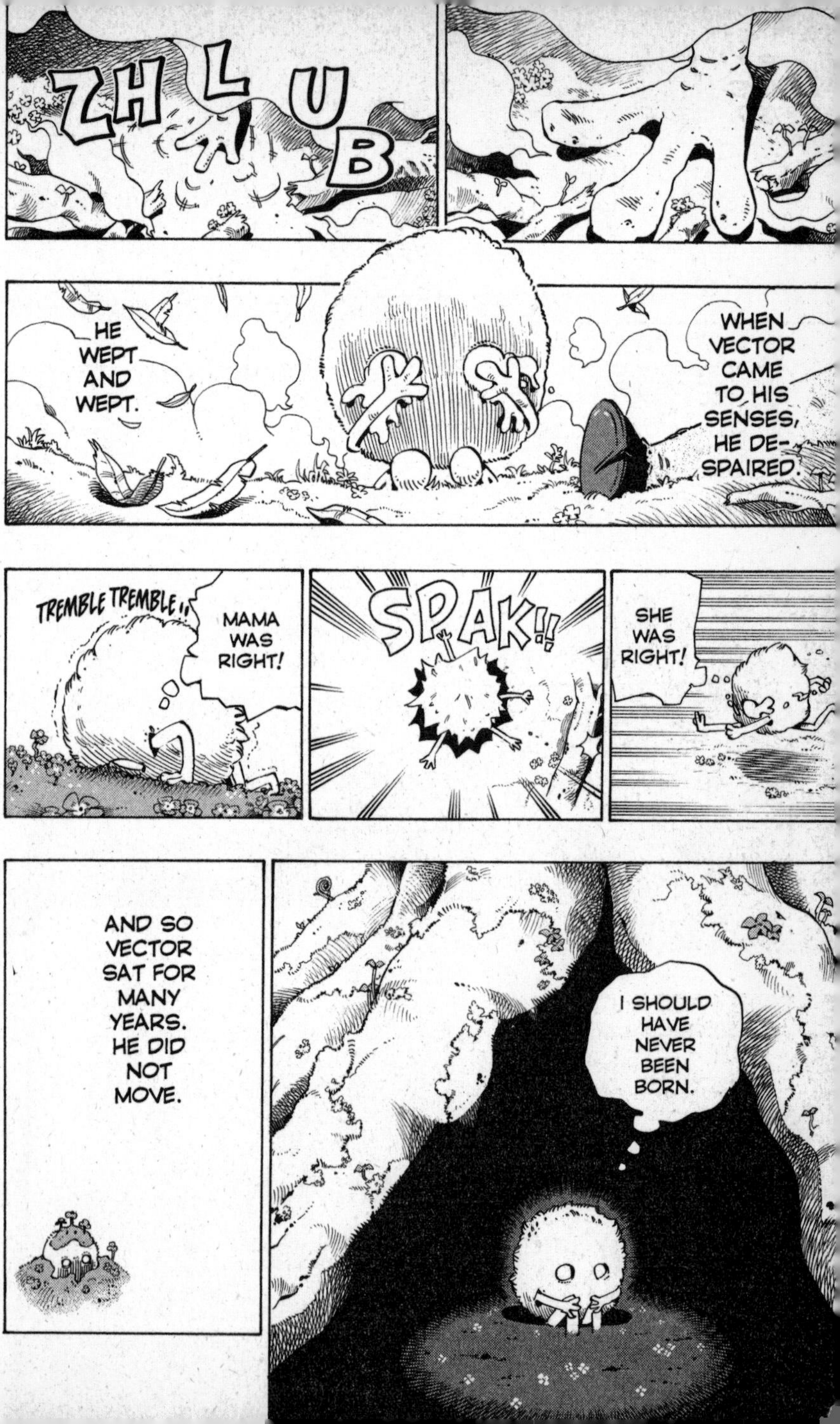
ZHLUB
WHEN VECTOR CAME TO HIS SENSES, HE DESPAIRED.
HE WEPT AND WEPT.
SHE WAS RIGHT!
SPAK!!
MAMA WAS RIGHT!
TREMBLE TREMBLE..
I SHOULD HAVE NEVER BEEN BORN.
AND SO VECTOR SAT FOR MANY YEARS. HE DID NOT MOVE.

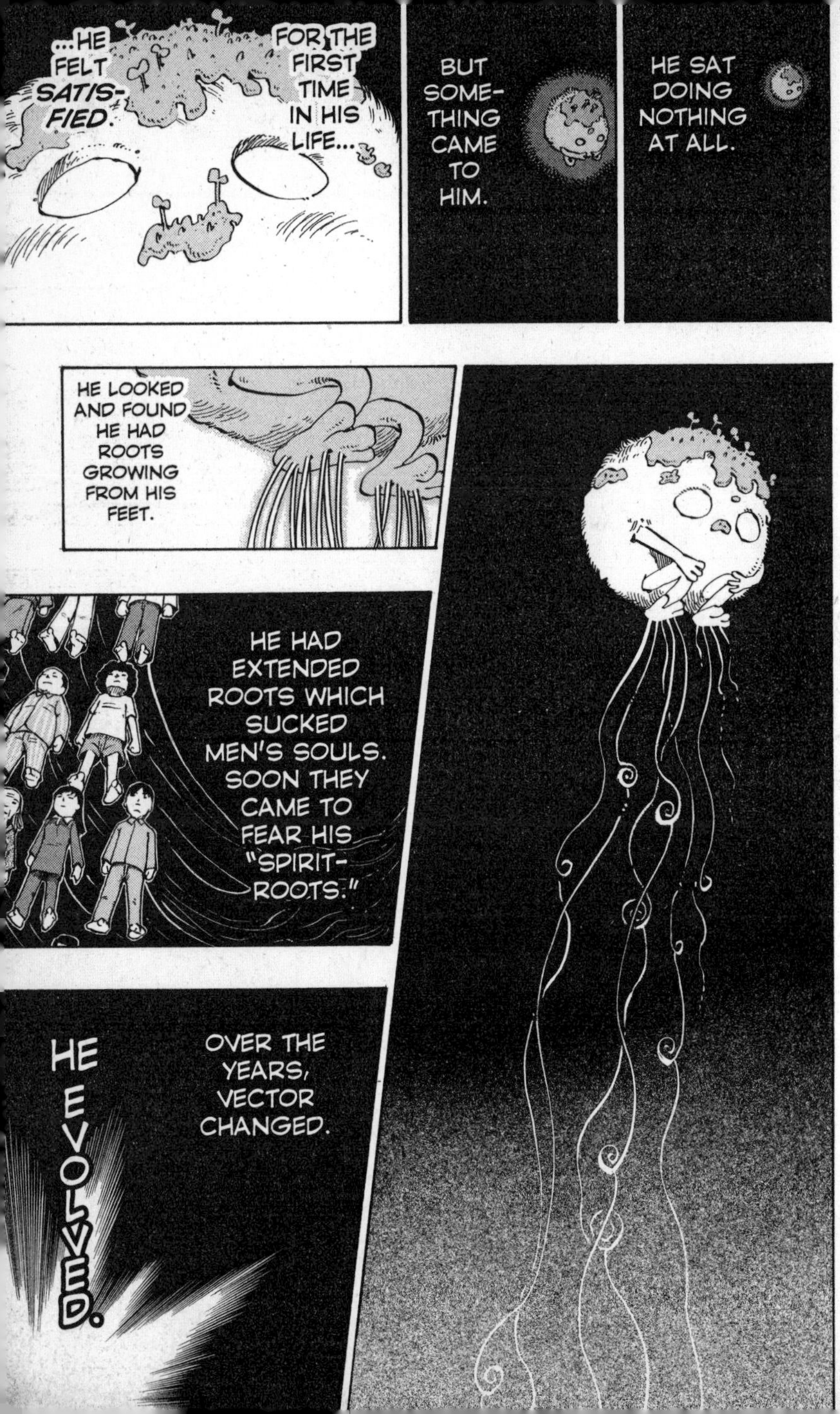
HE SAT DOING NOTHING AT ALL.
BUT SOME-THING CAME TO HIM.
FOR THE FIRST TIME IN HIS LIFE...
...HE FELT SATIS-FIED.
HE LOOKED AND FOUND HE HAD ROOTS GROWING FROM HIS FEET.
HE HAD EXTENDED ROOTS WHICH SUCKED MEN'S SOULS. SOON THEY CAME TO FEAR HIS "SPIRIT-ROOTS."
OVER THE YEARS, VECTOR CHANGED.
HE EVOLVED.

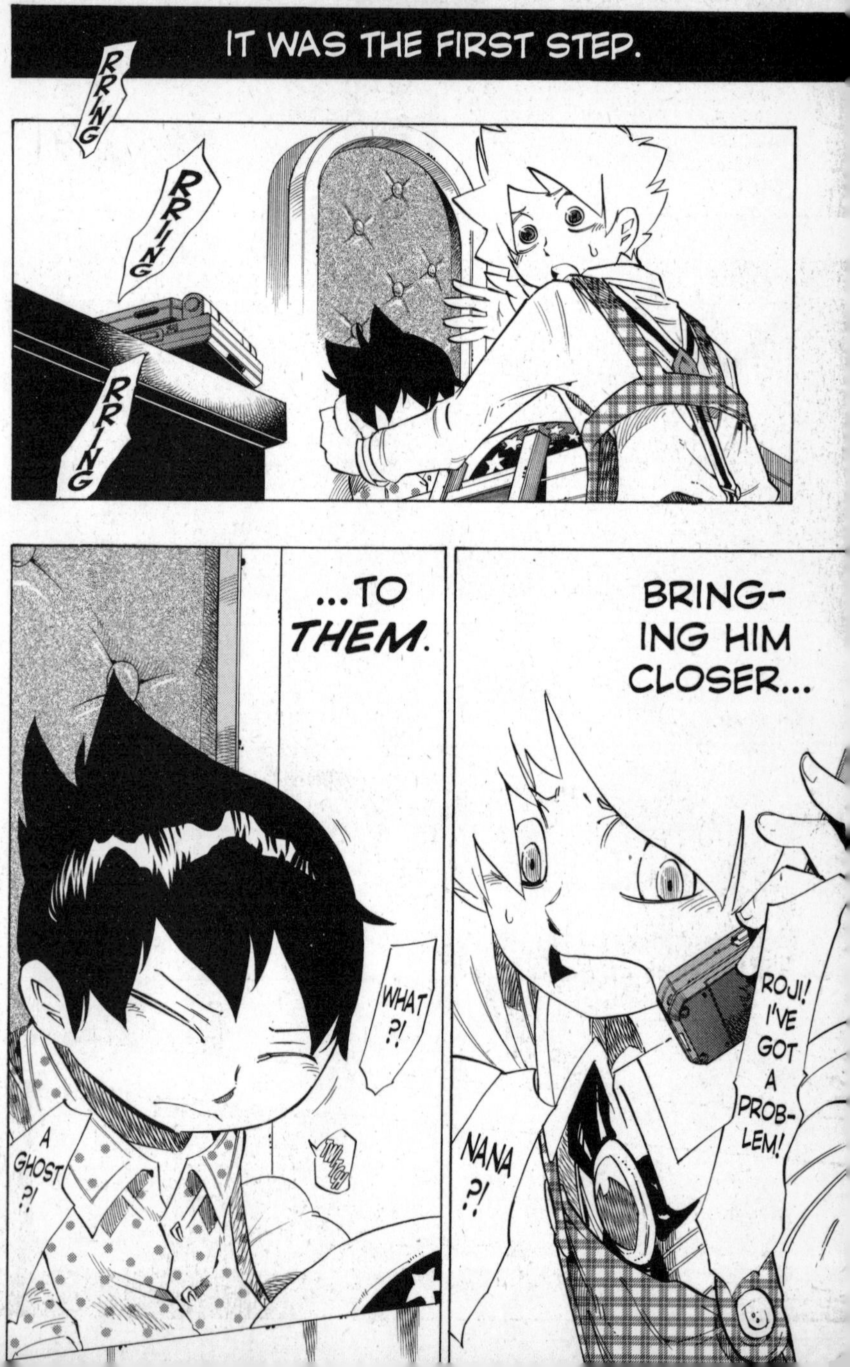
IT WAS THE FIRST STEP.
RRING
RRIING
RRING
BRINGING HIM CLOSER...
ROJI! I'VE GOT A PROBLEM!
NANA?!
...TO THEM.
WHAT?!
A GHOST?!

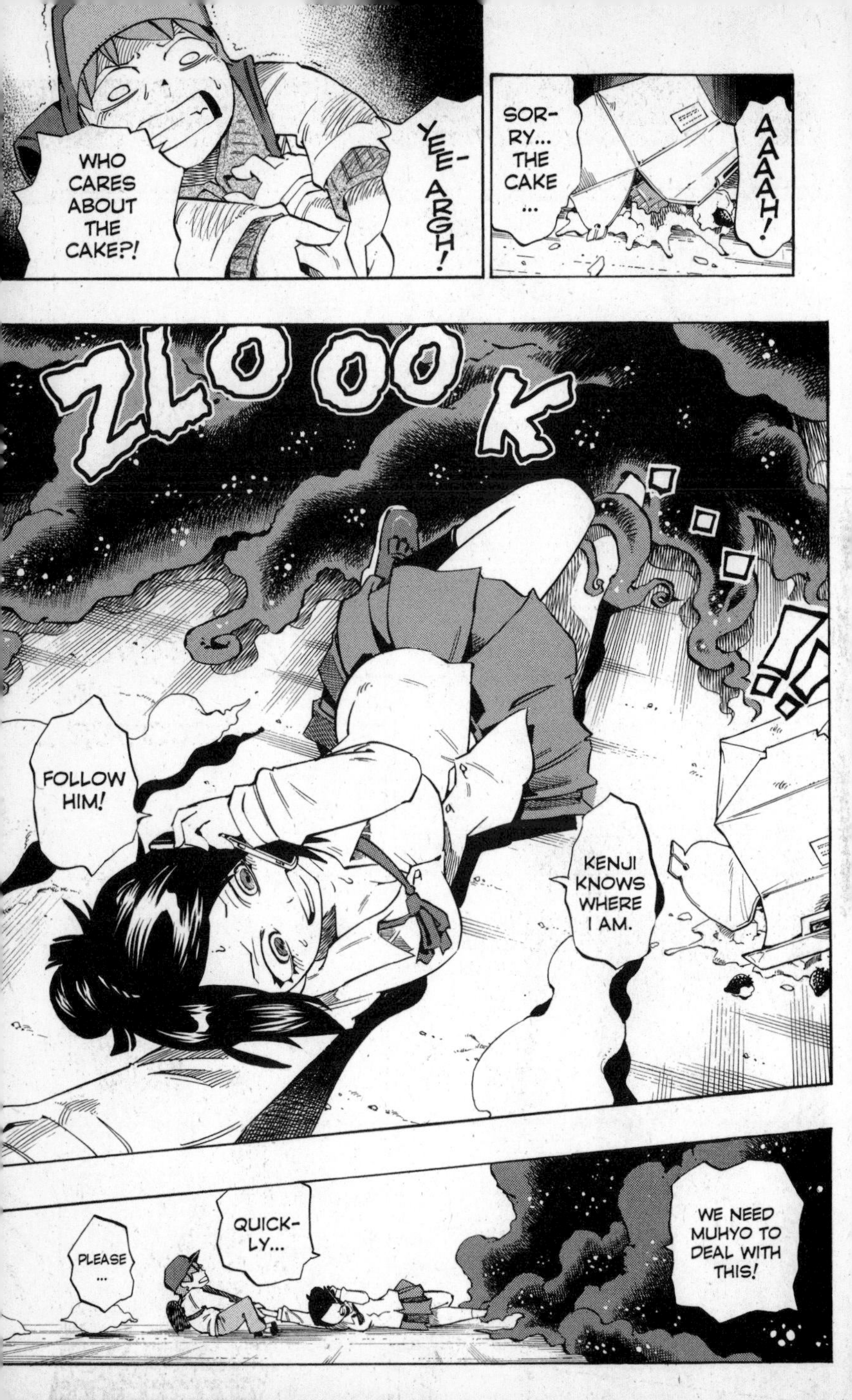
AAAAH!
SOR-RY... THE CAKE ...
YEE-ARGH!
WHO CARES ABOUT THE CAKE?!
ZLOOOK
!!
KENJI KNOWS WHERE I AM.
FOLLOW HIM!
WE NEED MUHYO TO DEAL WITH THIS!
QUICK-LY...
PLEASE ...

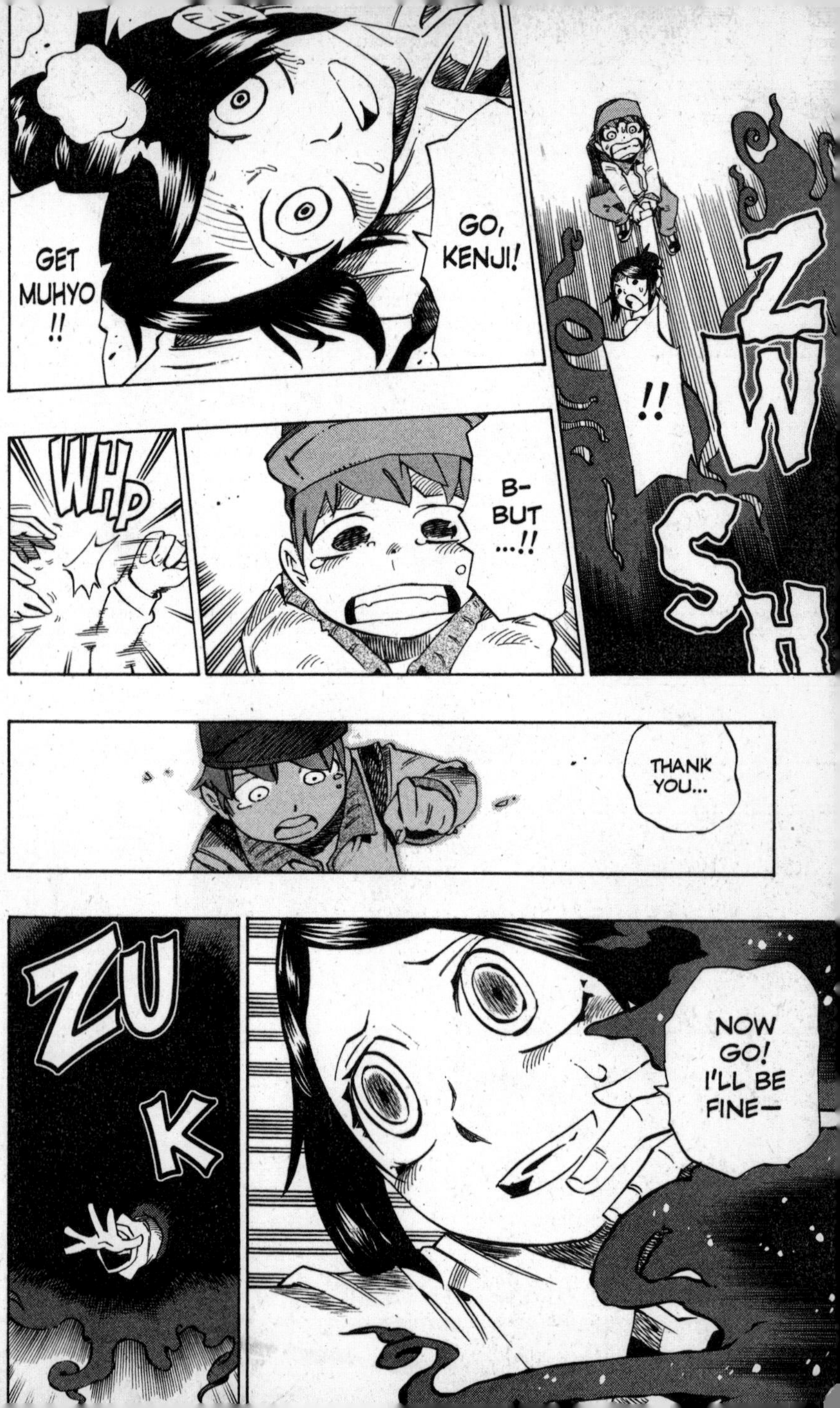
!!
ZWSH
GO, KENJI!
GET MUHYO !!
...
B-BUT ...!!
WHP
THANK YOU...
NOW GO! I'LL BE FINE—
ZUK

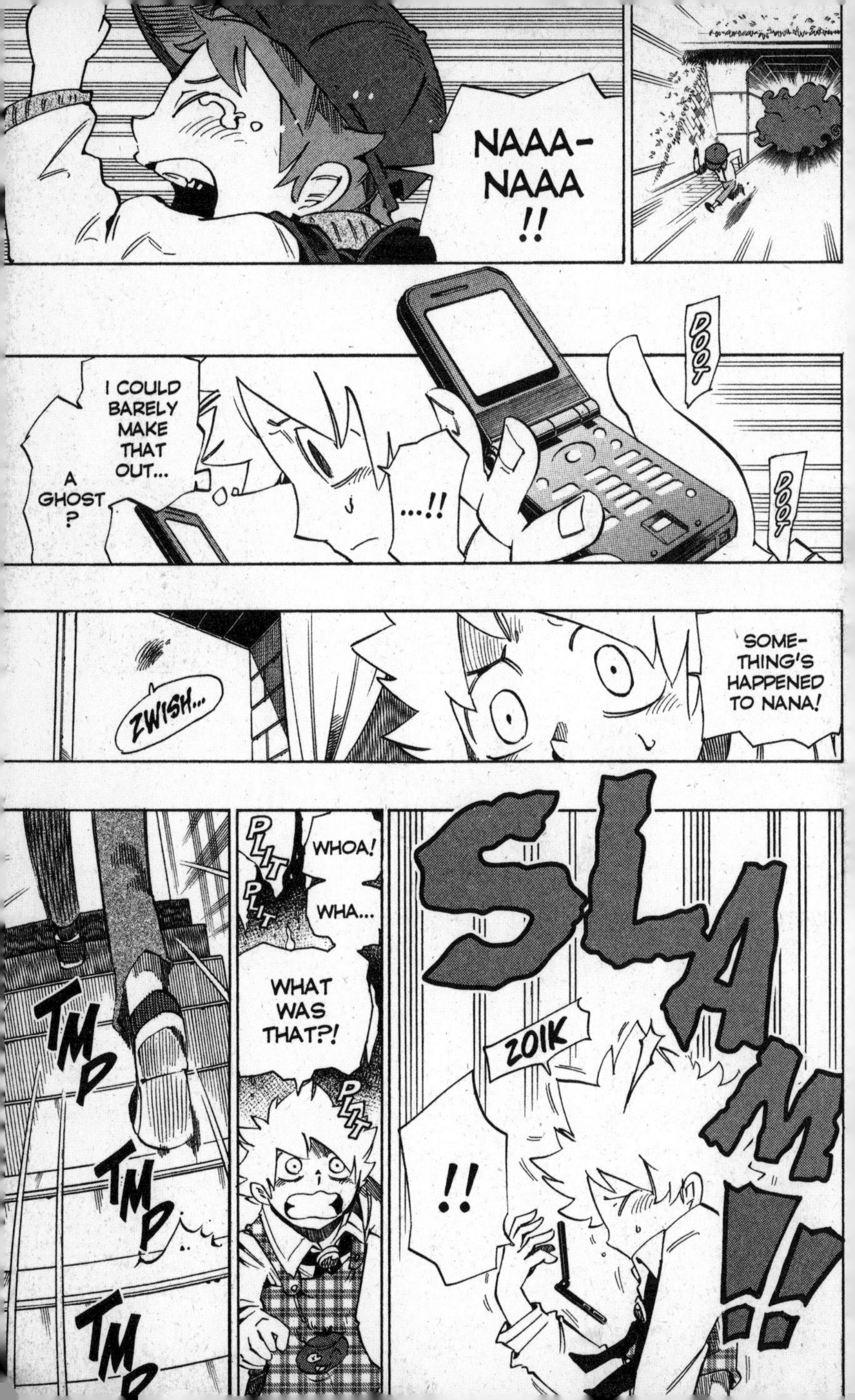
NAAA-NAAA!!
DOOT
DOOT
...!!
I COULD BARELY MAKE THAT OUT...
A GHOST?
SOME-THING'S HAPPENED TO NANA!
ZWISH...
SLAM!!
ZOIK
!!
WHOA!
PLIT
PLIT
WHA...
WHAT WAS THAT?!
PLIT
TMP
TMP
TMP

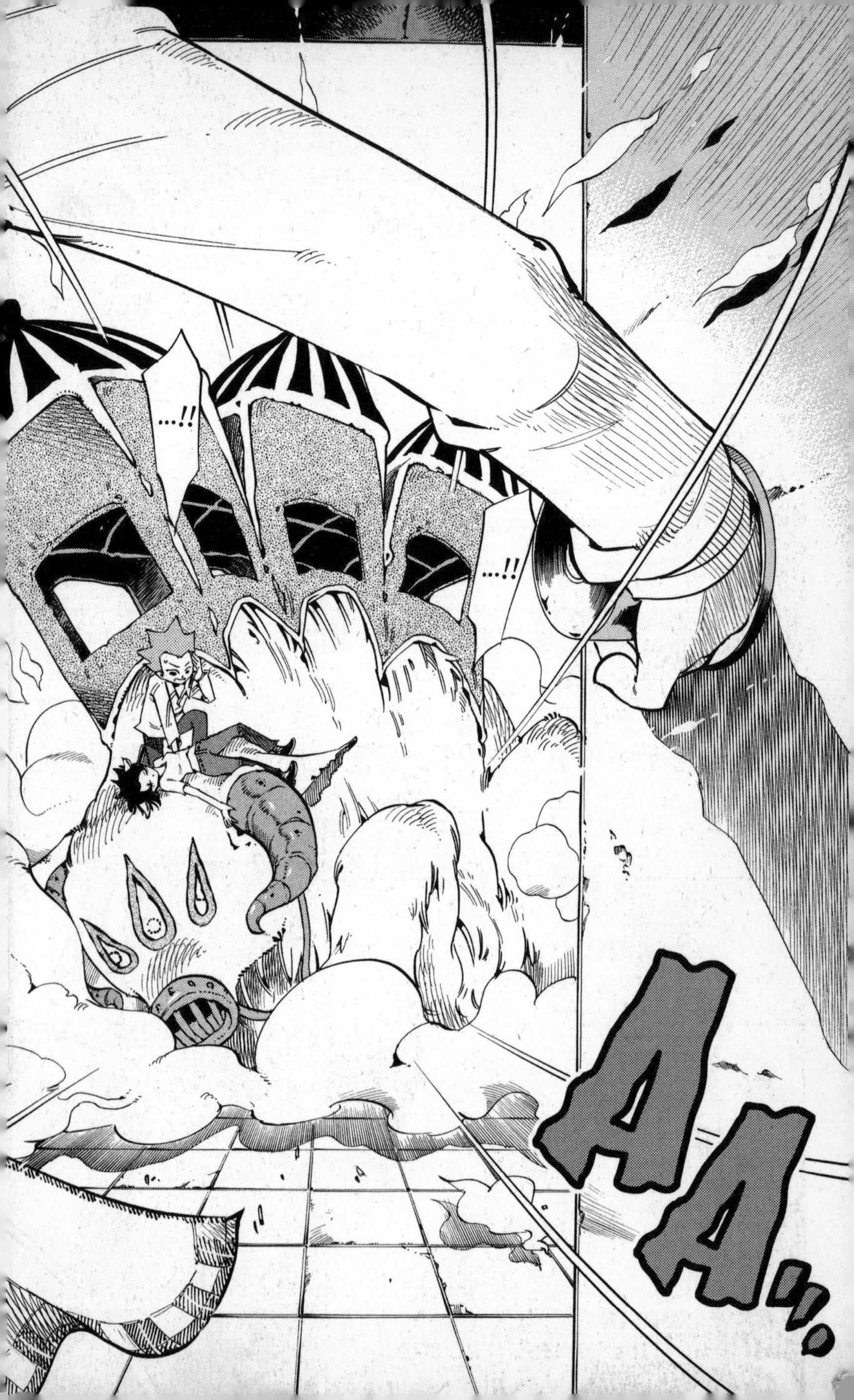
...!!
...!!
AA...

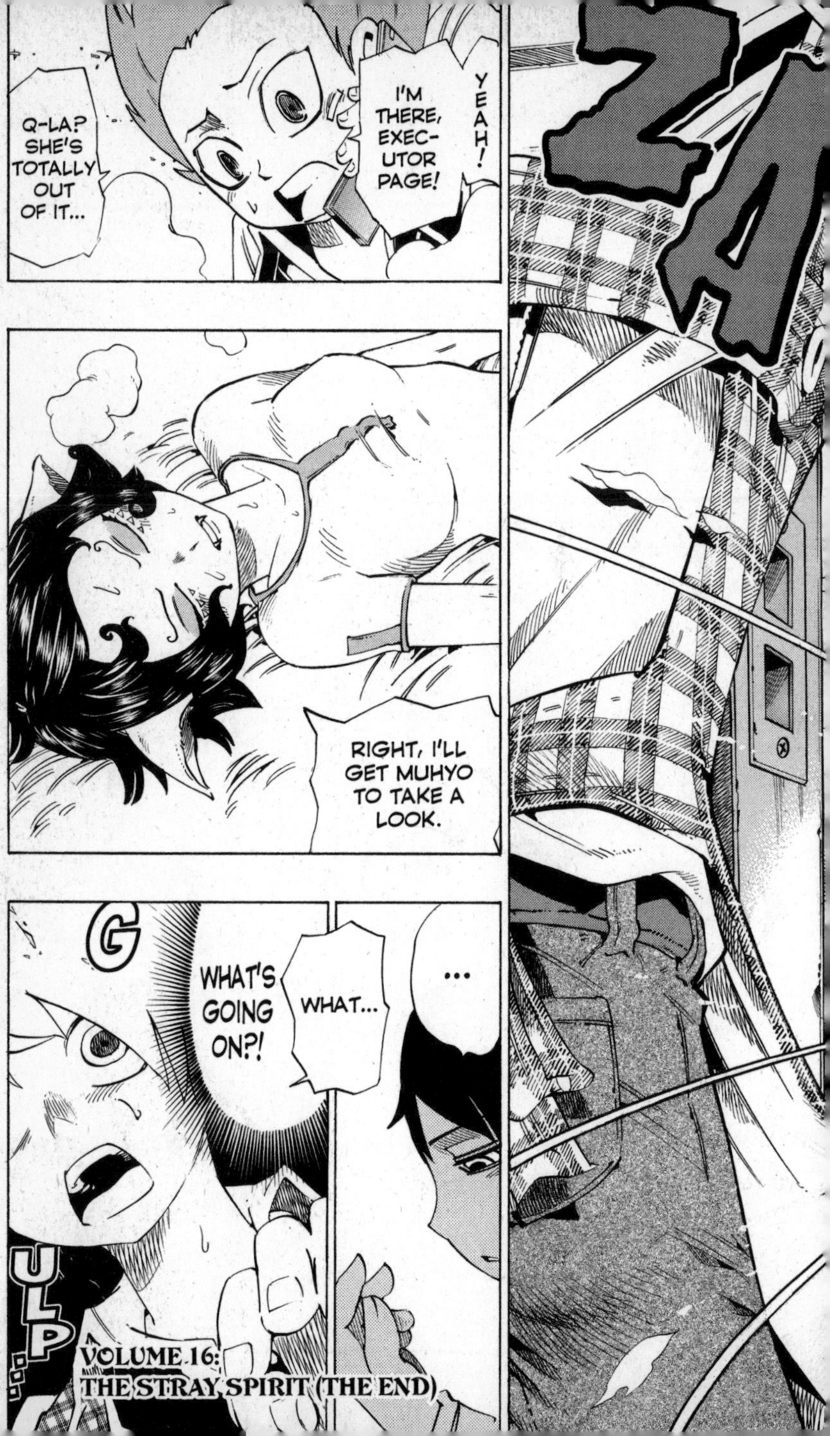
ZA
YEAH!
I'M THERE, EXECUTOR PAGE!
Q-LA? SHE'S TOTALLY OUT OF IT...
RIGHT, I'LL GET MUHYO TO TAKE A LOOK.
...
WHAT...
G
WHAT'S GOING ON?!
ULP...
VOLUME 16: THE STRAY SPIRIT (THE END)

In The Next Volume

Will these little guys play hero when the
Law Association falls under siege?

Available June 2010!

SHONEN JUMP

THE WORLD'S MOST POPULAR MANGA

BLEACH

STORY AND ART BY
TITE KUBO

ONE PIECE

STORY AND ART BY
EIICHIRO ODA

Tegami Bachi
LETTER BEE

STORY AND ART BY
HIROYUKI ASADA

JUMP INTO THE ACTION BY TELLING US WHAT YOU LOVE (AND WHAT YOU DON'T)

LET YOUR VOICE BE HEARD!

SHONENJUMP.VIZ.COM/MANGASURVEY

HELP US MAKE MORE OF THE WORLD'S MOST POPULAR MANGA!